AF685468

The *REAL* Drug Abusers

Palm Beach Community College
Library Learning Resource Center
4200 Congress Avenue
Lake Worth, FL 33461-4796

WITHDRAWN

The *REAL* Drug Abusers

Fred Leavitt

ROWMAN & LITTLEFIELD PUBLISHERS, INC.
Lanham • Boulder • New York • Oxford

ROWMAN & LITTLEFIELD PUBLISHERS, INC.

Published in the United States of America
by Rowman & Littlefield Publishers, Inc.
A Member of the Rowman & Littlefield Publishing Group
4501 Forbes Boulevard, Suite 200, Lanham, Maryland 20706
www.rowmanlittlefield.com

PO Box 317
Oxford
OX2 9RU, UK

Copyright © 2003 by Rowman & Littlefield Publishers, Inc.

All rights reserved. No part of this publication may be reproduced, stored in a retrieval system, or transmitted in any form or by any means, electronic, mechanical, photocopying, recording, or otherwise, without the prior permission of the publisher.

British Library Cataloguing in Publication Information Available

Library of Congress Cataloging-in-Publication Data

Leavitt, Fred.
The real drug abusers / Fred Leavitt.
p. cm.
Includes bibliographical references and index.
ISBN 0-7425-2517-1 (cloth : alk. paper) — ISBN 0-7425-2518-X (paper : alk. paper)
1. Drug utilization—United States. 2. Pharmaceutical policy—United States. 3. Medication errors—United States. 4. Pharmaceutical industry—United States. 5. Drug abuse—United States.
[DNLM: 1. Pharmaceutical Preparations—supply & distribution—United States. 2. Drug Industry—economics—United States. 3. Medication Errors—adverse effects—United States. 4. Substance-Related Disorders—prevention & control—United States. QV 736 L439r 2003] I. Title.
RM263 .L42 2003
362.1'782'0973—dc21

2002155387

∞™ The paper used in this publication meets the minimum requirements of American National Standard for Information Sciences—Permanence of Paper for Printed Library Materials, ANSI/NISO Z39.48-1992.

I had a personal crisis while writing this book and was helped through it because several people showed me the meaning of "friend in need." Art Smith has been a dear friend forever—or at least since Millard Fillmore was president. Art's support made a big difference. Uche Udemezue was always available to listen, be supportive, and set screens for my jump shots. Joe Martin kept me going with good advice and the ability to make me laugh. Martin Jaspovice was an oasis. Martin, you went way beyond the call of duty and are very special. I thank all of you and dedicate the book to Joe and Martin.

Diane, Jess, and Mel, I love the three of you so much.

Contents

Introduction

Drug abuse causes havoc over the entire globe and is considered one of the most pressing social problems in the United States.[1] It is the number one health problem in the United States. According to the Substance Abuse and Mental Health Services Administration, it causes more deaths, illnesses, and disabilities than any other preventable health condition.[2]

The news media thrive on lurid reports of drug-related dissolution and degradation. Readers and viewers avidly follow sensational stories about pushers soliciting junior high school children, strung-out addicts mugging people and terrorizing businesses, girls and young women turning to prostitution to support their habits, police officers being corrupted by the lure of easy money, informants turning on friends and relatives, gangs killing each other in wars over drug territory, and entire neighborhoods being destroyed while kingpins live in island villas with fleets of luxury cars and pleasure craft. But media reports often go well beyond what the facts about drugs warrant. The media are concerned more with ratings than accuracy, and sensationalized stories sell. The stories draw large audiences, whereas original research findings, described in technical language and published in specialized journals with limited readership, have little direct influence on public opinion.

Public opinion is also shaped by politicians, bureaucrats working within government agencies, and representatives from drug company marketing departments. They often refer to research findings and comment on isolated incidents involving drugs, but their pronouncements too often reflect vested interests rather than dedication to the truth. Nevertheless, they are influential and help keep the public woefully misinformed about the nature of drug abuse. For example, the view that drug addicts are qualitatively different from other people is entrenched in the public consciousness despite there being little support from research in biochemistry, neuroscience, psychology, sociology, or anthropology. See chapter 7.

SOCIETIES DIFFER IN THEIR STRATEGIES FOR MAKING BENEFICIAL DRUGS AVAILABLE AND RESTRICTING THE USE OF HARMFUL DRUGS

All societies have unique sets of behavioral norms, methods for discouraging deviation from the norms, and attitudes toward violators. Although drug abuse cuts across socioeconomic boundaries, certain groups—the mentally ill, the homeless, and people who do not receive proper medical care, who lack skills or motivation to find meaningful work, and who have been or merely feel oppressed—are especially vulnerable to relying on drugs in attempts to cope. Disparities in education, wealth, and power occur in all societies, but attitudes toward people at the lower end of the continuum differ greatly. Responses to both licit and illicit drugs, the likelihood that casual use will turn into addiction, and the harms caused by addiction depend to a great extent on these cultural factors.

The Molecule Is Not the Message

Advertisements directed at both doctors and laypersons suggest that drug actions depend almost exclusively on molecular structure. Authors describe effects in minute detail: "LSD, 1966, a presumptuous little pill, causes dilated pupils, increased heart rate, and vivid hallucinations of used car salesmen." The authors make subtle distinctions between structurally similar molecules, disregarding the fact that even experienced users cannot discriminate between heroin and morphine or between injected amphetamine and cocaine.[3] They consider humans passive respondents, little different from litmus paper or other forms of laboratory apparatus. Just as litmus paper reliably changes color if dipped into an acidic substance, human neurons change in reliable ways following exposure to certain drugs. But this perspective ignores the fact that changes in brain chemistry depend on many factors and are not the sole determinants of how recipients respond to drugs. People's expectations affect their responses to all experiences. Consider two studies by Martin Orne that do not involve drugs:

- Most subjects in early sensory deprivation experiments reported extreme stress. Orne manipulated expectations by asking some subjects to sign a frightening release form and showing them a panic button they could press if the stress became too great.[4] Then he ushered them into a quiet room and told them to sit there. He treated control subjects identically except for the release form and button. The experimentals experienced considerable stress, and many pressed the panic button. The controls did not. (As further evidence of the power of expectations, Suedfeld gave positive instructions to sensory-deprivation subjects and induced relaxation and calm.)[5]

- Orne told only one of two groups of students that the dominant hand of hypnotized subjects becomes rigid.[6] The information is false. Later, he asked for volunteers from both groups to be hypnotized. Several of the students in the first group and none in the second developed dominant hand rigidity.

Expectations can be manipulated so that sugar pills (placebos) affect recipients as though they are powerful drugs. Expectations induced by living in a particular society shape responses to real drugs. Following are a few examples. See chapter 7, pages 255–57, for further discussion.

Alcohol

Heath writes,

> A population that drinks daily may have a high rate of cirrhosis and other medical problems but few accidents, fights, homicides, or other violent alcohol-associated traumas; a population with predominantly binge drinking usually shows the opposite complex of drinking problems. . . . A group that views drinking as a ritually significant act is not likely to develop many alcohol-related problems of any sort, whereas another group, which sees it primarily as a way to escape from stress or to demonstrate one's strength, is at high risk of developing problems with drinking.

Heath gives several examples. He notes that aggression is much more likely to result from beer drinking in taverns than wine drinking at singles' bars and that drunken women are much less likely than drunken men to behave aggressively. He describes the Camba of Bolivia, who

> have gained considerable notoriety in the alcohol literature because more of them drink, they drink more often, and they drink more of the most potent alcoholic beverage in customary usage anywhere in the world, yet they have virtually no social, psychological, or economic problems in connection with drinking. . . . There is no verbal or sexual aggression, no destruction of property, no drunken homicide or suicide. On the contrary, drinking is a time for cordiality and easy social interaction that are rare in other times of their lives.[7]

Although several Scandinavian and English-speaking countries have strict regulations about when and where drinking can occur, relatively permissive societies such as Italy, France, Spain, Portugal, and Belgium report fewer behavioral drinking problems. Peele has hypothesized that people in the restrictive countries, if they drink, are at high risk for excessive consumption because they have no norms for moderate drinking or for drinking as part of daily life.[8] For the same reason, individuals who belong to groups with high abstinence rates and are exposed to alcohol become highly vulnerable to problem drinking.

Caffeine

Caffeine is the world's most widely used drug, but coffee was banned in Egypt several centuries ago. A sultan called it an exhilarating drink that inspired men and women to break Islamic laws.[9]

LSD

Metzner has noted that during the 1960s different subcultures had distinct, well-defined norms for the LSD experience.[10] Users responded accordingly:

- The "psychotomimetic" model treated the LSD experience like a psychosis.
- The CIA explored the brainwashing model for drugging enemy soldiers.
- Advocates of the hallucinogenic model used drugs as tools for studying the mechanisms of perception.
- People hoping for enlightenment and expansion of consciousness used the psychedelic model.
- The therapeutic model was used to treat people with psychiatric disorders.
- Writers, musicians, and artists used the creativity model as an aid for developing new problem-solving strategies.
- People seeking transcendent experiences used the religious-mystical model.

Marijuana

The physiological changes produced by marijuana are intrinsically neither pleasurable nor unpleasurable. Users must be taught that the state is pleasant. Becker writes about the reactions of novice marijuana smokers,

> Being high consists of two elements: the presence of symptoms caused by marijuana use and the recognition of these symptoms and their connection by the user with his use of the drug. It is not enough, that is, that the effects be present; they alone do not automatically provide the experience of being high. The user must be able to point them out to himself and consciously connect them with his smoked marijuana before he can have this experience. Otherwise, regardless of the actual effects produced, he considers that the drug has had no effect on him.[11]

Expectations also influence the reactions of highly experienced marijuana users. Most Americans surveyed reported that smoking increases their appetites, whereas most Jamaicans reported an appetite-suppressant effect.[12]

SOCIETAL NORMS AND LAWS RELATED TO DRUGS HAVE WIDESPREAD RAMIFICATIONS

Societal norms and laws have impacts that extend far beyond shaping the responses of drug users. They influence long-range prospects of users of illegal drugs, treatments of those in need of medical drugs, and people's general attitudes toward seeking alternatives to medical drugs and experimenting with recreational ones. The norms and laws affect safety, taxes, and quality of life for most citizens. Therefore, they should be frequently reevaluated. U.S. norms have changed dramatically during the past century. Several trends are clear for three different categories of drugs.

Illegal Drugs

Many once-acceptable drugs, including opium, cocaine, and marijuana, have been made illegal. In the United States, arrests for their use have skyrocketed, especially among minorities. And the rate of HIV infection among injection drug users, especially African Americans and Latinos, has soared.

Prescription Drugs

Each year, marketing departments get greater shares of drug companies' budgets. The companies promote their products for solving virtually all of life's problems. The campaigns have been effective. U.S. doctors prescribe drugs much more heavily today than in the past and much more heavily than in most other countries.

Over the Counter Drugs That Do Not Require a Prescription

The most widely used drugs in the world, including alcohol, caffeine, and nicotine, are sold over the counter. The usage trends for all three are in the same direction—up. Although per-capita nicotine consumption in the United States has declined during the past thirty years, the trend has been upward in developing countries and among women. As the ads proclaim, "You've come a long way baby." The World Health Organization estimates that, worldwide, 1.2 to 1.5 billion people smoke.[13] Unlike nicotine, alcohol and caffeine are not harmful in moderation. But chronic high-dose use is associated with a variety of problems—see chapter 10. High-dose alcoholic drinks have been heavily promoted in minority communities, and significant amounts of caffeine are added to soft drinks for young children.

DRUG ABUSE—AN EXPANDED PERSPECTIVE

Drug abuse, narrowly conceived, is any use of illicit substances or excessive use of legal ones. That is how government agencies define the term. But, though proscribed personal use makes headlines and gets people sent to prison, several less-publicized activities involving drugs cause great harm to the general public. The chapters that follow include examples from each of the following categories:

- Too many pharmacological researchers face strong conflicts between financial gain and accurate reporting of their findings. See pages 13–19.
- Individuals and institutions distort and suppress information to promote their objectives.
- The prescribing habits of some doctors depend less on the medical literature than on how drugs are promoted to them. Their diagnoses and prescriptions often demonstrate sexist and racist biases. See chapter 2 and pages 69–70.
- Some Health Maintenance Organizations (HMOs) are multidrug abusers. Many require their doctors to choose from a preselected formulary of drugs, with price overriding effectiveness as a criterion for inclusion in the formulary. See pages 68–70. Most HMOs are biased toward prescribing drugs for psychiatric patients rather than giving them lengthier, costlier (and probably more effective) access to someone to listen to their problems.[14]
- Hundreds of thousands of patients in U.S. hospitals experience bad drug reactions each year, and thousands die. The reported figures are probably an undercount, because many errors go undocumented and unreported. See page 62. The problem keeps growing, as doctors rely increasingly on drugs and pharmacists' workloads get heavier and heavier. Between 1983 and 1993, deaths due to medication errors more than doubled among hospital patients and increased eightfold among outpatients. A high proportion of residents of nursing facilities receives inappropriate prescriptions.[15]
- Patients in chronic pain, and especially the elderly, are often medicated inadequately. Health care professionals share an unwarranted fear that they will create narcotics addicts if they administer too much. So doctors underprescribe, and nurses underadminister pain medications to many patients, especially the elderly.[16]
- Politicians and other government officials are guilty of drug-related abuse when they spread misinformation and disinformation about drugs. Entire

societies abuse by encouraging the use of drugs for falling asleep, waking up, losing weight, overcoming shyness, and having bowel movements with clocklike regularity. The same societies, and the United States in particular, sentence staggering numbers of nonviolent drug offenders to longer prison terms than are given to rapists and murderers. See page 147. Alexander Shulgin writes: "Our generation is the first ever to have made the search for self-awareness a crime, if it is done with the use of plants or chemical compounds as the means of opening the psychic doors."[17] Shulgin's enlightened belief that the search for self-awareness should be encouraged can be contrasted with the view of Gerald Smith, who wrote a pamphlet distributed to schoolchildren in Utah. Entitled "How Parents Can Help Children Live Marijuana Free," the pamphlet includes a preface by Utah Senator Orrin Hatch and offers parents the following tip on how to recognize drug use by their children: "Excessive preoccupation with social causes, race relations, environmental issues, etc."

- Various state and federal asset-forfeiture laws allow government agencies to confiscate assets of convicted traffickers. A New Hampshire family with three small children had their home seized for growing four marijuana plants in the back garden. See pages 151–53 for additional examples. The practice has outraged civil libertarians.
- Many unethical medical experiments were conducted in the not-too-distant past. Powerful, dangerous, experimental drugs were administered to unwitting prisoners, soldiers, and civilian victims, including the mentally retarded and psychotic. Such abuses probably continue, although the extent may never be known. See pages 80–82.

The various categories of abuse can be traced to three types of causes:

1. Human error. Some human error is unavoidable, but errors occur in about 1 percent of drug prescriptions.[18] The rate is unacceptable. Arun Bhatt quotes W. E. Deming: "If we had to live with a 99.9 % (success rate in industry), we would have 2 unsafe plane landings per day at O'Hare, 16,000 pieces of lost mail every hour and 32,000 bank checks deducted from wrong bank account[s] every hour."[19] Chapter 3 gives tips for consumers to help them prevent medical error, but unfortunately consumer error-avoidance strategies are limited. The chapter also offers suggestions for pharmacists, doctors, nurses, and other hospital personnel and cites references to extensive discussions directed toward practitioners for improving safety practices.
2. Lack of information, misinformation, and disinformation. Debates about drug issues often resemble arguments about politics, religion, or sports.

That is, facts play a minor role. Nobody is an expert in all fields—the last Renaissance person probably lived during the Renaissance—so we rely for most of our information on the pronouncements of people we trust. Unfortunately, many of them are also nonexperts or have hidden interests in the positions they advocate. Consider what several authorities have written about the possibility that certain drugs enhance creativity:

> Donald Louria: LSD-induced creativity is a myth.
>
> Timothy Leary: Psychedelic drugs enhance the creative perspective.
>
> James Goddard: Mind-stretching claims for LSD are "pure bunk."
>
> John Finlater: Creatively, LSD is a complete bust. Users talk about creativity, but they don't do anything about it. The painter stops painting and fantasy replaces reality.
>
> Alan Watts: . . . LSD has been very beneficial (to the creative experience). . . . I can only say from my own point of view that I have derived all kinds of ideas for lectures and writings from it.
>
> Sidney Cohen: An overestimate of one's capabilities is not infrequent. Often mental productions are not as highly assessed when they are later examined in the sober state.
>
> Stanley Yolles: It may . . . lead to heightened suggestibility and a faulty perception, really an exaggerated notion of thinking more clearly, profoundly, and creatively.[20]

Their strong opinions notwithstanding, the authors do not refer to published research on drugs and creativity. They apparently count on the persuasive powers of their status.

Even research findings, even those published in the best scientific journals, are not sacred. As discussed in chapter 1, researchers have falsified data and, intentionally or otherwise, used faulty research designs, analyzed data incorrectly, and misinterpreted results.

Thousands of studies are published each year, so propagandists pick the ones that best serve their needs. If fifty studies show that drug X is ineffective and two show some beneficial effects, both the FDA and the general public are likely to hear only about the two favorable ones. Thus, probably all of us "know" lots of things that are not so.

3. Money. Throughout the drug field, money rules. Drug prescribers, pharmacists, and clinical researchers make comfortable livings; treatment providers for alcoholics and other drug abusers generate billions of dollars in annual income; and the pharmaceutical industry consistently returns excellent dividends on investments. Many people in those fields have opportunities to multiply profits by being unethical or dishonest. Human nature being what it is, some take advantage of the opportunities, which leads to the abuses described above.

Each of chapters 1 to 12 is headed with an assertion about one aspect of drug abuse. The text provides evidence and argument for the assertion.

NOTES

1. The Gallup Organization, *Consult with America: A Look at How Americans View the Country's Drug Problem, Summary Report* (Rockville, Md.: Gallup Organization, 1996).

2. Substance Abuse and Mental Health Services Administration, "Worker Drug Use and Workplace Policies Fact Sheet" (8 September 1999), available at www.samhsa.gov/PRESS/99/990908fs.htm (accessed on 12 December 2000).

3. H. Fraser et al., "Methods for Evaluating Addiction Liability. (A) Attitude of Opiate Addicts toward Opiate-like Drugs. (B) A Short-term 'Direct' Addiction Test," *Journal of Pharmacology and Experimental Therapeutics* 133 (1961): 371–87; J. Kramer et al., "Amphetamine Abuse," *Journal of the American Medical Association* 201 (1967): 305–09.

4. M. Orne, "On the Social Psychology of the Psychological Experiment," *American Psychologist* 17 (1962): 776–83.

5. P. Suedfeld, "Aloneness as a Healing Experience," in *Loneliness: A Sourcebook of Current Theory, Research, and Therapy,* ed. L. Peplau and D. Perlman (New York: Wiley-Interscience, 1981), 54–70.

6. M. Orne, "The Nature of Hypnosis: Artifact and Essence," *Journal of Abnormal and Social Psychology* 58 (1959): 277–99.

7. D. Heath, "Sociocultural Variants in Alcoholism," in *Encyclopedic Handbook of Alcoholism,* ed. E. Pattison and E. Kaufman (New York: Gardner Press, 1982), 426–40; D. Heath, "Alcohol and Aggression," in *Alcohol, Drug Abuse and Aggression,* ed. E. Gottheil et al. (Springfield, Ill.: Charles Thomas, 1983), 89–103.

8. S. Peele, "Utilizing Culture and Behavior in Epidemiological Models of Alcohol Consumption and Consequences for Western Nations," *Alcohol and Alcoholism* 32 (1997): 51–64.

9. P. Quimme, *The Signet Book of Coffee and Tea* (New York: Signet, 1976).

10. R. Metzner, "Reflections on LSD—Ten Years Later," *Journal of Psychedelic Drugs* 10 (1978): 137–40.

11. H. Becker, "Becoming a Marijuana User," *American Journal of Sociology* 59 (1953): 235–42.

12. C. Tart, *On Being Stoned: A Psychological Study of Marijuana Intoxication* (Palo Alto: Science and Behavior, 1971); V. Rubin and L. Comitas, *Ganja in Jamaica* (New York: Anchor, 1976).

13. These figures were kindly provided to me by Nina Rehn, a technical officer in Management of Substance Dependence, and Helen Green, of the Tobacco Free Initiative, World Health Organization, Geneva.

14. For one recent discussion of the problem, see T. Luhrmann, *Of Two Minds: The Growing Disorder in American Psychiatry* (New York: Knopf, 2000).

15. M. Beers et al., "Inappropriate Medication Prescribing in Skilled-Nursing Facilities," *Annals of Internal Medicine* 117 (1992): 684–89.

16. C. Novy and M. Jagmin, "Pain Management in the Elderly Orthopaedic Patient," *Orthopaedic Nursing* 16 (1997): 51–57.

17. A. Shulgin, "Confessions of a Psychedelic Alchemist," *Whole Earth Review* (fall 1991): 22–27.

18. L. Andrews et al., "An Alternative Strategy for Studying Adverse Events in Medical Care," *Lancet* 349: 309–13.

19. Arun D. Bhatt, "Medication Errors: Malpractice Implications and Prevention," available at www.expresshealthcaremgmt.com/20020630/edit2.shtml (accessed on 12 August 2002).

20. See F. Leavitt, *Drugs and Behavior,* 2d ed. (New York: Wiley-Interscience, 1982).

1

A Significant Portion of Medical Research Cannot Be Trusted

Imagine a headline in tomorrow's newspaper: MIRACLE DRUG DOUBLES LEARNING ABILITY IN RATS. Suppose the story told of an experiment in which drugged rats learned a complex task twice as quickly as untreated controls. Impulsive readers might bombard their doctors or pharmacists with prescription requests. Cautious ones would note that people are not rats, while sophisticates might track down the original article to check for flaws. But only the most cynical would question the integrity of the study's authors and suggest that the results might have been achieved dishonestly. Unless an ulterior motive is obvious, as when a scientist testifies as an expert witness in a courtroom and favors the side paying him, scientists are largely exempt from accusations of playing loose with the truth. By contrast, when salespeople expound on their products' virtues, or lawyers proclaim their clients' innocence, or politicians tell us that all hope of global peace and prosperity will vanish unless they are elected, we recognize that their arguments may be colored by self-interest.

—Jonathan King, "The Scientific Endeavor Is Based on Vigilance, Not Trust"

CONFLICTS OF INTEREST

Alliances between drug companies and the scientific community run deep. Schrag writes:

> Most of the major figures in drug research serve as consultants to drug firms and, at the same time, to [the National Institute of Mental Health (NIMH)] and the Food and Drug Administration [FDA], which licenses the drugs. They review each

other's grant proposals, sit on the same committees, work on the same studies, write for each other's journals. NIMH employees collaborate with drug-company consultants in mental health research; NIMH consultants appear before FDA review committees on behalf of drug companies; editors of journals heavily supported by drug-company advertising serve on "impartial" FDA committees reviewing the safety and efficacy of medication produced by their advertisers.[1]

Sponsoring Institutions

Whether or not the trust accorded to most scientists is justified, there is ample reason to be skeptical about pharmaceutical research. Crucial aspects of many studies are directed by parties motivated more by financial considerations than by the search for truth. Corporate support for U.S. science increased from less than $5 million in 1974 to hundreds of millions in the early 1990s; and 70 percent of the money for testing drugs comes from industry.[2] Companies rarely fund potentially important studies that might reduce sales, such as research to discover adverse effects of their drugs. To the contrary, reports of adverse effects are suppressed or minimized. For example, the information that serotonin reuptake inhibitors (SSRIs) cause sexual difficulties in many users was publicized only because of research conducted by manufacturers of non-SSRI antidepressants.[3] Marketing departments often rule on which studies to sponsor. The studies, in the words of former FDA commissioner David Kessler, are often "thinly veiled attempts to entice doctors to prescribe a new drug being marketed by the company."[4]

Most studies are designed by researchers working for drug companies, and they do not play fair. Johansen and Gotzsche have evaluated research comparing two antifungal drugs, fluconazole and amphotericin B.[5] The studies were funded by Pfizer, the manufacturer of fluconazole. Both drugs were administered orally, which is the appropriate route of administration for fluconazole. But amphotericin B is poorly absorbed through the gastrointestinal tract and so should be administered intravenously. Bodenheimer writes, "I've been in practice for 30 years and have never seen oral amphotericin B used for systemic infections; it's an intravenous drug. This design virtually guarantees that fluconazole—the funding company's drug—will produce better results."[6] Virtual guarantees were not good enough—additional studies were sponsored with a third drug, nystatin, known to be ineffective for invasive fungal infection. Then researchers combined the nystatin and amphotericin B data and compared them with the data from fluconazole. Bodenheimer gives other examples of designs biased in favor of the sponsoring company's drug. For example, in 54 percent of studies comparing nonsteroidal anti-inflammatory drugs, the doses of the funding company's drug were higher than those of the competitor's.

To prove a product's effectiveness and safety to the FDA, data must be gathered on many subjects. Only the largest hospitals, universities, or other institutions can ever provide enough subjects, so multiple sites are necessary. Yet investigators are often denied access to data except from their sites, which allows companies to spin the data in misleading ways. Bodenheimer cites a case in which a trial favorable to the company's drug was published and an unfavorable one by the same investigator was not. Another investigator demanded that his unfavorable findings be published, but company officials stalled until he lost interest. Another reported that the sponsor's drug caused adverse reactions; it vowed not to fund him again and published a competing article that barely mentions the adverse effects.

Some companies award funds on the condition that findings cannot be published without their approval, and they suppress unsatisfactory results. Researchers cooperate with their sponsors by delaying publication of undesired results.[7] Thirty-five percent of agreements signed between industry and academic researchers allowed the sponsor to delete information from publication; 53 percent allowed delays in publication; and 30 percent allowed both deletions and delays.[8] The results from many studies are never published, frequently because they are unfavorable to the sponsors' products.[9]

The British drug company Boots manufactures a drug, Synthroid, that had by the 1990s captured 84 percent of the U.S. market for drugs to control hypothyroidism. Then three much cheaper generics began making inroads into Boots's sales, so Boots awarded a grant to a team of researchers to compare Synthroid with the rivals. When the researchers submitted a paper showing that Synthroid is no better than the others, Boots forbade publication. Fortunately for the many people who need hypothyroid medication, Betty Dong and colleagues risked a lawsuit and reported their findings anyway.[10]

In 1995, the drug company Apotex funded research on the drug deferiprone. Researcher Nancy Olivieri concluded that the drug could lead to serious and potentially fatal problems. She told Apotex officials that she intended to submit the findings for publication. They cited their confidentiality clause and threatened legal action unless she desisted.[11] (Although she published, Apotex did not follow through on its threat.) It is scary to think that many less courageous researchers have probably buckled under to such pressures.

At least one company did follow through on its threats. Immune Response Corporation sponsored research on its AIDS drug Remune. The research team, led by University of California at San Francisco scientist James Kahn, concluded that Remune does not help HIV-positive people live longer or develop AIDS more slowly. When the team members prepared to publish their findings, the company requested that they analyze their data differently. The researchers balked, and Immune Response Corporation filed for arbitration against Kahn and the university, seeking $7–10 million.[12]

In 1995, the World Health Organization raised concerns that certain oral contraceptive pills increase the risk of deep blood clot formation. Although industry-sponsored studies reported no evidence to support the claim, twelve independent studies found strong evidence. In 1997, the drug manufacturer Wyeth-Ayerst conducted a study that, had it been published, would have been the first by the industry to show an increased risk of blood clot formation. But according to a Dutch team of investigative reporters, Wyeth tried to suppress publication of its own findings. Wyeth threatened legal action to prevent the reporters from broadcasting their charges on radio. Scientists who had published findings raising concern about the safety of the oral contraceptive claimed harassment from the drug companies.[13]

New drugs are protected by patent, so drug companies prefer having them turn out superior to older ones. Of the $100 billion spent on prescription drugs in 1998, more than 35 percent was for drugs introduced since 1991.[14] In studies comparing new with old drugs, 43 percent funded by a drug company and only 13 percent funded by other sources favored the new. Furthermore, "in no case was a therapeutic agent manufactured by the sponsoring company found to be inferior to an alternative product manufactured by another company."[15] Cho and Bero's literature review shows that 98 percent of published studies favored the company's drug.[16] Another analysis shows that drug studies reached unfavorable conclusions 38 percent of the time when funded by nonprofit groups but only 5 percent of the time when drug companies did the funding.[17]

Easterbrook, Dickersin, and their colleagues have analyzed the fates of approved research proposals. Of 285 studies approved by one committee between 1984 and 1987 that had been completed by 1990, 138 had been published. A smaller proportion of drug company–sponsored studies was published than that supported by government or voluntary organizations. The analysts cite data management by these companies as a major reason for nonpublication, inferring that drug companies discourage publication of studies they have funded that have negative results.[18]

Scientists who did original research were once the only ones who wrote up their work in reports, scholarly reviews, and editorials. Today, the writing is frequently turned over to professionals in the employ of drug companies who give their material a spin not justified by the evidence.[19] For example, a journal supplement sponsored by a drug company presented data showing that the drug gemfibrozil reduces the incidence of cardiac events. But the publication, which led to an increased rate of prescribing of gemfibrozil, omitted one bit of information that is more than slightly significant: patients who took gemfibrozil were more likely to die. Another group of authors wrote that "the results of our study suggest that foscarnet is highly effective in delaying progression of CMV retinitis in AIDS patients."[20] But the data were from one patient and did not support the conclusions. Gotzsche has found doubtful or invalid statements in the conclusions or abstracts of 76 percent of 196 studies, and the vast majority of them favored the sponsoring company.[21]

Direct profits are not a consideration for funding agencies of the federal government. Nevertheless, government agencies want their money to yield dividends, and their objectives may be incompatible with the search for truth. Organizations like the National Institute on Drug Abuse are committed to the position that marijuana, 3,4-methylenedioxymethamphetamine, and other illicit drugs are harmful. They grant far more money for studying adverse rather than beneficial effects of drugs. The agencies are not averse to exerting pressure. For example, the National Institutes of Health sponsored research on heart disease. Carl Selzer and his colleagues on the project found that men who drank moderate amounts of alcohol had a lower risk of heart disease than nondrinkers. They drafted a manuscript and forwarded it to the National Heart and Lung Institute for pre-publication review. The institute demanded the data back and denied them permission to publish.[22]

The only journals that most scientists take seriously are peer reviewed. These require that authors submit manuscripts to editors who send them to experts for review. The reviewers evaluate the research and recommend for or against publication. Although peer review has been criticized on various grounds, the process improves the likelihood that an article meets certain minimal standards. Several journals publish mostly peer-reviewed articles but also special supplementary issues under the aegis of corporate sponsors. Unwary readers may not distinguish between the two. The articles in supplements tend to be of lower quality and invariably favor the sponsor's products.[23] In some areas of therapeutics they dominate the medical literature and are listed in bibliographic data banks. Regular issues of the *Journal of Clinical Psychiatry* come out monthly, but the journal published at least thirteen supplements in 1997 and at least fifteen in 1999. The *Archives of Virology* published at least seventeen supplements in 2000.

A supplement to the *Journal of Psychopharmacology* (volume 10 [1996]) is entitled "Modern Management of Depression: Closing the Gap between Theory and Reality." The entire issue is heavily slanted toward one drug—the one manufactured by the supplement's sponsor. A supplement to the *Journal of Clinical Psychiatry* (volume 61 [2000]) is entitled "Norepinephrine: Neurotransmitter for the Millennium." The entire issue favors the drug of that supplement's sponsor. A supplement to the same journal (volume 62 [2001]) derives from a symposium in Atlanta, Georgia, supported through an "educational grant" from Pfizer Inc. The symposium faculty and contributing authors suggest off-label uses for several Pfizer drugs to treat social phobia. Two of the ten faculty report no monetary ties with any drug company. Six report ties with Pfizer. They received grant/research support, honoraria, and speaking and consultant fees and were on

Pfizer advisory boards. They were major stockholders in companies that had financial ties to Pfizer.

Researchers

Only a few years ago, most drug studies were conducted by career researchers at academic medical centers. Psychiatric drug researchers were specially trained and supervised. They interacted with their subjects and provided information about expected benefits and possible side effects. When the drugs they tested were administered in psychiatric clinics and hospitals to patients who received little more than a prescription, the results did not always generalize. Today, the situation is much worse. At the state Psychiatric Institute in Manhattan, at least ten psychiatrists and researchers in charge of drug experiments received huge speaking fees, consulting deals, board memberships, and subsidized international trips from drug companies. Beneficiaries included a top institute official and members of a panel that determines which proposed experiments may go forward and whether they meet federal and state rules to protect patients. Drug companies have paid panel members and then funded experiments approved by the panel. The researchers probably believed, probably correctly, that continued funding was contingent on results that cast company products in a favorable light.[24]

Now private practice physicians have joined the research business and are recruited by industry to persuade their patients to participate as subjects (see below). The license to practice medicine legally entitles them to do research, even if they have no research training. In 1997, 11,662 private physicians conducted drug studies, and 25 percent of those who conducted human experiments conducted only one. Many conducted research outside their specialties. Much of the work was methodologically unsound, and some unwitting patients/subjects received inadequate care.[25] Many doctors participate in postmarketing research and may be tempted to place their financial interests over the health of their patients.[26]

Doing research for drug companies, and reporting positive results, earns some scientists more than $1 million per year. The enormous financial incentives have induced investigators to falsify records and commit large-scale fraud.[27] In June 1992, the U.S. Department of Health and Human Services established an Office of Research Integrity (ORI). The office investigates allegations of scientific misconduct limited to Public Health Service–supported research, research training, or other research-related activities. By September 1994 ORI had found twenty-seven people guilty of scientific misconduct. Fourteen misconduct findings in 1997 equaled the annual average since 1992. In 1998, ORI opened fifty-four new cases.[28] The ORI website at http://ori.dhhs.gov lists ongoing investigations. Fraud occurs to a much greater extent in the biomedical sciences than in fields like physics, astronomy, and geology. Of twenty-six cases made public between 1980 and 1986, twenty-one came from biomedical science; two, from chemistry and biochemistry; one, from physiology; and the other two, from psychology.[29]

Fraud is hard to catch. Harvard physician John Darsee published nearly one hundred papers in two years, most based on forged data. Stewart and Feder have examined eighteen of his articles and found errors in all but two.[30] One article had twenty-eight errors, one had thirty-nine, and twelve had at least ten errors detectable from the text alone. Yet the articles had passed the scrutiny of reviewers and editors. Broad and Wade have estimated that for each case of major fraud uncovered, about one hundred thousand major and minor ones go undetected.[31]

People with sterling scientific reputations have published articles and taught medical students while serving as paid consultants to drug companies. The chief researcher in a study suggesting that zinc lozenges shorten the length of the common cold made $145,000 by selling stock in the lozenge company after the article was published. He also received options from the company to buy 10,000 shares.[32] In the first ten months of 1998, the Securities and Exchange Commission conducted at least five investigations into insider trading by clinical drug researchers.[33] An expert in diabetes conducted research for the National Institute of Health and praised a specific diabetes drug while on the payroll of the drug manufacturer. The drug was subsequently linked to liver injuries and thirty-three deaths.[34]

Confidential documents from the law firm of the Philip Morris tobacco company reveal that the company paid a network of scientists to cast doubt on the risks of passive smoking. The company's consultants included an editor of *The Lancet,* an adviser to a House of Commons select committee, and members of working groups of the International Agency for Research in Cancer. Scientists were "not paid unless and until they actually perform work"; they were "asked to cover all substantial scientific conferences where they can usefully influence scientific and public opinion."[35]

Barnes and Bero have identified 106 reviews of the health effects of passive smoking published from 1980 to 1995. Of the thirty-nine reviews that conclude that passive smoking is not harmful to health, thirty-one are written by authors who had affiliations with the tobacco industry. Three-quarters of the articles fail to disclose the sources of funding for the research. The authors infer that "the tobacco industry may be attempting to influence scientific opinion by flooding the scientific literature with large numbers of review articles supporting its position that passive smoking is not harmful to health."[36] Similarly, Walton has found 164 published papers on the artificial sweetener aspartame (NutraSweet). All of the seventy-four studies funded by the NutraSweet industry report that aspartame is safe; eighty-three of the other ninety studies identify potentially serious problems with aspartame.[37]

Drugs called calcium channel blockers are prescribed for heart spasms. After three studies published in the mid-1990s suggested that the drugs increase the risk of death from heart attack, a vigorous debate erupted within the medical literature between critics and defenders. Stelfox and colleagues identified seventy articles and letters related to the controversy and sent surveys to the eighty-nine authors asking them about their financial relationships with manufacturers of calcium channel blockers. Ninety-six percent of the authors who had written in support of the drugs, 60 percent of neutral authors, and 37 percent of critics reported financial relationships. Only two of the articles mention the authors' financial relationships.[38]

Of nearly eight hundred articles in major medical and biomedical journals, 34 percent list at least one author affiliated with a nonprofit academic or research institution who also had a financial interest in the research. The relationships with industry are almost never mentioned, so unsuspecting readers are likely to assume that the authors were unbiased. Krimsky and colleagues give several reasons for suspecting that their data underestimate the problem.[39]

In 1990, the *New England Journal of Medicine* (*NEJM*) initiated a policy requiring that only people with no financial interest in a product could write a review article or editorial about the product. In 2002, editors Jeffrey Drazen and Gregory Curfman abandoned the policy. They explained that they were unable to find enough experts without financial ties to drug companies.[40]

The *NEJM* does require that researchers and other contributors disclose their financial ties. The requirement has been breached many times. For example, an editorial in the 29 August 1996 issue maintains that the risk of obesity outweighs the dangers of appetite-suppressant drugs. Only after publication did the editors learn that the experts they had solicited to write the editorial had been paid consultants for companies that manufacture appetite-suppressant drugs.

Furthermore, disclosure does not banish concerns. Editor Marcia Angell has commented on one study that "the authors' ties with companies that make antidepressant drugs were so extensive that it would have used too much space to disclose them fully in the Journal" (see page 96 for more on Martin Keller, the lead author). Almost all research psychiatrists Angell spoke with had financial ties to drug companies that make antidepressants. The problem is not unique to psychiatry:

> The ties between clinical researchers and industry include not only grant support, but also a host of other financial arrangements. Researchers serve as consultants to companies whose products they are studying, join advisory boards and speakers' bureaus, enter into patent and royalty arrangements, agree to be the listed authors of articles ghostwritten by interested companies, promote drugs and devices at company-sponsored symposiums, and allow themselves to be plied with expensive gifts and trips to luxurious settings. Many also have equity interest in the companies.[41]

As they are so often on the payroll of drug companies, researchers are much more likely to report positive than adverse effects of drugs. Ioannidis and Lau analyzed 192 articles in seven different medical areas. Safety reporting was often inadequate and neglected, and was unsatisfactory in all seven areas. Only about one-third of the articles give sufficient information about toxicity levels or severity of side effects. Although many patients dropped out after experiencing toxicity, only 46 percent of the studies indicate the frequency of specific reasons. The typical study provides an enormous amount of information about safety and adverse effects, but authors selectively filter the data so that safety reporting typically takes up less than one-third of a page—less space than that taken to list the names and affiliations of the authors.[42]

The antidepressant sertraline (Zoloft) was compared with *Hypericum perforatum* (St. John's wort) and placebo. Previous studies failing to show a difference between antidepressants and placebo had been criticized for poor methodology, so the authors took precautions. They write, "Many of the presumed factors underlying this phenomenon were carefully attended to in this study, e.g., adherence to quality control by rater training, treatment adherence monitoring, inclusion of experienced investigators, and carefully defined entry criteria." Of the two primary outcome measures, neither sertraline nor *H. perforatum* differed significantly from placebo. The authors conclude: "This study fails to support the efficacy of *H. perforatum* in moderately severe major depression. The result may be due to low assay sensitivity of the trial, but the complete absence of trends suggestive of efficacy for *H. perforatum* is noteworthy."[43]

Two other points are noteworthy. First, even though sertraline-treated patients had done no better than those on placebo, the authors did not conclude: "This study fails to support the efficacy of sertraline in moderately severe major depression." Second, a possible reason for the omission is that ten of the authors held stock in or had received speaker, consulting, or other monies from Pfizer, the manufacturer of sertraline.

Jüni and Rutjes have discussed a widely cited study on selective cyclooxygenase 2 (COX-2) inhibitors.[44] Nonsteroidal anti-inflammatory drugs (NSAIDs) are effective in treating arthritis but cause gastrointestinal (GI) problems. Selective COX-2 inhibitors work by a different mechanism and were hypothesized to be as effective as NSAIDs while producing fewer GI problems. Pharmacia, the manufacturer of the selective COX-2 inhibitor celecoxib (Celebrex), sponsored a study and published the results in the *Journal of the American Medical Association* (*JAMA*). The main conclusion is that Celebrex causes fewer GI complications than NSAIDs.[45] About thirty thousand reprints were distributed.

But critics pointed out that the study was badly flawed.[46] The authors deviated from the protocol and introduced significant changes in design, outcomes, duration of follow-up, and analysis. Additional data available to the FDA when the manuscript was submitted contradicted the conclusion but were neither referred to in the article nor reported to *JAMA*. The criticisms were overlooked or ignored by most doctors, and sales of Celebrex soared.

Kjaergard and Als-Nielsen did a meta-analysis of randomized clinical trials published in the *British Medical Journal* from January 1997 to June 2001.[47] Studies in which the authors declare financial competing interests are significantly more likely than studies in which the authors do not declare financial competing interests to conclude that the experimental drug is better than placebo.

Editors

Because many journals are subsidized by industry, research critical of an industry product may create editorial discomfort. Seymour Fisher, the director of the Center for Medication Monitoring at the University of Texas, posted a series of articles on the Internet (www.psycom.net/fisher.html) describing what he believes is a clear case of editorial misfeasance. Fisher submitted a manuscript indicating that the drug sertraline (Zoloft) induces many adverse reactions. Although the three reviews were favorable, the journal's editor raised (what Fisher claims were inappropriate) barriers that delayed publication until fourteen months after acceptance. Fisher reviewed 119 articles published in the journal from July 1993 through April 1995 and reports a mean lag time from acceptance to publication of eight months. No other article had a lag time of as much as twelve months. Fisher thought it no coincidence that Pfizer Inc., which heavily subsidizes the journal to which he submitted the paper, manufactures Zoloft. Fisher claims that his experience is not unique and that he can document pharmaceutical company influences on National Institute of Health funding.

Industry money can corrupt editorials about research. The editor of the *British Journal of Psychiatry* published a favorable review of a drug while he was receiving an annual fee of 2,000 pounds from the drug's manufacturer.[48] A drug company representative asked Troyen Brennan to write an editorial for a medical journal: "The caller said that I would not really have to do much work on this project. I would discuss the matter with them, and they would then have a professional writer compose the editorial, which I could modify as I saw fit. I would earn $2,500 for what was estimated to be several hours of work." Brennan reviewed copies of other editorials the firm had commissioned. The few that acknowledged industry support did so in such a way that readers were likely to misconstrue the true nature of the support. Brennan writes further,

> Reading that editorial at the time of its publication, I had assumed the acknowledgment meant that at one time or another the author had received support from

> the drug company for a clinical trial. With this new information, the editorial seemed part of a deliberate strategy to change the opinion of readers, a goal that was also suggested by the memorandum from [the public relations firm] that accompanied the articles. The memorandum stated, "We are providing these materials to you in confidence, as we do not generally divulge the specific nature of projects conducted on behalf of our clients."[49]

Subjects

Drug companies pay doctors to enroll their patients in drug studies. A 1996 seminar for doctors was entitled "Successful Patient Recruitment: The Heart and Soul of Your Business." The top recruiters earn more than $1 million a year and are listed as authors of the studies even if they do nothing but recruit. When doctors in one study had trouble finding qualified patients, the drug company offered $3,495 instead of $2,955 for each subject enrolled, plus a bonus of $2,000 for doctors who enrolled their quota by a specified date.[50] Doctors who do not conduct research are also offered fees for finding test subjects. So are nurses and medical assistants who screen patients to see if they qualify.

The powerful incentives have encouraged some doctors to minimize risks while persuading patients to take unsafe drugs. There is an obvious ethical issue and another less obvious one—current practices sharply reduce the subject pool for researchers interested in important problems that are without great profit-making potential.

If test subjects differ from the typical future recipients of a drug, the findings on effectiveness and the frequency and seriousness of adverse effects may have little relevance for subsequent clinical use. Yet it is standard practice to test drugs on younger, healthier people than the eventual target population. Bodenheimer cites a study of drugs used primarily by elderly patients that produce a high incidence of side effects in the elderly.[51] Yet only 2.1 percent of the test subjects were sixty-five years of age or older. Although 63 percent of people in the United States with cancer are over sixty-five, only 25 percent of subjects in tests of cancer drugs are over sixty-five.

Some researchers exclude patients who have ever taken medication to treat their conditions, for those are the patients least likely to be helped by the test drug. Had they responded to prior treatments, they would probably not have volunteered for a new study.

Studies on the effectiveness of psychiatric drugs differ in important ways from the clinical usage of drugs. Researchers routinely give all prospective subjects placebos for seven–ten days. Usually about 20 percent improve substantially and would probably show a small drug/placebo difference, but they are disqualified from further participation. Also excluded are people with more than one disorder or a physical illness. About one-third of those accepted drop out, which further limits the generality of results. The issue is more than academic. Mildly depressed people are typically excluded from studies of antidepressants, yet they receive the bulk of prescriptions for antidepressants. The drugs are ineffective in mild depression.[52] Studies on Prozac excluded patients with serious suicidal tendencies, which is relevant to lawsuits charging that Prozac induced several patients to commit suicide.[53]

Information on the number of subjects used in studies is often inaccurate or misleading. An FDA report claims that 6,070 subjects were exposed to Prozac in U.S. studies. But only 1,730 were in placebo-controlled clinical trials, and only seventeen studies involving several hundred patients were found adequate enough to be used as evidence for FDA approval. Breggin obtained the data from those studies and counted the number of patients who completed the four-, five-, or six-week trials: The total was 286.[54]

The Food and Drug Administration

The FDA was established to protect consumers against dangerous and ineffective drugs, but FDA approval does not guarantee effectiveness and most certainly does not guarantee safety. The human studies conducted to meet FDA approval typically last four to six weeks.[55] Imagine if the dangers of cigarettes had been evaluated after only six weeks of tests. Furthermore, because most tests are conducted under the auspices of drug companies, adverse effects are often overlooked or minimized. Any that do occur are likely to be treated immediately, whereas real patients may continue taking their drugs until serious problems emerge. Less than 6 percent of research funds go toward testing drugs that have already received FDA approval, so adverse effects are not readily discovered after the initial testing period.[56] Also, as new drugs and medical devices enter the marketplace each year, they increase the potential for adverse interactions.

As indicated above, subjects often differ in important ways from the population that will ultimately receive the drugs. The number of subjects rarely exceeds 4,000, which is too small to reliably detect rare adverse reactions. To have a 95 percent chance of detecting an adverse reaction that affects one per 10,000 patients, 30,000 subjects would be needed.

The FDA has more than fourteen hundred employees with jobs related to approval of new drugs but only fifty-two (eight with medical degrees) who monitor the safety of drugs already approved.[57] New adverse effects are identified primarily through reports by consumers, doctors, pharmacists, and nurses either directly to the FDA or to the manufacturers (which are required by law to forward the information they receive). An estimated 51 percent of drugs produce adverse reactions not detected until after they have been approved. In 1997 the FDA received data showing cardiac problems in many people who used the diet drug fenfluramine. It was promptly withdrawn. But by then fenfluramine had been on the market for twenty-four years. Between 1997 and 2000, ten drugs that had been taken by about twenty-two million Americans were withdrawn for safety reasons. Top-selling anti-inflammatory drug bromfenac and antihistamine terfenadine were withdrawn between 1997 and 1998 after being prescribed to millions. Each caused serious side effects and deaths. Alosetron, approved to treat irritable bowel syndrome in women, was withdrawn in 2000 after the FDA received reports of seventy cases of serious adverse events including five deaths.

Doctors have little incentive to report adverse effects, so the majority go unreported. Although only 10 percent of men volunteered that an antihypertensive drug had made them impotent, 26 percent admitted it when asked directly, and 47 percent answered that it had on a questionnaire filled out in private.[58] Although Medicare records showed 202,211 hospitalizations for digoxin adverse effects in a seven-year period, the FDA received an average of only eighty-two adverse reaction reports on digoxin each year. An adverse event is not likely to be attributed to a drug if the event often occurs naturally in the patient population, such as cancer in the elderly or depression in people with thyroid problems, or if the event does not occur until long after drug administration. Former FDA commissioner David Kessler has estimated that only about 1 percent of adverse effects are ever reported.[59]

Problems with the FDA go deeper than insufficient staff and inadequate mechanisms for reporting adverse effects. FDA committees that evaluate the safety of substances are often packed with industry-funded scientists. The FDA established eighteen expert advisory committees to vote on the approval of new drugs and almost always follows their recommendations. The newspaper *USA Today* investigated financial conflicts such as stock ownership, consulting fees, and research grants that committee members disclosed at their 159 advisory meetings from 1 January 1998 through 30 June 2000.[60] At 146 of the meetings, at least one committee member had a financial stake in the outcome; at eighty-eight meetings, half or more members did; and at 102 meetings involving specific drugs, fifty-two committee members had a financial stake. Federal law prohibits the FDA from using experts with financial conflicts of interest unless a special waiver is granted. The FDA issued 803 waivers during the period under study. FDA spokesperson Linda Suydam defended the policy, stating that "the best experts for the FDA are often the best experts to consult with industry."

Despite more than sixteen thousand detailed adverse-reaction reports filed by consumers concerning the fat substitute olestra, an FDA committee voted to endorse its safety; at least nine of the seventeen positive votes came from consultants to food and drug companies.[61] Food industry observers call the FDA "Monsanto's Washington Office." Soon after the FDA approved and defended aspartame (made by a division of Monsanto), despite several reports indicating that it is toxic, eleven high-ranking officials closely tied to the approval took high-paying jobs in the NutraSweet industry.[62] (In a magazine for laypeople, the FDA stood behind its original approval of aspartame: "Subsequent evaluations have shown that the product is safe.")[63]

In 1991, an FDA committee heard testimony on the charge that fluoxetine (Prozac) induces suicidal and homicidal tendencies in some patients. The committee concluded that the assertion is unwarranted. Breggin and Breggin present compelling evidence that drug industry money influenced the decision of committee members.[64] For the same reason, FDA decisions about stimulant drugs to treat Attention Deficit/Hyperactivity Disorder should be regarded suspiciously.[65]

Patients in clinical studies who took the diabetes drug troglitazone (Rezulin) suffered severe liver damage. Executives at Warner-Lambert, the drug's manufacturer, claimed that the risk was trivial. The FDA medical officer assigned to evaluate Rezulin, John Gueriguian, disagreed and expressed concern about its potential toxicities. His boss acted promptly—he phoned a senior manager at Warner-Lambert and said that he would try to resolve the problem. If not, he promised, he would remove Gueriguian from the review of Rezulin. Shortly afterward, Gueriguian was removed and FDA staff withheld the existence of his review from the advisory committee. Company and FDA documents show that FDA officials provided Warner-Lambert with inside information and favors throughout the development and marketing of Rezulin. Rezulin was approved in December 1996 and withdrawn in March 2000, more than two years later than in Britain, after having being cited as the suspect in 391 deaths—and having generated $2.1 billion in sales.[66] Gueriguian commented, "The people in charge don't say, 'Should we approve this drug?' They say, 'Hey, how can we get this drug approved?'"

In 1993, the FDA official in charge of evaluating the drug cisapride (Propulsid) for approval was not a cardiac specialist. He reviewed studies showing that forty-eight patients who had taken Propulsid for easing nighttime heartburn had developed abnormal electrocardiogram patterns and eight young children given Propulsid had died. Still, he recommended approval. Within two years, adverse-reaction reports implicated Propulsid in several deaths. Scientists employed by the manufacturer, a subsidiary of Johnson & Johnson Co., argued that the deaths were due to other causes. They agreed to add a new safety label. The manufacturer donated money to the North American Society for Pediatric Gastroenterology and Nutrition, and Propulsid received the society's stamp of approval for treating gastric reflux in infants. Gastric reflux is a minor disorder that infants usually outgrow by the end of their first year. Safe, inexpensive, and effective therapies existed, but Propulsid became a popular treatment choice. Several children died. Seven years after approval, in 2000, Propulsid was finally taken off the market as a normally prescribed drug. It had generated U.S. sales of $2.5 billion and is suspected of killing more than three hundred people.[67]

Clinical tests of the antipsychotic drug Seroquel were conducted on 2,162 patients. Although the trials often lasted less than eight weeks, 80 percent of the patients did not last until the trial was over. The dropouts included 1,033 who were not helped by the drug, 398 who refused to continue or were lost to follow-up, and 86 who stopped because of adverse reactions. Nevertheless, in 1997, the FDA approved Seroquel. Soon afterward, an article in the *Archives of General Psychiatry* called Seroquel "an effective antipsychotic with a favorable safety profile," and an article in *Biological Psychiatry* claimed that it is "well tolerated and clinically effective in the treatment of schizophrenia."[68]

Richard Horton of *The Lancet* discusses the Alosetron case (see above) in a scathing editorial that accuses the FDA of failing in its mission to protect Americans from harmful drugs.[69] Horton claims that the FDA succumbs to funding from the drug industry and pressure from Congress to be favorable to the industry and that the FDA's Center for Drug Evaluation and Research is a servant of the industry. He writes that independent reviewers found serious flaws in research favorable to Alosetron and FDA officials were apprised of serious side effects. But scientists who raised concerns about its safety and called for more studies were ignored. Senior FDA officials are trying to reintroduce Alosetron.

Lurie and Wolfe of the nonprofit Public Citizen's Health Research Group surveyed doctors who review new drugs for the FDA.[70] The doctors were promised anonymity, and fifty-three of them (almost one-third) responded. They mentioned twenty-seven drugs that the FDA had approved in the previous three years even though the person most familiar with all the data on the drug opposed approval. The respondents described inappropriate phone calls from sponsors and pressure from Congress. In some instances, supervisors did not permit them to present data critical of drugs to FDA advisory committees. Most of the new drugs offered no benefit over their predecessors.

Expert Panels

Choudhry and colleagues contacted 100 authors who had served on committees to write clinical practice guidelines (CPGs) on common adult diseases.[71] CPGs are designed to influence doctors' prescribing practices. Eighty-seven of the authors had received money from the drug industry, fifty-nine had financial relationships with companies whose drugs were considered in the CPG they authored, and all but two had relationships that predated their work on the CPG. Only two authors acknowledged their relationships in published CPGs.

In May 2001, a twenty-two-member panel of government-selected cholesterol specialists broadened the definition of high cholesterol level. The new definition reclassified more than twenty-three million people as borderline at-risks who should join the ranks of those taking cholesterol-lowering drugs to battle heart disease. Drug company sales prospects and stock prices soared with the announcement. But critics noted that (1) at least five panel members had received funding or grants from companies selling or developing cholesterol-lowering drugs; (2) the companies funded some of the key studies; and (3) the recommendations were skewed in favor of drugs while placing too little emphasis on diet, exercise, and a healthy lifestyle.[72]

The 2000 annual report of the American Heart Association (AHA) includes the statement: "[Tissue plasminogen activator (tPA)] holds enormous potential for the treatment of ischemic stroke, which accounts for 70 to 80 percent of all strokes."[73] The report recommends upgrading tPA from optional to definitely recommended for stroke. But tPA probably increases mortality rates in acute ischemic stroke. The panel ignored studies in which tPA-treated patients did poorly, including one in which they had twice the death rate of similar patients not treated. The panel based its recommendations on one positive study, but in that study tPA-treated patients had milder initial stroke scores than patients treated with placebo.

Jeanne Lenzer learned that Genentech, tPA's manufacturer, had contributed more than $11 million to the AHA over the previous decade.[74] Eight of the nine panelists who evaluated tPA for the AHA report had financial ties to Genentech. The exception, Jerome Hoffman, dissented from the recommendation and was asked to write a paper giving his reasons. He did, but the paper was never published, and the guidelines do not mention it.

Lenzer's article provoked heated discussion. In a commentary immediately following, Saver and others, all of whom disclosed financial ties with several drug companies including Genentech, write that her recommendation that experts avoid all appearance of potential bias "is presently unworkable and undesirable. Such extreme 'financial correctness' would leave treatment guideline development largely to individuals who are not experts in the disease being treated and therefore presumably ill equipped to reach reliable conclusions."[75] They also claim that Lenzer's article abounds with innuendo and misinformation.

The Media

Prominent astronomer Carl Sagan noted shortly before his death that "almost every newspaper in America has a daily astrology column. Most do not even have a weekly science column." Yet the media have a huge impact on laypersons' views of science. For example, surveyors found that 64 percent of people get their information about cancer prevention from magazines; 60 percent, from newspapers; and 58 percent, from television.[76] Most probably assume that science stories are free. But scientific discoveries and controversies often have political or economic ramifications, and media outlets with leftist, rightist, business, or environmental leanings may slant their coverage accordingly. Brian Trench has concluded, after comparing reports of the same story in major Irish, French, German, Spanish, and British newspapers, that readers of different papers might not realize they're reading about the same research.[77]

Articles published in scientific journals are read primarily by trained professionals, whereas stories about the articles in newspapers and magazines and on television reach a much greater audience. Conventional wisdom is not newsworthy, so the media play on public fears while emphasizing the frontiers and fringes of science. Reporters with limited scientific training and under severe time constraints sometimes use just one source and thus present just one point of view. They fail to distinguish among preliminary findings, conference reports, small pilot studies, and more substantial works. They compress lengthy, complex articles into brief stories or sixty-second time slots, omitting important details in the process. They ask interviewees for definitive answers, which leads to speculations beyond what the data warrant.

Editors issue press releases in advance of publication to alert reporters to potentially interesting stories, and reporters often accept them uncritically. De Semir and colleagues collected press releases and tables of contents from major scientific journals and stories on scientific research in major newspapers worldwide. Of the 142 newspaper stories that referred to journal articles, only twenty-three covered articles that had not been mentioned in press releases.[78]

Vendors of scientific products capitalize on reporters' quotas and deadlines. The vendors' public relations departments produce and distribute press kits including entire scripts for television science reporters. Their dramatic, slick video news releases are essentially lengthy commercials but are more compelling than most reporters' best efforts. So they are often shown in their entirety, masquerading as news. Schwitzer cites a survey of 2,500 editors and reporters that found that 90 percent of ideas for health articles had originated with a public relations person.[79]

A research team led by Ray Moynihan analyzed more than two hundred stories on new drugs that had been published in newspapers or presented on television. Most of the accounts overstated benefits, did not mention risks, and ignored the source of funding. Forty percent of the reports that quoted an expert failed to mention that the expert had financial ties to the drug's manufacturer.[80]

ADDITIONAL METHODOLOGICAL ISSUES

A set of statistical techniques called meta-analysis enables reviewers to combine results from separate studies to answer questions such as "What is the average effect of a treatment?" It is noteworthy that much of the research on the effectiveness of drugs is seriously deficient methodologically, and the smallest improvements generally come from the most carefully conducted studies.[81]

Washout Procedure

Experimenters routinely initiate studies of antidepressants and certain other psychiatric drugs by giving placebos for seven to ten days to all potential subjects. Those who markedly improve are disqualified from further participation. The washout procedure eliminates placebo responders; they constitute a significant portion of the psychiatric population and would be expected to show the smallest drug/placebo differences.

Double Blind

The best method for evaluating a drug's effectiveness is the controlled experiment. Experimenters randomly assign subjects to receive either a drug or a placebo (or a different drug) and treat the groups identically in all other respects. Treatment is not identical if either experimenters or subjects know who is in which group, for the knowledge can affect their expectations and subsequent behavior. The solution is to conduct double-blind experiments in which neither experimenter nor subjects know who received what. A research aide administers treatments and hides a code that indicates group assignment until the data have been collected. One problem is that subjects are often assigned to groups nonrandomly, which undermines the purpose of the double blind, introduces serious bias, and leads to inflated measures of effectiveness. But summaries of the research nevertheless falsely use the word *randomized.* Two studies identified by a MEDLINE search as "randomized controlled trials" had one patient each.[82]

Drugs have side effects, so even blinded experimenters and subjects often figure out who has received which treatment.[83] Furthermore, write-ups of double-blind experiments do not always reflect the actual conduct of researchers. Schulz and his colleagues visited laboratories and found that, when the codes indicating group assignment were poorly concealed, the experimental treatment was reported effective by an average of 30 percent more than when codes were kept strictly confidential. Schulz quizzed 400 researchers after promising them anonymity. More than half admitted to opening unsealed envelopes containing the assignments, cracking simple codes meant to hide the identity of the two groups, searching for a master list of codes, or holding sealed envelopes up to the light.[84] Researchers frequently deviate from written protocols.[85]

An acceptable variation on the drug/placebo comparison is to give one group of subjects a drug and the other group a different treatment, for example, psychotherapy. But it is acceptable only if the alternative treatment is adequate. In six widely cited studies that compared drugs with psychotherapy for schizophrenia, the psychotherapists were either generally inexperienced or inexperienced in treating chronic schizophrenics.[86] The National Institute of Mental Health sponsored a study that compared stimulant drugs with other treatments for attention deficit/hyperactivity disorder. Proponents claimed that the study demonstrated the superiority of stimulants over behavioral treatment. Among the many flaws is that the behavioral treatments were inadequate.[87]

Thornley and Adams rated the methodological quality of 2,000 trials over a fifty-year period on people with schizophrenia, serious or chronic mental illness, psychosis, or movement disorders.[88] Although several types of treatment were considered, 86 percent (1,725) of the trials evaluated the effects of drugs. The maximum score was 5, for which the report had to have given appropriate methods of generating random assignment, appropriate blinding of participants and raters, and details on those who withdrew from the trial before its conclusion. Only twenty trials received a rating of 5, slightly more than one-third received a score of 3 or more, and 1,280 scored 2 or less. Scores did not improve with time. From 1950 to 1997 the mean quality score was consistently under 2.5. More than half of the trials (1,082) lasted six weeks or less, and less than one-fifth lasted longer than six months.

In most recent trials, haloperidol was the control drug. Side effects from haloperidol make blind conditions difficult to maintain, so even studies labeled as double blind are vulnerable to bias. In addition, because haloperidol's side effects are often very unpleasant, drugs with even moderate antipsychotic properties are likely to be favorable by comparison.

Statistical Tricks

For a drug to gain FDA approval, at least two studies must be published showing that the drug has outperformed placebo. If there are negative findings (no difference between drug and placebo groups), they do not count for much. M. Thase reports that 50 percent of trials funded by the drug industry are negative, and most of them go unpublished.[89] Researchers, reviewers for journals, and journal editors all prefer positive to negative studies. This preference, called publication bias, has serious consequences. Suppose, for example, that fifty published studies indicate that a certain drug is 25 percent more effective than placebo, whereas fifty equally well-done studies produce negative results and hence go unpublished. Meta-analysts will overestimate the drug effect at 25 percent. The problem is exacerbated by the large dropout rate from individual studies, often as high as 50 percent of the subjects. People are likely to drop out if the drug is producing unpleasant side effects or not working.

Although sixteen published studies on advanced ovarian cancer indicate a significant survival advantage of combination chemotherapy, the advantage was found to be illusory when several unpublished studies were located and added to the database.[90] Publication bias in reviews of studies on the treatment of obesity have resulted in overestimates of the effectiveness of the treatments.[91]

Some researchers conduct a single study and then publish their results in more than one journal. Meta-analysts may be fooled into thinking the studies are independent, especially if different authors are listed. The result is an overestimation of treatment effects, as happened with ondansetron for treating postoperative nausea.[92] Huston and Moher have identified twenty articles describing randomized, double-blind trials of the antipsychotic drug risperidone. But the articles were not independent. All the data came from seven small and two large trials. Huston and Moher write, "Multiple renditions of the same information is self-serving, wasteful, abuses the volunteer time of peer reviewers, and can be profoundly misleading; it brings into question the integrity of medical research."[93]

The previous examples concern misleading methods of combining and presenting results, but even individual studies in good medical journals often have inappropriate statistical analyses.[94] Methodological impurity can be subtle. Spiro describes a study on a potential treatment for peptic ulcers:

> At the end of two weeks, the ulcer crater had healed in more than half the patients given the active drug and in only a third of patients taking placebos; that one observation point provided the desired statistical significance to permit the claim that the active drug, in this case cimetidine, "speeded the healing" of peptic ulcer. . . . But at every other period of assessment, cimetidine and the placebo proved equally effective. . . . Statisticians often select the best answers to magnify the claims for the agent.[95]

Pharmaceutical giant Upjohn manufactures the benzodiazepine alprazolam (Xanax). In the 1980s, Upjohn sponsored a large-scale study to assess the efficacy of Xanax in treating panic disorder. Even before all the data were in, Upjohn used the research to promote Xanax at company-sponsored conferences and symposia and in supplements to journals sent to thousands of psychiatrists. Then the results were published in four separate articles in the May 1988 issue of the *Archives of General Psychiatry* (which accepts advertising for Upjohn drugs). The results, which were promoted in ads for Xanax, indicate that panic attack sufferers who took Xanax were much more likely to be free of panic attacks than those given placebo. The ads were true as far as they went. But they did not mention three key points:

- The drug phase of the study was supposed to last eight weeks. Many subjects dropped out before the end.
- Although the Xanax recipients had fewer panic attacks during the first four weeks than those given placebo, by the eighth week the two groups were virtually identical. (The ads cited only the four-week results.)

- At the end of the eight weeks the Xanax subjects were gradually withdrawn from the drug. They suffered rebound panic attacks at a slightly greater frequency than they had been experiencing at the beginning. They were worse off. By contrast, the number of panic attacks in placebo subjects declined significantly throughout the study.[96]

Nuovo and colleagues examined the statistics reported in studies claiming a significant drug effect. They investigated all issues of five prestigious medical journals for the years 1989, 1992, 1995, and 1998. The statistics in most articles exaggerate effectiveness. Suppose, for example, that 2 percent of placebo- and 1 percent of drug-treated patients have relapses. The drug reduces relapse rate by 50 percent. A more informative but less impressive statistic is that the drug saves one patient in 100 from relapse. Statistics of the first type are used much more frequently.[97]

If drug company executives were motivated to improve health care rather than maximize profits, then they would market only those drugs that are at least as good as existing ones. The typical study would compare a new drug with the best treatment currently available. Such studies are rare. Statistically significant results—which companies need for FDA approval—are most easily achieved by comparing the drug with a placebo. If a drug were compared with the best available treatment and came up short, the marketing department would have to work overtime to give the results a positive spin.

End Points

Some variables cannot be measured easily, so surrogate end points are used instead. For example, high blood pressure is a surrogate end point for subsequent heart disease. A good surrogate end point correlates strongly with the more important clinical end point and can reduce the length and cost of a research project. Much can be said for streamlining the drug approval process, but it is both scientifically unsound and dangerous to approve drugs for sale solely on the basis of their effects on surrogate end points. One problem is that some researchers study many surrogate end points and publish results only for those that favor their product.

If a fair coin is tossed five times, the probability that it will come up heads each time is about 3 percent. But if fifty fair coins are each tossed five times, the probability is almost 80 percent that at least one coin will come up heads each time. By the same reasoning, a researcher who tests multiple end points increases the probability that at least one will appear statistically significant. It is likely to be a false positive. One study tested 857 end points.[98]

Fleming and DeMets discuss a second problem: The fact that a surrogate normally correlates strongly with a clinical outcome does not ensure that a treatment-induced change in the surrogate will produce a corresponding change in the clinical outcome.[99] For example, obesity is a risk factor for many diseases. The drug dexfenfluramine helps people lose weight, so the FDA approved dexfenfluramine on the grounds that the benefits of weight loss more than offset any dangers of the drug. But doctors found that the dangers outweigh the benefits, and dexfenfluramine was eventually withdrawn.

Psaty and colleagues discuss another strategy for approving drugs based on their action on surrogates. The reasoning takes the following form: "(1) in large, long-term clinical trials, drug A reduces both the surrogate end point and the disease incidence; (2) in short-term trials, drug B reduces the level of the surrogate end point; (3) in clinical practice, drug B will behave like drug A in its effect on disease incidence."[100] Psaty and colleagues write that the reasoning has some merit if drugs A and B are from the same drug class. Still, clinical outcome should be the ultimate criterion of a drug's value; they note cases where the generalization from A to B failed for clinical outcome. And if A and B are from different classes with different mechanisms of action and side effect profiles, drug B's hypothesized benefit is much less certain.

Below are some additional examples in which changes in surrogate end points did not accurately predict clinical outcomes:

- Tumor response is a frequent surrogate end point in trials of advanced cancer. But many drugs reduce tumors without changing mortality rates.
- CD4 cells (helper T-cells) release molecules that signal other cells to produce antibodies to HIV. Change in CD4 cell count is the most popular surrogate for tests of drugs for treating HIV and AIDS. But CD4 cell count change does not accurately predict progression to AIDS or time to death.
- Postmenopausal women lose bone mass, which ultimately leads to an increased risk for fractures of the hip and other bones. Sodium fluoride stimulates bone formation and increases bone mass, so it came into widespread use. But patients treated with fluoride experienced a higher incidence of fractures than patients who received placebo.
- Quinidine prevents atrial fibrillation, which is life threatening. But among patients with atrial fibrillation, quinidine increased mortality rate more than threefold.
- High cholesterol levels are associated with heart disease. Clofibrate (Atromid-S) and pravastatin (Pravachol) both reduce cholesterol levels. The death rate was reduced in patients taking Pravachol but increased in Atromid-S patients.
- Hypertension is a risk factor for cardiovascular-related mortality. Low-dose diuretics and beta blockers both lower blood pressure and reduce the risk. Two newer classes of drugs, angiotensin-converting enzyme inhibitors and calcium channel blockers, also lower blood pressure and were believed to

> have a better side effect profile than the older drugs. Although they are much more expensive, they took over a large share of the market. But their overall effects are probably harmful. Blood pressure, although a reliable surrogate end point for the evaluation of low-dose diuretics, is not a good surrogate for other antihypertensive drugs. Nevertheless, manufacturers of calcium channel blockers use surrogate endpoints in their advertising.
>
> Ventricular arrhythmia is associated with a large increase in the risk for death related to cardiac complications. In the 1980s and early 1990s, three new drugs that suppressed arrhythmias were approved by the FDA and taken by hundreds of thousands of people with life-threatening arrhythmias. But the drugs were deadly. Investigative journalist Thomas Moore has estimated that 50,000 patients died over a two-year period from taking them. Moore also shows that the doctors who were paid by drug companies to develop the drugs also worked with the FDA to approve the drugs and then worked to promote them.[101]

Greenhalgh writes, "It would be wrong to suggest that the pharmaceutical industry develops surrogate end points with the deliberate intention to mislead the licensing authorities and health professionals. Surrogate end points have both ethical and economic imperatives. The industry does, however, have a vested interest in overstating its case on the strength of these end points."[102]

CONCLUDING COMMENTS

The methods of science are the most powerful ever developed for learning how the world works. But it is rare for somebody to become a competent researcher without extensive training, which few medical students receive. Yet many medical doctors do research. Their work is often flawed, and their conclusions, untrustworthy.

Financial considerations play a huge role in determining which proposals get funded; how data are recorded, analyzed, and interpreted; and whether the results are ever published. Money also influences the actions of government agencies and recommendations of expert committees concerning medical practices. Few methodology textbooks devote space to the motives of researchers, but people whose health and well-being depend on research should do so.

NOTES

1. P. Schrag, *Mind Control* (New York: Pantheon, 1978).
2. E. Haber, "Industry and the University," *Nature Biotechnology* 14 (1996): 441–42.
3. J. Glenmullen, *Prozac Backlash* (New York: Simon and Schuster, 2000).

4. D. Kessler et al., "Therapeutic Class Wars—Drug Promotion in a Competitive Marketplace," *New England Journal of Medicine* (*NEJM*) 331 (1994): 1350–53.

5. H. Johansen and P. Gotzsche, "Problems in the Design and Reporting of Trials of Antifungal Agents Encountered during Meta-analysis," *Journal of the American Medical Association* (*JAMA*) 282 (1999): 1752–59.

6. T. Bodenheimer, "Uneasy Alliance: Clinical Investigators and the Pharmaceutical Industry," *Health Policy Report* 342 (2000): 1539–44.

7. D. Blumenthal et al., "Withholding Research Results by Academic Life Scientists: Evidence from a National Survey of Faculty," *JAMA* 277 (1997): 1224–28.

8. W. Cohen et al., *University-Industry Research Centers in the United States* (Pittsburgh: Carnegie-Mellon University Press, 1994).

9. I. Chalmers, "Underreporting Research Is Scientific Misconduct," *JAMA* 263 (1990): 405–08; K. Dickersin, "The Existence of Publication Bias and Risk Factors for Its Occurrence," *JAMA* 263 (1990): 1385–89.

10. Bodenheimer, "Uneasy Alliance."

11. Bodenheimer, "Uneasy Alliance."

12. U. Torassa, "Drug Firm Battles UCSF on Research Results," *San Francisco Examiner,* 1 November 2000: A1, A16.

13. "News," *British Medical Journal* (*BMJ*) 322 (2001): 571, 1086.

14. F. Teitelbaum et al., *Express Scripts Drug Trend Report* (St. Louis: Express Scripts, Inc., June 1999), 20.

15. R. Davidson, "Source of Funding and Outcome of Clinical Trials," *Journal of General Internal Medicine* 1 (1986): 155–58.

16. M. Cho and L. Bero, "The Quality of Drug Studies Published in Symposium Proceedings," *Annals of Internal Medicine* 124 (1996): 485–89.

17. C. Bennett et al., "Evaluation of Conflict of Interest in Economic Analyses of New Drugs Used in Oncology," *JAMA* 282 (1999): 1453–57.

18. P. Easterbrook et al., "Publication Bias in Clinical Research," *The Lancet* 337 (1991): 867–72; K. Dickersin et al., "Factors Influencing Publication of Research Results: Follow-up of Applications Submitted to Two Institutional Review Boards," *JAMA* 267 (1992): 374–78.

19. Bodenheimer, "Uneasy Alliance."

20. L. Bero and D. Rennie, "Influences on the Quality of Published Drug Studies," *International Journal of Technology Assessment in Health Care* 12 (1996): 209–37.

21. P. Gotzsche, "Methodology and Overt and Hidden Bias in Reports of 196 Double-Blind Trials of Nonsteroidal Anti-inflammatory Drugs in Rheumatoid Arthritis," *Controlled Clinical Trials* 10 (1989): 31–56.

22. C. Selzer, "Second Thoughts: 'Conflicts of Interest' and 'Political Science,'" *Journal of Clinical Epidemiology* 50 (1997): 627–29.

23. P. Rochon et al., "A Study of Manufacturer Supported Trials of Nonsteroidal Anti-inflammatory Drugs in the Treatment of Arthritis," *Archives of Internal Medicine* 154 (1994): 157–63.

24. G. Birnbaum and D. Montero, "Analyze This: Docs Get Drug Co. $$," *New York Post,* 28 February 1999, available at www.ferris.edu/isar/arcade/psycho/analyze.htm (accessed on 16 December 2002).

25. K. Eichenwald and G. Kolata, "Drug Trials Hide Conflicts for Doctors," *New York Times,* 16 May 1999: sec. 1, 1.

26. J. La Puma, "Physicians' Conflicts of Interest in Post-marketing Research: What the Public Should Know, and Why Industry Should Tell Them," in *The Ethics of Research Involving Human Subjects: Facing the 21st Century,* ed. H. Vanderpool (Frederick, Md.: University Publishing Group, 1996), 203–19.

27. P. Breggin and D. Cohen, *Your Drug May Be Your Problem* (Reading, Mass.: Perseus Books, 1999); J. Glenmullen, *Prozac Backlash* (New York: Simon and Schuster, 2000).

28. Office of Research Integrity, *Annual Report* (Rockville, Md.: Department of Health and Human Services, 1996); Office of Research Integrity, *Highlights for 1997* (Rockville, Md.: Department of Health and Human Services, 1999).

29. P. Woolf, "Projection on Science Fraud and Misconduct," Report on Workshop Number One (Washington, D.C.: American Association for the Advancement of Science, 1988), 37.

30. W. Stewart and N. Feder, "The Integrity of the Scientific Literature," *Nature* 325 (1987): 207–14.

31. W. Broad and N. Wade, *Betrayers of the Truth* (New York: Simon and Schuster, 1982).

32. "Cold Researcher Made Profit on Quigley Shares; Stock Soared after Release of Study Favorable to Lozenges," *Washington Post,* 31 January 1997: G1.

33. "Insider Traders in White Coats; Drug Researchers in Rare Position to Exploit Stocks," *New York Times,* 11 April 1998: D1.

34. D. William, "Drug Maker Hired NIH Researcher," *Los Angeles Times,* 7 December 1998: 1, 14.

35. "News," *BMJ* 316 (1998): 1553.

36. D. Barnes and L. Bero, "Why Review Articles on the Health Effects of Passive Smoking Reach Different Conclusions," *JAMA* 279 (1998): 1566–70.

37. R. Walton, "Survey of Aspartame Studies: Correlation of Outcome and Funding Sources," unpublished study, compiled for *60 Minutes* (1994).

38. H. Stelfox et al., "Conflict in the Debate over Calcium-Channel Antagonists," *NEJM* 338 (1998): 101–06.

39. S. Krimsky et al., "Financial Interests of Authors in Scientific Journals: A Pilot Study of 14 Publications," *Science and Engineering Ethics* 2 (1996): 395–410.

40. J. Drazen and G. Curfman, "Editorial," *NEJM* 346 (2002): 1901–02.

41. M. Angell, "Is Academic Medicine for Sale?" *NEJM* 342 (2000): 1516–18.

42. J. Ioannidis and J. Lau, "Completeness of Safety Reporting in Randomized Trials: An Evaluation of 7 Medical Areas," *JAMA* 285 (2001): 437–43.

43. Hypericum Depression Trial Study Group, "Effect of Hypericum perforatum (St John's Wort) in Major Depressive Disorder: A Randomized Controlled Trial," *JAMA* 287 (2002): 1812.

44. P. Jüni and A. Rutjes, "Editorial," *BMJ* 324 (2002): 1287–88.

45. F. Silverstein et al., "Gastrointestinal Toxicity with Celecoxib vs Nonsteroidal Anti-inflammatory Drugs for Osteoarthritis and Rheumatoid Arthritis: The CLASS Study: A Randomized Controlled Trial. Celecoxib Long-term Arthritis Safety Study," *JAMA* 284 (2000): 1247–55.

46. S. Okie, "Missing Data on Celebrex. Full Study Altered Picture of Drug," *Washington Post,* 5 August 2001: A11; J. Berg Hrachovec and M. Mora, "Reporting of 6-Month vs 12-Month Data in a Clinical Trial of Celecoxib," *JAMA* 286 (2001): 2398; J. Wright et al., "Reporting of 6-Month vs 12-Month Data in a Clinical Trial of Celecoxib," *JAMA* 286 (2001): 2398–99.

47. L. Kjaergard and B. Als-Nielsen, "Association between Competing Interests and Authors' Conclusions: Epidemiological Study of Randomised Clinical Trials Published in the *BMJ*," *BMJ* 325 (2002): 249–58.

48. Editorial, "Just How Tainted Has Medicine Become?" *The Lancet* 359 (2002): 1167.

49. T. Brennan, "Buying Editorials," *NEJM* 331 (1994): 673–75.

50. Eichenwald and Kolata, "Drug Trials Hide Conflicts for Doctors," 1.

51. Bodenheimer, "Uneasy Alliance."

52. R. Peveler et al., "Effect of Antidepressant Drug Counseling and Information Leaflets on Adherence to Drug Treatment in Primary Care: Randomized Controlled Trial," *BMJ* 319 (1999): 612–15.

53. P. Breggin and G. Breggin, *Talking Back to Prozac* (New York: St. Martin's Press, 1994).

54. In an otherwise kind review of a previous book of mine, Andrade writes that "the views of cranks such as Peter Breggin are entertained without adequate rebuttal" (*National Institute of Mental Health and Neuroscience Journal* 14 [1996]: 63–68). Many in the medical establishment view Breggin as a crank. However, he presents important data and arguments. They should be considered by anyone who wants to make informed decisions about psychiatric drugs. See Breggin and Breggin, *Talking Back to Prozac.*

55. Breggin and Cohen, *Your Drug May Be Your Problem.*

56. See www.phrma.org/publications/industry/profile99/chap2.html#growth (accessed on 20 September 2000).

57. T. Moore et al., "Commentary—Time to Act on Drug Safety," *JAMA* 279 (1998): 1571–73.

58. D. DeLeo and G. Magni, "Sexual Side Effects of Antidepressant Drugs," *Psychosomatics* 24 (1983): 1076–82.
59. D. Kessler, "Introducing MedWatch," *JAMA* 269 (1993): 2765–68.
60. D. Cauchon, "FDA Advisers Tied to Industry," *USA Today,* 25 September 2000.
61. M. Jacobson, "Fake Fat, Ersatz Sugar," *The Nation,* 24 May 1999: 2.
62. M. Anderson, "Sweetheart Deal," *Berkeley Monthly,* October 1999: 20–21, 37.
63. "Sugar Substitutes," *FDA Consumer,* November–December 1999: 12–16.
64. Breggin and Breggin, *Talking Back to Prozac.*
65. Breggin and Cohen, *Your Drug May Be Your Problem.*
66. D. Williams, "How Withdrawn Diabetes Drug Got an OK," *San Francisco Chronicle,* 11 March 2001: A3–A4.
67. D. Willman, "A Heartburn Drug, Now Linked to Children's Deaths," *Los Angeles Times,* 20 December 2000: front page.
68. R. Whitaker, "Lure of Riches Fuels Testing," *Boston Globe,* 17 November 1998: A1.
69. R. Horton, "Lotronex and the FDA: A Fatal Erosion of Integrity," *The Lancet* 357 (2001): 1544–45.
70. P. Lurie and S. Wolfe, "Troubling Climate at FDA," *Washington Post,* 30 December 1998: A19.
71. N. Choudhry et al., "Relationships between Authors of Clinical Practice Guidelines and the Pharmaceutical Industry," *JAMA* 287 (2002): 612–17.
72. "U.S. Cholesterol Guidelines Have Some Suspecting Bias," *San Francisco Chronicle,* 4 June 2001: B4.
73. J. Lenzer, "Alteplase for Stroke: Money and Optimistic Claims Buttress the 'Brain Attack' Campaign," *BMJ* 324 (2002): 725.
74. Lenzer, "Alteplase for Stroke," 723–29.
75. J. Saver et al., "Commentary: Thrombolysis in Stroke: It Works!" *BMJ* 324 (2002): 727. For further comments, see "Letters, Alteplase for Stroke," *BMJ* 324 (2002): 1581.
76. D. Nelkin, *Selling Science* (New York: W. H. Freeman, 1987).
77. I. Lowe, "Forum: Tell It Like It Is," *New Scientist,* 24 October 1998: 52.
78. V. De Semir et al., "Press Releases of Science Journal Articles and Subsequent Newspaper Stories on the Same Topic," *JAMA* 280 (1998): 294–95.
79. G. Schwitzer, "The Magical Medical Media Tour," *JAMA* 267 (1992): 1969–71.
80. R. Moynihan et al., "Coverage by the News Media of the Benefits and Risks of Medications," *NEJM* 342 (2000): 1645–51.
81. D. Moher et al., "Does Quality of Reports of Randomised Trials Affect Estimates of Intervention Efficacy Reported in Meta-analyses?" *The Lancet* 352 (1998): 609–13; A. Smith et al., eds., "Studies on the Effectiveness of Antidepressant Drugs," theme issue, *Psychopharmacology Bulletin* (1969); S. Fisher and R. Greenberg, *The Limits of Biological Treatments for Psychological Distress* (Hillsdale, N.J.: Lawrence Erlbaum, 1989).
82. L. Bero and D. Rennie, "Influences on the Quality of Published Drug Studies," *International Journal of Technology Assessment in Health Care* 12 (1996): 209–37.
83. J. Margraf et al., "How 'Blind' Are Double-Blind Studies?" *Journal of Consulting and Clinical Psychology* 59 (1991): 184–87; R. Greenberg and S. Fisher, "Seeing through the Double-Masked Design: A Commentary," *Controlled Clinical Trials* 15 (1994): 244–46.
84. K. Schulz, "Empirical Evidence of Bias. Dimensions of Methodological Quality Associated with Estimates of Treatment Effects in Controlled Trials," *JAMA* 273 (1995): 408–12.
85. M. Shapiro, "Data Audit in Investigational Drug Trials and Their Implications for Detection of Misconduct in Science," in *Fraud and Misconduct in Medical Research,* ed. S. Lock and F. Wells (London: BMJ Publishing Group, 1993), 128–41.
86. B. Karon, "Psychotherapy versus Medication for Schizophrenia: Empirical Comparisons," in *The Limits of Biological Treatments for Psychological Distress,* ed. S. Fisher and R. Greenberg (Hillsdale, N.J.: Lawrence Erlbaum, 1989), 105–50.
87. P. Breggin, "A Critical Analysis of the NIMH Multimodal Treatment Study for Attention-Deficit Hyperactivity Disorder (the MTA Study)," *Ethical Human Sciences and Services* 2 (2000): 63–72.

88. B. Thornley and C. Adams, "Content and Quality of 2000 Controlled Trials in Schizophrenia over 50 Years," *BMJ* 317 (1998): 1181–84.

89. M. Thase, "Antidepressant Effects: The Suit May Be Small, but the Fabric Is Real. Commentary on the Emperor's New Drugs: An Analysis of Antidepressant Medication Data Submitted to the U.S. Food and Drug Administration," *Prevention and Treatment* 5 (2002): article 25.

90. R. Simes, "Publication Bias: The Case for an International Registry of Clinical Trials," *Journal of Clinical Oncology* 4 (1986): 1529–41.

91. D. Allison et al., "Publication Bias in Obesity Treatment Trials?" *International Journal of Obesity and Related Metabolic Disorders* 20 (1996): 931–37.

92. M. Tramer et al., "Impact of Covert Duplicate Publication on Meta-analysis: A Case Study," *BMJ* 315 (1997): 635–40.

93. P. Huston and D. Moher, "Redundancy, Disaggregation, and the Integrity of Medical Research," *The Lancet* 347 (1996): 1024.

94. D. Altman, "Statistics in Medical Journals," *Statistics in Medicine* 1 (1982): 59–71.

95. H. Spiro, "Clinical Reflections on the Placebo Phenomenon," in *The Placebo Effect: An Interdisciplinary Exploration,* ed. A. Harrington (Cambridge: Harvard University Press, 1997), 37–55.

96. "High Anxiety," *Consumer Reports,* January 1993: 19–24.

97. J. Nuovo et al., "Reporting Number Needed to Treat and Absolute Risk Reduction in Randomized Controlled Trials," *JAMA* 287 (2002): 2813–14.

98. Gotzsche, "Methodology and Overt and Hidden Bias in Reports of 196 Double-Blind Trials of Nonsteroidal Anti-inflammatory Drugs in Rheumatoid Arthritis."

99. T. Fleming and D. DeMets, "Surrogate End Points in Clinical Trials: Are We Being Misled?" *Annals of Internal Medicine* 125 (1996): 605–13.

100. B. Psaty et al., "Surrogate End Points, Health Outcomes, and the Drug-Approval Process for the Treatment of Risk Factors for Cardiovascular Disease," *JAMA* 282 (1999): 788.

101. Fleming and DeMets, "Surrogate End Points in Clinical Trials." Regarding high cholesterol levels, see also J. Shepard et al., "Prevention of Coronary Heart Disease with Pravastatin in Men with Hypercholesterolemia," *NEJM* 333 (1995): 1301–07; F. Sacks et al., "The Effect of Pravastatin on Coronary Events after Myocardial Infarction in Patients with Average Cholesterol Levels," *NEJM* 335 (1996): 1001–09; and M. Oliver, "W.H.O. Cooperative Trial on Primary Prevention of Ischaemic Heart Disease Using Clofibrate to Lower Serum Cholesterol: Mortality Follow-up," *The Lancet* (1980): 379–85. Regarding arrhythmia, see also T. Moore, *Deadly Medicine* (New York: Simon and Schuster, 1995).

102. T. Greenhalgh, "How to Read a Paper: Papers That Report Drug Trials," *BMJ* 315 (1997): 480–83.

2

Drug Companies Place Profits over Progress

Research financed by drug companies has been crucial for the development of new drugs to treat chronic diseases and increase life expectancy. Insulin allows thousands of diabetics to lead normal lives, cardiac drugs prolong the lives of people with heart problems, antibiotics cure many formerly deadly infectious diseases, and general anesthetics make operations bearable. Fuchs and Sox contacted 225 general internists nominated by their peers as highly respected.[1] The respondents ranked the importance of thirty medical innovations in treating patients. They ranked four drugs in the top ten innovations and eleven in the top twenty.

But the companies are beholden to their shareholders, so the bottom line is making money. Profits, thank you, have been spectacular. *Fortune* magazine has reported that the drug industry's 18.5 percent return on investment led all U.S. industries in 2001 for the third time in ten years. Although overall profits of Fortune 500 companies declined by 53 percent in 2001, the top ten U.S. drug makers increased profits by 32 percent. Total spending on prescription drugs increased each year between 1997 and 2001. The trend has been toward more drugs and more expensive drugs.[2]

Spokespeople claim that companies need high profit margins to support research and development. They must demonstrate to the Food and Drug Administration (FDA) that their drugs work, which requires expensive animal and human clinical studies. Pharmaceutical Research and Manufacturers of America, a Washington-based private trade organization, has presented the industry's arguments on the Internet. Box 2.1 gives several excerpts.

One response to the drug companies' defense is that 90 percent of their research is directed at diseases that cause 10 percent of the global burden of disease.[3]

Box 2.1. Excerpts from the Pharmaceutical Research and Manufacturers Association Comments on Drug Development and Pricing

Just as the price of a textbook is not determined by the cost of the paper of its pages and the cost of surgery has little to do with the price of the surgeon's scalpel, the cost of a medicine is not simply the cost of its ingredients. Like other products that result from research and creativity, medicines are really made of knowledge—knowledge that prevents and cures disease and relieves suffering. The knowledge needed to discover and develop new medicines does not come cheap. Discovering, developing, testing, and gaining regulatory approval for new medicines is expensive, time consuming and risky.

Of every 5,000 medicines tested, on average, only 5 are tested in clinical trials, and only 1 of those is approved for patient use. Revenues from successful medicines must cover the costs of the "dry holes." The average cost of bringing one new medicine to market is $500 million. It takes an average of 12–15 years to discover and develop a new medicine. Most of that time is spent testing the drug to make sure it is safe.

On average, only 3 of every 10 prescription drugs available to treat Americans generate revenues that meet or exceed average R&D costs.

Although the cost of developing drugs is soaring, the time that companies have to recoup their investment is shrinking due to stepped-up competition from generic drugs.

The U.S. is the world leader in pharmaceutical innovation—at least in part because of its relatively free market for pharmaceuticals. Nearly half of the world-class medicines developed over the past two decades originated in the U.S. It is no accident that the U.S., where free market competition is allowed to determine prices, produces the most innovation and that countries with price controls on pharmaceuticals produce the least.

Source: Available at www.phrma.org/publications/publications/brochure/questions/whycostmuch.phtml (accessed on 10 July 2002).

That is where the profits are. Furthermore, although the research is needed for FDA approval, companies spend 40 to 70 cents of each prescription drug dollar on marketing, selling, and administration. As with laundry detergents and shampoos, marketing strategies take precedence over identifying the most effective products. Ron Pollack, the executive director of a Washington, D.C.–based health care consumers' group, Families USA, has said, "The industry is hiding behind research and development as a way of increasing prices and therefore increasing profits. The research and development mantra they use is clearly extremely misleading."[4]

A report from the watchdog group Public Citizen has challenged the industry's claim that the average cost of developing a new drug is $500 million. Public Citizen analysts have estimated that the actual average is closer to $100 million.[5]

A recent report from the National Institute for Health Care Management Research and Educational Foundation describes the FDA's method of reviewing and classifying drugs for approval.[6] Drugs that offer significant clinical improvement over available products qualify for fast priority review, whereas all other drugs get standard reviews. The FDA has an additional way of classifying:

- New Molecular Entity (NME): a drug whose active ingredient has never before been approved by the FDA
- Incrementally Modified Drug (IMD): a drug that has been modified by the manufacturer but whose active ingredient is identical with or a close chemical derivative of an ingredient of an already approved drug
- Other Drug: a drug using an active ingredient already available in an identical marketed product

From 1989 to 2000 the FDA approved 1,035 new drug applications. Of these, 361 (35 percent of the total) were NMEs, and 153 of them received a priority rating; 558 (54 percent) were IMDs, and 86 received a priority rating; 116 (11 percent) were other drugs, and five received a priority rating. In the six years between 1989 and 1994, priority NMEs (the only category offering both new active ingredient and significant clinical improvement) accounted for 17 percent of total approvals. During 1995–2000, they accounted for only 13 percent.

Between 1995 and 2000, retail spending on prescription drugs increased from $64.7 billion to $132 billion. Two-thirds of the increase came from new drugs approved by the FDA in 1995 or later, and two-thirds of those were standard rated, that is, providing no significant clinical improvement over existing products. In 2000, the average cost per prescription was $91.20 for new priority NMEs, $81.92 for new standard NMEs, $142 for priority IMDs ($84.14 if very expensive HIV antiviral drugs are excluded), $65.07 for standard IMDs, and $37.20 for older branded and generic drugs approved prior to 1995. The price differences between new IMDs and older drugs illustrate the incentives to manufacturers for making insignificant changes to aging products.

Blockbuster drugs (annual sales of at least $1 billion) accounted for 48 to 80 percent of the total prescription drug sales of the five largest drug companies in 2001. In the past, many blockbusters were NMEs that treated common and previously untreatable conditions. But from 1990 to 1999, only five drug companies introduced at least ten NMEs. IMDs feature an active ingredient whose safety and efficacy have already been established and whose name is known to doctors and consumers, so they offer a much less risky route to big profits.

The report acknowledges a study that complicates matters somewhat. Lichetenberg has analyzed 1996 data from the Medical Expenditure Panel Survey of health care use and spending by the U.S. population.[7] He found that people who took newer drugs lost fewer days from work than people with the same conditions who took older drugs. They spent less money on nondrug medical concerns, including money to hospitals, and they were less likely to have died by the end of the survey.

Lichetenberg's findings are important but must be interpreted cautiously. One problem is that patients were not randomly assigned to get new or old drugs. (See pages 178–79 for discussion of the importance of random assignment.) The patients may have differed in the severity of their illnesses or the quality of the medical care they received. Furthermore, Lichetenberg analyzes just thirteen of about five hundred medical conditions treated with prescription drugs. Newer drugs improved outcomes for only a few conditions. They reduced lost workdays for four conditions (chronic sinusitis, disease of lipoid metabolism, allergic rhinitis, and diabetes mellitus), reduced nondrug medical expenditures for two (ill-defined heart disease and arthropathies), and reduced mortality rates for two (ill-defined heart disease and disease of lipoid metabolism).

LOBBYING

The drug industry spent $235.7 million from 1997 to 1999 to lobby government officials, and it spent millions more on television spots, radio and newspaper ads, direct mailings, and telemarketing efforts. The industry contributed $23 million to Republicans and $10.4 million to Democrats between 1993 and 1999. It ranks number one in direct lobbying expenditures—at least $83.6 million in 1999—and hired 297 lobbyists just to oppose Medicare drug coverage.[8] The reason is that drug purchases for seniors are currently covered by many different groups within the private sector. Medicare, if it did all the purchasing, would have considerable leverage in negotiations over prices. That would reduce industry profits.

ALLIANCES

Some drug companies sponsor organizations for patients with specific disabilities and then promote their own drug for treating the disability. According to one industry executive, patient groups help companies to "rapidly disseminate information about a product to patients."[9] Speaking tours and television exposure are arranged for articulate, personable leaders of the patient groups. For example, Eli Lilly, manufacturer of Prozac, arranged for a support group of Prozac users to appear on the *Oprah Winfrey Show* and tell how Prozac had transformed their lives.[10] The nonprofit group Children and Adults with Attention Deficit Disorder, which encourages parents to place their children on Ritalin, receives much of its financial support from Ritalin's manufacturer. Boots/Knoll, the company that manufactures the thyroid drug Synthroid, helps fund the American Thyroid Association. When Boots/Knoll delayed publication of a study showing that three much less expensive generic drugs are as effective as Synthroid, the association defeated a motion to ask the company to allow publication. As one observer has noted, "The ability of the association to influence these events by speaking with moral authority was weakened by its heavy dependence on money from Knoll."[11]

An article in *Mother Jones* magazine discusses the National Alliance for the Mentally Ill (NAMI), which bills itself as "a grassroots organization of individuals with brain disorders and their family members." According to *Mother Jones,* eighteen drug firms gave NAMI a total of $11.72 million between 1996 and mid-1999.[12] One drug company executive helped NAMI with strategic planning.

The attorneys general of sixteen states issued a report in 1999 decrying the ties between nonprofit and commercial organizations.[13] Commercial organizations have paid nonprofits substantial amounts of money to use their names and logos in advertising and marketing campaigns. For example, advertisements for the cholesterol drug Pravachol, made by Bristol-Meyers Squibb, display the name and logo of the American Heart Association and provide health information messages about cholesterol and heart disease from the association. The alliances are usually exclusive, which increases the potential for deceiving the public into the belief that the product bearing the nonprofit's name is superior. Other alliances include those between AstraZeneca and the American Cancer Society and between Eli Lilly and NAMI. SmithKline Beecham pays the American Cancer Society $1 million for the right to display the society logo in its ads for antismoking aid Nicorette.

SmithKline Beecham manufactures the antidepressant paroxetine (Paxil). Shortly after Paxil became the first drug of its class approved by the FDA for treating social anxiety disorder and social phobia, posters appeared nationwide alerting readers to the possibility that they might have the disorder and that treatment is available. Nonprofit organizations devoted to helping people with psychiatric disorders backed the campaign. The posters bore the imprimatur of the American Psychiatric Association, the Anxiety Disorders Association of America, and Freedom from Fear. The organizations benefited from an increase in the number of people who concluded that they were socially phobic. The big beneficiary was SmithKline Beecham. Valenstein comments on the cynical nature of the campaign: "Shyness can't be marketed because most people recognize it as a normal variation on personality. But 'social phobia' sounds like a disease."[14]

The National Cancer Institute (NCI) and the American Cancer Society (ACS) are funded to a great extent by the drug industry. The programs of the two large nonprofits focus on diagnosis and treatment while explaining away escalating cancer rates as caused by faulty lifestyle. They divert attention from the major role of industrial carcinogens that contaminate air, water, food, cosmetics, toiletries, and the workplace. NCI and ACS have neither educated the public about these avoidable risks nor promoted corrective legislative and regulatory actions. Their policies are influenced by relationships and conflicts of interest with the drug industry. NCI funded research and development for the anticancer drug Taxol and then gave its manufacturer the exclusive sales rights at more than twenty times the production cost. Taxol is not an isolated example. Former NCI director Samuel Broder said, "The NCI has become what amounts to a government pharmaceutical company." NCI has blocked funding for research on promising nontoxic alternative cancer therapies in favor of patented drugs. Additionally, the cancer establishment has harassed proponents of alternative cancer treatments.[15]

In *The Politics of Cancer Revisited,* Samuel Epstein describes how priorities of the NCI and ACS have impeded efforts to prevent various cancers.[16] His well-documented book shows that the ACS receives substantial financial support from large corporations that discharge known and potential pollutants into the environment. A consequence is that ACS funding largely ignores those pollutants while focusing on research on new (patentable) drugs to fight cancer and on people's lifestyle choices that increase cancer risk.

Universities that depend on research funds from drug companies have been intolerant to critics of the companies. The University of Toronto offered a professorship to Dr. David Healy and then rescinded the offer after Healy stated in a seminar there that selective serotonin reuptake inhibitors (SSRIs) sometimes lead to anxiety and suicidal thoughts. Healy also claimed that psychiatrists overmedicate their patients. Eli Lilly, the manufacturer of top-selling SSRI Prozac, was a major contributor to the university. Twenty-seven scientists, including two Nobel laureates, signed a letter saying that the university's decision had besmirched its name.[17] (In 2002, Healy accepted a joint position at the university and its affiliated Centre for Addiction and Mental Health. The center's website announced the appointment and "the settlement of all litigation and other outstanding disputes.")

PHONY ALLIANCES

About 35 million people in the United States are members of the American Association of Retired People (AARP). While this book was in production, the AARP Bulletin (February 2003) wrote about three organizations that claim to be nonpartisan advocates for seniors. In fact, the organizations back political candidates friendly to the pharmaceutical industry and support various ultraconservative issues. For example, one of the three worked to defeat a government-operated prescription plan for older Americans. The pharmaceutical industry is the biggest donor to the organizations. According to the article, "When the pharmaceutical industry speaks these days, many Americans may not be able to recognize its voice. That's because the industry often uses 'front groups' that work to advance its agenda under the veil of other interests" (p. 4).

ADVERTISEMENTS, PROMOTIONS, AND DETAILMEN

Direct to Consumer Advertising

Until about fifteen years ago, printed advertisements for prescription-only drugs were found almost exclusively in medical journals. Today, drug companies spend more on direct-to-consumer (DTC) advertising than on ads to doctors and other health professionals.[18] In the year 2000, DTC expenditures reached $2.5 billion. Advertising works. The number of prescriptions dispensed in 2000 for the fifty most heavily advertised drugs (of a total of approximately nine thousand nine hundred prescription drugs) increased 24.6 percent, whereas the number of prescriptions dispensed for all other drugs increased 4.3 percent.[19] (As the National Institute for Health Care Management Research and Education noted, other factors affect prescription patterns. These include (1) an increase in the number of drugs being approved in recent years for chronic conditions, (2) a rise in the incidence of many chronic conditions, (3) an aging population, and (4) increased spending on the promotion of prescription drugs to doctors.)

Drug company Eli Lilly ran ads offering university scholarships to schizophrenic patients who switched to Lilly's antipsychotic drug Zyprexa. The ads were effective—patients pressured their psychiatrists to prescribe Zyprexa even when other treatments were more suitable. The patients had their hopes raised, but most were ill-equipped to endure a rigorous academic environment. On the other hand, Lilly executives delighted in $550 million first-year sales of Zyprexa.[20]

Television advertising has become big business, costing companies about $2 billion in 1999. In 1987, during the infancy of DTC advertising, only 18 percent of patients asked their doctors about specific drugs; by 1992, 54 percent were asking.[21] Of survey respondents who had seen a drug ad on television or in a magazine, nearly 20 percent reported that they subsequently asked their doctors to prescribe the drug.[22] Doctors working for HMOs are pressured to see as many patients per day as possible, and arguments make examinations go slowly, so the doctors can usually be persuaded to prescribe requested drugs. In one survey, 84 percent of doctors said they would consider prescribing a drug requested by a patient, and 16 percent said they were very likely to prescribe the drug.[23] HMOs typically require that patients be seen by a general practitioner before referral to a specialist. GPs who lack experience with a patient's condition and are uncertain about the best drug for the condition are especially susceptible to the patient's demands. Doctors claimed that the main reason for their occasional inappropriate prescriptions was perceived patient demands.[24] (As documented in chapter 3, inappropriate prescriptions are more than occasional.)

Promotional tactics of drug companies might raise the hackles of ethicists:

- The companies pay freelance writers to develop stories on their products and place them in national magazines—without telling the magazine's editors about the arrangement.
- The companies threaten to withhold advertising if a magazine publishes articles unfavorable to its products.
- The companies pay attractive doctors to be spokespeople for new products. The doctors are taught how to charm the media. They are booked as medical experts on talk shows and do not disclose their ties to the companies.
- The companies pay celebrities to tell reporters how they have been helped by the companies' products. Celebrity product endorsement campaigns are typically aimed at the news sections of newspapers and TV.
- Companies sponsor chat rooms and newsgroups on the Internet. They promote drugs for unapproved uses without revealing their ties to the companies.
- Some advertisements are very direct. Drug companies pay managers of prescription databases to identify people who have specific medical conditions or have used specific drugs. The invasion of privacy culminates in a personalized letter from a pharmacist promoting a company's products.[25]

A substantial proportion of print and TV ads is misleading and even factually wrong. The ads exaggerate benefits, minimize side effects, and make unapproved claims. Benefits are displayed more prominently than potential risks, and the layouts discourage patients from reading safety information. If a drug is ineffective for a certain segment of the population, that fact is rarely mentioned.[26] Nor is there mention of alternative treatments or lifestyle changes that might improve the condition and reduce the need for the drug.

After analyzing several issues of popular women's magazines, Whelan has concluded that health advice columns in the magazines distort scientific findings to service their advertisers. The columns focus on controversial and relatively trivial ill effects of eating imported fresh fruit, being exposed to electromagnetic fields emanating from refrigerators and radiation from computers, and enjoying thrill rides at amusement parks. They rarely mention smoking and other lifestyle factors that undisputedly lead to preventable deaths. On the other hand, the magazines carried 147 cigarette advertisements (an average of 7.3 per issue). Whelan notes the hypocrisy: "*Cosmopolitan* in a 'What We Want Now' feature, surrounded by cigarette ads, demands 'increased funding for research on women's health.' Meanwhile, no reference is made to the fact that lung cancer has replaced breast cancer as the leading cause of cancer death among women."[27]

Ads Directed at Doctors

Most newly introduced drugs offer no therapeutic gains over existing drugs; they are developed only to get the manufacturer a share of the market. Thus, doctors have dozens of virtually identical decongestants, penicillins, beta blockers, and antidepressants to choose from and little time to evaluate subtle variations. Furthermore, the formal pharmacological training of doctors occurs early in medical school, at which time they learn about drugs for treating diseases they have never seen in clinical situations. Five years usually elapse between the pharmacology course and their three-year residencies. After medical school doctors receive no systematic, informed exposure to unbiased assessments of drug therapy, yet new drugs are introduced each year. So doctors routinely prescribe drugs about which they have had no formal education. Under the circumstances, drug company promotions have a huge impact.

Many advertisements to doctors are no more objective than those designed to sell cars and toothpaste. The ads skew information on risks and benefits, and, because references to scientific studies impress doctors, they often include extensive reference lists. But the lists frequently include irrelevant or seriously flawed studies. Former FDA commissioner David Kessler writes, "Prescription drug advertisements sometimes distort information in ways that may be difficult to detect even by the trained observer."[28]

Most doctors have reported that advertising has minimal influence on their prescribing habits. They are either fooling themselves or lying. Despite the absence of scientific support, they tend to believe in the effectiveness of heavily promoted products.[29] Abt Associates randomly assigned doctors to receive either low, medium, or high frequencies of exposure to advertisements for a specific cardiovascular drug. The publishers of journals to which the doctors subscribed agreed to place the ads with the appropriate frequency. During the year-long study, doctors in each of the three groups wrote more prescriptions for the drug than they had written previously. The ones exposed to the most ads increased their prescriptions the most.[30] A meta-analysis of twenty-nine studies shows a strong relationship between gifts or meals given by drug representatives to doctors and the doctors' subsequent prescribing habits and requests for formulary additions. The altered patterns were still evident two years later.[31]

Promotions Aimed at Doctors

Drug company promotions to doctors are creative, many, and varied:

- Ciba-Geigy offered Caribbean vacations to doctors who attended lectures on Ciba-Geigy's estrogen patch.
- Wyeth-Ayerst Laboratories gave 1,000 frequent-flyer miles each time doctors prescribed Wyeth's hypertensive drug.
- Roche paid doctors $1,200 for prescribing its antibiotic to twenty patients.
- Searle told Canadian doctors that it would contribute to a charitable campaign to help battered women if they prescribed its oral contraceptives.
- Connaught Labs awarded points redeemable for merchandise to doctors who bought Connaught vaccines.[32]

Most doctors who attended all-expense-paid trips to symposia to promote drugs claimed that their prescribing habits would be unaffected. But pharmacy inventory reports show that, after the symposia, they prescribed the promoted drugs more frequently.[33]

Doctors must take continuing medical education (CME) courses each year to maintain their hospital privileges. The financial support for CME courses comes largely from the drug industry, and the sponsors pick speakers whose opinions match their marketing needs. After each course, attendees typically begin prescribing more of the sponsor's drug.[34] One witness testified before the U.S. Senate, "The physicians of this country have . . . accepted a situation in which their continuing professional education and growth is largely paid for by the drug companies, whose main purpose is to buy access to the physician, assure whenever possible attention to their products, and provide a setting where they can directly market their drugs."[35]

Steinman and his colleagues sent questionnaires to first- and second-year medical residents at the University of California in San Francisco asking them about nine types of drug company promotions.[36] Most respondents considered seven of the types appropriate; the most important factor seemed to be cost rather than educational value of the items. All respondents who considered free conference lunches and pens inappropriate had accepted these gifts. Thirty-nine percent reported that industry promotions and contacts influenced their own prescribing, and 84 percent believed that other doctors' prescribing was affected.

Other health professionals should not feel slighted by the attention given to doctors. Drug companies try to influence pharmacists, nurses, and hospital administrators who pick the drugs used within the hospital. In 1995, Parke-Davis promised Peruvian pharmacists a complimentary bottle of red wine to celebrate Father's Day if they sold three boxes of Sinutab Maximum Strength or Sinutab

Non-drowsy.[37] A subsidiary of Eli Lilly paid bonuses to U.S. pharmacists who recommended any of eighty-nine drugs from a special list.[38] Both Merck and Miles pharmaceuticals paid pharmacists for switching patients to drugs that profited the manufacturer. Pharmacists were not required to tell patients of the arrangement.[39]

Detailmen

U.S. drug companies spend more than $5 billion each year to send about sixty thousand sales representatives—attractive, personable people called "detailmen"—into doctors' offices and hospitals. Detailmen present information about drugs and leave gifts. In 1990, the American Medical Association banned exorbitant gifts and cash payments of any amount while continuing to allow small items such as pens, pads, and small toys. But in 1992, 80 percent of doctors surveyed said that during the previous year detailmen had offered them cash or expensive gifts such as textbooks, tickets to sporting events, and lavish dinners at fancy restaurants.[40]

Detailmen are paid to promote their company's products. They receive printouts with information on doctors' backgrounds, likes, dislikes, and prescribing histories. They are given advice on dealing with doctors who prescribe another company's drugs. The information they offer invariably favors the sponsor's drug and so is often biased and inaccurate. Few doctors notice. Detailmen emphasize the drugs' benefits and rarely mention safety issues such as side effects and contraindications.[41]

The likelihood that a doctor will associate a particular drug with a particular disorder increases substantially following visits by detailmen.[42] Promotional meals increase sales by as much as 80 percent.[43] Most importantly, doctors who rely heavily on the information provided by detailmen are most likely to prescribe inappropriately.[44]

Warner-Lambert's drug gabapentin was approved for treating epilepsy. A former employee alleged in a lawsuit that the company's sales representatives encouraged doctors to prescribe gabapentin for pain, bipolar disorder, and attention deficit disorder in children. The sales representatives paid doctors for letting them meet with patients in examining rooms, review medical charts, and recommend what drugs to prescribe. High-volume prescribers were given speaker and consultant fees and were paid for entering patients in clinical trials.[45]

American Medical Association guidelines state that doctors should not accept cash payments from drug companies. Nevertheless, some drug companies pay Time-Concepts LLC to arrange meetings between company sales representatives and doctors. Time-Concepts LLC receives $105 for each meeting, keeps $50.00, pays $50.00 to the doctor for listening to a sales pitch, and gives $5.00 to a charity selected by the doctor.[46]

Many doctors encourage detailmen. Pomper quotes one: "If you talk to the representatives and get them to let down their hair about things, they will tell you horrifying stories of out-right extortion by physicians, as in 'I won't prescribe any more of your product unless you get me good seats to the Yankee game next Saturday.' I used to think that these were few and far between, but the more reps I talk to, the more stories I hear."[47]

INCREASING SALES

Special Bonuses

Drug company lobbyists persuaded the Department of Education to classify children diagnosed with attention deficit/hyperactivity disorder (ADHD) as health impaired. The decision entitles schools to receive approximately $420 for each enrolled ADHD child. A school that does nothing for the children but dispense Ritalin can put the money into a general fund. The schools profit, and Ritalin sales stay high.[48] (Some children may also benefit. Wealthy parents have bought ADHD diagnoses to improve their children's chances of getting into a good college. The reason is that the diagnosis gives students the right to take entrance exams untimed.)[49]

Medicare pays for some prescription drugs that doctors administer in their offices and reimburses the doctors at 95 percent of the drugs' average wholesale prices. Drug companies report one wholesale price publicly but charge doctors a much lower price, and Medicare reimburses the doctors at a rate similar to the publicly announced price. The practice is legal.[50] Thus, the doctors may be tempted to prescribe drugs with the highest profit margins even if they are not the most appropriate. For example, doctors make $84.59 in profit each time they administer Glaxo Wellcome Plc's antinausea drug Zofran. Glaxo informed doctors that the profit is $12.32 more than that from a competing drug by Smith-Kline Beecham. For a practice that administered 165,000 Zofran doses, additional profits could top $2 million. Medicare patients pay a 20 percent copayment for covered drugs. According to Virginia Congressman Tom Bliley, they have paid billions of dollars in inflated drug prices.[51]

Expiration Dates

Drug makers must prove that their drugs are safe and effective until whatever expiration date the company puts on the package, but the expiration date does not mean that the drug will deteriorate immediately afterward. In fact, tests conducted by the FDA show that about 90 percent of drugs are safe and effective far past their listed expiration dates. Listed dates are often even earlier than the manufacturer's, because pharmacists transfer many drugs from their original packaging and then routinely cut the expiration date to one year after the transfer. Most tablets and capsules stored in unopened packages in a cool, dry place retain at least 70 to 80 percent of their potency for ten years or more. Even after a package has been opened, most drugs stored in relatively low humidity retain at least 70 to 80 percent of their potency for at least one to two years after the expiration date. Nitroglycerin, insulin, and some liquid antibiotics are exceptions. Tetracycline is the only drug known to become toxic when stored too long.[52]

Expiration dates increase sales. Companies do not want products sitting on a shelf for ten years. That explains why several big drug retailers fund the National Expired and Unused Medication Drive, which has collected and destroyed about forty tons of drugs since 1991.

Outreach

Drug companies extend their markets by promoting drugs for treating behaviors such as bulimia, nail biting, and compulsive shopping and gambling. Public service messages and educational campaigns are little more than drug-selling strategies. Genentech and Lilly fund the Human Growth Foundation charity, and their officials are on its board of directors. The foundation instituted a program of free height screening for schoolchildren. Then it wrote parents of children in the bottom fifth percentile for their age group to alert them about a potential treatment, a drug manufactured by Genentech and Lilly.[53] The drug is expensive, ineffective, potentially dangerous, and must be injected five times a week for years. Yet shortness is rarely caused by a medical disorder and requires no special treatment. It is a logical necessity that the distribution of height includes a bottom 5 percent.

On the opposite end of the height spectrum, many pediatric endocrinologists prescribe estrogens to tall adolescent girls to suppress their growth. But tall stature, like shortness, is not a disease. The treatment frequently causes weight gain, nausea/vomiting, areolar or nipple pigmentation, headache, and irregular menses. The long-term risks are unknown.[54]

Additional Outreach

Medical supplies sent by drug companies to assist victims of catastrophes frequently assist only the donors. During the war in Bosnia and Herzegovina, many areas depended on foreign help for medicines and medical supplies. An estimated 27,800 to 34,800 metric tons of drugs and medical materials entered the area between 1992 and mid-1996, and 50 to 60 percent were inappropriate. By mid-1996, there were an estimated seventeen thousand metric tons of useless and unusable medicines stockpiled in warehouses and clinics in Bosnia and Herzegovina. The inventory included Chap Stick, Preparation H, and anti-smoking inhalers. For each ton of inappropriate drugs, donors avoid destruction costs of $2,000, which the recipients must then pay. The donors also get tax deductions and favorable publicity for their "humanitarian gifts."[55]

The drug companies have had opportunities to do good works. Almost twenty-three million South Africans are HIV positive and need drugs to stave off common AIDS infections like tuberculosis and pneumonia. But their average annual income is less than $3,000, and the patent-protected drugs cost $12,000 per year in the United States. The South African government's solution, legal under current international trade agreements, was to give licenses to local companies to produce inexpensive generic versions. But the Clinton administration bowed to pressure from Pharmaceutical Research and Manufacturers of America and threatened trade sanctions against South Africa if it produced generic drugs. Thailand, India, and other developing countries experiencing similar public health crises were also pressured by the United States to halt production of generic drugs.

Pfizer, the world's largest drug company, enforces its patents aggressively in poor countries. Pfizer keeps prices beyond the reach of most people in those countries and does not issue licenses to generic manufacturers for the antifungal fluconazole, the antibiotic azithromycin, or the antiretroviral nelfinavir. The three are important drugs for treating infectious diseases.[56]

On 7 March 2001, Merck & Co., Inc., bowed to international pressure and announced that it would greatly reduce prices of two AIDS drugs to governments in developing countries. It would make no profit on their sale. Other companies also pledged discounted prices. Drug activists welcomed the announcement but said that as long as companies defended their patents, developing countries would be prevented from securing the lowest-cost medicines. Sophia Tickell, a spokeswoman for the United Kingdom charity Oxfam, said, "As long as these kinds of price cuts are not seen as a solution to this problem, then they are welcome. But if it is seen as an alternative, then it is going to be a flawed alternative."[57]

Bristol-Myers Squibb holds the patent on a drug that treats two distinct conditions: it removes facial hair in women and cures trypanosomiasis (sleeping sickness), a disease that kills thousands of people in Central Africa each year. There is big money in facial hair removal (about $50.00 for a month's supply), but there is none in trypanosomiasis cures. Very few Central Africans can afford the drug. Under intense pressure from the group Doctors without Borders, Bristol-Myers Squibb agreed to donate 60,000 doses for the approximately three hundred thousand people infected annually. That is currently the extent of the contribution.[58]

U.S. drug companies pay doctors to test human subjects in Africa, Asia, Eastern Europe, and Latin America. The experiments are poorly regulated and often fail to meet the standards demanded by U.S. ethics committees. One standard, widely endorsed around the world, is that participants in experiments be fully informed of the risks they face and of their right to withdraw from a test at any time for any reason. A *Washington Post* series documented repeated violations of this standard. The series described many examples of unethical research, such as an experiment by Pfizer in response to a meningitis epidemic in Nigeria in 1996. Pfizer executives were excited about a new antibiotic that had not yet been approved in the United States, so they developed protocols over a six-week period (instead of the year or longer common in the United States) and set up camp in Nigeria. Only a few yards away, a humanitarian charity with volunteer doctors worked solely to save lives. But Pfizer employees persuaded 200 children, who did not understand that they were guinea pigs, to enroll in their study. Children unresponsive to the Pfizer drug were not switched to proven medicines, as is normally done. Eleven died, and others became permanently disabled. Pfizer's doctors left after three weeks and returned only once to examine the patients. They did not track long-term recovery.[59]

In an eight-month study at Buenos Aires Naval Hospital, researchers for Hoechst Marion Roussel (now part of Aventis) gave 137 patients an experimental drug. Thirteen patients died, and prosecutors investigated. They interviewed nearly all of the patients or their families and concluded that at least eighty consent document signatures were forged. None of the other signatories understood what they were signing. Patients' medical records were changed to make them seem eligible for the study. Prosecutors claim that at least three of the deaths constitute murder.[60]

Still More Outreach

The American Psychiatric Association and the National Alliance for the Mentally Ill have joined forces to promote a national program, versions of which are already in force in forty-one states, that requires people in homeless shelters or living on the street to take psychiatric drugs against their will—even if they have not violated any laws or been proven dangerous. People who refuse could be forcibly injected—with drugs made by the companies that finance NAMI.

The laws ignore research showing that people discharged from psychiatric hospitals are no more likely to show violent behavior than other people living in their communities.[61] Moreover, discharged patients who choose their own treatment fare as well as those required under threat of commitment to receive a specific treatment plan.[62] Volunteers for treatment are more likely to develop a trusting relationship with their service providers, to be more optimistic about the outcome, and to improve.[63]

PROMOTING DRUGS FOR SPECIAL CONDITIONS

Heart disease is the major cause of death of postmenopausal women. Women experience an apparent sizeable leap in coronary risk at menopause. But according to Hugh Tunstall-Pedoe, the increased risk is a myth perpetuated by the drug industry to promote sales of hormone-replacement therapy. American women spent $2.75 billion on hormone-replacement therapy in 2001. Tunstall-Pedoe has analyzed the death rates in women of all ages from heart disease and has found nothing to substantiate the drug companies' claims.[64]

The rate of heart disease in both women and men increases with age, but the rate in women is ten years behind. That is, sixty-year-old women have approximately the same rate as fifty-year-old men. But the increased rate does not accelerate at menopause. Women live longer, so there are far more elderly women than elderly men. Thus, relatively more elderly women die of heart disease and most other diseases. Another reason that hormone therapy seems to protect post-menopausal women from heart disease is that women who take hormones tend to smoke less, have better diets, and are more physically active. Hormone therapy does help protect women from certain symptoms of menopause, but there is a cost. It increases the risk of blood clots, breast cancer, and, possibly, ovarian cancer.[65] An extensive report by the National Heart, Lung and Blood Institute cites studies showing that hormone replacement actually increases women's risk of having heart attacks and strokes.[66]

Soon after the report was published came an interesting revelation: Hormone-replacement therapy was first promoted in *Feminine Forever,* a 1966 book that became a best-seller. The author, Dr. Robert Wilson, went on a countrywide promotional tour to tell audiences that estrogen could keep women young, healthy, and attractive. Without it, once they passed fifty, their breasts and genital organs would shrivel and they would become dull and unattractive. In 2002, Wilson's son Ronald said that Wyeth-Ayerst, the manufacturer of the highly profitable hormone-replacement drug Premarin, had paid his father to write the book and to lecture.[67]

EXTENDING THE USES

Once a drug has been approved by the FDA for at least one use, doctors can prescribe it to treat any disease condition and patient population and at any dosage level. Nonapproved use is called off-label prescribing. Drug companies encourage doctors to prescribe off-label by promoting approved drugs for uses that have not been adequately tested. Then they can increase sales without expending resources to get FDA approval. Off-label prescriptions constitute about 2 percent of the total number of prescriptions written each year; a 1991 national survey reveals that 56 percent of cancer patients were receiving at least one drug off-label.[68] Failure to use off-label drugs where appropriate may constitute malpractice.[69]

In 1999, the U.S. District Court for the District of Columbia ruled that the FDA cannot restrict manufacturers from promoting their drugs for off-label uses.[70] The ruling permits manufacturers to give doctors articles from peer-reviewed journals and reference texts. A positive report that has appeared in print, even if preliminary and contradicted by several negative findings, can be distributed.

The occasional benefits of off-label uses should be weighed against their potential for harm. For example, several years ago the FDA approved fenfluramine for treating obesity and, in a separate action, approved phentermine. Following a 1984 study suggesting that the two in combination are more effective than either alone the combination (Fen-Phen) became a popular off-label prescription item. But two 1997 articles report damaged heart valves in Fen-Phen users.[71] Had the 1999 court ruling been in effect at the time of the positive study, doctors would undoubtedly have been deluged with copies of the 1984 study results and the number of victims would have been much higher.

Many drugs approved on the basis of tests on adults are prescribed off-label to children.[72] If prescriptions to children constitute a small proportion of the total market, then the drug's manufacturer has little incentive to conduct additional tests to determine safety and efficacy in children. So, until recently, such studies were rarely conducted.[73] Cote and colleagues give examples of unfortunate and tragic outcomes because of insufficient information on children.[74]

In 1997, the FDA began requiring companies to test almost all new medicines in children. Then Congress passed legislation giving complying companies extended pediatric exclusivity to protect them from generic competition. Thus, the cost of a pediatric trial can be recouped many times over from increased sales. Eli Lilly studied the effects of Prozac in children and received a six-month patent extension; sales increased by an estimated $1 billion and profits by $700 million. The FDA estimates that pediatric exclusivity will cost consumers $13.9 billion over the next twenty years. Over that time, brand-name drug makers will gain $29.6 billion, and the generic industry will lose $10.7 billion.[75] Children are also bearing a cost—eight died in medical experiments over the past seven years, and at least thirty-six research institutions were cited for violating federal rules to protect children.[76] (In March 2002, the FDA suspended the rule requiring testing of new medicines in children; the incentives to companies that test remain.)

POSTAPPROVAL TESTING

To get a drug approved by the FDA, the manufacturer must show only that it is safe and effective. But even after approval, manufacturers often continue testing and comparing their drugs with those of competitors. They pass the costs on to consumers. The purpose is to find some advantage of the drug, even a trivial one, that can be highlighted in a marketing campaign. In 1985, Genentech developed a drug, a tissue plasminogen activator (tPA: Activase, alteplase), which seemed far superior to an older rival drug, streptokinase, in dissolving deadly blood clots. The exciting results encouraged Genentech to price Activase at $2,200 a dose, more than ten times the price of streptokinase. But subsequent studies gave Activase only a trivial advantage at best in improving heart function or prolonging survival. Undaunted, Genentech publicized the advantage, captured 65 percent of the market, and grossed $58 million in Activase sales in just the last six weeks of 1987. Doctors eventually caught on; sales dropped precipitously, and Genentech temporarily halted production of Activase in October 1988.[77] See page 25 for more on tPA.

BUSINESS DEALS

Pharmacy benefit managers (PBMs) contract with HMOs to track all prescriptions written by the HMO physicians. PBMs also develop lists of drugs, called formularies, for prescribing to HMO members. Because they buy in bulk, PBMs can negotiate big discounts from drug companies. The practice threatened companies' profits, and the companies responded by buying PBMs. Today, PBMs often add or remove drugs from formulary lists because of the manufacturer rather than for medical reasons. Under threat of taking their business elsewhere, they pressure pharmacists to persuade doctors to prescribe drugs on the list. PBMs and drug companies curb discounts to HMOs unless the HMOs use their products exclusively. They offer steep discounts on their popular drugs in exchange for putting their less popular or newer drugs on the formulary.[78] When PBMs process benefit claims, they collect information about patients and often forward it to the parent drug companies to use in their marketing efforts. They also send the information to employers, who may use it to discriminate against employees with certain conditions.

TAP Pharmaceutical Products agreed to pay a fine of more than $840 million to settle federal allegations that it offered an HMO $65,000 to get it to use TAP's prostate cancer drug rather than a competing drug. TAP manipulated the average government reimbursement to ensure that prescribing doctors would make at least $100 profit per dose.[79]

Zeneca, a company that manufactures a drug for treating prostate and breast cancer, bought Salick Health Care, the largest private chain of cancer clinics in the United States. Clinic managers have a financial incentive to encourage prescriptions for Zeneca's drug even if better alternatives are available.

Generic drug makers threaten the profits of the larger companies, but the two groups of manufacturers worked out a solution that helps everybody—except consumers. The larger companies pay the generic manufacturers to postpone producing their low-cost versions of top-selling brand-name drugs. For example, in the year 2000, sales of Schering-Plough Corporation's slow-release potassium supplement K-Dur reached $300 million. Schering paid $90 million to the American Home Products Corporation and Upsher-Smith Laboratories to postpone sales of their generic versions of K-Dur. The collusion among the three companies cost consumers more than $100 million.[80] In April 2001, the Bush administration announced that the U.S. Federal Trade Commission would start a probe to determine the extent of such activities.

PRICES

Most countries have price controls on prescription drugs, but the United States does not. As a result, most drugs cost less outside the United States. For example, in 2001 a year's supply of tamoxifen, widely prescribed for survivors of breast cancer, cost about $1,400 in the United States and $125 in Canada. Many Americans on limited budgets must organize periodic trips to Canada or Mexico to buy their needed drugs. When legislation was proposed to Congress to allow pharmacists to reimport drugs and thus sell them at lower prices, eleven FDA commissioners issued statements claiming that prescription drug reimportation would be unsafe. On 19 September 2000, one of the sponsors of the legislation, Vermont Congressman Bernard Sanders, released a report indicating that at least seven of the eleven had strong financial ties to the pharmaceutical and medical equipment industry. (On 27 October 2000, President Clinton signed a bill allowing reimportation.)

During the 2000 presidential campaign, Vice President Al Gore criticized the manufacturer of the arthritis drug Lodine. Lodine cost $108 a month when prescribed for humans and $38.00 when prescribed for dogs.

MAKING THE MOST OF PATENT PROTECTION

Another strategy of the larger companies is to patent some trivial feature of the drug, such as its pill coating or delivery mechanism, just before the patent expiration date. Technological advances make such maneuvering relatively easy. For example, one day before the patent was due to expire on the top-selling antianxiety drug BuSpar, Bristol-Myers Squibb Co. secured a new patent covering a "molecule patients create when they ingest BuSpar." The patent prevented two companies from introducing generic versions.[81]

Generics must conform to the dosage schedule of the brand drugs they replace. So, shortly prior to patent expirations on their products, some brand manufacturers introduce and promote new versions that differ from the originals only in dosage schedule. Patients switched to the new version cannot substitute a generic developed to conform to the dosage schedule of the original.

When a firm applies to the FDA for approval of a generic product, the brand manufacturer is notified and can sue for patent infringement. The generic firm must then wait thirty months or until the issue is decided in court. The courts almost never decide before thirty months. In 2002, U.S. Senators Charles Schumer, a New York Democrat, and John McCain, an Arizona Republican, introduced a bill to eliminate the automatic thirty-month extension. Their bill would let the courts decide on a case-by-case basis whether to allow a generic drug on the market. As of June 2002 the bill was being debated in the Senate.

Manufacturers apply for patents even before drugs are approved, and the timing of approval typically leaves them with about twelve years of patent protection. They promote the drugs immediately, to maximize sales before generics can compete. Their promotional strategies conflict with good medical practice.

Safety information accumulates as a drug is used and, therefore, is limited for new drugs. The first users are guinea pigs. For example, shortly after Oraflex was approved in 1982, a highly successful DTC marketing campaign began. About five hundred thousand people took Oraflex within two months of its debut. Many suffered severe side effects, some died, and Oraflex was taken off the market. Had Oraflex been introduced more cautiously, it probably would have produced substantially less damage. Oraflex is not an isolated case. Between 1997 and 2000, eleven popular drugs, each created to rival an effective existing drug, were pulled off the market. While available, the drugs were heavily prescribed and caused many deaths.[82]

In 1999, five top-selling drugs were withdrawn from the market because of unexpected adverse events. Wood estimates that, prior to their removal, 19.8 million patients (almost 10 percent of the U.S. population) were exposed to them. He adds that "none of the drugs was indicated for a life-threatening condition nor, in many cases, were they the only drugs available for that indication."[83]

Lasser and colleagues examined the *Physicians' Desk Reference* for all new chemical entities approved by the FDA between 1975 and 1999.[84] There were 548. They also counted how many drugs between 1975 and 2000 were either withdrawn from the market or tagged with warnings that they might cause serious injury or death. There were fifty-six (10.2 percent), which undercounts the eventual number because some of the drugs had only recently come on the market. Most of the warnings and withdrawals occurred within seven years of approval; some, much earlier. Thus, unless a new drug represents a breakthrough, doctors should wait at least five years before prescribing it.

Clinical trials of new drugs use relatively few subjects for relatively short periods of time, so they cannot be expected to discover every potential problem. They are likely to miss even serious side effects, even death, if they occur in less than one of 1,000 patients. That is why the FDA has postapproval surveillance.

The *Diagnostic and Statistical Manual of Mental Disorders* of the American Psychiatric Association lists premenstrual dysphoric disorder (PMDD) as a severe form of premenstrual syndrome. Symptoms of PMDD include depression, anxiety, difficulty concentrating, decreased energy, and changes in sleep and appetite. Physical symptoms include headache, joint and muscle pain, bloating, weight gain, and breast tenderness. Television commercials commissioned by drug manufacturer Eli Lilly suggested that many women suffer from PMDD. The commercials promoted a Lilly product, Sarafem, for treating PMDD. Sarafem's active ingredient, fluoxetine, is also the active ingredient in Lilly's best-seller Prozac. Sarafem and Prozac are essentially the same. So why did Lilly bother with a new drug?

One likely reason is that women dissuaded from taking a drug to treat depression, a mental illness, might be more inclined to take the drug to treat a hormonal problem. Second, the patent protections on Prozac had recently expired. By marketing the same drug under a new trade name, Lilly received new patent protections.

CONCLUDING COMMENTS

This chapter has continued a theme that recurs throughout the book—money is the driving force behind decisions in the drug field. In approaches to research and development, advertising, promotions, ensuring consumer safety, lobbying, and forming alliances, there are no important differences between the drug industry and other powerful U.S. industries. But, whereas defective computers, clothing, and home entertainment systems are annoying, defective medicines can kill.

NOTES

1. V. Fuchs and H. Sox, "Physicians' Views of the Relative Importance of Thirty Medical Innovations," *Health Affairs,* September–October 2001: 30–42.

2. Public Citizen, "Pharmaceuticals Rank as Most Profitable Industry, Again," available at www.citizen.org/congress/reform/drug_industry/profits/articles.cfm?ID=7416 (accessed on 6 June 2002); S. Gottlieb, "Drug Companies Maintain 'Astounding' Profits," *British Medical Journal* (*BMJ*) 324 (2002): 1054.

3. Commission on Health Research for Development, *Health Research: Essential Link to Equity in Development* (Oxford: Oxford University Press, 1990).

4. T. Zwillich, "Drug Firms Spend Small Portion on Research: Report," *Reuters Health,* 10 July 2001, available at www.health4us.org/news/2001_07_10_02.htm.

5. Public Citizen, "Rx R&D Myths: The Case against the Drug Industry's R&D 'Scare Card,'" available at www.citizen.org/publications/release.cfm?ID=7065 (accessed on 23 July 2001).

6. National Institute for Health Care Management Research and Educational Foundation, *Changing Patterns of Pharmaceutical Innovation* (Washington, D.C.: National Institute for Health Care Management Research and Educational Foundation, 28 May 2002).

7. F. Lichetenberg, "Are the Benefits of Newer Drugs Worth Their Cost? Evidence from the 1996 MEPS," *Health Affairs,* September–October 2001: 241–51.

8. F. Clemente et al., "Addicting Congress: Drug Companies' Campaign Cash and Lobbying Expenses," Public Citizen News Release, 6 July 2000.

9. J. Willis, "You and Patients Can Pull Together," *Pharmaceutical Marketing,* July 1997: 26.

10. C. Thomson, "Woke Up This Morning Feelin' So Blue. Took an Antidepressant but What'll It Do?" *The Bulletin* 5 (1997): 24–31.

11. D. Rennie, "Thyroid Storm," *Journal of the American Medical Association* (*JAMA*) 277 (1997): 1238–43.

12. K. Silverstein, "Prozac.org: An Influential Mental Health Nonprofit Finds Its 'Grassroots' Watered by Pharmaceutical Millions," (November–December 1999), available at www.motherjones.com/mother_jones/ND99/nami.html (accessed on 9 September 2000).

13. B. Lockyer, "What's in a Nonprofit's Name? Public Trust, Profit and the Potential for Public Deception: A Preliminary Multistate Report on Corporate-Commercial/Nonprofit Product Marketing Advertising of Commercial Products" (Office of the Attorney General of California, April 1999), available at http://caag.state.ca.us/publications/nonprofit/table_of_contents.html (accessed on 29 June 2002).

14. E. Valenstein, *Blaming the Brain: The Real Truth about Drugs and Mental Health* (New York: Free Press, 1998).

15. "The Cancer Drug Industry 'March' Seriously Misleads the Nation," *PR Newswire,* 24 September 1998.

16. S. Epstein, *The Politics of Cancer Revisited* (Fremont Center, N.Y.: East Ridge Press, 1998).

17. O. Dyer, "University Accused of Violating Academic Freedom to Safeguard Funding from Drug Companies," *BMJ* 323 (2001): 591.

18. "US DTC Advertising Spend Tops $700 Million," *Scrip Magazine* 2203 (1997): 14.

19. National Institute for Health Care Management Research and Educational Foundation, *Prescription Drugs and Mass Media Advertising* (Washington, D.C.: National Institute for Health Care Management Research and Educational Foundation, 21 November 2001).

20. D. Josefson, "Marketing of Antipsychotic Drugs Attacked," *BMJ* 316 (1998): 645.

21. M. Rachlis and C. Kushner, *Strong Medicine: How to Save Canada's Health Care System* (New York: HarperCollins, 1994).

22. R. Bell et al., "Direct-to-Consumer Prescription Drug Advertising and the Public," *Journal of General Internal Medicine* 14 (1999): 651–57.

23. C. Ukens, "Consumer Advertising Found to Pack Prescribing Punch," *Drug Topics* 136 (1992): 24–26.

24. R. Schwartz et al., "Physician Motivations for Nonscientific Drug Prescribing," *Social Science and Medicine* 28 (1989): 577–82.

25. "Pushing Drugs to Doctors," *Consumer Reports,* February 1992: 87–94; "Miracle Drugs or Media Drugs?" *Consumer Reports,* March 1992: 142–46; "Celebrity Endorsements Take a Deceptive Turn," *San Francisco Chronicle,* 3 January 2000: A3; R. O'Harrow, "Prescription Sales, Privacy Fears; CVS, Giant Share Customer Records with Drug Marketing Firm," *Washington Post,* 15 February 1998: A1.

26. "Drug Advertising: Is This Good Medicine?" *Consumer Reports,* June 1996: 62.

27. E. Whelan, "Inverted Priorities: Health Hazards in Women's Magazines," *American Council on Science and Health* 4 (1992), available at www.acsh.org/publications/priorities/0404/hazards.html (accessed on 5 December 2002).

28. D. Kessler, "Addressing the Problem of Misleading Advertising," *Annals of Internal Medicine* 116 (1992): 950–51.

29. J. Avorn et al., "Scientific versus Commercial Sources of Influence on the Prescribing Behavior of Physicians," *American Journal of Medicine* 73 (1982): 4–8.

30. N. Matalia, "Journal Advertising Works! Three Studies Say So!" *Medical Marketing and Media,* 5 May 1994: 12.

31. A. Wazana, "Physicians and the Pharmaceutical Industry: Is a Gift Ever Just a Gift?" *JAMA* 283 (2000): 373–80.

32. "Cheaper Can Be Better," *Time Magazine,* 18 March 1991: 70.

33. J. Orlowski and L. Wateska, "The Effects of Pharmaceutical Firm Enticements on Physician Prescribing Patterns. There's No Such Thing as a Free Lunch," *Chest* 102 (1992): 270–73.

34. J. Lexchin, "Interactions between Physicians and the Pharmaceutical Industry: What Does the Literature Say?" *Canadian Medical Association Journal* 149 (1993): 1401–07.

35. U.S. Senate, Committee on Labor and Human Resources, Hearings before the Committee on Labor and Human Resources of the U.S. Senate, 101st Congress, 2d sess., "Examining Practices of United States Pharmaceutical Companies and How Drug Prices and Prescriptions Are Affected," 11–12 December (Washington, D.C.: Government Printing Office, 1990).

36. M. Steinman et al., "Of Principles and Pens: Attitudes and Practices of Medicine Housestaff toward Pharmaceutical Industry Promotions," *American Journal of Medicine* 110 (2001): 551–57.

37. Public Citizen Health Research Group, "Promoting Health in Developing Countries? Parke-Davis Offers Free Wine with Sinutab in Peru," *Worst Pills Best Pills News*, September 1995: 3–4.

38. P. Keating, "Why You May Be Getting the Wrong Medicine," *Money Magazine,* June 1997: 142–57.

39. "Druggist Payments Ending," *Wall Street Journal,* 5 April 1994: D16.

40. D. Podolski and R. Newman, "Prescription Prizes," *U.S. News and World Report,* 29 March 1993: 56–60.

41. M. Ziegler et al., "The Accuracy of Drug Information from Pharmaceutical Sales Representatives," *JAMA* 273 (1995): 1296–98; J. Lexchin, "What Information Do Physicians Receive from Pharmaceutical Representatives?" *Canadian Family Physician* 43 (1997): 941–45.

42. R. Ferguson et al., "Encounters with Pharmaceutical Sales Representatives among Practicing Internists," *American Journal of Medicine* 107 (1999): 149–52.

43. T. Randall, "AMA, Pharmaceutical Association Form 'Solid Front' on Gift-Giving Guidelines," *JAMA* 265 (1991): 2304–05.

44. Lexchin, "What Information Do Physicians Receive from Pharmaceutical Representatives?"; Wazana, "Physicians and the Pharmaceutical Industry."

45. F. Charatan, "Doctor Sues Company over Unethical Marketing," *BMJ* 324 (2002): 1234.

46. D. Spurgeon, "Doctors Accept $50 a Time to Listen to Drug Representatives," *BMJ* 324 (2002): 1113.

47. S. Pomper, "Drug Rush," *Washington Monthly,* 12 May 2000, available at www.alternet.org/print.html?StoryID=9140 (accessed on 15 March 2001).

48. N. Shapiro, "Is Johnny a Cash Cow?" *Eastside Week* (Seattle), 11 December 1996: 7.

49. T. Ready, "The Religion of Ritalin," *The Stranger* (Seattle), 10 July 1997: 12–14.

50. "Drug Companies Give Physicians Profits at Medicare's Expense," *CongressDailyAM,* 28 September 2000.

51. L. Richwine, "U.S. Probe Details Drug Pricing, Promotion," *Reuters,* 27 September 2000.

52. "Drugs Past Their Expiration Date," *The Medical Letter* 38 (19 July 1996).

53. "Questions on US Growth Charity," *Scrip Magazine* 1960 (1994): 19.

54. N. Barnard et al., "The Current Use of Estrogens for Growth-Suppressant Therapy in Adolescent Girls," *Journal of Pediatric and Adolescent Gynecology* 15 (2002): 23–26.

55. P. Berckmans et al., "Inappropriate Drug-Donation Practices in Bosnia and Herzegovina, 1992 to 1996," *New England Journal of Medicine* (*NEJM*)337 (1997): 1842–45.

56. R. Watson, "Oxfam Accuses Pfizer of 'Moral Bankruptcy,'" *BMJ* 323 (2001): 186.

57. Watson, "Oxfam Accuses Pfizer," 186.

58. From *60 Minutes,* 11 February 2001.

59. J. Stephens, "The Body Hunters: As Drug Testing Spreads, Profits and Lives Hang in Balance," *Washington Post,* 17 December 2000: A1; S. LaFraniere et al., "The Dilemma: Submit or Suffer," *Washington Post,* 19 December 2000: A1.

60. K. DeYoung and D. Nelson, "Latin America Is Ripe for Trials, and Fraud," *Washington Post,* 21 December 2000: A1.

61. H. Steadman et al., "Violence by People Discharged from Acute Psychiatric Inpatient Facilities and by Others in the Same Neighborhoods," *Archives of General Psychiatry* 55 (1998): 393–401.

62. Policy Research Associates, Inc., "1998 Final Report, Research Study of the New York City Involuntary Outpatient Commitment Pilot Program," 4 December 1998.

63. V. Hiday, "Coercion in Civil Commitment: Process, Preferences, and Outcomes," *International Journal of Law and Psychiatry* 15 (1992): 359–77; B. Winick, *The Right to Refuse Mental Health Treatment* (Washington, D.C.: American Psychological Association, 1997); R. Kaltiala-Heino et al., "Impact of Coercion on Treatment Outcome," *International Journal of Law and Psychiatry* 20 (1997): 311–22.

64. H. Tunstall-Pedoe, "Myth and Paradox of Coronary Risk and the Menopause," *Lancet* 351 (1998): 1425–27.

65. J. Manson and K. Martin, "Clinical Practice: Postmenopausal Hormone-Replacement Therapy," *NEJM* 345 (2001): 34–40.

66. "International Position Paper on Women's Health and Menopause: A Comprehensive Approach," NIH Publication 3284 (Bethesda, Md.: National Heart, Lung, and Blood Institute, NIH Office of Research on Women's Health, and Giovanni Lorenzini Medical Science Foundation, 2002).

67. G. Kolata and M. Petersen, "Hormone Replacement Study a Shock to the Medical System," *New York Times,* 10 July 2002: A1, A16.

68. General Accounting Office, "Off-Label Drugs: Initial Results of a National Survey: Briefing Report to the Chairman, Committee on Labor and Human Resources, U.S. Senate" (Washington, D.C.: General Accounting Office, 1991).

69. American Academy of Pediatrics Committee on Drugs, "Unapproved Uses of Approved Drugs: The Physician, the Package Insert, and the Food and Drug Administration: Subject Review," *Pediatrics* 98 (1996): 118–23.

70. *Washington Legal Foundation v. Henney,* D.D.C., No. 94-1306 (RCL), 28 July 1999.

71. H. Connolly et al., "Valvular Heart Disease Associated with Fenfluramine-Phentermine," *NEJM* 337 (1997): 581–88 (correction in *NEJM* 337 [1997]: 1783); D. Graham and L. Green, "Further Cases of Valvular Heart Disease Associated with Fenfluramine-Phentermine [letter]," *NEJM* 337 (1997): 635.

72. M. Riddle et al., "Pediatric Psychopharmacology: Problems and Prospects," *Journal of Child and Adolescent Psychopharmacology* 8 (1998): 87–97; B. Vitiello and P. Jensen, "Medication Development and Testing in Children and Adolescents. Current Problems, Future Directions," *Archives of General Psychiatry* 54 (1997): 871–76.

73. R. Kauffman, "Status of Drug Approval Processes and Regulation of Medications for Children," *Current Opinion in Pediatrics* 7 (1995): 195–98.

74. C. Cote et al., "Is the Therapeutic Orphan about to Be Adopted?" *Pediatrics* 98 (1996): 118–23.

75. S. Stolberg, "Children Test New Medicines Despite Doubts," *New York Times,* 11 February 2001: 1.

76. A. Dembner, "Drug Research on Children Raises Concerns," *Boston Globe,* 18 November 2001: A1.

77. M. Chase, "Genentech Halts TPA Production for Rest of '88," *Wall Street Journal,* 14 October 1988, available at www.aidsinfobbs.org/articles/wallstj/88/335 (accessed on 12 December 2002).

78. M. Freudenheim, "Merck Reports Major Shift in Its Marketing on Drugs," *New York Times,* 18 November 1991: D17.

79. "Drug Firm Facing Record Penalty," *Oakland Tribune,* 2001: B1–B2.

80. K. Scannell, "Generics Have New Way to Make Millions," *Oakland Tribune,* 22 April 2001: L9.

81. Scannell, "Generics Have New Way to Make Millions."

82. "Government Issues Warning over Misprescribed Drugs," *Oakland Tribune,* 12 December 2000: A5.

83. A. Wood, "The Safety of New Medicines: The Importance of Asking the Right Questions [editorial]," *JAMA* 281 (1999): 1753–54.

84. K. Lasser et al., "Timing of New Black Box Warnings and Withdrawals for Prescription Medications," *JAMA* 287 (2002): 2273–75.

3

Medical Personnel Prescribe Incorrectly Too Often

To err is human. The most skilled shortstop in baseball commits several errors a year, basketball's best marksmen miss about half their shots, great actors occasionally flub lines, and musicians miss notes. But the potential consequences of medical errors are so terrible that they should be kept to an absolute minimum. They are not.

Considering the information from the previous chapters, it should not surprise that the system is less than optimal. In fact, the extent of medical error is substantial enough to verge on and merge with abuse. For every dollar spent on drugs, another dollar is spent to treat new health problems caused by the drug.[1] The Institute of Medicine has listed medical errors as the fifth leading cause of death in the United States, behind only heart disease, cancer, stroke, and lung disease.[2] Errors kill between 44,000 and 98,000 Americans in hospitals each year, and about seven thousand of the deaths are attributable to drug errors.[3] The actual rate is probably considerably higher, for estimates are based only on cases identified by doctors. Galvin gives an interesting perspective: airplane crashes make headlines, but the statistic of 0.43 fatalities per million miles traveled in airplanes is miniscule compared with the 1,250 fatalities per million patients from drug errors; and although baggage-handling errors are a source of frustration, the baggage-handling error rate of 10,000 per million is trivial compared with inpatient drug errors of 140,000 per million doses.[4]

PRESCRIBING ERRORS

Serious adverse drug events (ADEs) are reported in almost 7 percent of hospital inpatients, and nonserious ADEs are reported in another 8 percent.[5] At least 2 percent of hospital patients suffer preventable ADEs, and estimates go as high as 50 percent.[6] In one hospital study, 64 percent of cardiac arrests were judged preventable and most were caused by drugs.[7] Yet most error studies rely exclusively on what doctors and nurses write down in the medical record, so most ADEs probably go unreported. Of 731 ADEs identified in one study, only ninety-two were indicated on patients' charts.[8] When Andrews and colleagues used trained observers to listen to discussions between doctors and nurses during clinical meetings, they identified serious ADEs in about 18 percent of the patients.[9] The error rate in preparing and administering drugs in hospitals is about 12 percent, and about 15 percent of hospital days in the United States are devoted to treating ADEs.[10] A major concern is the failure of doctors to routinely screen for drug interactions. Almost half of 424 randomly selected visits to a hospital emergency department led to prescriptions for drugs in addition to what the patient was already receiving; in 10 percent of those visits in which at least one drug was added, and despite the fact that the patient's drug history was available, the new drug made an adverse interaction likely.[11] The average number of different drugs taken by patients prior to experiencing an ADE was twelve.[12]

In addition to the threats they pose to patients already in hospitals, drug errors are a major contributor to the high rate of occupancy of hospital beds. About 60 percent of people who take prescribed drugs end up with a drug-related problem, and eight million people annually—about 17 percent of admissions—are hospitalized for diseases caused by prescription drugs.[13] Outside of hospitals, doctors make errors by prescribing the wrong dosage or dosage form, missing allergy warnings, or duplicating treatment.[14]

Doctors prescribe inappropriately for about 25 percent of older people living in the community,[15] and sometimes the drugs cause new diseases. In one study, most new cases of parkinsonism in elderly patients were caused by prescribed drugs.[16] Substantial percentages of elderly patients who received antidepressants, oral hypoglycemics, sedatives, or nonsteroidal anti-inflammatory drugs (NSAIDs) were given a potentially inappropriate drug.[17] NSAIDs were prescribed for 42 percent of patients with a history of peptic ulcer disease. Both peptic ulcer disease and hypertension increase the risk of gastrointestinal bleeding and perforation, but those risk factors were assessed in only nineteen of the fifty-seven visits during which NSAIDs were prescribed. That may explain why NSAIDs account for an estimated seven thousand six hundred deaths and seventy-six thousand hospitalizations each year in the United States.[18]

Horlen and colleagues reviewed hospital charts of 100 randomly selected patients for whom doctors had prescribed the type 2 diabetes drug metformin.[19] The packaging of the generally safe drug, for which more than twenty-five million prescriptions are written each year, states that it should not be prescribed to patients suffering from congestive heart failure or kidney dysfunction. The warning has a black border around it to attract attention. Yet twenty-two of the 100 metformin patients had one or both of the contraindications.

Mort and Aparasu studied the frequency of inappropriately prescribed psychiatric drugs in elderly outpatients.[20] They considered a prescription inappropriate only if it involved a drug that (a) should always be avoided in the elderly or (b) should be avoided because of a patient's preexisting condition. They did not analyze the incidence of inappropriate dosing. (Johnson cites a study by the Physician Insurers Association of America indicating that incorrect or inappropriate dosage is among the most frequent mistakes doctors make.)[21] The prescriptions were inappropriate in 27.2 percent of cases, primarily because doctors prescribed drugs that should generally be avoided by the elderly. Doctors prescribed psychiatric drugs in 8.7 percent of visits by the elderly. Antidepressants and antianxiety drugs were most often inappropriately prescribed, and the potential adverse reactions were serious.

Children are frequent victims of drug errors.[22] The most common error is prescription of incorrect dosages.[23] Pediatricians treat patients ranging in size from premature infants to burly adolescents, so they often prescribe very different doses of the same drug. The process of calculating dosages entails a risk of error. In one study, pediatricians made 4.94 errors per 1,000 patient days.[24] In another, twenty-eight of sixty-four medical residents made at least one error on a test evaluating their ability to assess correct dosages for children; and seven of the residents, despite using calculators, made a tenfold dosing calculation error.[25] Registered nurses fared little better. They had a mean miscalculation dosing error rate of 19 percent on intramuscular/subcutaneous dosing questions, 36 percent on oral dosing questions, and 48 percent on intravenous dosing questions.[26]

A different type of problem occurs because manufacturers try to establish dosage early in the developmental process, when information is sparse. The initially recommended dose of many prescription drugs is often too high, and about 20 percent of drugs undergo substantial reductions in recommended dosage after having been on the market. The primary reason for lowering the recommended dosage is safety. The problem has gotten worse in recent years. Drugs released in the last five years are more likely than older ones to have their recommended dosage reduced (see www.nytimes.com/2002/09/17/health/17DOSE.html?ex=1033351849&ei=1&en=e6eda5bfceb170d8 [accessed on 13 December 2002]).

Even when the dose is right, errors may occur. The time at which drugs are administered is often crucial. See pages 246–47. In one study, antibiotics given prior to surgery as a preventative measure were correctly timed in only 40 percent of cases.[27]

Some drugs are prescribed unnecessarily. Twenty-six percent of patients who were hypertensive while being evaluated by a doctor had normal blood pressure outside the doctor's office (as assessed with portable blood pressure–monitoring devices). The patients suffered no ill effects after discontinuing their drug for lowering blood pressure.[28]

Gandhi and colleagues telephoned 2,858 randomly selected twenty- to seventy-five-year-old outpatients from eleven Boston-area clinics. Of the 2,248 who said they were taking prescription drugs, 394 (18 percent) reported a drug complication (defined as a problem or symptom in the past year related to prescription medications). The most common offenders were antibiotics, antidepressants, and NSAIDs. Only sixty-four of the patients' medical charts listed a drug complication.[29]

Doctors overprescribe antibiotic drugs. About 10 percent of doctor visits by U.S. adults and 13 percent of visits by children are for treatment of colds, upper respiratory tract infections, or bronchitis.[30] In 30 to 70 percent of the cases, doctors prescribe antibiotics.[31] Yet the illnesses are most commonly caused by viruses, which antibiotics do not effectively treat. They are worse than ineffective—they kill benign bacteria that help protect the body against invading pathogens.

One estimate is that at least half the human use of antibiotics in the United States is unnecessary or inappropriate.[32] The Centers for Disease Control developed guidelines for appropriate use, but the guidelines are often ignored. (Antibiotics are also used to promote growth of meat animals, to control bacterial infections in trees, and in household cleaning products.) The more they are used, the more bacteria mutate and become resistant to them. At least twenty-four kinds of bacteria have become resistant to one or more antibiotics.

Antibiotics are underprescribed for at least one condition. Following the discovery that a bacterium causes peptic ulcers, a National Institutes of Health panel convened to reevaluate treatment options for ulcers. The panel released a statement with the unambiguous conclusion that antibiotic therapy is the treatment of choice. Yet, as of 1998, doctors continued to prescribe a traditional and ineffective class of drugs for 72 percent of their Medicaid patients.[33]

Other drugs are also underprescribed. Both the American College of Cardiology/American Heart Association and the Agency for Health Care Policy and Research published guidelines for treating heart attacks and congestive heart failure.[34] The guidelines indicate that, in the absence of specific contraindications, patients should be treated with angiotensin converting enzyme (ACE) inhibitors. ACE inhibitor therapy is the only treatment to date known to improve symptoms and prolong life. Yet ACE inhibitors are not prescribed for more than 30 percent of patients who should be receiving them.[35]

Drugs that relieve pain (analgesics) are underprescribed, especially for the elderly. Morphine has been called "God's own medicine" because of its ability to relieve pain, but many doctors prescribe it reluctantly and in insufficient dosage or for an insufficient period of time.[36] Then nurses tend to underadminister the prescribed doses.[37]

Elderly patients were prescribed smaller doses of analgesics than younger patients undergoing the same surgery, and on average only about 25 percent of prescribed regimens were administered; the percentage declined with advancing age.[38] Elderly burn patients in great pain received significantly less than the minimum dose of prescribed analgesic.[39] More than 25 percent of elderly cancer patients with daily pain received no analgesics, and others received weak ones.[40] Many nursing facility residents receive only acetaminophen, codeine, or a combination of the two, and the inadequate treatment devastates their lives: More than half reported that daily pain impaired their ability to enjoy activities or even move about, and 45 percent reported sleep disturbances; 32 percent, depression; and 26 percent, anxiety.[41] Burn victims aged seventy-six to ninety-two years received significantly less than the minimum prescribed medication, less than those aged sixty-six to seventy-five years, and less still than patients aged fifty-five to sixty-five years.[42]

A major reason for the tendency toward underprescribing narcotic analgesics has been a fear on the part of doctors that their patients would become addicted. The concern about fostering addiction seems terribly misplaced when applied to elderly patients with serious and even terminal illnesses. Furthermore, even younger patients are highly unlikely to become addicted in a hospital setting.[43] Outpatients given weak drugs to treat their severe pain often try to compensate by taking large doses. Unfortunately, many weak analgesics are more damaging to the liver and kidneys than morphine and related drugs.

In a well-publicized case, hospital personnel administered morphine to control the pain of an elderly man with prostate cancer and a six-month life expectancy. Then he was transferred to a long-term care facility where a nurse concluded that he was addicted. She substituted a mild tranquilizer. His estate sued and won a $15 million verdict against the owner of the nursing facility for failing to provide adequate pain relief.[44] Several similar cases prompted a reevaluation of common practices; this led to the enactment of laws to protect patients. Starting in January 2001, hospitals, nursing homes, and outpatient clinics accredited by the Joint Commission on Accreditation of Healthcare Organizations were required to give patients proper pain relief. Failure to do so will result in loss of accreditation.

Pharmacists make errors in dispensing.[45] From 1989 to 1999, the number of prescriptions filled by U.S. pharmacists doubled while the number of pharmacists rose just 5 percent. In 2000, retail pharmacies filled 2.9 billion prescriptions.[46] The greater workload of individual pharmacists correlates with an increase in errors. Carmen Catizone of the National Association of Boards of Pharmacy has claimed that about 5 percent of the three billion U.S. prescriptions filled each year are incorrect.[47] According to estimates by pharmacists interviewed for an Associated Press story, about 3 to 5 percent of the errors are clinically significant.[48] The Associated Press reported that the number of complaints of pharmacy malpractice reflects only a small fraction of the total number of errors. Many customers do not complain, and others settle by accepting small payments. Walgreens pharmacists can pay up to $500 to settle a claim before contacting Walgreens' insurance company. Resolved claim reports remain in the store.

Many pharmacists have insufficient knowledge of herbal supplements. *Consumer Reports* sent shoppers to twenty-five different pharmacies and had them pick up a bottle of ginkgo while waiting for a Coumadin prescription. The combination of Coumadin and ginkgo is dangerous. Yet none of the pharmacists volunteered information about the two drugs, and sixteen gave wrong or incomplete advice when asked.[49]

Between 25 and 80 percent of patients do not comply with their prescribed drug regimen, and nearly 9 percent never have their prescriptions filled.[50] Doctors' perceptions of patients' compliance bear little relationship to actual behaviors.[51] Among the many reasons for noncompliance are misleading or unclear instructions, inconvenience, expense, forgetting, unpleasant side effects, difficulty adhering to a complex dosing schedule, embarrassment at taking drugs in front of others, and use of alternative treatments. Doctors who incorrectly assume that patients are taking their drugs as prescribed may increase the dose or prescribe a new one.

SOLUTIONS

A 1999 Institute of Medicine Report got people's attention about medical error,[52] and since then several individuals and organizations have worked on finding solutions. An excellent starting place is Bogner's edited volume.[53] And the American Academy of Pediatrics and the Pediatric Pharmacy Advocacy Group have published guidelines for reducing pediatric drug errors.[54]

For Patients

One reason why doctors overprescribe antibiotic drugs is that patients demand them and stop going to reluctant prescribers. Patients must learn to accept that drugs are not always the best solution. They should read prescriptions aloud and ask their doctors to confirm drug names and dosages. They should go to a pharmacy where the pharmacists do not seem overburdened. Patients can check with state pharmacy boards to learn if a pharmacist has ever been disciplined. Upon picking up prescriptions, patients should read the labels to make sure that drug names and dosages match what they have written down. If they are refilling, they should make sure the pills are the same color, size, and shape as what they had previously.

For Doctors

Verbal orders are less likely to produce error than handwritten orders; computer-entered orders that can be checked on-line for problems are even better. Having a clinical pharmacist follow an intensive care unit team on hospital rounds can substantially reduce preventable ADEs.[55]

Before prescribing, dispensing, or administering a drug, doctors should know a patient's diagnosis, age, weight, allergies, drug history, current drug usage, and pregnancy status. Collecting that and other relevant information would prevent about 18 percent of ADEs. Use of abbreviations, acronyms, and other shortcuts can cause miscommunication among doctors, pharmacists, and nurses. So can vague instructions such as, "Take as needed." Miscommunication leads to errors in drug administration.[56] Gruchalla presents a classification system for ADEs and suggests how doctors can question patients and use diagnostic tests to minimize the incidence of serious problems.[57]

For Hospitals

Hospitals should restrict certain substances to their pharmacies. For example, although weak potassium chloride solution is frequently prescribed as a beneficial electrolyte, the undiluted chemical is so deadly that it is used in executing criminals. In 1991, between forty and fifty accidental deaths in hospitals were attributed to concentrated potassium chloride. In March 1995, the nonprofit Institute for Safe Medication Practices sent a warning letter to every hospital pharmacy and nursing director in the country recommending that undiluted potassium chloride be removed from all patient care areas. Since then, there have been at least seven deaths in hospitals from accidental undiluted potassium chloride injections.

For Pharmacists

Pharmacists should recognize that dispensing errors occur most often when they are rushed, distracted, or not paying attention.[58] Pharmacists should consult with patients, preferably in a quiet, private setting, to ensure that instructions will be followed properly. Pharmacists must familiarize themselves with drugs that look alike, have sound-alike names, or are packaged or labeled similarly.

Such drugs increase the error rate and merit special precautions.[59] Spelling is similar for the arthritis drug Celebrex, the antidepressant Celexa, and the antiepileptic drug Cerebyx. The cervical dilator Lamicel is pronounced the same as the antifungal drug Lamisil. Several fatalities occurred when the diuretic Lasix was dispensed instead of the antiulcer drug Losec.

According to the Food and Drug Administration (FDA) site at www.fda.gov/oc/workshops/errorsum.htm: "FDA has received 6000 medication error reports since 1992 and 50 percent are related to confusion in the labeling or packaging of the drug. The total number of serious adverse events that are related to errors number 1,273 with 326 deaths. These numbers only represent a snapshot of what is actually occurring and FDA believes that there are a correspondingly greater number of unreported events." Schommer and colleagues set up one-on-one hour-long discussions between pharmacists and patients in the patients' churches. The patients spent part of the time listening to a general talk about the dangers of taking drugs incorrectly and part of the time talking individually with a pharmacist. At six-month follow-ups, the participants reported using fewer drugs and having far fewer drug-related problems than they had in the six months prior to the sessions.[60]

SEXISM AND RACISM IN PRESCRIBING

The preceding sections describe careless, tragic, but generally unintentional errors. Unfortunately, however, the medical field is not immune to the gender and racial biases that pervade our society. Biases occur in advertising for psychiatric drugs, diagnosis of disorders for which drugs are prescribed, and drug treatment. Some treatment disparities may be caused by ignorance of gender and racial differences in response to drugs, but the ignorance is borne of discrimination. Until 1993, women were excluded from most trials of new drugs. Research conducted solely on men was often generalized to women, even for drugs prescribed mostly to women.[61] An American Medical Association report has concluded that the typical clinical trial rarely provided sufficient evidence of applicability to women.[62] Also, most tests are on young volunteers. Women outlive men and constitute a much greater proportion of senior citizens, so they are more likely than men to receive a drug that has been inadequately tested for their age group.

In the 1990s, the FDA reversed its policy of excluding women of child-bearing age from clinical trials. The FDA has recommended that studies include analyses of gender-specific responses. Additional guidelines urge that previously excluded groups, such as the elderly, be routinely evaluated so that subjects in clinical trials reflect the population that ultimately receives the drug. But after analyzing studies on drug therapy for heart attack survivors, Rochon and others concluded that gender differences are still typically ignored.[63] The studies, conducted worldwide and published between 1992 and 1996 in leading medical journals, had on average only 25 percent women subjects. Even when women were included, the articles rarely discussed gender-related results. Whether or not a study was funded by an agency with a gender-related policy had little impact on the inclusion of women or reporting of results. An analysis of studies funded by the National Heart, Lung, and Blood Institute yields similar findings.[64]

Below are a few examples in which women and men were treated differently. Then follow several examples of differential treatment due to race.

- When the symptoms of mental health problems are held constant, women receive more prescriptions than men for psychiatric drugs.[65]
- For adults diagnosed with colds, upper respiratory tract infections, or bronchitis, doctors prescribe antibiotics more frequently to women and to whites.[66]
- The conclusion that *all survivors* of heart attacks at high or medium risk should be treated with long-term beta-adrenergic-antagonist therapy is based on research involving 13,385 men and no women.[67]
- Institutionalized elderly women receive more tranquilizers than men. Women of all ages are prescribed at least twice as many tranquilizers and antianxiety drugs as men.[68]
- People with coronary artery disease (CAD) benefit from drugs that lower levels of lipids. The drugs reduce future cardiovascular events. Yet the drugs have been underprescribed to CAD patients and especially to women.[69]
- Commenting on the frequent recall of drugs during the past few years, R. Woosley, the Pharmacology Department chairman at Georgetown University, said, "One of the things we're beginning to realize is that many of the drugs being taken off the market are being withdrawn because of harm to women. Seldane, Hismanal, Posicor, Raxar, Propulsid—all had more than twofold greater harm in women. There are another 40 drugs still out there that potentially have this same problem of causing arrhythmias in women."[70]

Examples of differential drug treatment due to race are as follows:

- In both clinics and psychiatric emergency services in general hospitals, clinicians spend less time evaluating blacks than other patients. They prescribe more and higher doses of antipsychotic drugs to blacks, which may account for the greater incidence of tardive dyskinesia in blacks than whites.[71]
- Symptoms of depression are often ignored in elderly black people. Elderly whites are more likely to be prescribed antidepressant drugs, whereas older,

depressed blacks are less likely to be treated until they require hospitalization. For all ages, antidepressants are prescribed to depressed black and Hispanic patients at less than half the rate at which they are prescribed to similarly diagnosed white patients. Blazer and colleagues surveyed more than four thousand people aged sixty-five and older. In 1986, when the survey began, more than twice as many elderly whites as blacks were using antidepressants. By 1996, almost three times as many whites as blacks were taking the drugs (in light of the discussion on pages 97–100, maybe people of color are better off).[72]

For treating depression, tricyclics and selective serotonin reuptake inhibitors (SSRIs) are the standards. Most prescribers prefer SSRIs because they produce fewer aversive side effects and better compliance. Doctors prescribe SSRIs to a higher proportion of whites than blacks. They also prescribe larger amounts to whites, which increases compliance.[73]

- For psychotropic drugs generally, whites are more likely than nonwhites to receive prescriptions.[74]
- Whites were more likely than blacks to report that their doctors told them to stop smoking. Whites were more likely to be enrolled in formal cessation programs to quit smoking.[75]
- For adults diagnosed with colds, upper respiratory tract infections, or bronchitis, doctors prescribe antibiotics more frequently to whites (antibiotics are ineffective in those cases and increase bacterial resistance, so people of color are better off).[76]
- Hispanic and black patients are less likely than whites with similar pain complaints in the medical record to receive emergency department analgesics.[77] Anderson and colleagues surveyed African American and Hispanic cancer patients and the doctors who treated them. The doctors underestimated pain severity for 64 percent of the Hispanic and 74 percent of the African American patients, especially for female minority patients. Many of the patients, despite reporting high levels of pain and limited relief from prescribed drugs, did not receive guideline-recommended analgesic prescriptions.[78]
- Morrison and colleagues telephoned 347 New York pharmacies and asked whether they stocked enough morphine to dispense to a patient in severe pain with a properly written prescription. Only 25 percent of drugstores in black and Hispanic neighborhoods could fill the prescription. In largely white areas, nearly 75 percent could.[79]
- Blacks are less likely than whites to receive antiretroviral therapy when first referred to an HIV clinic.[80]
- Even in the nations' top hospitals, whites are five times more likely than blacks to receive the tissue plasminogen activator (tPA) drug as an emergency clot-busting treatment for stroke.[81] (But see pages 25 and 53 on tPA.)

COUNTERFEIT DRUGS: AN EMERGING PROBLEM EVEN FOR THOSE WHO RECEIVE THE CORRECT PRESCRIPTION

The World Health Organization has estimated that more than 7 percent of the global supply of prescription drugs is counterfeit. Until recently, officials believed that the United States had sufficient safeguards against counterfeits, but the landscape is changing. In 2001 and 2002, at least eight different adulterated and counterfeit prescription drugs from several different manufacturers were discovered in warehouses of U.S. distributors and on pharmacy shelves. Some patients received and took counterfeits. The drugs included Gamimune N, to treat weakened immune systems; antianemia drug Epogen; antipsychotic drug Zyprexa; Combivir, to treat HIV; and Serostim, for the wasting caused by AIDS. Tom Kubic, executive director of the Pharmaceutical Security Institute in Virginia, said, "The US is and will continue to be a likely target for counterfeiters. . . . The population on the whole spends quite a bit of money on pharmaceuticals, and in illegal activity, you're going to go where the money is."[82] (The cost of a three-month supply of Serostim is about $20,000.)

Counterfeiters get hold of expired drugs and buy cheap generics. They remove old labels and attach phony new ones. They water down drugs and sell bathtub mixtures, ranging from sugar pills to toxic concoctions, as genuine drugs.

Nonprofit hospitals, nursing home pharmacies, charities, and foreign countries receive deeply discounted prices on drugs. Unscrupulous wholesalers and distributors buy drugs diverted from these sources. Pharmacy professor Marvin Shepherd has monitored the transmission of drugs across the border from Mexico for several years. He reports that they show up at flea markets and garage sales all over the country. Lewis Kontni, of Reconnaissance International, the sponsor of a 2002 pharmaceutical anticounterfeiting conference, said, "Wherever you have diversion you have counterfeits. . . . It's true with perfume, ink jet printer cartridges, sunglasses and sweatshirts—why would it be any different with pharmaceuticals? In fact, there is a lot of money to be made, and you destroy the evidence as you consume the fake 'medicine.' Really, it's the perfect crime."[83]

Counterfeiting drugs is a white-collar crime with lesser penalties than those carried by trafficking of illegal drugs. Kubic said that criminals "are doing the risk-benefit analysis, and they're choosing to shift to diverting and counterfeiting prescription drugs."[84]

The American Pharmaceutical Association has issued advice on how to avoid counterfeit drugs:

- Be observant about the appearance of the packaging and medicine you receive and alert to any changes from one prescription lot number to the next. Talk to your pharmacist if you have any questions about your medication.

- Always buy medications from a highly reputable source.
- Be wary of "special deals" or marked reductions in product price that may represent promotion of a counterfeit.
- Be careful when buying medications on-line. Avoid buying medications from on-line pharmacies not licensed in the United States, or from on-line stores that offer either to sell medications without prescriptions or to write prescriptions. Reputable on-line pharmacies will have a seal of approval called VIPPS, or a Verified Internet Pharmacy Practice Site, provided.[85]

CONCLUDING COMMENTS

Error is inevitable in all human endeavors, but the error rate in prescribing and administering drugs is intolerably high and on the rise. Between 1983 and 1998, U.S. fatalities from acknowledged prescription errors increased by 243 percent, more than the increase for almost any other cause of death. The percentage increase in fatalities far outpaced the increase in the number of prescriptions.[86] A few easily implemented procedures, such as requiring that doctors print rather than write prescriptions in cursive, would probably reduce error rate considerably. Other changes would be more costly. Only if the costs to the people and institutions responsible for making errors exceed the costs of reducing them is change likely. It is a business decision. Consumers should fight for legislation to increase the costs to error makers.

NOTES

1. Alliance for Aging Research, *When Medicine Hurts Instead of Helps* (Washington, D.C.: Alliance for Aging Research, 1998).
2. L. Kohn et al., eds., *To Err Is Human: Building a Safer Health System,* Institute of Medicine (Washington, D.C.: National Academy Press, 1999).
3. D. Phillips et al., "Increase in U.S. Medication-Error Deaths between 1983 and 1993," *Lancet* 351 (1998): 643–44.
4. R. Galvin, "What Do Employers Mean by 'Value'?" *Integrated Healthcare Report,* September–October 1998: 1–15.
5. J. Lazarou, "Incidence of Adverse Drug Reactions in Hospitalized Patients: A Meta-analysis of Prospective Studies," *Journal of the American Medical Association* (*JAMA*) 279 (1998): 1200–05.
6. D. Bates et al., "Relationship between Medication Errors and Adverse Drug Events," *Journal of General Internal Medicine* 10 (1995): 199–205; E. Holland and F. Degruy, "Drug-Induced Disorders," *American Family Physician* 56 (1997): 1781–88.
7. L. Leape, "Error in Medicine," *JAMA* 272 (1994): 1851–57.
8. D. Classen et al., "Computerized Surveillance of Adverse Drug Events in Hospital Patients," *JAMA* 266 (1991): 2847–51.
9. L. Andrews et al., "An Alternative Strategy for Studying Adverse Events in Medical Care," *Lancet* 349 (1997): 309–13.

10. N. Davis and M. Cohen, *Medication Errors: Causes and Prevention* (Philadelphia: George F. Stickley, Co., 1981); K. Isselbacher et al., eds., *Harrison's Principles of Internal Medicine,* 13th edition (New York: McGraw-Hill, 1994).

11. M. Beers et al., "Potential Adverse Drug Interactions in the Emergency Room," *Annals of Internal Medicine* 112 (1990): 61–64.

12. D. Classen et al., "Adverse Drug Events in Hospitalized Patients," *JAMA* 277 (1997): 301–06.

13. J. Johnson and J. Bootman, "Drug-Related Morbidity and Mortality," *Archives of Internal Medicine* 155 (1995): 1949–56; K. Beard, "Adverse Reactions as a Cause of Hospital Admissions in the Aged," *Drugs and Aging* 2 (1992): 356–61; O. Schneitman-McIntire et al., "Medication Misadventures Resulting in Emergency Department Visits at an HMO Medical Center," *American Journal of Health-System Pharmacy* 3 (1996): 1416–22.

14. J. Hallas et al., "Drug Related Admissions to a Cardiology Department: Frequency and Avoidability," *Journal of Internal Medicine* 228 (1990): 379–84; T. Lesar et al., "Factors Related to Errors in Medication Prescribing," *JAMA* 277 (1997): 312–17.

15. S. Willcox et al., "Inappropriate Drug Prescribing for the Community Dwelling Elderly," *JAMA* 272 (1994): 292–96.

16. P. Stephen and J. Williamson, "Drug-Induced Parkinsonism in the Elderly," *Lancet* 2 (1984): 1082–83.

17. G. Anderson et al., "Auditing Prescription Practice Using Explicit Criteria and Computerized Drug Benefit Claims Data," *Journal of Evaluation in Clinical Practice* 3 (1997): 283–94.

18. R. Tamblyn et al., "Unnecessary Prescribing of NSAIDs and the Management of NSAID-Related Gastropathy in Medical Practice," *Annals of Internal Medicine* 127 (1997): 429–38.

19. C. Horlen et al., "Frequency of Inappropriate Metformin Prescriptions," *JAMA* 287 (2002): 2504–05.

20. J. Mort and R. Aparasu, "Prescribing Potentially Inappropriate Psychotropic Medications to the Ambulatory Elderly," *Archives of Internal Medicine* 160 (2000): 2825–31.

21. L. Johnson, "Avoiding Lawsuits for Careless Prescribing Errors," *Medical Economics,* 27 April 1998: 190.

22. G. Koren and R. Haslam, "Pediatric Medication Errors: Predicting and Preventing Tenfold Disasters," *Journal of Clinical Pharmacology* 34 (1994): 1043–45.

23. H. Folli et al., "Medication Error Prevention by Clinical Pharmacists in Two Children's Hospitals," *Pediatrics* 79 (1987): 718–22.

24. T. Lesar, "Errors in the Use of Medication Dosage Equations," *Archives of Pediatrics and Adolescent Medicine* 152 (1998): 340–44.

25. C. Rowe et al., "Errors by Paediatric Residents in Calculating Drug Doses," *Archives of Disease in Childhood* 79 (1998): 56–58.

26. R. Bindler and T. Bayne, "Medication Calculation Ability of Registered Nurses," *Image: Journal of Nursing Scholarship* 23 (1991): 221–24.

27. S. Pestotnik et al., "Implementing Antibiotic Practice Guidelines through Computer-Assisted Decision Support: Clinical and Financial Outcomes," *Annals of Internal Medicine* 124 (1996): 884–90.

28. J. Staessen et al., "Antihypertensive Treatment Based on Conventional or Ambulatory Blood Pressure Measurement: A Randomized Controlled Trial," *JAMA* 278 (1997): 1065–72.

29. T. Gandhi et al., "Drug Complications in Outpatients," *Journal of General Internal Medicine* 15 (2000): 149–54.

30. National Center for Health Statistics, *Current Estimates from the National Health Interview Survey, 1993* (Hyattsville, Md.: U.S. Department of Health and Human Services, 1994); National Center for Health Statistics, National Ambulatory Medical Care Survey, *1991 Summary* (Hyattsville, Md.: U.S. Department of Health and Human Services, 1994).

31. R. Gonzales et al., "Antibiotic Prescribing for Adults with Colds, Upper Respiratory Tract Infections, and Bronchitis by Ambulatory Care Physicians," *JAMA* 278 (1997): 901–4; J. Metlay et al., "National Trends in the Use of Antibiotics by Primary Care Physicians for Adult Patients with Cough," *Archives of Internal Medicine* 158 (1998): 1813–18; A. Mainous et al., "Antibiotics and Upper Respiratory

Infection: Do Some Folks Think There Is a Cure for the Common Cold?" *Journal of Family Practice* 42 (1996): 357–61; L. Mccaig and J. Hughes, "Trends in Antimicrobial Drug Prescribing among Office-Based Physicians in the United States," *JAMA* 273 (1995): 214–19; R. Watson, "Antimicrobial Use for Pediatric Upper Respiratory Infections: Reported Practice, Actual Practice, and Parent Beliefs," *Pediatrics* 104 (1999): 1251–57.

32. P. Radetsky, "Last Days of the Wonder Drugs," *Discover,* November 1998: 76–85.

33. M. Thamer et al., "Influence of NIH Consensus Conference on Helicobacter pylori on Physician Prescribing among a Medicaid Population," *Medical Care,* May 1998: 646–60.

34. T. Ryan et al., "ACC/AHA Guidelines for the Management of Patients with Acute Myocardial Infarction: A Report of the American College of Cardiology/American Heart Association Task Force on Practice Guidelines," *Journal of the American College of Cardiology* 28 (1996): 1328–1428; Agency for Health Care Policy and Research, *Heart Failure: Management of Patients with Left Ventricular Systolic Dysfunction,* Publication No. 94-0613 (Rockville, Md.: Agency for Health Care Policy and Research, 1994).

35. E. Ellerbeck et al., "Quality of Care for Medicare Patients with Acute Myocardial Infarction. A Four-State Pilot Study from the Cooperative Cardiovascular Project," *JAMA* 273 (1995): 1509–14; R. Stafford et al., "National Patterns of Angiotensin-Converting Enzyme Inhibitor Use in Congestive Heart Failure," *Archives of Internal Medicine* 157 (1997): 2460–64; C. Sueta et al., "Recommended Management of Hyperlipidemia and Heart Failure: Are We Following the Guidelines?" *Circulation* 96 (supplement) (1997): 1–66.

36. R. Marks and E. Sachar, "Undertreatment of Medical Inpatients with Narcotic Analgesics," *Annals of Internal Medicine* 78 (1973): 173–81; S. Perry, "The Undermedication for Pain," *Psychiatric Annals* 4 (1984): 808–11; R. Portenoy, *Textbook of Pain Management: Theory and Practice* (Baltimore: Williams and Wilkins, 1996).

37. C. Novy and M. Jagmin, "Pain Management in the Elderly Orthopaedic Patient," *Orthopaedic Nursing* 16 (1997): 51–57.

38. A. Egbert, "Postoperative Pain Management in the Frail Elderly," *Clinics in Geriatric Medicine* 12 (1996): 583–99.

39. S. Honari et al., "Comparison of Pain Control Medication in Three Age Groups of Elderly Patients," *Journal of Burn Care and Rehabilitation* 18 (1997): 500–04.

40. R. Bernabei et al., "Management of Pain in Elderly Patients with Cancer," *JAMA* 279 (1998): 1877–82.

41. B. Ferrell et al., "Pain in the Nursing Home," *Journal of the American Geriatrics Society* 38 (1990): 409–14.

42. Honari et al., "Comparison of Pain Control Medication in Three Age Groups of Elderly Patients."

43. M. Zenz et al., "Long-term Oral Opioid Therapy in Patients with Chronic Non-malignant Pain," *Journal of Pain and Symptom Management* 7 (1992): 69–77; E. Rosenthal, "Patients in Pain Find Relief, Not Addiction in Narcotics," *New York Times,* 28 March 1993: sect. 1, 24; R. Portenoy, "Chronic Opioid Therapy in Nonmalignant Pain," *Journal of Pain and Symptom Management* 5 (supplement) (1990): S46–S62.

44. W. Stein and B. Ferrell, "Pain in the Nursing Home," *Clinics in Geriatric Medicine* 12 (1996): 601–13.

45. R. Knox, "Prescription Errors Tied to Lack of Advice: Pharmacists Skirting Law, Massachusetts Study Finds," *Boston Globe,* 10 February 1999: Metro B1.

46. National Institute for Health Care Management, Research and Educational Foundation, "Prescription Drug Expenditures in 2001: May 2002" (Washington, D.C.: National Institute for Health Care Management, May 2002).

47. Available at www.consumeraffairs.com/news/pharmacy_errors.html (accessed on 12 December 2000).

48. Associated Press Release, 1 March 2000.

49. "Putting Druggists to the Test: Prescription for Disaster," *Consumer Reports,* October 1999: 40.

50. D. Sackett, "Is There a Compliance Problem? If So, What Do We Do about It?" in *Controversies in Therapeutics,* ed. L. Lasagna (Philadelphia: Saunders, 1980), 552–56; J. Robbins, "Improving Patient Compliance: Is There a Pharmacist in the House?" *Schering Report* 14 (1992): 1–16.

51. A. Mushlin and F. Appel, "Diagnosing Patient Noncompliance," *Archives of Internal Medicine* 137 (1977): 318–21.

52. Kohn et al., *To Err Is Human.*

53. M. Bogner, ed., *Human Error in Medicine* (Hillsdale, N.J.: L. Erlbaum Associates, 1994).

54. Committee on Drugs and Committee on Hospital Care, American Academy of Pediatrics, "Prevention of Medication Errors in the Pediatric Inpatient Setting," *Pediatrics* 102 (1998): 428–30; Institute for Safe Medication Practices and Pediatric Pharmacy Advocacy Group, "Draft Guidelines for Preventing Medication Errors in Pediatrics," *Journal of Pediatric Pharmacy Practice* 3 (1998): 189–202.

55. D. West et al., "Pediatric Medication Order Error Rates Related to the Mode of Order Transmission," *Archives of Pediatrics and Adolescent Medicine* 148 (1994): 1322–26; L. Leape et al., "Pharmacist Participation on Physician Rounds and Adverse Drug Events in the Intensive Care Unit," *JAMA* 282 (1999): 267–70.

56. L. Leape et al., "Systems Analysis of Adverse Drug Events," *JAMA* 274 (1995): 35–43; M. Cohen and N. Davis, "Systems That Prevent Error," *American Pharmacy* NS33(5) (1993): 20.

57. R. Gruchalla, "Clinical Assessment of Drug-Induced Disease," *Lancet* 356 (2000): 1505–11.

58. A. Grasha and M. O'Neill, "Cognitive Processes in Medication Errors," *U.S. Pharmacist* 21 (1996): 96–109.

59. Leape et al., "Systems Analysis of Adverse Drug Events"; K. Baker and E. Cowley, "Liability for Errors in Expanded Pharmacy Practice: Issues for Technicians and Pharmacists," presented at the American Pharmaceutical Association Annual Meeting, Washington, D.C., 10–14 March 2000.

60. J. Schommer et al., "Interdisciplinary Medication Education in a Church Environment," *American Journal of Health-System Pharmacy* 59 (2002): 423–28.

61. A. Kimberly et al., "Gender Differences in Pharmacokinetics and Pharmacodynamics of Psychotropic Medication," *American Journal of Psychiatry* 149 (1992): 587–95.

62. Council on Ethical and Judicial Affairs, American Medical Association, "Gender Disparities in Clinical Decision Making," *JAMA* 266 (1991): 559–62.

63. P. Rochon et al., "Reporting of Gender-Related Information in Clinical Trials of Drug Therapy for Myocardial Infarction," *Canadian Medical Association Journal* 159 (1998): 321–27.

64. D. Harris and P. Douglas, "Enrollment of Women in Cardiovascular Clinical Trials Funded by the National Heart, Lung, and Blood Institute," *New England Journal of Medicine* (*NEJM*) 343 (2000): 475–80.

65. R. Marinier et al., "Psychotropic Drug Use by Women: Demographic, Lifestyle, and Personality Correlates," *Drug Intelligence and Clinical Pharmacy* 19 (1985): 40–41.

66. Gonzales et al., "Antibiotic Prescribing for Adults with Colds, Upper Respiratory Tract Infections, and Bronchitis by Ambulatory Care Physicians."

67. L. Goldman et al., "Costs and Effectiveness of Routine Therapy and Long-term Beta-Adrenergic Antagonists after Acute Myocardial Infarction," *NEJM* 319 (1988): 152–56.

68. J. W. Milliren, "Some Contingencies Affecting the Utilization of Tranquilizers in Long Term Care of the Elderly," *Journal of Health and Social Behavior* 18 (1977): 206; H. Ashton, "Psychotropic-Drug Prescribing for Women," *British Journal of Psychiatry* 158 (1991): 30–35.

69. M. Miller et al., "Sex Bias and Underutilization of Lipid-Lowering Therapy in Patients with Coronary Artery Disease at Academic Medical Centers in the United States and Canada," *Archives of Internal Medicine* 160 (2000): 343–47.

70. R. Woosley and D. Flockart, "Evaluating Drugs after Their Approval for Clinical Use," *NEJM* 330 (1994): 1394–95; R. Woosley, "Centers for Education and Research in Therapeutics," *Clinical Pharmacology and Therapeutics* 55 (1994): 249–55; R. Woosley, "A Prescription for Better Prescriptions," *Issues in Science and Technology* 10 (1994): 61–66.

71. S. Segal et al., "Race, Quality of Care, and Antipsychotic Prescribing Practices in Psychiatric Emergency Services," *Psychiatric Services* 47 (1996): 282–86; W. Glazer et al., "Race and Tardive Dyskinesia among Outpatients at a CMHC," *Hospital and Community Psychiatry* 45 (1994): 38–42.

72. D. Blazer, "Marked Differences in Antidepressant Use by Race in an Elderly Community Sample: 1986–1996," *American Journal of Psychiatry* 157 (2000): 1089–94; D. Sclar et al., "Ethnicity and

the Prescribing of Antidepressant Pharmacotherapy: 1992–1995," *Harvard Review of Psychiatry* 7 (May–June 1999): 29–36.

73. D. Sclar et al., "Antidepressant Prescribing Patterns: A Comparison of Blacks and Whites in a Medicaid Population," *Clinical Drug Investigation* 16 (1998): 135–40.

74. B. Sleath et al., "Patient Race and Psychotropic Prescribing during Medical Encounters," *Patient Education and Counseling* 34 (1998): 227–38.

75. N. Hymowitz et al., "Past Quit Smoking Assistance and Doctors' Advice for White and African-American Smokers," *Journal of the National Medical Association* 88 (1996): 249–52.

76. Gonzales et al., "Antibiotic Prescribing for Adults with Colds, Upper Respiratory Tract Infections, and Bronchitis by Ambulatory Care Physicians."

77. K. Todd et al., "Ethnicity as a Risk Factor for Inadequate Emergency Department Analgesia," *JAMA* 269 (1993): 1537–39; K. Todd et al., "Ethnicity and Analgesic Practice," *Annals of Emergency Medicine* 35 (2000): 11–16.

78. K. Anderson et al., "Minority Cancer Patients and Their Providers: Pain Management Attitudes and Practice," *Cancer* 88 (2000): 1929–38.

79. R. Morrison et al., "'We Don't Carry That'—Failure of Pharmacies in Predominantly Nonwhite Neighborhoods to Stock Opioid Analgesics," *NEJM* 342 (2000): 1023–26.

80. R. Moore et al., "Racial Differences in the Use of Drug Therapy for HIV Diseases in an Urban Community," *NEJM* 330 (1994): 763–68.

81. S. Claiborne Johnston et al., "Utilization of Intravenous Tissue-Type Plasminogen Activator for Ischemic Stroke at Academic Medical Centers: The Influence of Ethnicity," *Stroke* 32 (2001): 1061–68.

82. See Naomi Aoki, "Real Fears over Phony Drugs: US Health Officials View Spate of Recent Cases as Evidence of Rising Trend," available at www.psi-inc.org/fears.pdf (accessed on 23 December 2002).

83. See Susan J. Landers, "Pharmaceutical Fakes, Knockoffs a Growing Problem: The Prevalence of Counterfeit Drugs in Other Nations Is Sparking Concern about the Reimportation of Pharmaceuticals," available at www.ama-assn.org/sci-pubs/amnews/pick_01/hlsb1126.htm (accessed on 23 December 2002).

84. See Aoki, "Real Fears over Phony Drugs."

85. See Michael F. Conlan, "How Safe Is the Drug Supply? Reports of Counterfeit Drugs and the Growth of e-Tailing Are Fanning Concerns about Drug Quality," available at www.findarticles.com/cf_0/m3045/20_145/80325787/print.jhtml (accessed on 23 December 2002).

86. D. Phillips and C. Bredder, "Morbidity and Mortality from Medical Errors: An Increasingly Serious Public Health Problem," *Annual Review of Public Health* 23 (2002): 135–50.

4

Human Subjects Have Often Been Treated Inhumanely

Terrible things have been done to people in the name of science. The most infamous involved the Nazi regime. Nazi scientists conducted experiments such as measuring survival times of concentration camp prisoners after forcing them to eat poison or sit in ice water. As horrific as those were, research conducted by reputable U.S. scientists both before and after World War II is not strikingly different. Many of the studies involved drugs. The Nazis experimented on Jews, gypsies, homosexuals, and others they considered of little value to society. The victims of U.S. scientists have been poor people in developing countries and, within the United States, prisoners, people in mental institutions, and soldiers. A few cases have been described on earlier pages, and other authors provide chilling examples.[1]

Until a few decades ago, U.S. scientists with financial backing did pretty much what they wanted with human subjects. There was little oversight. Then, in 1966, Henry Beecher published a landmark article.[2] Beecher examined 100 consecutive published reports of medical studies involving humans and reported that at least twelve violated widely accepted ethical principles. For example, victims of typhoid fever were given either chloramphenicol or placebo even after chlor-amphenicol had been recognized as effective. Approximately three times as many placebo patients as drug patients died. Beecher's work stimulated the National Research Act of 1974, which requires that institutions that accept federal funds for research establish institutional review boards (IRBs). Today, approximately five thousand IRBs (panels of five to twenty scientists, ethicists, and others) are appointed by hospitals, universities, managed care organizations, and government agencies to examine the institutions' research projects. Their mandate is to ensure that subjects understand the risks involved and give willing consent. Fourteen officials with the National Institutes of Health oversee them. (No federal agency regulates drug company–sponsored research that does not result in a Food and Drug Administration [FDA] application.) IRBs have cut down on abuses but, as will be seen, not sufficiently.

INFORMED CONSENT

The first commandment in the Nuremberg Code (written following the trials of Nazi war criminals) is that patients must be told that they are not required to accept any treatment for other than therapeutic reasons. They must also be told of any risks. But lawyers who work for research institutions devise the consent forms, and their goal is to protect the institutions rather than inform patients. So zealous researchers adhere to the letter of the law while trampling over patients' rights. Grunder analyzed consent forms from five hospitals and concluded, "The readability of all 5 was approximately equivalent to that of material intended for upper division undergraduates or graduate students. Four of the 5 forms were written at the level of a scientific journal, and the fifth at the level of a specialized academic magazine."[3] A standardized, informed consent form was beyond the reading level of 40 to 74.7 percent of all patients.[4]

Gray interviewed fifty-one women who had signed a consent form to receive a new labor-inducing drug.[5] Having been told that the drug was new, most assumed it was superior, and only twenty realized that it was experimental. Few women understood that they were not required to participate and might be exposed to hazards. Of 200 cancer patients who had signed a consent form for chemotherapy and were later questioned, only 40 percent had read it carefully, only 60 percent understood the purpose of chemotherapy, only 55 percent were able to list even a single major risk, and only 27 percent could name even one alternative treatment.[6]

The informed consent procedure is especially problematic when the subjects are poor, uneducated, or recent immigrants or refugees. Many foreign-born Asians and Pacific Islanders, particularly elderly women, were never permitted to question authorities in their country of origin. They consent because a doctor or professor has asked them to, not because they understand the forms.[7]

Animal tests on a new drug cannot detect common adverse effects in humans such as depression and headaches, and positive effects may not generalize. So new drugs must be tested on humans. The first human subjects are either healthy volunteers or patients with the disease the drug is meant to treat. The studies are called phase I or phase I/II trials. The goals are to evaluate toxicity and pharmacokinetics. The typical strategy is to give a very low dose to the first group of subjects and steadily increasing doses to later groups until signs of toxicity appear. The previous dose level then becomes the recommended one. That dose level is then tested for efficacy in a phase II trial. Brody cites a survey of phase I trials showing that the eventual recommended dose averaged forty times the dose given to the first group.[8] In other words, the first few groups did not get enough drug to do them any good. Then he raises an important informed consent issue. When cancer patients were asked why they had participated in phase I studies, 100 percent reported that they had hoped to benefit, and only 33 percent mentioned helping future patients. Yet only 33 percent had understood that they were unlikely to receive anywhere near a therapeutic dose and that late participants were likely to experience toxicity.

A 1998 *Boston Globe* series described experiments in which researchers administered drugs to intensify the symptoms of psychiatric patients (see below).[9] The consent forms frequently deceived patients about what would be done and the risks. Leonard Glantz said, "Why would anyone agree to be in these studies? If you were really well-informed and you really knew what was going on, could you possibly say yes? You don't make psychotic people psychotic. You don't put diabetic people into shock. You don't give people with heart disease heart attacks. It's not an appropriate use of human beings." Adil Shamoo reports that some researchers recruit psychotic patients from emergency rooms for experiments that either delay treatment with antipsychotic drugs or administer psychosis-provoking agents: "How could people give informed consent when they are psychotic and delusional?"[10]

Shamoo and Keay searched MEDLINE for the years 1966–93 and found forty-one U.S. studies relevant to the topic of schizophrenia relapse during experimental withdrawal from antipsychotic drugs.[11] In twenty-three articles the subjects are reported to have signed an informed consent form, though in only one article do the authors mention using an independent psychiatrist to judge whether the subjects were competent to sign. (Federal regulations require that subjects must be able to comprehend what they have signed.) In fifteen articles the authors do not report obtaining informed consent, and in three they report that the next of kin gave consent. In only one study do the authors indicate that subjects or their next of kin had the right to withdraw.

Sharav and Shamoo cite a 1997 Veterans Administration (VA) publication on informed consent: "It is standard practice to provide full detailed information in written form covering all aspects of the proposed research. . . . The potential participant has every possible piece of information that might be important . . . in making a decision."[12] Then they quote the chief of psychiatry at the Bronx VA Medical Center, who testified under oath: "I have had occasion to review many consent forms for psychiatric studies during the late 1970s and 1980s. I can state that I have seen not one single consent form during that period of time that discussed any risk associated with a drug-free period or the withdrawal of medication."[13]

IN DEFENSE OF EXPERIMENTS THAT HARM HUMAN SUBJECTS

People whose lives are governed by the principle "Do unto others as you would have others do unto you" will have no indecision about condemning harmful research. But for people who adhere to an alternative ethical principle, such as "The end justifies the means," "Knowledge is the greatest good," or "Seek the greatest good for the greatest number," the issues are complex. Many medical advances that have saved thousands of lives originated from experiments in which a few subjects died. Walter Reed's identification of the *Aedes* mosquito as the carrier of yellow fever is a prominent example. Public health would suffer if dangerous experiments were banned. Tests for possible toxicity of drugs and chemical additives would be disallowed—they entail risks and no direct gain for participants. No treatment, having once gained acceptance, would ever be withheld to further test its value. People would still be treated with exorcisms, leeches, cold-water baths, and blood letting.

The points for the defense are valid. Still, I am opposed to experiments such as the ones described next.

RESEARCH DONE SINCE THE ESTABLISHMENT OF INSTITUTIONAL REVIEW BOARDS

Researchers who need actively psychotic subjects for testing antipsychotic drugs have withheld drugs from patients in hospital emergency rooms, administered drugs to intensify the symptoms of psychiatric patients, and discontinued drugs to stabilized patients to see how quickly relapses occur. They justify their work on the grounds that it leads to improved treatments. As noted above, active psychotics cannot give meaningful informed consent. They do not benefit and are exposed to pain and long-term harm. No other type of patient has symptoms deliberately made worse for research purposes only. According to a 1998 *Boston Globe* series, more than two thousand mentally ill patients over the past twenty-five years were victimized:

> Psychiatric researchers have used a variety of agents—L-dopa, amphetamine, methylphenidate, m-cholorophenyl piperazine, ketamine, and tetrahydrocannabinol—to deliberately provoke psychotic symptoms in more than 1,200 schizophrenia patients. Symptom-provocation experiments like these have been conducted by prominent researchers at the National Institute of Mental Health and at close to a dozen leading medical schools. They have drawn their psychotic subjects largely from outpatient clinics, Veterans Affairs hospitals, state mental institutions, and emergency rooms—settings that regularly provide care to the poor and uninsured. In the few studies that recorded the ethnic makeup of patients, 54 percent were minorities.[14]

> In the '80s and early '90s, researchers conducted experiments in which they withdrew medications from schizophrenic patients whose condition was stabilized, including some living in community settings, and studied them until they had a full relapse. The prevailing view is that following a relapse, particularly the first one after a psychotic break, patients may never return to the same level of functioning. During a relapse, schizophrenic patients are also at a dramatically higher risk of self-injury and suicide.[15]

Sharav and Shamoo cite "sudden medication withdrawal" experiments such as a 1995 study involving eighty-eight schizophrenic veterans at a VA medical center.[16] About 50 percent of the veterans relapsed. They cite dozens of "deliberate exacerbation of schizophrenia symptoms" experiments. A study published in 1994 involved withdrawing medication from forty-one stable outpatient schizophrenics for fifty-two weeks or until relapse. Subjects were injected with methylphenidate four times to provoke psychosis. Amphetamine, which worsens the symptoms of schizophrenia, was injected in studies in 1996 and 1998. Ketamine was injected in two studies published in 1995. The consent form for a 1987 VA study on schizophrenics in remission and living in the community states: "We think that by giving you this drug and evaluating your response to it, we may be able to tell if your regular medication is safe for you."[17] Nothing is mentioned about the possibility of relapse. But in the published article, the authors write that the study was designed to predict time to relapse in twenty-eight schizophrenic patients withdrawn from an effective antipsychotic drug and challenged with L-dopa until relapse. All twenty-eight subjects relapsed.[18]

The nonprofit organization Citizens for Responsible Care and Research has listed dozens of federally funded relapse-producing experiments, many conducted since 1995. The citations can be seen (as of 17 July 2002) at www.networksplus.net/fhp/madnation/citations/circarebib2.htm.

In the forty-one studies analyzed by Shamoo and Keay, 900 subjects (39 percent of them) relapsed and 243 dropped out. In thirty-six of the studies, the number of dropouts is not specified. The dropouts were not followed up to ensure that they were safe. Shamoo and Dunigan write that "in 30 years of reported research in the United States, there was not a single case of reported suicides despite the fact that, in general, about 1 percent of schizophrenic patients commit suicide each year. The lack of reported suicides is also in direct contrast to both the recent testimonies of families and patients to the National Bioethics Advisory Commission and the reported suicide rates in non-U.S. studies."[19] In other words, American investigators have almost certainly suppressed information.

Los Angeles County has more than two thousand severely disabled people, primarily schizophrenics, in its care. Called "conservatees," they are placed in nursing homes, board and care facilities, and convalescent or state hospitals. They lose their right to vote and can be forced to take certain drugs. The county had banned the testing of psychiatric drugs on conservatees but lifted the ban in 1999. Critics charged that drug companies lobbied for rescinding the ban so they could increase their population of test subjects. Conservatees are especially desirable because they usually remain in one place, which makes for easy monitoring. Proponents of the new policy note that some new drugs have greatly improved the conditions of some conservatees. Opponents are skeptical. Edward Opton, an attorney and psychologist who sits on the state's Committee for the Protection of Human Subjects, said, "Any drug might benefit anyone. But when you're looking for new psychotropic drugs you're looking for a needle in a haystack."[20]

Doctors at the New York State Psychiatric Institute and three other hospitals recruited healthy African American and Hispanic boys, aged six to ten, whose older brothers were convicted delinquents. The children were offered gift certificates for toys to take part in a study on the biology and sociology of criminal behavior. They fasted for twelve hours and were given a drug, fenfluramine, that was never approved for use in minors and was eventually withdrawn by the FDA after causing several deaths.[21]

TREATMENT OF HIV-POSITIVE PREGNANT WOMEN

About one-third of untreated HIV-positive women transmit the virus to their newborn babies. The drug AZT, given over a period of six months during pregnancy and immediately after delivery to the newborn, reduces the transmission rate to about 8 percent. So HIV-positive women in American hospitals are routinely treated with AZT. But the treatment costs about $800. Some clinicians believed that AZT would be almost as protective if given only during late pregnancy and childbirth, and the shorter course of treatment would be more affordable. The hypothesis spurred clinical trials to test the effectiveness of a short course of AZT and led to a controversy that divided the medical community.[22]

A proper test required comparing transmission rates of women who had received the short course of treatment with those of women who had not. As David Rothman notes in his excellent summary of the controversy, the ethical question involved the nature of the comparison group.[23] There were two possibilities: The comparison group could be given either placebo or the standard effective treatment that American women received. Several projects were begun, most in Africa and Thailand. In fifteen of sixteen projects under way by 1997, involving about seventeen thousand women, the researchers gave the comparison group placebo.[24] *New England Journal of Medicine* editor Marcia Angell wrote a blistering attack in response. She argued that the work violated a provision of the 1964 World Medical Association's Declaration of Helsinki stating that control groups should always be given the best proven therapy. She compared the withholding of AZT from black female AIDS victims in Africa with the withholding of penicillin from black men with syphilis in Tuskegee.[25]

Researchers in several ongoing AIDS studies in African countries continue to withhold AZT from their subjects. Rothman mentions an investigation of couples in which one partner is HIV-positive and the other is HIV-negative.[26] The couples are given general health education and drugs to treat infectious diseases but no contraceptives or AZT. The researchers want to find out when and under what conditions the negative partner turns positive, and providing AZT would undermine the project.

Defenders of such research have rebutted the criticisms as too simplistic.[27] They write that local ethics committees approved the projects, that the subjects never would have received a long course of AZT under any conditions, and that the research is likely to lead to treatments that will help people in Africa and Asia. Maybe the criticisms are too simplistic, but I will give Rothman the last words:

> To date the results of placebo-based AIDS trials have not brought medical benefits to Africa. Short-course AZT was supposed to be helpful, but it is infrequently used.
>
> . . . [M]aking human rights relative to social and economic conditions in distant countries could come back to haunt us. Appalachia is not Westchester County and the mortality statistics in Harlem are worse than those in Bangladesh. Will American researchers be allowed to provide less treatment in our own impoverished regions than in prosperous ones? The question is not idle, for this is the position that the US Public Health Service adopted in conducting and rationalizing the Tuskegee research.
>
> . . . [A]bject poverty is harsh enough without people having to bear the additional burdens of serving as research subjects.[28]

CONCLUDING COMMENTS

Stronger oversight is needed. Institutional review boards are charged with the task of examining research projects for violations of ethical principles. But in most IRBs, all but one or two board members work for the research institutions and review studies sponsored by companies that contribute to the institutions' budgets. They review studies of colleagues who may someday return the favor. They rarely interview subjects or review research once it has been approved, so they do not know how carefully investigators are adhering to the written protocol. According to a General Accounting Office (GAO) report, IRBs "rely largely on investigators' self-assessments," "do not verify the accuracy of the reported information," and "spend only 1 or 2 minutes of review per study."[29] The GAO report notes that, in one FDA district, twelve IRBs had not been inspected in over ten years.

The inspector general's office evaluated IRBs and issued a report in 1998 noting that both the number and the types of research projects had increased enormously during the previous few years.[30] Whereas most earlier projects had been conducted by one or a few investigators at a single location, research by 1998 frequently involved hundreds of researchers at many different sites. The report includes six sets of recommendations. A second report, issued in 2000, includes the following comments:

> **Several promising steps have been taken.**
> NIH [National Institute of Health] and FDA have enacted two of our recommendations. NIH now requires data and safety monitoring boards to share summary information with IRBs and FDA now informs sponsors and IRBs about its findings of clinical investigator misconduct. In addition, both agencies have ongoing initiatives, particularly in the area of education. NIH and FDA continue to be active in educational outreach and programs, conducting numerous training presentations and seminars. . . . FDA convened a national meeting addressing current issues in human subject protections and has had numerous workgroups examining specific issues. NIH, also, has constructed a website containing bioethics resources.
> **But overall, few of our recommended reforms have been enacted.**
> **Flexibility and Accountability.** Minimal progress had been made in recasting Federal IRB requirements so that they grant IRBs greater flexibility and hold them more accountable for results. Too much IRB attention now focuses on review responsibilities of questionable protective value.
> **Oversight and Protections.** Minimal progress has been made in strengthening continuing protections for human subjects participating in research.[31]

Concerned scientists and other citizens continue to discuss ways to protect research subjects.[32]

NOTES

1. J. Jones, *Bad Blood: The Tuskegee Syphilis Experiment* (New York: Free Press, 1981); J. Moreno, *Undue Risk: Secret State Experiments on Humans* (New York: W. H. Freeman, 1999); J. Kaye, "Retin-A's Wrinkled Past," *Pennsylvania History Review* (spring 1997); L. Bender, "Autonomic Nervous System Responses in Hospitalized Children Treated with LSD and UML," presented at the 19th Annual Convention and Scientific Program of the Society of Biological Psychiatry, Los Angeles, 13 May 1964; G. Gardos, "Are Antipsychotic Drugs Interchangeable?" *Journal of Nervous and Mental Disease* 159 (1974): 343–48; B. Shlain and M. Lee, *Acid Dreams: The CIA, LSD, and the Sixties Rebellion* (New York: Grove, 1985); J. Marks, *The Search for the "Manchurian Candidate": The CIA and Mind Control* (New York: Times Books, 1979).
2. H. Beecher, "Ethics and Clinical Research," *New England Journal of Medicine* (*NEJM*) 274 (1966): 1354–60.

3. T. Grunder, "On Readability of Surgical Consent Forms," *NEJM* 302 (1980): 900.

4. M. Williams et al., "Inadequate Functional Health Literacy among Patients at Two Public Hospitals," *Journal of the American Medical Association* 274 (1995): 1677–82.

5. B. Gray, *Human Subjects in Medical Experimentation* (New York: Wiley, 1975).

6. B. Cassileth et al., "Informed Consent—Why Are Its Goals Imperfectly Realized?" *NEJM* 302 (1980): 896–900.

7. E. Yu and W. Liu, "Methodological Problems and Policy Implications in Vietnamese Refugee Research," *International Migration Review* 20 (1986): 483–501.

8. B. Brody, *The Ethics of Biomedical Research* (New York: Oxford University Press, 1998).

9. D. Kong, "Doing Harm: Research on the Mentally Ill. Still No Solution in the Struggle on Safeguards," *Boston Globe,* 18 November 1998: A1; R. Whitaker and D. Kong, "Doing Harm: Research on the Mentally Ill. Testing Takes Human Toll," *Boston Globe,* 15 November 1998: A1.

10. D. Kong, "Doing Harm: Research on the Mentally Ill. Debatable Forms of Consent," *Boston Globe,* 16 November 1998: A1.

11. A. Shamoo and T. Keay, "Ethical Concerns about Relapse Studies," *Cambridge Quarterly of Healthcare Ethics* 5 (1996): 373–86.

12. V. Sharav and A. Shamoo, "Are Experiments That Chemically Induce Psychosis in Patients Ethical?" *BioLaw 2000* 2 (2000): S14.

13. Sharav and Shamoo, "Are Experiments That Chemically Induce Psychosis in Patients Ethical?" S15.

14. Kong, "Doing Harm: Research on the Mentally Ill. Still No Solution in the Struggle on Safeguards," A1.

15. Whitaker and Kong, "Doing Harm," A1.

16. Sharav and Shamoo, "Are Experiments That Chemically Induce Psychosis in Patients Ethical?"

17. Sharav and Shamoo, "Are Experiments That Chemically Induce Psychosis in Patients Ethical?" S14.

18. M. Davidson et al., "L-dopa Challenge and Relapse in Schizophrenia," *American Journal of Psychiatry* 144 (1987): 934–38; Shamoo and Keay, "Ethical Concerns about Relapse Studies."

19. A. Shamoo and C. Dunigan, "Ethics in Research," *Experimental Biology and Medicine* 224 (2000): 209.

20. N. Riccardi, "County Lifts Ban on Testing Drugs on Mentally Ill," *Los Angeles Times,* 29 November 1999: A1.

21. D. Pine et al., "Neuroendocrine Response to Fenfluramine Challenge in Boys," *Archives of General Psychiatry* 54 (1997): 839–46.

22. A short course of AZT offers substantial protection although it is not as good as the standard treatment.

23. D. Rothman, "The Shame of Medical Research," *New York Review of Books,* 30 November 2000: 60–64.

24. P. Lurie and S. Wolfe, "Unethical Trials of Interventions to Reduce Perinatal Transmission of the Human Immunodeficiency Virus in Developing Countries," *NEJM* 337 (1997): 853–56.

25. M. Angell, "The Ethics of Clinical Research in the Third World," *NEJM* 337 (1997): 847–49.

26. Rothman, "The Shame of Medical Research."

27. See H. Varmus and D. Satcher, "Ethical Complexities of Conducting Research in Developing Countries," *NEJM* 338 (1997): 836–44.

28. Rothman, "The Shame of Medical Research," 64.

29. General Accounting Office, *Scientific Research: Continued Vigilance Critical to Protecting Human Subjects,* Report to the Senate Committee on Government Affairs, GAO/HEHS-96-72 (Washington, D.C.: U.S. General Accounting Office, 1996).

30. Department of Health and Human Services Office of Inspector General, *Institutional Review Boards: A Time for Reform,* OEI-01-97-00193 (Washington, D.C.: Department of Health and Human Services, 1998).

31. Department of Health and Human Services Office of Inspector General, *Protecting Human Research Subjects: Status of Recommendations,* OEI-01-97-00197 (Washington, D.C.: Department of Health and Human Services, 2000).

32. For recent suggestions, see M. Christian et al., "A Central Institutional Review Board for Multi-institutional Trials," *NEJM* 346 (2002): 1405–08; and R. Steinbrook, "Improving Protection for Research Subjects," *NEJM* 346 (2002): 1425–30.

5

U.S. Citizens Are Overmedicated with Psychiatric Drugs

Doctors in most medical specialties do not recruit patients. People know either directly or from diagnostic tests when they are ill. Psychiatrists, by contrast, must persuade troubled people that they are sick and in need of professional help.[1] For this they rely on drug companies. Drug companies help in three ways. First, they finance "educational" campaigns to persuade the public that sadness, shyness, boisterousness, anxiety, and other symptoms within the normal realm of human experience are actually diseases that require treatment with drugs. Second, they subsidize journals, conferences, and symposia. Between 20 and 30 percent of the American Psychiatric Association's operating budget comes from drug companies.

Third, drug companies join with the psychiatric profession and the National Institute of Mental Health (the federal agency that funds much psychiatric research) to promote the view that brain defects are the primary cause of mental disorders. One observer asserted that "the pharmaceutical industry is a lobby within psychiatry, pushing for biological findings in etiological research and thus justifying biological treatments."[2] Their spokespeople argue that modern drugs correct chemical imbalances and should therefore be the treatment of choice. They portray the therapeutic effects of their products in terms of actions on specific neurotransmitters (NTs). For example, the effectiveness of the first generation of antipsychotic drugs mirrored their ability to block a subset of dopamine receptors. That led to the hypothesis that schizophrenia is caused by hyperactivity of brain dopaminergic systems. Similarly, antidepressant drugs target the presumed biological cause by enhancing the functioning of norepinephrine, serotonin, or both. Antianxiety drugs increase the efficiency of gamma aminobutyric acid (GABA) synapses, which are presumed defective in anxiety disorders. Hobson writes, "There is no doubt that the development of drugs that interact with the brain-mind's chemical system is the most important advance in the history of modern psychiatry."[3]

But scores of critics have expressed doubt. Whereas debates about drug industry profits typically feature adversaries who differ professionally and economically—company executives versus consumers—both advocates and dissenters on the issue of effectiveness of psychiatric drugs come from the ranks of therapists and researchers. Biopsychologist Elliot Valenstein has written, "Contrary to what is claimed, no biochemical, anatomical, or functional signs have been found that reliably distinguish the brains of mental patients"; he adds that "people with mental disorders may be encouraged when they are told that the prescribed drugs will do for them just what insulin does for a diabetic, but the analogy is certainly not justified."[4]

Fred Baughman cites Surgeon General David Satcher: "Mental illness is no different than diabetes, asthma or other physical ailments. Mental illnesses are physical illnesses. We know the chemical disorders we are treating." Then Baughman responds:

> The presence of any bona fide disease, like diabetes, cancer, or epilepsy is confirmed by an objective finding—a physical or chemical abnormality. No demonstrable physical or chemical abnormality: no disease! . . . [T]here is no physical or chemical abnormality to be found, in life, or at autopsy in depression, bipolar disorder and other mental illnesses. Why, then, are you telling the American people that "mental illnesses" are "physical" and that they are due to "chemical disorders"?[5]

The theories relating schizophrenia to dopamine excess, and depression to insufficient norepinephrine or serotonin, originated when only a few NTs were known. Since then, researchers have identified many more—plus other features of neurotransmission that allow for enormous complexity and gradation of response. It is simplistic to reduce emotional state and cognitive functioning to the activity of single NTs. Recent evidence points to roles for the neuropeptide substance P, dopamine, and acetylcholine in depression.[6]

One reason for the disagreement between proponents and critics of psychiatric drugs is a turf war. Psychotherapists with degrees in psychology cannot prescribe drugs, whereas psychiatrists, with M.D.s, can. So the psychotherapists prefer environmental explanations of abnormality, and psychiatrists seek neuroanatomical and biochemical causes and cures.[7]

Even if it were shown unambiguously that victims of psychiatric disorders have brain defects, the finding would not prove that defects cause the disorders. Painful life experiences might be at the root of both the disorders and the defects. Trauma, stress, sexual abuse, neglect, and boredom not only cause emotional problems but can also change brain chemistry. People born after 1945 have a five- to twenty-fold higher lifetime prevalence rate of depression than those born before 1934.[8]

During those years, family structures, schooling, and other environmental factors changed considerably; inherited brain chemistry almost certainly did not.

Although mental illness increases the likelihood that a person will become homeless, many homeless people are merely victims of unfortunate circumstances. Yet society devalues them. The homeless are exposed to daily privation, dangers, powerful stressors, and loss of self-esteem. Such factors often precipitate the onset of mental health problems. Previously healthy homeless people may start to behave outside the norm and be diagnosed as mentally ill.

In addition to the alliance between drug companies and psychiatrists, at least two other factors lead to overprescription of psychiatric drugs. First, most health maintenance organizations limit the number of sessions for which they reimburse therapists who treat psychiatric disorders. Talking therapies require frequent visits, whereas drugs, after the initial visit, can be prescribed by telephone. Thus, economic pressures force even those psychiatrists who would prefer to do psychotherapy into prescribing drugs. Psychiatrists must often evaluate a patient after a single session, and some HMOs relieve them of even that task. Psychiatrist Thomas Jensen filed suit against the Kaiser Permanente Medical Group in San Diego, claiming that it fired him after he refused to prescribe drugs to patients solely on the recommendations of social workers.[9]

Second, primary care doctors are less likely to refer patients to psychiatrists than to other specialists. The primary care doctors prescribe drugs as their first line of treatment when various alternatives would often be preferable.[10] As psychiatry is not their specialty, they have limited knowledge about the drugs and are especially susceptible to the tactics of detailmen.

Even staunch advocates of psychiatric drugs acknowledge that the vast majority relieve symptoms without curing. Thus, patients must take the drugs for life or run a substantial risk of relapse. If the drugs were clearly better than alternatives, there would be no controversy. But they cause side effects (which are probably substantially underreported—see below), cost money, and are often aversive to patients, so the burden of proof should be with the prescribers. Nevertheless, the psychopharmacological treatment of psychiatric disorders has become a multibillion-dollar business.[11] Psychiatric drugs account for almost 11 percent of covered prescription drug costs and are the largest single drug-cost category for nearly half of pharmacy benefit management companies.[12]

Psychiatric drugs are far less selective than their proponents claim, and their initial actions on the brain do not necessarily indicate how they affect behavior. A drug may initiate a cascade of responses that eventually involves the entire central nervous system. And, although a drug may act on a specific NT, NTs are involved in diverse bodily processes. The selective serotonin reuptake inhibitors (such as Prozac) are promoted for their selectivity—but about 95 percent of serotonin in humans is found outside the brain, and serotonin regulates activity within the gastrointestinal, cardiovascular, and reproductive systems. Interestingly, many drugs are promoted, on the one hand, for their selectivity and, on the other, for treating a broad (and ever increasing) array of emotional problems.

As indicated in chapter 13, if a drug blocks the receptors for an NT, more NT is synthesized and released; if reuptake is blocked, synthesis and release slow down. Because many different compensatory mechanisms regulate brain NT activity, and drugs do not impair all mechanisms simultaneously, the activity tends to return to its baseline state. Therefore, concludes Mandell, drugs cannot provide other than transient euphoric states.[13] If Mandell is right, drug effects would be temporary even if they did correct chemical imbalances.

As discussed below, psychiatric drugs are drastically over- and misprescribed. Nevertheless, some recipients claim that they work wonders. For example, actress Patty Duke and Broadway director Joshua Logan testified that lithium profoundly improved their lives.[14] There are several plausible reasons in addition to the ones offered by the chemical imbalance advocates. Taking a drug is decisive and proactive. The drugs produce discernible effects to recipients who, in Western society, have great faith in them. Therefore, their nonspecific effects are considerable. Drugs that stimulate, such as Prozac, may temporarily boost the mood of a lethargic, depressed person. Whatever the reason, critics of the drugs should acknowledge that successes have occurred.

Although methodological problems plague much of the research purporting to show the value of the drugs, certain factors work against observation of positive effects:

- Responses to an active drug may be weakened if recipients are uncertain about the drug's effectiveness. Patients told that they may receive placebo may be wary about stating that a possibly inactive medication has helped them, perhaps especially because they suffer psychiatric illness.
- Laboratory scientists typically restrict their experiments to homogeneous subjects such as college sophomore women or male rats of the same strain, age, and weight. Psychiatric patients, by contrast, are heterogeneous in length and severity of illness and pre- and post-treatment life situations. Only rarely do they all receive medication at the same time from the same therapist. Because of the great variability, only very strong effects reach statistical significance.
- The more accurate the measuring instrument, the easier it is to detect changes in whatever is being measured. The measurements of height and white blood cell count are accurate, but the measurements of depression, hyperactivity, and anxiety are much less so.

Yet the archives of prestigious scientific journals list hundreds of apparently error-free positive studies. Below are references to a few published materials that present psychiatric drugs favorably:

Schizophrenia:

- G. Beaumont, "Antipsychotics—The Future of Schizophrenia Treatment," *Current Medical Research and Opinion* 16 (2000): 37–42.
- J. Kane, "The Effectiveness of Novel Antipsychotics in Preventing Relapse," *International Journal of Neuropsychopharmacology* 3 (supplement 1) (2000): Abstract, S.01.2.
- K. Wahlbeck et al., "Evidence of Clozapine's Effectiveness in Schizophrenia: A Systematic Review and Meta-analysis of Randomized Trials," *American Journal of Psychiatry* 156 (1999): 990–99.

Depression:

- S. Kasper and A. Heiden, "Do SSRIs Differ in Their Antidepressant Efficacy," *Human Psychopharmacology* 10 (1995): S163–72.
- S. Preskorn, "The Revolution in Psychiatry," *Phi Kappa Phi,* winter 1993: 22–25.
- O. Spigset and B. Mårtensson, "Fortnightly Review: Drug Treatment of Depression," *British Medical Journal* 318 (1999): 1188–91.

Anxiety:

- R. Durham and T. Allan, "Psychological Treatment of Generalised Anxiety Disorder. A Review of the Clinical Significance of the Results since 1980," *British Journal of Psychiatry* 163 (1993): 19–26.
- J. Roerig, "Diagnosis and Management of Generalized Anxiety Disorder," *Journal of the American Pharmaceutical Association* 39 (1999): 811–21.

Attention Deficit/Hyperactivity Disorder (ADHD):

- P. Wender, "Attention Deficit Hyperactivity Disorder in Adults: A Wide View of a Widespread Condition," *Psychiatric Annals* 27 (1997): 556–62.
- MTA Cooperative Group, "A 14-Month Randomized Clinical Trial of Treatment Strategies for Attention Deficit/Hyperactivity Disorder," *Archives of General Psychiatry* 56 (1999): 1073–86.

The next section briefly describes the drugs used to treat four major psychiatric disorders, results of research on the drugs, and a few common side effects for each drug category. Virtually all the drugs produce serious effects if taken over a long enough period, yet many of them are prescribed indefinitely.[15] The next chapter discusses alternatives to the drugs.

DRUGS USED TO TREAT SCHIZOPHRENIA

In 1954, mental institutions in the United States housed approximately half a million inmates. The majority were schizophrenics kept in straitjackets or other restraints. They exhibited so-called positive symptoms, such as hallucinations and delusions, and negative symptoms such as flat affect and lack of motivation.

Then, in 1956, chlorpromazine was introduced, and for the first time ever housed fewer people in public mental hospitals at the end of the year than at the beginning. Advocates claim that chlorpromazine and to an even greater extent several newer drugs help patients feel in control while reducing or eliminating their terrifying hallucinations; thus, psychiatrists can release patients from institutions to live and work outside. The total sales of antipsychotic drugs quadrupled from 1996 to 2000, to $4 billion per year, primarily because of increased sales of the newer drugs.[16]

Many biologically oriented theorists believe that schizophrenia is caused by hyperactivity of brain dopaminergic systems. But, although the first generation of antipsychotic drugs rapidly block a subset of dopamine receptors (called D2 receptors), their effects are delayed for three–six weeks; and several new antipsychotics with weak D2 receptor activity are equally effective. Tandon argues that the balance between acetylcholine and dopamine is critical in the pathology of schizophrenia.[17]

Results of Research

In the literature on psychiatric drugs, there is a strong relationship between skimpiness of methodological detail and strength of reported effect. Thornley and Adams conclude that the effects of antipsychotic drugs are consistently overestimated.[18] In addition, most studies designed to show the effectiveness of antipsychotic drugs covered time periods of a year or less, and the difference between drug and placebo groups decreased with time.[19] Moreover, whereas a high proportion of drug-free schizophrenics shows long-term trends toward improvement, those maintained on antipsychotic drugs do not; 82 percent of drug-treated patients relapse within five years of their first psychotic episodes.[20] (Abrupt discontinuation of an antipsychotic drug can produce withdrawal effects that are mistakenly taken as signs of relapse and lead to the false conclusion that the drug has been effective.)[21] Several studies suggesting that drugs are better than psychotherapy had serious flaws. They used inexperienced therapists, were not done double-blind, had high drop-out rates, and measured adjustment in hospital wards rather than more meaningful predictors of long-term success.[22]

In one study, placebos produced greater long-term improvement than did antipsychotic drugs; readmission rates were 47 percent for drugged patients and 8 percent for those given placebo.[23] The two-year recovery rates of schizophrenics in Nigeria and India, where drugs are not used heavily, are 58 and 50 percent, respectively. Denmark's schizophrenics are treated much more extensively with drugs and have a two-year recovery rate of 8 percent.[24]

The literature is unclear on the relative merits of traditional antipsychotics such as haloperidol and atypical, more expensive ones such as clozapine, olanzapine, risperidone, and quetiapine. Atypicals often induce unwanted weight gain but cause fewer severe movement disorders. Most studies on atypicals lasted only thirteen weeks or less, yet more than half the patients in several large-scale studies dropped out before completion.[25] Although clozapine reduced symptoms of schizophrenia, clozapine-treated patients were no more successful in maintaining jobs or being discharged from the hospital.[26]

In one study, 157 schizophrenics who had failed to improve on traditional antipsychotics despite lengthy treatments were randomly assigned to receive clozapine, olanzapine, risperidone, or haloperidol. Only the three atypicals improved symptoms, but their effects were small. In an accompanying editorial, Lewis writes that the study "clearly underscores the need for identification of more effective treatments."[27] To complicate matters further, the authors of a recent meta-analysis conclude that the atypical antipsychotics are neither more effective nor better tolerated. The authors advise psychiatrists to treat schizophrenics initially with the less expensive traditional drugs.[28]

And to complicate still further, Hegarty and colleagues reviewed 320 studies from 1895 to 1992 on long-term clinical improvement in schizophrenia.[29] During the years 1956–85, 48.5 percent of treated patients were reported improved compared with only 35.4 percent improved during 1895–1955. But during 1985–94, the proportion improved declined to 36.4 percent. The authors suggest as a partial explanation that diagnostic concepts had changed. Whatever the reason, for none of the time periods did more than half the patients diagnosed with schizophrenia show substantial long-term improvement.

Although antipsychotic drugs are given credit for reducing the schizophrenic population in psychiatric hospitals, heavy budget cuts played the major role. With less space available, the hospitals released large numbers of patients to communities that offered little structure or support. Even so, schizophrenic patients occupy 10 percent of hospital beds in the United States.[30] In addition, about 6 percent of prison inmates and 30 percent of homeless people are schizophrenic.[31]

A focal point of the debate on antipsychotic drugs concerns the behaviors they modify. Suppose that hallucinating, delusional, aggressive schizophrenics treated with a drug show fewer of those behaviors than similar patients given placebo. Although the results appear favorable, effectiveness should not be judged solely by reduction of negative symptoms. Otherwise, rendering patients unconscious by cracking them over the head with a baseball bat would be considered an outstanding outcome.

Laboratory animals injected with high doses of antipsychotic drugs can be molded into bizarre positions where they remain for extended periods. The duration of the immobility is correlated with antipsychotic efficacy in humans, and, in that respect, people treated with antipsychotics behave comparably to rats. Guess whether the statement below describing a typical drugged patient was written by advocates or critics of chlorpromazine for treating schizophrenia:

> Sitting or lying, the patient is motionless in his bed, often pale and with eyelids lowered. He remains silent most of the time. If he is questioned, he answers slowly and deliberately in a monotonous, indifferent voice; he expresses himself in a few words and becomes silent. Without exception the response is fairly appropriate and adaptable, showing that the subject is capable of attention and of thought. But he rarely initiates a question and he does not express his anxieties, desires, or preferences.[32]

The statement was written by two strong advocates. Not surprisingly, critics charge that antipsychotic drugs are prescribed exclusively to sedate, for sedated patients place less burden on caretakers and increase profits for the institutions that house them. That seems the most probable reason for the endemic prescriptions of antipsychotic drugs to nonpsychotic inmates in nursing homes, prisons, and institutions for the mentally retarded.[33] Plotkin and Rigling write, "Phenothiazines [a class of antipsychotics] satisfy the institution's need to reduce objectionable behavior by reducing virtually all behavior."[34] It also seems the best explanation for their extensive use in homes for the mentally retarded, despite literature reviews showing their ineffectiveness with that population. (The few positive studies had serious methodological flaws.)[35] On the other hand, advocates argue that antipsychotics, especially the newer ones such as clozapine, olanzapine, and quetiapine, improve both positive and negative symptoms of schizophrenia. They say that sedation is irrelevant.[36]

Side Effects

Patients on antipsychotic drugs complain that they feel lethargic, old, tired, slow of thought, lacking in enthusiasm, and depressed. Many experience movement disorders more unpleasant than their original symptoms.[37] Permanent, incapacitating effects on bodily movement and cognition, called tardive dyskinesia, occur in 30 percent of middle-aged and elderly patients treated with conventional antipsychotics for even one year and are almost inevitable in patients exposed for fifteen years or more.[38] Many doctors fail to recognize tardive dyskinesia and drug-induced parkinsonism in their patients.[39] Newer antipsychotics produce less tardive dyskinesia but still induce movement disorders. The drugs cause cognitive decline and, if used long-term, brain atrophy.[40] Prior to the advent of the antipsychotics, autopsy studies of schizophrenics failed to show atrophy.[41] Antipsychotics also cause other structural changes such as swelling of the brain.[42]

The dopamine system, which antipsychotic drugs block, plays an important role in reward and the experience of pleasure. The reduced ability of drugged patients to feel pleasure may explain Breggin's report that many secretly dispose of their drugs. He writes, "Time and again in my clinical experience I have witnessed patients driven to extreme anguish and outrage by having major tranquilizers [antipsychotics] forced on them. The problem is so great in routine hospital practice that a large percentage of patients have to be threatened with forced intramuscular injection before they will take their drugs."[43] Harrow studied a group of schizophrenics and found a strong relationship between antipsychotic use and major depression almost five years later.[44]

Correlational data suggest that clozapine, olanzapine, and other antipsychotic drugs may precipitate or unmask diabetes in susceptible patients.[45] Patients on antipsychotic drugs are seven times more likely than drug-free study participants to develop blood clots, especially during their first three months on the drugs. Yet, even though the problem has been known for about forty years, blood clots are not listed as a potential side effect of antipsychotics.[46]

As part of a World Health Organization program to monitor the effects of drugs, sixty countries report adverse reactions to a central database maintained in Sweden. Coulter and colleagues analyzed summaries of case histories in the database. They found that infection and other diseases of heart muscle were more frequently reported for clozapine, other antipsychotic drugs, and lithium than for other drugs.[47] The associations raise concern that the drugs cause heart problems, although it is also possible that people already at high risk for heart problems are the most likely recipients of antipsychotics. A third possibility is that some other factor causes both psychotic behavior and proneness to diseases of heart muscle. Still, the study raises an additional reason for caution in using antipsychotics, especially because there have been many unexplained sudden deaths in psychotic patients.

ANTIDEPRESSANTS

Because of its prevalence, depression has been called the common cold of psychological disturbances. In any given six-month period, about 3 percent of U.S. adults experience severe depression, and it is the impetus for an estimated 20 percent of visits to family practitioners.[48] According to one estimate, only 30 to 40 percent of depressed patients are accurately diagnosed during these visits.[49] A conference held under the auspices of the National Depressive and Manic-Depressive Association (NDMDA), a patient alliance group, concludes with a lengthy consensus statement that begins as follows: "There is overwhelming evidence that individuals with depression are being seriously undertreated. Safe, effective and economical treatments are available. The cost to individuals and society of this undertreatment is substantial."[50]

However, before calling your friendly psychiatrist, consider that the conference was funded by Bristol-Myers-Squibb, the maker of the antidepressant nefazodone. Dr. Martin Keller (also see page 17) was a cochair. Keller was on the Executive Committee of the Scientific Advisory Board of the NDMDA, and he earned about $1 million over a two-year period from drug companies that market antidepressants (ADs). During that time he published several articles and presented the results at scientific meetings. He praised the ADs lavishly but did not disclose his financial ties to either the journal editors or the meetings' sponsors.[51]

Even if the market has not been fully tapped, sales of ADs are fine. Olfson and colleagues compared the rates of outpatient treatment for depression in 1987 and 1997.[52] In 1987, seven of every 1,000 people received treatment. In 1997, twenty-three of every 1,000 did. The proportion of treated individuals who used ADs increased from 37.3 percent to 74.5 percent. The number of prescriptions to children and adolescents also increased dramatically.[53] Spending growth on outpatient prescription drugs increased by $22.5 billion in 2001. Antidepressants were responsible for the largest share (9.4 percent) of the one-year increase. Antidepressants were the top-selling drug category, with $12.5 billion in retail sales.[54]

All of the popular ADs act on norepinephrine, serotonin, or both. Some are highly selective, and others have multiple mechanisms of action. There are three main classes:

- Tricyclics (TCAs) inhibit the reuptake of norepinephrine and serotonin. Reuptake is the major mechanism by which their actions are terminated, so reuptake inhibition lets the NTs stay longer in contact with postsynaptic receptors. Although the inhibition is produced rapidly, mood elevation may not occur for two weeks, and full effects may take up to six weeks. Until about 1990, TCAs were the drugs of first choice for treating depression.
- Monoamine oxidase inhibitors (MAOIs) prolong the actions of norepinephrine and serotonin plus dopamine by blocking the enzyme that metabolizes them. The first generation of MAOIs fell out of favor because they interact with many drugs and foods to increase blood pressure to dangerous levels. Several newer MAOIs have briefer actions and are safer.
- Selective serotonin reuptake inhibitors (SSRIs) are, as the name indicates, selective in their reuptake blockade. SSRIs are the most widely used drugs for the treatment of depression.

An alternative biological hypothesis of depression has sparked interest in a different class of drugs. Stress frequently precipitates depression, and stress also triggers the release of several hormones including cortisol and other glucocorticoids from the adrenal glands. Many depressed people show excess glucocorticoid activity. These observations stimulated the idea that substances that reduce glucocorticoid activity (antiglucocorticoids) might improve depressive symptoms.

Wolkowitz and colleagues administered ketoconazole, which inhibits the synthesis of cortisol, to drug-free depressed patients. Some of the patients were hypercortisolemic (produced excess cortisol), and some were not. Ketoconazole improved symptoms in the former but not the latter.[55]

Results of Research

A meta-analysis has shown that long-term treatment with SSRIs produces superior outcomes to long-term treatment with placebo.[56] Although SSRIs are newer than TCAs and, thus, more expensive, a meta-analysis of ninety-eight studies has found no clinically significant differences in effectiveness between the two classes of drugs.[57] People taking SSRIs are more likely to withdraw from a study because of lack of efficacy, less likely because of unpleasant side effects, and slightly less likely overall.[58]

But the extent of benefits caused by treatment is difficult to quantify. Patients whose depression scores improve by at least 50 percent are typically counted as successes even if they still meet the diagnostic criteria for major depression. Kirsch and Sapirstein analyzed data from nineteen studies; they defined drug effect as the difference in response between patients given drug and placebo and concluded that ADs have only a 25 percent advantage over placebos.[59] That is, a patient whose depression rating improves twelve points would owe nine of those points to the placebo response. Walach and Maidhof analyzed additional studies and found that 65 percent of the patients in drug groups and 46 percent of patients in placebo groups improved.[60] More recently, Kirsch and colleagues analyzed data from clinical trials submitted to the Food and Drug Administration by the manufacturers of fluoxetine (Prozac), paroxetine (Paxil), sertraline (Zoloft), venlafaxine (Effexor), nefazodone (Serzone), and citalopram (Celexa).[61] The data constituted the basis on which the drugs were approved. Although most trials were brief (thirty-three trials lasted six weeks, six lasted four weeks, two lasted five weeks, and six lasted eight weeks), of those for which attrition rates were reported, only 60 percent of the placebo patients and 63 percent of the drug patients completed the trials.

When data from all trials were combined, the overall drug effect was 18 percent. Kirsch and colleagues called the effects small. But a 25 percent advantage, or even an 18 percent advantage, can be substantial. I would be delighted with an 18 percent raise in my salary. Furthermore, if the average effect was 18 percent, some patients must have done substantially better than 18 percent. It would make sense for researchers and clinicians to try to identify the best candidates for improvement. On the other hand, the drug/placebo differences might be overestimates:

- ADs produce discernible side effects that probably increase their effectiveness as placebos. Atropine does not directly affect depression but produces some of the same side effects, so atropine has occasionally been used instead of inert placebos. In only two of nine studies did ADs outperform atropine, and in one the difference was small.[62]

- Expectations can strengthen or weaken reactions to both placebos and active drugs. See pages 254–57. In laboratories, unlike doctors' offices, subjects start trials not knowing which they will get. If they then figure out that they have gotten the drug, they are likely to develop positive expectations and react strongly. Effects are likely to be diminished in subjects who later conclude that they have gotten placebo. (Both experimenters and subjects often figure out who has received which treatment.)[63]

Zimmerman and colleagues tested the idea that people who participate in clinical trials of ADs differ in important ways from people to whom the ADs are typically prescribed.[64] The researchers evaluated 346 patients with major depression for coexisting conditions such as suicide risk, unstable medical illnesses, eating disorders, obsessive-compulsive disorder, panic disorder, anxiety disorder, and a history of manic episodes or drug abuse. Any one condition is sufficient to exclude a person from most clinical trials of ADs. People with only mild depression are also typically excluded, for drug company researchers worry that they will respond as well to a placebo as to the drug. (Depression is the only condition for which people with the disorder are routinely excluded from clinical trials because they are not sick enough.)

About 85 percent of the 346 patients would not have been eligible for inclusion in most clinical trials. Yet more than 90 percent of them for whom prescribing information was available were being treated with ADs. The authors conclude that subjects in AD trials represent a minority of patients treated for major depression in routine clinical practice. The effectiveness of ADs for most of the patients who receive them is unknown.

Side Effects

TCAs frequently cause dry mouth, constipation, blurred vision, difficulty urinating, increased sensitivity to the sun, dizziness after standing up quickly, weight gain, and drowsiness. Although many of these side effects disappear within a few days, they typically appear well before any positive effects and can add considerably to the burden of an already clinically depressed person. That helps explain why TCA overdose has been the most common cause of death from prescription drugs.[65] Self-poisoning is the method of choice used by most women who attempt suicide.[66]

Saliva protects teeth by washing away sugars and other substances that promote cavities and by neutralizing mouth acidity. Dry mouth increases the risk for tooth decay. Atropine, clonidine, and more than six hundred other drugs produce dry mouth. Rats, which develop cavities much as humans do, were given atropine or clonidine. They developed significantly more cavities on both the smooth and the chewing surfaces of their teeth than did untreated rats. TCAs have atropine-like effects on salivary flow. Clonidine is used to treat high blood pressure in adults and ADHD in children.[67]

SSRIs produce little sedation or lowered blood pressure. Although SSRIs have been promoted as causing little weight gain, long-term users often gain weight. Common side effects include insomnia, nervousness, nausea, diarrhea, and headache. About 60 percent of users experience decreased libido, decreased arousal, or delayed orgasm. (The manufacturers' official figures are 2–5 percent.)[68] Toxicity from overdose is less serious with SSRIs than TCAs and probably could be reduced. Eli Lilly, Prozac's manufacturer, recommends that most patients get an initial 20 milligram dose, even though many patients do well on 10 or even 5 milligrams, and larger doses cause more side effects.[69]

The increase in prescribing of SSRIs during the past several years has paralleled an increase in the potentially fatal condition called serotonin syndrome. Symptoms of serotonin syndrome include drowsiness, abnormal foot movements, muscle twitching, high body temperature, shivering, diarrhea, and a drunk, dizzy feeling. Any treatment that raises serotonin levels can bring on the condition.

SSRIs have been considered the safest ADs for treating depression in the elderly, especially those at high risk for falls. Working from observational data of nursing home residents, Thapa and colleagues compared the number of falls of new users of TCAs, SSRIs, or trazodone with the number of falls of nonusers. The users of each type had higher rates of falls than the nonusers, and the elevated rates increased with dosage and persisted through the first 180 days of therapy and beyond.[70]

Abrupt cessation of an AD may produce discontinuation symptoms that vary with the class of drug. Frequent complaints after TCA withdrawal include gastrointestinal effects, flu-like symptoms, and sleep disturbance; after MAOI withdrawal, disorientation, confusion, cognitive impairment, suicidal thoughts, and sleep disturbance; and after SSRI withdrawal, dizziness, nausea, lethargy, and headache.[71] A patient can eliminate discontinuation symptoms by taking more drug, so dependence becomes a concern.

Preda and colleagues reviewed all admissions to a university-based general hospital psychiatric unit during a fourteen-month period.[72] There were 533. Of those, forty-three (8.1 percent) were admitted because of AD-associated mania or psychosis.

Syndicated columnist Arianna Huffington wrote that Lilly's patent for a new version of Prozac claimed that it would reduce the usual adverse effects, including suicidal thoughts, self-mutilation, and manic behavior. Yet Lilly has faced more than two hundred Prozac lawsuits over a ten-year period in which plaintiffs charged that Prozac contributed to user suicide or homicide; Lilly's lawyers and witnesses repeatedly denied under oath that violent acts are a side effect. Lilly has not lost a case, although many were secretly settled. Huffington quotes the president of Lilly's neuroscience product group: "There is absolutely no medically sound evidence of an association between . . . Prozac and the induction of suicidal ideation or violence." She also cites an article from the *Boston Globe* indicating that, according to the company's own figures, "One in 100 previously nonsuicidal patients who took the drug in early clinical trials developed a severe form of anxiety . . . causing them to attempt or commit suicide during the studies."[73] She cites another study estimating that fifty thousand people who committed suicide on Prozac would not have done so if they had not been on the drug.

In 1998, within weeks of being prescribed paroxetine (Paxil) for mild depression, a man killed his wife, daughter, granddaughter, and then himself. His surviving family sued Paxil manufacturer GlaxoSmithKline. An expert witness for the plaintiffs testified that both his own research and that of GlaxoSmithKline show that up to 25 percent of previously healthy volunteers who took SSRIs became extremely agitated. In June 2001, a Wyoming jury found GlaxoSmithKline 80 percent responsible for the deaths; it was the first time a drug company was found liable for the suicidal or homicidal actions of an individual taking its antidepressant. The jury awarded $6.4 million to the plaintiffs.[74]

ANTIANXIETY DRUGS

Anxiety affects twenty million people in the United States and is our most common mental health problem.[75] It comes in three primary forms. Phobias are specific fears, such as fear of flying, snakes, or embarrassing oneself in public (called generalized social phobia or SAD). Panic attacks are sudden terrifying bursts of fear with no obvious precipitating event; and generalized anxiety disorder (GAD) is marked by overall fear and worry. SAD is the most common anxiety disorder, with a lifetime prevalence of 13.3 percent. In a large-scale survey, 1.6 percent of respondents reported experiencing symptoms of GAD during the previous six months, and 3.1 percent during the previous twelve months. The lifetime prevalence is 5.1 percent, with women slightly more likely than men to receive the diagnosis.[76]

Antianxiety drugs (also called sedatives and anxiolytics) decrease anxiety and relax muscle spasms. The primary ones are a family of structurally similar compounds called benzodiazepines. In 1990, six of the twenty-five top-selling prescription drugs in the United States were benzodiazepines, and about one million people had become dependent on them.[77] Most prescriptions for antianxiety drugs are written by primary care doctors rather than psychiatrists.[78]

Results of Research

Benzodiazepines differ from each other primarily in time to take effect, duration of action, and the extent to which they sedate and impair performance. Some start to work within an hour after being taken. Most induce sleep at higher doses and, if taken for that purpose, are called hypnotics. The benzodiazepines enhance functioning of the neurotransmitter GABA. They are all about equally effective.[79]

Buspirone is a nonbenzodiazepine antianxiety drug that interacts with serotonin rather than GABA receptors. Buspirone is neither sedating nor muscle relaxing and must be taken daily for two–three weeks before effects are noticed.[80]

Positive results in patients with GAD and with SAD have been reported following antidepressant treatment.[81] ADs take about four weeks to begin producing favorable effects, compared with one week for benzodiazepines, but ADs are less likely to be abused. SSRIs are the first-line treatment for panic disorder.[82] Alprazolam and other benzodiazepines are also frequently prescribed.[83] See pages 29–30 for further comments on alprazolam.

Although antianxiety drugs reduce anxiety and induce sleep in the short term, their effectiveness wanes within about sixty days. About 25 percent of patients relapse within one month of discontinuing the drugs, and 60 to 80 percent relapse within one year.[84] Discontinuation may cause a rebound anxiety more severe than the original symptoms. A frequent solution is to take more drug, so addiction is a serious concern.

Side Effects

Given that high doses of benzodiazepines induce sleep, it should not surprise that lower doses cause drowsiness and sedation. Other common side effects include blurred vision, loss of motor coordination, impaired memory, and confusion. Buspirone is less sedating and does not alter psychomotor functioning, but recipients may experience dizziness, headaches, nausea, and nervousness. Although long-term users become tolerant to the sleep-promoting effects, approximately two-thirds of prescriptions for hypnotics go to people who have been using nightly for several years. During the daytime, they suffer cognitive and memory impairment and are more prone to automobile accidents. Their mortality rate is similar to that of people who smoke more than one pack of cigarettes per day.[85] When fifteen doctors who had prescribed benzodiazepines during the previous two years were surveyed, seven reported observing serious adverse effects including a fatal overdose that may have been a suicide; yet they had not filed any adverse reaction reports.[86]

DRUGS USED TO TREAT ATTENTION DEFICIT/ HYPERACTIVITY DISORDER

ADHD, the most commonly diagnosed behavioral disorder in children, is characterized by inattentiveness, impulsiveness, and hyperactivity. ADHD children fidget, squirm, blurt out answers, interrupt others, and have difficulty completing tasks. Many have learning disabilities and problems interacting with family and peers. There is no widely accepted hypothesis about the cause of ADHD. The participants at a 1998 National Institute of Health Consensus Conference on ADHD concluded that "we do not have an independent, valid test for ADHD, and there are no data to indicate that ADHD is due to a brain malfunction."[87]

The American Academy of Pediatrics estimated that between 4 and 12 percent of children have ADHD.[88] But pediatricians and family doctors vary widely in their diagnostic criteria, and school psychologists have complained that they felt pressed to recommend pills even before beginning an evaluation.[89] Walker writes that many children receive the diagnosis only because they are smart and get bored in school.[90] A U.N. International Narcotics Control Board report indicates that ADHD is greatly overdiagnosed in the United States.[91] ADHD was virtually unknown in the United Kingdom until the late 1980s, yet it is now widely diagnosed and called a genetic disorder. Rose points out that human genes barely change within such a short time period. Rose attributes the increased diagnoses to

> the invention of new diagnostic categories to feed into the ever burgeoning diagnostic and statistical manual, along with age associated memory impairment, dissociative identity disorder, and many more. All part of the medicalisation of daily life. Naughty and disruptive children have doubtless always existed. In the past their unruly behaviour might have been ascribed to poor parenting, poverty, impoverished schools, or unsympathetic teachers. Of course we might all have conceded that some children were simply wicked. Now we blame the victim instead; there is original sin in them there genes.[92]

On the other hand, many believe that the disorder is both underdiagnosed and undertreated. In one study of children diagnosed with ADHD, only about 50 percent were receiving treatment.[93]

Boys are much more likely than girls to be diagnosed with ADHD, but the percentage of afflicted men and women is about the same (2 percent to 4 percent). Quinn and Nadeau argue that the ratio is also similar in children, but girls are less often hyperactive and oppositional, two traits that alert parents, teachers, and doctors to the possibility of ADHD.[94]

Jacobson found that children in England and the United States are not significantly different in the frequency with which they display so-called ADHD behaviors such as fidgeting and blurting out.[95] But, whereas English children with behavioral problems are typically entered into behavior modification programs, their U.S. counterparts are more likely to receive an ADHD diagnosis and Ritalin. Jacobson also finds no significant differences between children diagnosed as ADHD and those considered normal. He writes that the normal, natural condition for childhood looks a lot like ADHD, so adults can easily find ADHD wherever they want to.

Stimulants such as amphetamine and methylphenidate (Ritalin) are the primary drugs for treating ADHD, a practice encouraged by the American Academy of Pediatrics guidelines.[96] Clonidine is frequently prescribed to counter insomnia produced by the stimulants. Whether properly diagnosed or not, an estimated 10 to 12 percent of American boys aged between six and fourteen years are using Ritalin or similar drugs. About 90 percent of the prescriptions worldwide are to Americans. In 1991, Zito and colleagues started analyzing pharmacy records of more than two hundred thousand two to four year olds in various parts of the United States. By 1995, 1.5 percent of the children were receiving a stimulant, antidepressant, or other psychoactive drug—an increase over the four years of 50 percent.[97] While psychiatrists were reporting that about half the children referred to them as ADHD cases were actually suffering from a variety of other ailments, Ritalin became so freely available that children sold it as a recreational drug for $3.00 to $15.00 per pill.[98] By 1999, the number of children on Ritalin had risen to approximately four or five million, with boys accounting for about 80 percent of the cases.[99]

Rappley and colleagues identified 223 children in Michigan aged three years or younger, diagnosed with ADHD, and receiving Medicaid. Drug treatment varied markedly. Twenty-two different drugs were used, and 46 percent of the children received more than one drug.[100]

Results of Research

Because about 60 percent of ADHD children still have their condition in adulthood, parents have been pressured to continue their children on the drugs indefinitely. Breggin notes that children who grew up to have behavioral problems had all been treated with Ritalin.[101] He has reviewed research showing that the popular drugs for treating attention deficit disorder reduce spontaneous activity, curiosity, and initiative and flatten the emotions. On page 12 of his book is a table summarizing serious and common adverse effects of the drugs on the cardiovascular system, central nervous system, gastrointestinal system, endocrine/metabolic system, and other systems. The children themselves often complain of loss of sleep, stomach pains, and irritability, particularly when the dose is wearing off.[102] Clonidine, often prescribed as an adjunct to Ritalin, suppresses REM (dream) sleep. REM sleep has an important role in development.[103]

Whatever benefits the drugs produce occur primarily in the first few months and dissipate when they are withdrawn.[104] Long-term treatment does not lead to better outcomes. Claude and Firestone did a twelve-year follow-up on sixty children, most of whom had received Ritalin; most were doing poorly.[105] Schachter and colleagues reviewed sixty-two studies involving 2,897 children diagnosed with ADHD.[106] Each study demonstrated an apparently beneficial effect of Ritalin, but the authors suggest that negative studies were suppressed because of publication bias. The studies lasted three weeks on average, none longer than twenty-eight weeks. During that time, many children suffered adverse events.

Drugs may work on only a subset of ADHD children. Swanson and Volkow speculate that Ritalin-induced behavioral changes are secondary to Ritalin-induced increases in dopamine concentration at synaptic junctions.[107] They gave volunteers a standard dose of dopamine and measured levels of dopamine in the synapse. There was considerable variability. They hypothesize that people who are relatively insensitive to Ritalin may be receiving an insufficient dose to produce positive behavioral changes. Anderson and colleagues also report that boys with ADHD who display high levels of activity in a specific brain area—the midline vermis of the cerebellum—benefit most from Ritalin.[108]

Advocates claim that children like the drugs, but Sleator and colleagues present evidence that many children lied to their doctors. Raters who evaluated the evidence did not catch the lies. Of twenty-three interviews proven totally or partially unreliable, twenty-one were coded by raters as having good credibility.[109] Eichlseder reports that all of 872 children who received drugs for ADHD complained about how the drugs made them feel.[110]

On 1 May 2000, a class action suit was filed charging that the American Psychiatric Association, the organization Children and Adults with Attention Deficit Disorder, and Novartis, the manufacturer of Ritalin, had "planned, conspired, and colluded to create, develop, promote and confirm the diagnoses of Attention Deficit Disorder and Attention Deficit Hyperactivity Disorder, in a highly successful effort to increase the market for its product Ritalin." Several more suits have since been filed (see www.bio-medical.com/adhd_0002.htm).

CONCLUDING COMMENTS

Thousands of psychiatrists and hundreds of thousands of patients and their relatives swear to the beneficial effects of psychiatric drugs. They may be right. Before summarizing the reasons for doubt, I will present the case for drugs.

Reasons for Believing That the Drugs Work

Psychiatric disorders are not monolithic. Unlike diseases such as malaria and hepatitis, they have a variety of causes and manifestations. For example, depression may result from a single precipitating event or occur seemingly spontaneously, and it may be associated with reduced levels of dopamine, norepinephrine, or serotonin. Therefore, any one drug may help only a small subgroup of afflicted individuals. Experiments in which large numbers of subjects are randomly assigned to receive drug or placebo may be insufficiently sensitive to detect changes in just a few. Even if those few improve significantly, an experimenter may conclude that the drug is ineffective. In the clinic, however, observant psychiatrists may be able to prescribe the right drug and dosage for each patient.

Most psychiatric drugs are taken willingly and repeatedly by people who must believe they are benefiting. It seems arrogant for others to say, "We know better than you; the drugs don't work." Critics who claim that a drug is just a placebo ignore the fact that placebo effects are real. Drugs that produce a recognizable constellation of physiological effects, are heavily advertised, and receive favorable media coverage including accounts of miraculous cures are likely to become exceptionally effective and powerful placebos.

Reasons for Remaining Skeptical

Most positive studies were either flawed methodologically or reported by researchers with financial stakes in the outcome. Wahlbeck and colleagues reviewed studies on antipsychotic drugs for schizophrenia.[111] The studies funded by drug companies invariably report greater benefits of treatment. For each drug considered in this chapter, many negative studies have been published.

All drugs produce side effects. A drug may alleviate certain symptoms but cause negative effects that outweigh the good. Recipients of psychiatric drugs may not be able to perform proper cost/benefit analyses, especially if the side effects occur only after chronic, long-term use. Most patients who receive the drugs discussed in this chapter take them chronically and long term.

Using drugs as a front-line defense against psychiatric illnesses relegates alternative solutions to second-class status. But, as shown in the next chapter, many alternatives are safer, less costly, and at least as effective.

NOTES

1. Estimates of incidence of psychological disorders are probably inflated, probably considerably. Clinical psychologist Tana Dineen lumps together, under the rubric "psychology industry," all people who call themselves psychotherapists and work to create a market for their services. Therapists must persuade people

that normal problems of living are actually psychological disorders. In Dineen's words, they must manufacture victims to stay in business. Their manufacturing skills are excellent. Fifty years ago, about 14 percent of the U.S. population had received psychological services. By 1990, it was 33 percent, and, in 1995, it was 46 percent. Industry estimates of the number of sufferers of seventeen psychological disorders total more than double the U.S. population. See T. Dineen, *Manufacturing Victims: What the Psychology Industry Is Doing to People,* 2d edition (Toronto: Robert Davies Pub., 1998).

2. A. Pam, "A Critique of the Scientific Status of Biological Psychiatry," *Acta Psychiatrica Scandinavica* 82 (1990): 1–35.

3. J. Hobson, *The Chemistry of Conscious States* (Boston: Little, Brown, 1994).

4. E. Valenstein, *Blaming the Brain* (New York: Free Press, 1998).

5. F. Baughman, "The Rise and Fall of ADD/ADHD" (25 September 2000), available at www.house.gov/ed_workforce/hearings/106th/oi/ritalin92900/baughman.htm (accessed on 20 June 2002).

6. D. Charney, "Substance P Antagonists: Mechanisms of Action and Clinical Implications," presented at the 153rd Annual Meeting of the American Psychiatric Association, Chicago, 13–18 May 2000; N. Kalpana et al., "Biology of Mood Disorders," in *Textbook of Psychopharmacology,* 2d edition, ed. A. Schatzberg and C. Nemeroff (Washington, D.C.: American Psychiatric Press, 1998), 439–78; D. Janowsky and D. Overstreet, "The Role of Acetylcholine Mechanisms in Mood Disorders," in *Psychopharmacology: The Fourth Generation of Progress,* ed. F. Bloom and D. Kupfer (New York: Raven Press, 1994), 945–56.

7. But some of the most eloquent voices against the medicalization of mental illness and overuse of drugs, Loren Mosher, Joseph Glenmullen, and Peter Breggin among them, are psychiatrists. Mosher publicized his concerns on the Internet. Below are excerpts from his letter of resignation:

> After nearly three decades as a member it is with a mixture of pleasure and disappointment that I submit this letter of resignation from the American Psychiatric Association. The major reason for this action is my belief that I am actually resigning from the American Psychopharmacological Association.
>
> . . . APA likes only those drugs from which it can derive a profit—directly or indirectly.
>
> . . . [P]sychiatry has been almost completely bought out by the drug companies. The APA could not continue without the pharmaceutical company support of meetings, symposia, workshops, journal advertising, grand rounds luncheons, unrestricted educational grants etc. etc. Psychiatrists have become the minions of drug company promotions.
>
> . . . [T]he most important part of a resident curriculum is the art and quasi-science of dealing drugs, i.e., prescription writing. (available at www.connix.com/~narpa/mosher.htm [accessed on 6 September 2000])

8. G. Klerman and M. Weissman, "Increasing Rates of Depression," *Journal of the American Medical Association (JAMA)* 261 (1989): 2229–35.

9. Available at www.psychiatrictimes.com/p000601a.html (accessed on 5 December 2002).

10. H. Pincus et al., "Prescribing Trends in Psychotropic Medications, Primary Care, Psychiatry, and Other Medical Specialties," *JAMA* 279 (1998): 526–31; D. Regier et al., "The De Facto U.S. Mental Health and Addictive Disorders Services System: Epidemiologic Catchment Area Prospective 1 Year Prevalence Rates of Disorders and Services," *Archives of General Psychiatry* 50 (1993): 85–94.

11. E. Fried, "Visits from Pharmaceutical Reps," *Psychiatric Times* 14(1) (January 2001): 21.

12. S. Namovicz-Peat, "Drug Cost Management Report" 1(1) (Washington, D.C.: Atlantic Information Services, Inc., May 2000), 1–19.

13. A. Mandell, "Neurobiological Barriers to Euphoria," *American Scientist* 61 (1973): 565–73.

14. P. Duke and K. Turan, *Call Me Anna: The Autobiography of Patty Duke* (Toronto: Bantam, 1987); J. Logan, *Movie Stars, Real People, and Me* (New York: Delacorte, 1978).

15. P. Breggin and D. Cohen, *Your Drug May Be Your Problem* (Reading, Mass.: Perseus Books, 1999).

16. Z. Moukheiber, "Silencing the Voices," *Forbes Magazine,* 14 May 2001: 266–68.

17. R. Tandon, "Cholinergic Aspects of Schizophrenia," *British Journal of Psychiatry* 37(supplement) (1999): 7–11.

18. B. Thornley and C. Adams, "Content and Quality of 2000 Controlled Trials in Schizophrenia over 50 Years," *British Medical Journal (BMJ)* 317 (1998): 1181–84.

19. B. Karon, "Psychotherapy versus Medication for Schizophrenia: Empirical Comparisons," in *The Limits of Biological Treatments for Psychological Distress,* ed. S. Fisher and R. Greenberg (Hillsdale, N.J.: Lawrence Erlbaum, 1989), 105–50.

20. C. Harding et al., "Chronicity in Schizophrenia: Fact, Partial Fact, or Artifact?" *Hospital and Community Psychiatry* 38 (1987): 477–86; D. Robinson et al., "Predictors of Relapse Following Response from a First Episode of Schizophrenia or Schizoaffective Disorder," *Archives of General Psychiatry* 56 (1999): 241–47.

21. N. Lehrman and V. Sharav, "Ethical Problems in Psychiatric Research," *Journal of Mental Health Administration* 24 (1997): 227–50.

22. Karon, "Psychotherapy versus Medication for Schizophrenia."

23. P. Breggin, *Toxic Psychiatry* (London: Fontana, 1992).

24. A. Jablensky et al., "Schizophrenia: Manifestations, Incidence and Course in Different Cultures. A World Health Organisation Ten Country Study," *Psychological Medicine* 20 (supplement) (1992): 1–97.

25. L. Duggan et al., "Olanzapine for Schizophrenia (Cochrane Review)," *The Cochrane Library* 2 (2002); M. Srisurapanont et al., "Quetiapine for Schizophrenia (Cochrane Review)," *The Cochrane Library* 2 (2002).

26. K. Wahlbeck et al., "Clozapine versus Typical Neuroleptic Medication for Schizophrenia (Cochrane Review)," *The Cochrane Library* 2 (2002).

27. D. Lewis, "Atypical Antipsychotic Medications and the Treatment of Schizophrenia," *American Journal of Psychiatry* 159 (2002): 177–79; see also J. Volavka et al., "Clozapine, Olanzapine, Risperidone, and Haloperidol in the Treatment of Patients with Chronic Schizophrenia and Schizoaffective Disorder," *American Journal of Psychiatry* 159 (2002): 255–62.

28. J. Geddes and P. Harrison, "Atypical Antipsychotics in the Treatment of Schizophrenia: Systematic Overview and Meta-regression Analysis," *BMJ* 321 (2000): 1371–76.

29. J. Hegarty et al., "One Hundred Years of Schizophrenia: A Meta-analysis of the Outcome Literature," *American Journal of Psychiatry* 151 (1994): 1409–16.

30. Schizophrenia, available at www.mentalhealthchannel.net/schizophrenia (accessed on 5 December 2002).

31. A. Kopelowicz and R. P. Liberman, "Psychosocial Treatments for Schizophrenia," in *A Guide to Treatments That Work,* ed. P. Nathan and J. Gorman (New York: Oxford University Press, 1998), 190–211.

32. Delay and Deniker, cited in D. Marholin and D. Phillips, "Methodological Issues in Psychopharmacological Research: Chlorpromazine—A Case in Point," *American Journal of Orthopsychiatry* 46 (1976): 480.

33. F. Leavitt, *Drugs and Behavior,* 3d edition (Thousand Oaks, Calif.: Sage Publications, 1995).

34. R. Plotkin and K. Rigling, "Invisible Manacles: Drugging the Mentally Retarded," *Stanford Law Review* 31 (1979): 637–78.

35. A. Rifkin, "Antipsychotic Drugs in Mentally Retarded Persons: A Critical Review," *NADD Bulletin* 2 (1999): 27–30; L. Duggan and J. Brylewski, "Effectiveness of Antipsychotic Medication in People with Intellectual Disability and Schizophrenia: A Systematic Review," *Journal of Intellectual Disability Research* 43(2) (1999): 94–104.

36. G. Remington and S. Kapur, "Atypical Antipsychotics: Are Some More Atypical Than Others?" *Psychopharmacology* (Berlin) 148 (2000): 3–15.

37. T. Van Putten, "Why Do Schizophrenic Patients Refuse to Take Their Drugs?" *Archives of General Psychiatry* 31 (1974): 67–72.

38. Breggin, *Toxic Psychiatry*; D. Jeste et al., "Conventional vs. Newer Antipsychotics in Elderly Patients," *American Journal of Geriatric Psychiatry* 7 (1999): 70–76.

39. T. Hansen et al., "Underrecognition of Tardive Dyskinesia and Drug-Induced Parkinsonism by Psychiatric Residents," *General Hospital Psychiatry* 14 (1992): 340–44.

40. R. McShane et al., "Do Neuroleptic Drugs Hasten Cognitive Decline in Dementia? Prospective Study with Necropsy Follow Up," *BMJ* 314 (1997): 266.

41. P. Breggin, "Brain Damage, Dementia and Persistent Cognitive Dysfunction Associated with Neuroleptic Drugs: Evidence, Etiology, Implications," *Journal of Mind and Behavior* 11 (1990): 425–64.

42. R. Gur et al., "Subcortical MRI Volumes in Neuroleptic-Naive and Treated Patients with Schizophrenia," *American Journal of Psychiatry* 155 (1998): 1711–17; A. Madsen, "Neuroleptics in Progressive Structural Brain Abnormalities in Psychiatric Illness," *Lancet* 352 (1998): 784; P. Harrison, "Review: The Neuropathological Effects of Antipsychotic Drugs," *Schizophrenia Research* 40 (1999): 87–99.

43. P. Breggin, *Psychiatric Drugs: Hazards to the Brain* (New York: Springer, 1983), 45.

44. M. Harrow, "Depression in Schizophrenia: Are Neuroleptics, Akinesia, or Ahedonia Involved?" *Schizophrenia Bulletin* 20 (1994): 327–38.

45. E. Koller and P. Doraiswamy, "Olanzapine-Associated Diabetes Mellitus," *Pharmacotherapy* 22 (2002): 841–52; E. Koller et al., "Clozapine-Associated Diabetes," *American Journal of Medicine* 111 (2001): 716–23.

46. G. Zornberg and H. Jick, "Antipsychotic Drug Use and Risk of First-Time Idiopathic Venous Thromboembolism: A Case-Control Study," *Lancet* 356 (2000): 1219–23.

47. D. Coulter et al., "Antipsychotic Drugs and Heart Muscle Disorder in International Pharmacovigilance: Data Mining Study," *BMJ* 322 (2001): 1207–09.

48. S. Yudofsky et al., *What You Need to Know about Psychiatric Drugs* (New York: Ballantine, 1991).

49. J. Docherty, "Barriers to the Diagnosis of Depression in Primary Care," *Journal of Clinical Psychiatry* 58 (supplement 1) (1997): S5–S10.

50. R. Hirschfeld et al., "Undertreatment of Depression," *JAMA* 277 (1997): 333.

51. A. Bass, "Drug Companies Enrich Brown Professor," *Boston Globe,* 4 October 1999: Metro, A1.

52. M. Olfson et al., "National Trends in the Outpatient Treatment of Depression," *JAMA* 287 (2002): 203–09.

53. J. Zito et al., "Rising Prevalence of Antidepressants among US Youths," *Pediatrics* 109 (2002): 721–27.

54. National Institute for Health Care Management Foundation, "Prescription Drug Expenditures in 2001: Another Year of Escalating Costs" (Washington, D.C.: National Institute for Health Care Management Foundation, May 2002).

55. O. Wolkowitz et al., "Antiglucocorticoid Treatment of Depression: Double-Blind Ketoconazole," *Biological Psychiatry* 45 (1999): 1070–74.

56. S. Kasper and A. Heiden, "Do SSRIs Differ in Their Antidepressant Efficacy?" *Human Psychopharmacology* 10 (1995): S163–72.

57. J. Geddes et al., "Selective Serotonin Reuptake Inhibitors (SSRIs) for Depression (Cochrane Review)," *The Cochrane Library* 2 (2002).

58. C. Barbui et al., "Treatment Discontinuation with Selective Serotonin Reuptake Inhibitors (SSRIs) versus Tricyclic Antidepressants (TCAs) (Cochrane Review)," *The Cochrane Library* 2 (2002).

59. I. Kirsch and G. Sapirstein, "Listening to Prozac but Hearing Placebo: A Meta-analysis of Antidepressant Medication," *Prevention and Treatment* 1 (1998): 32, 595, available at www.journals.apa.org/prevention/volume1/pre0010002a.html (accessed on 10 August 2002).

60. H. Walach, and C. Maidhof, "Is the Placebo Effect Dependent on Time? A Meta-analysis," in *How Expectancies Shape Experience,* ed. I. Kirsch (Washington, D.C.: American Psychological Association, 1999), 321–32.

61. I. Kirsch et al., "The Emperor's New Drugs: An Analysis of Antidepressant Medication Data Submitted to the U.S. Food and Drug Administration," *Prevention and Treatment* 5 (2002): Article 23, available at www.journals.apa.org/prevention/volume5/pre0050023a.html (accessed on 15 July 2002).

62. J. Moncrieff et al., "Meta-analysis of Trials Comparing Antidepressants with Active Placebos," *British Journal of Psychiatry* 172 (1998): 227–31.

63. J. Margraf et al., "How 'Blind' Are Double-Blind Studies?" *Journal of Consulting and Clinical Psychology* 59 (1991): 184–87.

64. M. Zimmerman et al., "Are Subjects in Pharmacological Treatment Trials of Depression Representative of Patients in Routine Clinical Practice?" *American Journal of Psychiatry* 159 (2002): 469–73.

65. L. Haddad, "Managing Tricyclic Antidepressant Overdose," *American Family Physician* 46 (1992): 153–59.

66. Agency for Health Care Policy and Research, "Depression in Primary Care: Detection, Diagnosis, and Treatment," AHCPR Publication No. 93-0552 (Rockville, Md.: U.S. Department of Health and Human Services, Public Health Service, 1993).

67. G. Watson et al., "The Effect of Chronic Clonidine Administration on Salivary Glands and Caries in the Rat," *Caries Research* 34 (2000): 194–200.

68. J. Glenmullen, *Prozac Backlash* (New York: Simon and Schuster, 2000).

69. J. Wernicke et al., "Low-Dose Fluoxetine Therapy for Depression," *Psychopharmacology Bulletin* 24 (1988): 183–88; A. Louie et al., "Use of Low-Dose Fluoxetine in Major Depression and Panic Disorder," *Journal of Clinical Psychiatry* 54 (1993): 435–38.

70. P. Thapa et al., "Antidepressants and the Risk of Falls among Nursing Home Residents," *New England Journal of Medicine* (*NEJM*) 339 (1998): 875–82.

71. P. Delgado, "Approaches to the Enhancement of Patient Adherence to Antidepressant Medication Treatment," *Journal of Clinical Psychiatry* 61(supplement 2) (2000): 6–9; C. Thompson, "Discontinuation of Antidepressant Therapy: Emerging Complications and Their Relevance," *Journal of Clinical Psychiatry* 59 (1998): 541–48.

72. A. Preda et al., "Antidepressant-Associated Mania and Psychosis Resulting in Psychiatric Admissions," *Journal of Clinical Psychiatry* 62 (2001): 30–33.

73. A. Huffington, "Depressing Problems Bedevil Prozac Pills," *San Francisco Examiner,* 25 October 2000: A19.

74. D. Josefson, "News Extra," *BMJ* 322 (2001): 1446.

75. G. Winokur and W. Coryell, "Anxiety Disorders: The Magnitude of the Problem," in *The Clinical Management of Anxiety Disorders,* ed. W. Coryell and G. Winokur (New York: Oxford University Press, 1991), 9.

76. R. Kessler et al., "Lifetime and Two Month Prevalence of *DSM-III-R* Psychiatric Disorders in the United States," *Archives of General Psychiatry* 51 (1994): 8–19; H. Wittchen et al., "*DSM-III-R* Generalized Anxiety Disorder in the National Co-morbidity Survey," *Archives of General Psychiatry* 51 (1994): 355–64.

77. Yudofsky, *What You Need to Know about Psychiatric Drugs*; M. Lader, "History of Benzodiazepine Dependence," *Journal of Substance Abuse Treatment* 8 (1991): 53–59.

78. M. Shear and H. Schulberg, "Anxiety Disorders in Primary Care," *Bulletin of the Menninger Clinic* 59 (1995): A73–A85.

79. A. Schatzberg et al., *Manual of Clinical Psychopharmacology,* 3d edition (Washington, D.C.: American Psychiatric Press, 1997); P. Thompson, "Generalized Anxiety Disorder Treatment Algorithm," *Psychiatric Annals* 26 (1996): 227–32; R. Shader and D. Greenblatt, "Use of Benzodiazepines in Anxiety Disorders," *NEJM* 328 (1993): 1398–405; K. Connor and J. Davidson, "Generalized Anxiety Disorder: Neurobiological and Pharmacotherapeutic Perspectives," *Biological Psychiatry* 44 (1998): 1286–94.

80. D. Chiaie et al., "Assessment of the Efficacy of Buspirone in Patients Affected by Generalized Anxiety Disorder, Shifting to Buspirone from Prior Treatment with Lorazepam: A Placebo-Controlled, Double-Blind Study," *Journal of Clinical Psychopharmacology* 15 (1995): 12–19.

81. A. Gelenberg et al., "Efficacy of Venlafaxine Extended-Release Capsules in Nondepressed Outpatients with Generalized Anxiety Disorder: A 6-Month Randomized Controlled Trial," *JAMA* 283 (2000): 3082–88; P. Rocca et al., "Paroxetine Efficacy in the Treatment of Generalized Anxiety Disorder," *Acta Psychiatrica Scandinavica* 95 (1997): 444–50; N. Brunello et al., "Social Phobia: Diagnosis and Epidemiology, Neurobiology and Pharmacology, Comorbidity and Treatment," *Journal of Affective Disorder* 60 (2000): 61–74; M. Stein et al., "Paroxetine Treatment of Generalized Social Phobia (Social Anxiety Disorder)," *JAMA* 280 (1998): 708–13; I. Van Vliet et al., "Psychopharmacological Treatment of Social Phobia; a Double Blind Placebo Controlled Study with Fluvoxamine," *Psychopharmacology* 115 (1994): 128–34.

82. P. Blier, "Serotonergic Drugs and Panic Disorder," *Journal of Psychiatry and Neuroscience* 25 (2000): 237–38.

83. J. Davidson, "Long-term Treatment of Panic Disorder," *Journal of Clinical Psychiatry* 59 (supplement 8) (1998): 17–21.

84. R. Hales et al., "A Treatment Algorithm for the Management of Anxiety in Primary Care Practice," *Journal of Clinical Psychiatry* 58 (supplement 3) (1997): 76–80.

85. D. Kripke, "Chronic Hypnotic Use: Deadly Risks, Doubtful Benefit [review]," *Sleep Medicine Reviews* 4 (2000): 5–20.

86. D. Cohen and S. Karsenty (1998), cited in Breggin and Cohen, *Your Drug May Be Your Problem.*

87. Cited in F. Baughman, "The Rise and Fall of ADD/ADHD," available at www.house.gov/ed_workforce/hearings/106th/oi/ritalin92900/baughman.htm (accessed on 20 June 2002).

88. American Academy of Pediatrics, "Clinical Practice Guideline: Diagnosis and Evaluation of the Child with Attention Deficit/Hyperactivity Disorder," *Pediatrics* 105 (2000): 1158–70.

89. M. Wolraich et al., "Stimulant Medication Use by Primary Care Physicians in the Treatment of Attention Deficit Hyperactivity Disorder," *Pediatrics* 86 (1990): 95–101.

90. S. Walker, *The Hyperactivity Hoax* (New York: St. Martin's Paperbacks, 1998).

91. "News: Behavioural Disorders Are Overdiagnosed in US," *BMJ* 312 (1996): 657.

92. S. Rose, "Clinical Review: Neurogenetic Determinism and the New Euphenics," *BMJ* 317 (1998): 1707.

93. R. Bussing et al., "Children in Special Education Programs: Attention Deficit Hyperactivity Disorder, Use of Services, and Unmet Needs," *American Journal of Public Health* 88 (1998): 880–86.

94. P. Quinn and K. Nadeau, "Diagnosis and Treatment of ADHD for the Primary Care Provider," presented at the National Conference for Nurse Practitioners, Baltimore, 7–10 November 2001.

95. K. Jacobson, "ADHD in Cross-Cultural Perspective: Some Empirical Results," *American Anthropologist* 104 (2002): 283–86.

96. American Academy of Pediatrics, "Clinical Practice Guideline: Treatment of the School-Aged Child with Attention-Deficit/Hyperactivity Disorder," *Pediatrics* 108 (2001): 1033–44.

97. J. Zito et al., "Trends in Prescribing of Psychotropic Medications to Preschoolers," and J. Coyle, accompanying editorial, *JAMA* 283 (2000): 1025–30.

98. L. Hancock, "Mother's Little Helper," *Newsweek,* 18 March 1996: 50–56.

99. Breggin and Cohen, *Your Drug May Be Your Problem.*

100. M. Rappley, "Diagnosis of Attention-Deficit/Hyperactivity Disorder and Use of Psychotropic Medication in Very Young Children," *Archives of Pediatrics and Adolescent Medicine* 153 (1999): 1039–45.

101. P. Breggin, *Talking Back to Ritalin: What Doctors Aren't Telling You about Stimulants for Children* (Monroe, Maine: Common Courage Press, 1998).

102. "Mother's Little Helper."

103. A. Rechtschaffen, "Current Perspectives on the Function of Sleep," *Perspectives in Biology and Medicine* 41 (1998): 359–90.

104. L. Charles and R. Schain, "A Four-Year Follow-Up Study of the Effects of Methylphenidate on the Behavior and Academic Achievement of Hyperactive Children," *Journal of Abnormal Child Psychology* 9 (1981): 495–505.

105. D. Claude and P. Firestone, "The Development of ADHD Boys: A 12-Year Follow-Up," *Canadian Journal of Behavioural Science* 27 (1995): 226–49.

106. H. Schachter et al., "How Efficacious and Safe Is Short-Acting Methylphenidate for the Treatment of Attention-Deficit Disorder in Children and Adolescents? A Meta-Analysis," *Canadian Medical Association Journal* 165 (2001): 1475–88.

107. J. Swanson and N. Volkow, "Pharmacokinetic and Pharmacodynamic Properties of Stimulants: Implications for the Design of New Treatments for ADHD," *Behavioural Brain Research* 10 (2002): 73–78.

108. C. Anderson et al., "Effects of Methylphenidate on Functional Magnetic Resonance Relaxometry of the Cerebellar Vermis in Boys with ADHD," *American Journal of Psychiatry* 159 (2002): 1322–28.

109. E. Sleator et al., "How Do Hyperactive Children Feel about Taking Stimulants and Will They Tell the Doctor?" *Clinical Pediatrics* 21 (1982): 475–79.

110. W. Eichlseder, "Ten Years of Experience with 1,000 Hyperactive Children in a Private Practice," *Pediatrics* 76 (1985): 176–84.

111. Wahlbeck et al., "Clozapine versus Typical Neuroleptic Medication for Schizophrenia."

6

There Are Effective Alternatives to Psychiatric Drugs

Although psychiatric drugs might temporarily relieve symptoms, they do not provide a permanent solution.[1] Benzodiazepines may reduce a student's test anxiety, but if the anxiety stems from being unprepared because of poor study habits, and the now carefree student loses motivation to change those habits, the student's long-range prospects will be diminished.

Drugs that merely treat psychiatric symptoms may do more harm than good. That is the point of the schizophrenia/baseball bat example of the previous chapter. Certain surgical procedures may eliminate depression and anxiety, but only at the expense of large chunks of useful brain. Antipsychotic drugs may be the equivalent of surgery—prominent psychiatrist Heinz Lehmann called them a "pharmacological substitute for lobotomy"—and that is why they should be a last rather than first resort for treating psychiatric disorders.[2] Many alternatives to drugs have been proposed, as can easily be verified by getting on the Internet and typing in the appropriate terms. In contrast to the health-impairing side effects of drugs, many alternatives promote physical as well as mental health. But before briefly describing some of them, an important preliminary note must be made. Methodological defects and biases are not restricted to the psychopharmacology community. Although the rationale for many alternative therapies is sound, and their use is supported by a substantial body of scientific research published in reputable journals, the evidence for others is scant and largely anecdotal. Some glowing reports have their origins in attempts to promote sales of commercial products. These possibly beneficial but less well established alternatives are grouped under a miscellaneous category at the end of the chapter. Even if they do elevate mood or relieve anxiety, they are inadequate for treating people with serious psychiatric disturbances.

IS THERE REALLY A PROBLEM?

Everitt and colleagues presented 501 primary care doctors with a hypothetical case of a man complaining of sleeping difficulties.[3] The doctors were all volunteers and aware that their decisions would be analyzed. They were encouraged to ask questions. If they asked, they were told that the man typically goes to bed at 9:00 p.m., wakes at 4:00 a.m., and cannot get back to sleep. If they asked about medical problems, they were told that he has severe arthritis and treats it with Tylenol. Other questions elicited the information that he has two cups of coffee with dinner, his spouse was recently diagnosed with lung cancer, and his exercise consists of getting in and out of his car.

The patient had many reasons for sleep problems—undertreated chronic pain, evening caffeine consumption, psychological stress, and lack of exercise—but most doctors never found out because they did not ask. Almost two-thirds of them recommended a hypnotic drug. Yet the problem may have been imaginary, as the patient was getting seven hours of sleep per night.

Randolph Nesse and George Williams have been at the forefront of a movement to apply evolutionary principles to medicine.[4] A key feature of their approach is to distinguish between bodily defects and evolutionary adaptations. They note that many common medical symptoms are actually sophisticated defenses for fighting illness. Pain, for example, is not an abnormality but, rather, a cue that indicates tissue damage. People born without the capacity for pain usually die before the age of forty. Coughing helps keep respiratory airways clear. People with asthma, cystic fibrosis, and a variety of inflammatory conditions produce abnormal secretions that block their airways. Cough suppression would harm them. Similarly, fever defends against infection, vomiting eliminates toxins from the stomach, diarrhea clears the colon, and the low iron levels of chronic infection limit the growth of pathogens. In many circumstances, treating these conditions with drugs, nutritional supplements, or other procedures makes people sicker.

Psychiatric symptoms may also be defenses that represent extremes of normal forms of behavior. Although excessive anxiety is disabling, moderate levels increase fitness in dangerous situations. Dugatkin classified guppies in a fish tank according to their reaction to a smallmouth bass.[5] Some hid, some swam away, and several apparently nonanxious guppies faced the bass while maintaining their ground. Each guppy group was then left alone in a tank with a bass. After sixty hours, 40 percent of the hiders had survived, 15 percent of the fleers, and none of the nonanxious. People with insufficient anxiety may also suffer serious consequences. They do not typically complain about their condition, but Nesse suggests that they are likely to be found in emergency rooms, jails, and unemployment lines.

Behaviors associated with the different subtypes of anxiety disorder would have been adaptive in the environments of our distant ancestors. The sight of blood causes fainting, which slows bleeding. Fear of heights is manifested by freezing. A looming predator causes flight. Similarly, depression may increase fitness by causing people to withdraw from situations in which they have little prospect of winning. Nesse writes: "In a propitious situation, organisms gain by up-regulating effort and risk taking. In an unpropitious situation, down-regulation of effort and risk taking is adaptive. Mood thus regulates the allocation of effort and resources—toward enterprises, strategies, and times likely to give a high payoff and away from unprofitable enterprises and times when efforts will likely be wasted or dangerous."[6]

Just as people vary in height, we vary in propensity to exhibit psychiatric symptoms. The symptoms are less harmful than what they protect against, so most of us probably err on the side of safety. That is, we occasionally develop symptoms to insignificant threats. In such cases, drugs that block the symptoms may do no harm and lead to the false conclusion that the symptoms are not useful.

If depression increases passivity in situations in which withdrawal or assertive action would be futile or dangerous, then it should appear most frequently in people who are anxious, duty bound, ambitious, lacking alternatives, or unable to accomplish their goals. This has implications for treatment, because antidepressant drugs are likely to promote activity. Nesse speculates that people in bad marriages who receive antidepressants (ADs) are more likely to leave because the drugs give them new confidence. The confidence is unlikely to serve them if they are given only drugs and gain no insights into their situations. Commenting on a study in which ADs failed to help women with marital problems, Yeats writes, "Trying to treat depression without treating the marital distress is like trying to treat hay fever when the patient works in a flower shop."[7]

IDENTIFY THE CAUSE

Brain neurochemistry undoubtedly affects vulnerability to psychiatric disorders, but external factors play a considerable role. Depression and anxiety are symptoms that must sometimes be expressed to promote healing, as when people grieve over a loss. Drug advertisements ignore the factors that might have caused distress and instead focus on biochemistry. They put all the blame on the victims and fail to acknowledge that people who live under conditions of privation are likely to become depressed; stressful environments increase anxiety levels; and sterile, boring schools and homes produce children who have difficulty focusing their attention.

Women are about twice as likely as men to suffer from a major depressive episode.[8] Many factors are involved: Women live longer, are more likely to lose a spouse, and have less power and status in our society. In addition, women are more prone than men to hypothyroidism, a condition frequently associated with depression. Oral contraceptives and drugs used in hormone-replacement therapy may also precipitate depression.[9]

Identifying the cause of a problem often points toward a solution. Eliminating a causal agent is surely preferable to administering powerful drugs for life. But keep in mind that correlation does not prove causation. Even if it were established that schizophrenics have a specific nutritional deficiency, the deficiency might not cause schizophrenia. The schizophrenia might cause the deficiency, or some third factor might cause both problems.

ILLNESS

Many physical illnesses cause psychiatric symptoms. Here is a partial list: endocrine disorders such as Cushing's disease, Addison's disease, and thyroid, parathyroid, and adrenal dysfunction; hypoglycemia and hyperglycemia; infections (mononucleosis, influenza, syphilis, and AIDS); Parkinson's disease; brain tumors; lupus; cardiac conditions (arrhythmias and tachycardia); multiple sclerosis; and vitamin deficiencies. Patients with hypertension, irritable bowel syndrome, or diabetes are prone to anxiety disorders, particularly panic disorder.[10]

Koran, Sox, and their colleagues examined patients in community mental health programs in California. Thirty-nine percent of patients had an active, important physical disease. The disease had not been detected in 47.5 percent of the affected patients. Sixteen percent of patients had a physical disease that was either causing their mental disorder or making it worse.[11] Other studies have shown that from 4 to 32 percent of patients have a physical disease either causing or exacerbating their mental disorder.[12] Evidence suggests that physical illness is the sole cause of symptoms in about 20 percent of psychiatric patients and makes symptoms worse in about 67 percent.[13] About 15 percent of elderly inpatients are depressed because of organic causes such as an endocrine disorder.[14] A variety of conditions cause Attention Deficit/Hyperactivity Disorder (ADHD) symptoms in children.[15] Charlton hypothesizes that when a person is physically ill, the body's all-out attack on invading microbes precipitates fatigue, sleepiness, and the inability to feel pleasure. In his view, ADs act primarily as painkillers.[16]

Compromised Immune System

When the immune system detects something foreign, such as an invading virus or bacteria, it produces immune mediators. The primary ones, peptides called cytokines, come in several varieties including interleukins, interferons, and tumor necrosis factor. Some cytokines cause depression.[17] Cancer and hepatitis C patients are often treated with cytokines. They exhibit flu-like symptoms almost immediately afterward, and they become depressed. The symptoms usually disappear shortly after the treatment is terminated.[18] The evidence is mixed, but ADs may act by suppressing immune function and cytokine secretion.[19]

Infectious Diseases

Psychiatric symptoms accompany many different infectious diseases, and psychotic patients often report that their symptoms first appeared after a viral infection. The later stages of syphilis, which is caused by a bacterium, are marked by dementia, mania, depression, and delusions. Creutzfeldt-Jakob (mad cow) disease is probably caused by infectious proteins that act like viruses. Symptoms include continual screaming, inappropriate laughter, failure to bathe, and compulsive walking. The HIV virus can cause anxiety, delirium, psychosis, and depression severe enough to lead to suicide. A virus may cause Alzheimer's disease. The bacteria that cause strep throat may be at least partially responsible for childhood obsessive-compulsive disorder, Tourette's syndrome, and anorexia nervosa. In several countries, influenza epidemics have been followed by a high incidence of schizophrenia in the next generation.[20] Viruses including ones transmitted from house cats have been implicated as a cause of schizophrenia.[21] Depressive symptoms are frequent sequels to the common cold, influenza, and other upper respiratory tract illnesses.[22]

Borna disease virus (BDV), named for a 1984 outbreak among horses near Borna, Germany, can attack many other animals, including humans. BDV is called "Sad Horse" disease because the horses became somnolent, apathetic, anorexic, and seemingly depressed before they died. A high percentage of people with neuropsychiatric symptoms test positive for BDV.[23] Ferszt and colleagues gave the antiviral agent amantadine to thirty BDV-infected depressed patients. In nineteen of them, depressive symptoms improved significantly.[24]

Battaglia and colleagues identified forty-three depressed patients who had several symptoms or risk factors for Lyme disease and a poor response to antidepressants. After an antibiotic was added to the treatment regimen, the psychiatric symptoms lessened or disappeared within ninety days.[25]

Fifty children who had streptococcal infections developed a set of symptoms shortly afterward that included Tourette-like tics, obsessive-compulsive behaviors, hyperactivity, impulsivity, distractibility, mood swings, separation anxiety, obsessive bedtime rituals, cognitive deficits, and oppositional behaviors. Swedo and colleagues treated them with immunoglobulin or plasma exchange to remove the streptococcal antibodies from their blood. Several of the children improved.[26]

Morag and colleagues vaccinated teenaged girls with live attenuated rubella virus. Some of the girls were already immune and showed no mood changes.

Others developed a mild case of rubella and a significant rise in several standard measures of depressed mood.[27]

Lithium, used to treat both bipolar disorder and major depression, kills viruses in a test tube. Amsterdam speculates that lithium's antidepressant activity might be caused by its ability to suppress viruses. He recruited mentally healthy women with genital herpes and gave them small doses of lithium. After a year, nine of ten patients reported that the herpes had either gotten better or disappeared. One inference is that some psychiatric disorders are caused by a latent herpes virus that gets out of control and creates a mild brain inflammation.[28]

Buka and colleagues matched twenty-seven adults with schizophrenia and other psychotic illnesses with fifty-four healthy controls. All of their mothers had given blood samples at the end of pregnancy as part of a research project. The mothers of adults with psychotic disorders were more likely to have had a herpes simplex virus type 2 (HSV-2) infection at the time of delivery. HSV-2 is a sexually transmitted disease.[29]

Clozapine and nine of its metabolites were studied for possible antiviral activity. Four of the metabolites stopped the replication of HIV in human cell cultures. If clozapine and other antipsychotic drugs work by suppressing an unknown virus, then antivirals might have a place in treating schizophrenia.[30]

Impaired Absorption

The intestinal wall is a barrier that protects the rest of the body from viral and bacterial agents and undegraded or partly degraded dietary proteins. The protection is compromised by a group of diseases given the umbrella term *malabsorption syndrome.* Malabsorption diseases are characterized by impaired absorption of nutrients from the intestinal wall into the body and by increased intestinal permeability to foreign substances. Many apparently healthy people with malabsorption syndrome do not fully digest proteins in wheat, rye, barley, oats, and dairy products. Dohan suggests that incomplete digests (now called "exorphins") affect the brain and produce the symptoms associated with autism and schizophrenia.[31]

Exorphins are absorbed through the intestinal wall and pass into the circulation.[32] Five have been identified as incomplete digests of gluten, and eight others as incomplete digests of milk.[33] Exorphins, so-named to indicate their pharmacological similarity to endorphins, have morphine-like effects. They bind to opioid receptors and are blocked from binding by narcotic antagonists.[34] Incomplete digests of wheat also contain non-opioid, psychoactive materials.[35]

Malabsorption syndrome is a major feature of celiac disease, a probably greatly underdiagnosed hereditary condition that may affect as many as one in 250 people in the United States.[36] Victims of celiac disease are prone to depression, schizophrenia, and ADHD.[37] The symptoms of each of those conditions have been at least partially relieved by feeding patients a diet free of cereals and milk. Both hemodialysis, which removes low-molecular weight peptides from blood, and a casein- and gluten-free diet improved symptoms in schizophrenics and autistic patients.

Beta-casomorphin-7 is an exorphin produced by digestion of casein in milk. Cade and others showed that the concentration of beta-casomorphin-7 is higher in urine, blood, and cerebrospinal fluid of schizophrenics and autistic patients than in normal subjects. Beta-casomorphin-7 crosses the blood–brain barrier. It activates opioid receptors, and its effects are blocked by naloxone. It produces several strong effects in rats including tooth chattering, pupillary dilation, and rapid running around the cage.[38]

Cade and colleagues examined the blood and urine of schizophrenics and autistic children. They had up to 100 times the normal level of exorphins. When the patients were treated with dialysis or a gluten/casein-free diet, symptoms of schizophrenia abated, and 81 percent of the autistic children showed considerable improvement within three months.[39]

MEDICATIONS AND EVERYDAY DRUGS

Many medications, including antihypertensives, calcium channel blockers, beta blockers, and analgesics, cause depression or anxiety.[40] Approximately ten million new prescriptions are written annually in the United States for oral corticosteroids to treat asthma. Corticosteroids may cause depression, mood disturbances, and hallucinations.[41] In a family practice clinic, 43 percent of patients diagnosed as depressed were taking at least one drug that might have been the causative agent.[42] Caffeine, a mild AD for most people, induces depression in some and in high doses causes anxiety.[43] Cigarette smoking increases stress.[44] A correlational study of more than one hundred twenty thousand women found that cigarette smokers are far more likely than nonsmokers to commit suicide.[45]

ALLERGIES

Boris and Mandel claim that allergies precipitate symptoms of ADHD in many children.[46] In one study, nineteen ADHD children responded to specific foods or additives with both a worsening of behavior and impaired psychological test performance. The provoking substances had significantly greater negative effects than placebos. Forty other children (out of an initial group of seventy-four) showed similar food allergies, but the authors were unable to disguise the provoking substances sufficiently to test the children double blind.[47] Other research suggests an unusually high incidence of allergy, possibly exceeding 70 percent, among people with a diagnosis of depression.[48]

NUTRITIONAL DEFICIENCIES

Because vitamins and plants cannot be patented, the potential for profit in the vitamin business is much less than that for synthetic drugs. As a result, little research has been done in the United States on such substances. But note that, according to the definition of *drug* given on page 225, they are drugs if they affect behavior. They can interact with other drugs and cause toxicity in overdose.

There is a strong negative correlation between intake of junk foods and likelihood of having adequate intake of important vitamins and minerals.[49] Many Americans eat so much junk food that they do not get the recommended daily allowances. Hoffer argued for decades that even recommended allowances may not be enough for some people. He claims, on the basis of his own psychiatric practice plus a few double-blind experiments, that psychiatric disorders respond well to large doses of vitamins, especially B vitamins and vitamin C.[50]

The dominant biochemical theory of mood is that depressed people have insufficient levels of serotonin or norepinephrine. Folic acid is needed for the synthesis of both neurotransmitters, and low folate levels may cause depression. More than one-third of adults diagnosed with depression may have borderline or deficient folate levels, and folate supplements improved depressive symptoms as much as an AD.[51] Folic acid enhanced the AD effects of fluoxetine, especially in women.[52]

Thiamin (vitamin B_1) deficiency causes irritability and depression, and thiamin supplements relieve some symptoms.[53] Vitamin B_6 (pyridoxine) is needed for converting tryptophan to serotonin and tyrosine to norepinephrine. A volunteer who lived on a pyridoxine-free diet for fifty-five days became severely depressed, and he quickly improved when given pyridoxine.[54] Modern diets may not provide enough pyridoxine, and a substantial percentage of depressed patients have low plasma levels of the vitamin.[55] Vitamin B_{12} deficiency may cause depression, and administration of B_{12} has led to rapid improvement.[56]

Vitamin C is also necessary for converting tryptophan to serotonin. Psychiatric inpatients who received large doses of vitamin C showed significant improvements in depressive, manic, and paranoid symptoms and in overall functioning.[57] In one study, schizophrenic patients had lower levels of vitamin C in their blood than control group patients maintained on the same hospital diet. The authors infer that schizophrenics need more vitamin C than other people.[58]

Selenium deprivation affects serotonin and dopamine neurotransmission, and subclinical deficiencies are common. Volunteers given selenium supplements reported elevated moods and reduced anxiety. The effects were greatest in subjects with low initial selenium levels.[59]

In another study, depressed and manic patients had abnormal calcium metabolism.[60] Copper levels were elevated in depressed patients compared with controls, and levels dropped in the depressed patients as they recovered. Zinc levels were lower in depressed patients than in controls, and levels rose during recovery.[61]

Magnesium deficiency causes many symptoms of depression, and surveys suggest that subclinical magnesium deficiency is common in the United States.[62] A high proportion of depressed patients have low plasma magnesium levels.[63] Magnesium deficiency occurs more frequently in ADHD children than healthy children, and there is a positive correlation between magnesium level and freedom from distractibility.[64] Magnesium supplements given over a six-month period corrected deficiencies and reduced hyperactivity and disruptive behaviors of fifty ADHD children. Untreated control subjects did not improve.[65]

An estimated 16 percent of children under the age of six suffer from lead poisoning.[66] Tuthill reports a strong correlation between level of lead in first grade pupils (as measured by scalp hair samples) and teacher ratings of attention-deficit behaviors and an even stronger correlation between level of lead and physician-diagnosed attention-deficit hyperactivity.[67] Chelation therapy can remove lead stores.

TREATMENTS

Just as drugs do not correct environmental problems that precipitate emotional distress, neither do the treatments listed below (with the occasional exception of psychotherapy). However, some of them reduce distress and can be valuable adjuncts to a comprehensive treatment program.

Psychotherapy

The primary alternative to drugs is psychotherapy. Unlike drug prescribers, psychotherapists try to give their clients insights and coping skills to use in difficult and threatening life situations. Many studies show that parents and teachers who spend time with children and are free with praise and affection are far superior to drugs in treating ADHD.[68] Literature reviews show that psychotherapy, especially cognitive therapy, is at least as effective as drugs for treating depression and is probably the preferred treatment.[69] Cognitive therapy is also probably best for anxiety disorders.[70] In some cases, improvements because of drugs were more rapid, but relapse rates were higher.[71] Schizophrenics treated with talk therapy plus drugs did better than those treated with drugs alone and were less likely to suffer relapses.[72] But money to do experiments, so lavishly provided by drug companies to pharmacology researchers, is in much shorter supply for talk therapists. Because of the unavailability of funds, little research has been done in recent years on schizophrenia outcomes following talk therapy alone.

Self-Therapy: Writing about Traumatic Events

Pennebaker asked one group of college students to write about the most traumatic event in their lives while a control group wrote on an emotionally neutral topic. Both groups wrote continuously for fifteen minutes a day for four consecutive days. They were told not to worry about grammar or spelling because their writing would be anonymous and they would get no feedback on it. Not surprisingly, students in the traumatic-writing group showed some emotional distress during and shortly after the exercise; but the impressive finding is that, during the next several months, they made far fewer visits to their doctors than the control students did.[73] In subsequent studies, Pennebaker and colleagues showed that the exercise improves subjective well-being; it also confers physical benefits such as improving lung function in asthmatics and reducing symptoms in people with rheumatoid arthritis.[74] Pennebaker believes that trying to suppress a painful memory may be counterproductive; suppression is likely to increase both the intensity and the frequency with which the memory pops into consciousness. It may impair the immune system. Writing about a traumatic event may help people make sense of the event.

To Do the Exercise. In a place where you will have at least thirty minutes of uninterrupted time, write about your deepest thoughts and feelings about any experiences or topics that are of great concern to you; alternatively, write about the most stressful event of your life and what it means to you. Write continuously for twenty minutes without regard for grammar or spelling; then reflect for ten minutes on what you have written. Do this for three or four days within a period of a week. Explore how the topic or event is related to your childhood, your relationships, who you are today, who you would most like to be, and your plans for your future. If possible, explore both positive and negative aspects.

Dietary Supplements

Even in the absence of obvious nutritional deficiency, certain supplements have proven beneficial. Diet and supplements can affect amino acid levels and thereby modulate neurochemical brain function.[75] Tryptophan, one of the least common amino acids in dietary protein, is required for the synthesis of brain serotonin. That is, tryptophan is a serotonin precursor. Protein-rich meals raise the blood level of amino acids that compete with tryptophan for entry into the brain; thus, even if they contain small amounts of tryptophan, they reduce serotonin synthesis. High-carbohydrate/low-protein meals and tryptophan-rich foods, such as turkey, chicken, fish, beans, peas, brewer's yeast, peanut butter, nuts (especially almonds), cottage cheese, tofu, and soybeans, facilitate tryptophan entry into the brain. Tryptophan is converted into 5-hydroxytryptophan (5-HTP) and then to serotonin. So both tryptophan and 5-HTP increase brain levels of serotonin, whereas selective serotonin reuptake inhibitors prevent reuptake of existing serotonin and may not help people who do not produce enough on their own. Depressed patients given 5-HTP improved more and more rapidly (within three to seven days) than those given fluvoxamine.[76] After six hours of tryptophan depletion, volunteers reported a lowering of mood; the effect was especially pronounced in first-degree relatives of people who had experienced serious depression.[77]

5-HTP has successfully treated weight loss, depression, sleep problems, migraine headaches, seasonal affective disorder, menstrual distress, and other medical complaints.[78] Tyrosine and L-phenylalanine are precursors for both dopamine and norepinephrine. Tryptophan, 5-HTP, tyrosine, and L-phenylalanine all have a place in treating mildly or moderately depressed people.[79]

Phenylethylamine (PEA) is a naturally occurring brain compound with mood-elevating effects. Some depressed patients have a PEA deficiency, and PEA elevates mood rapidly after the inhibition of monoamine oxidase type B.[80] D-phenylalanine, which does not normally occur in the body or in food but can be bought in health food stores, is metabolized to PEA.

S-Adenosyl-Methionine (SAMe) is produced endogenously (within our bodies) and is needed for the metabolism of norepinephrine, dopamine, and serotonin. Several reports indicate that SAMe is safe, superior to placebo, and approximately as effective as standard ADs.[81]

Two large meta-analyses of double-blind studies led to the conclusion that the herb St. John's wort (active ingredient hypericum) is better than placebo and at least as effective as standard ADs for treating mild to moderately severe depressive disorders. A smaller percentage of hypericum recipients than standard AD recipients reported untoward side effects.[82] More recently, hypericum was compared with the tricyclic AD imipramine for treating mildly depressed people. Improvements were greater, and side effects, fewer, with hypericum.[83] Concurrent administration of hypericum with a monoamine oxidase inhibitor (MAOI) may increase the MAOI effect.[84] However, there have also been negative studies.[85]

Kava (*Piper methysticum*) was superior to placebo in reducing the anxiety of anxious outpatients. Kava produces few side effects but can potentiate the adverse effects of antipsychotic drugs.[86] In March 2002, the Food and Drug Administration issued an advisory warning that kava-containing supplements may cause severe liver injury. The advisory said that liver damage appears to be rare, but consumers should be informed of the risk.

Two types of polyunsaturated fatty acids, omega-3 and omega-6, must be obtained in food because the body cannot synthesize them. They are called essential fatty acids (EFAs). A typical red meat diet contains sufficient omega-6 fatty acids but not enough omega-3s; thus, mild deficiencies are probably common. Omega-3s are found in high concentrations in fish such as salmon, herring, sardines, tuna, anchovies, and mackerel and in nuts, whole grains, beans, and other seeds. EFA deficiencies have been linked to ADHD, dyslexia, senile dementia, clinical depression, bipolar disorder, schizophrenia, and other psychiatric problems; and EFA supplements improve symptoms.[87] Pregnancy uses up omega-3s, which may account for postpartum depression.

In the past one hundred years, the lifetime risk of developing major clinical depression has increased substantially in North America and correlates with greatly reduced omega-3 fatty acid consumption. Across nineteen different countries, the incidence of both major and postpartum depression increased as fish intake decreased.[88] Depressed patients had low levels of omega-3 fatty acids, and boys with ADHD had low concentrations of omega-3 or omega-6 fatty acids. Boys with lower omega-3 fatty acid concentrations had more temper tantrums and other behavior, sleep, learning, and health problems than controls.[89]

Schizophrenics have an abnormal ratio of fatty acids in their cell membranes. When given omega-3 fatty acid supplements, their membrane abnormalities were corrected and their schizophrenic symptoms were reduced.[90]

INSIGHT-PROMOTING DRUGS

During the period from 1950 to the mid-1960s, psychiatrists administered LSD (lysergic acid diethylamide) and other psychedelic drugs to more than forty thousand patients. Psychedelic drug therapy is vastly different from psychiatric drug therapy. The goal is not to sedate or relieve pain but to promote insights into such problems as alcoholism, sexual difficulties, obsessional neuroses, and sociopathy. The drugs are administered once or a few times at most, so side effects are minimal or nonexistent. The psychedelic drug experience may help people to confront their guilt directly, as in the following example taken from the report of a man who had been seriously neglecting his family:

> I opened my eyes and there was a picture over the mantle. . . . There seemed to be in front of the picture many veils hanging and I pushed each veil aside one by one, knowing that as I got the last veil aside I would finally see God. . . . Finally the last

> veil was to be removed. I knew it was the last veil and tried to prepare myself for the great experience of seeing God. I raised my hand over my head and then leaned backwards to make myself more receptive in order to feel the full force of God. And finally the last veil was pulled aside and there were my three children crying for their father. . . . Before me was going all the selfish feelings—all the selfish attitudes that I had had throughout my entire married life.[91]

Most psychiatrists who tried LSD therapy described the results glowingly. Their patients undoubtedly provided more entertainment than run-of-the-mill sibling rivalries, Oedipal complexes, and so forth; and heightened therapist interest leads to more favorable outcomes. The religious and mystical aspects may have invested patients' lives with new meanings—LSD is more likely than maintenance Haldol to promote spiritual awakening. But well-controlled experimental support for long-range improvement was minimal. Few researchers used control groups, random assignment, double blinds, objective measures, or postsession follow-ups. Most of the well-designed studies yielded negative results. For example, Johnson randomly assigned alcoholics to one of four treatment groups:

1. LSD was given with a nurse present throughout.
2. LSD was given in the presence of both a nurse and a therapist.
3. A combination of amobarbital and methamphetamine was given in the presence of both a nurse and a therapist.
4. Patients received routine clinical care.[92]

The drug recipients got split doses, with the second dose adjusted according to the therapist's assessment. The procedure ensured that everybody received an optimal dose. The LSD recipients improved substantially on several measures such as degree of abstinence and response to alcohol, and the changes persisted for at least a year. But the crucial finding is that patients in every group improved, and there were no significant differences among the groups on any measure. LSD treatment was no better than routine care or the amobarbital and methamphetamine combination. Score another for placebos.

Psychiatrist Claudio Naranjo wrote a very readable, almost poetic book describing his experiences as a psychedelic drug therapist.[93] He worked with harmaline, ibogaine, MDMA (3,4-methylenedioxymethamphetamine), and MDA (3,4-methylenedioxyamphetamine), all of which have unique properties that make them valuable therapeutic tools. Naranjo's humanity and insightfulness are enthralling, but his work is limited by the same design defects that plague other studies on psychedelic drugs. On the other hand, he makes clear that therapy involves more than administering a drug and waiting for a cure. He prepared his patients for weeks, sometimes months, in advance. They wrote autobiographies and brought photographs from important times in their lives, like the first day of school or their wedding day. Then, while they were intoxicated, Naranjo showed them the photographs and discussed them. He believed that his technique brought unconscious conflicts to the forefront. Reading through his case histories shows that failure to achieve satisfactory results with a drug may reflect more on the (lack of) skills of the therapist than on the drug itself. That will not be known for sure unless scientists perform double-blind studies in which patients who receive placebos also write autobiographies and collect photographs. One safe conclusion is that psychiatrists who freely dispense Prozac, Xanax, and similar drugs but do not spend time with their patients are not providing optimal therapy.

Although Grinspoon and Bakalar agree that the optimism about LSD and other psychedelic drugs was excessive, they criticize laws that ban psychiatrists from conducting studies on new psychedelics. They write:

> A generation of physicians and scientists has grown up without the opportunity to pursue human research with these drugs, and the financial and administrative obstacles remain serious. These drugs should not be regarded either as a panacea or as entirely worthless and extraordinarily dangerous. If the therapeutic results have been inconsistent, that is partly because of the complexity of psychedelic drug effects. For the same reason we may not yet have had enough time to sort out the best uses of these drugs.[94]

Grinspoon and Bakalar note that psychedelics are used in many preindustrial cultures to enhance psychotherapeutic healing. The drugs facilitate diagnosis, strengthen the therapeutic alliance, and help patients generate memories, fantasies, and insights. Contrast those effects with the description on page 94 of the effects in a typical chlorpromazine patient.

MDMA (street name Ecstasy) is structurally similar to amphetamine. It is not hallucinogenic. Advocates claim that MDMA increases capacity for introspection and intimacy while providing temporary relief from anxiety and depression. Greer and Tolbert report many favorable outcomes following single MDMA sessions in a clinical setting.[95] Gallagher writes that MDMA helps "grease the emotional and cognitive gears that produce insight"; he also quotes psychiatrist Richard Ingrasci: "You've been seeing this patient for six months, and you think you know him pretty well. Then you give him some MDMA, and suddenly you're hearing all kinds of stuff you haven't heard before. That's when the therapy really takes off."[96] Samuel Widmer, the administrator of an MDMA therapy research project in Switzerland, writes, "We have not observed any negative effects, either of a psychological or physical kind. No addictions to MDMA have been observed after use of MDMA. To the contrary, we have been able to confirm that other addictions (alcohol, medical drugs, heroin, etc) were greatly reduced by MDMA-supported therapy."[97] Unfortunately, none of the comments is based on double-blind studies.

MDMA was patented in 1914 and is no longer patentable, so drug companies were uninterested in supporting research on it. In 1985, MDMA was classified as a Schedule I drug (high potential for abuse, no currently accepted medical use). Grinspoon and Bakalar decry the decision. They conclude their article by writing, "To ignore the possibility of reviving the centuries-old but now neglected tradition of drug-enhanced psychotherapeutic healing would mean unnecessarily limiting the potential of psychotherapy itself to help people gain insight into their problems and bring more perspective to their lives."[98]

ELECTROCONVULSIVE THERAPY

Electroconvulsive therapy (ECT) involves passing small amounts of electric current through electrodes attached to a person's head. The current stimulates a small brain seizure. Patients are first given a muscle relaxant to minimize bodily convulsions, and they are anesthetized during the procedure. ECT is probably the most controversial of all psychiatric techniques. One psychiatrist has called it "the most effective antidepressant, antipsychotic, anticatatonic we have today."[99] But detractors point to side effects such as memory loss, sometimes long-lasting, and other types of cognitive deterioration.

MISCELLANEOUS THERAPIES

Light

Some people become depressed each year as days get shorter with the approach of winter. Victims of seasonal affective disorder respond well to exposure to bright light for several hours each day.[100]

Massage

Massage has relieved anxiety and improved the mood of cancer patients, child and adolescent psychiatric patients, and teenage mothers. Some of the effects were immediate and long-lasting.[101]

Scents

Exposure to citrus fragrance improved the moods of patients with depressive symptoms. Exposure to a vanilla-like scent reduced anxiety.[102]

Vagus Nerve Stimulation

The vagus nerve carries information to brain areas that control mood, sleep, and other functions. George and colleagues electrically stimulated the left vagus nerve in the neck through a small surgically implanted wire attached to a pulse generator in the chest of several depressed patients. In a pilot study (with no placebo group and raters of people's moods who were not blinded), depression scores of many patients improved. The study was funded by the manufacturers of the devices.[103]

Exercise

Exercise may increase brain serotonin and reduce both depression and anxiety with benefits that can last for at least a year.[104] Hospitalized depressed patients who do aerobic exercises benefit, and so do nonclinically depressed people at high risk for depression. Men interviewed in 1962 or 1966 who reported low levels of physical activity were more likely than active men to be diagnosed with depression in 1988.[105]

Over a four-month period, Blumenthal and colleagues gave depressed people either sertraline, an exercise program, or a combination of the two. Each treatment reduced depression scores. But six months after the treatments ended, depression relapse rates were lower in the exercise group than in the sertraline or combination groups. The researchers speculate that the combination group members had higher relapse rates than the exercise-alone group because they attributed their success to the drug. By contrast, the exercise-alone group incorporated the belief: "I was dedicated and worked hard with the exercise program; it wasn't easy, but I beat this depression."[106]

But the effectiveness of exercise is still in dispute. Lawlor and Hopker did a meta-analysis of fourteen studies reporting that exercise reduced symptoms of depression. The effects were greatest in the studies with shortest follow-up. All the studies had serious methodological weaknesses.[107]

Pets

Barker summarizes a growing literature on the positive effects of pets on both physical and psychological well-being.[108] Heart attack victims who owned pets had a higher one-year postattack survival rate than those without pets. People who bought pets had fewer minor health problems. Women's stress levels were lower when with their dogs than with their human best friends. Children with pets scored higher on measures of empathy, self-esteem, and self-concept than children without pets. Children awaiting painful medical procedures had lower stress levels when a dog was present.

Visits by animals reduced depression in nursing home residents. The presence of caged birds improved group attendance and reduced psychiatric symptoms of hospitalized psychiatric patients. The presence of a dog increased responsiveness of autistic children to their therapist. When hospitalized psychiatry patients were given the opportunity to hug and pet a dog, their anxiety levels dropped significantly.

Acupuncture

Following reports that stimulation of certain acupuncture points can promote the release of brain serotonin, Chen administered electroacupuncture (EA) to patients diagnosed with chronic physical disorders complicated by depression. Almost 80 percent of the depressed patients improved.[109] Luo and colleagues have published extensively on EA and report that it is as effective as standard ADs and more effective than antianxiety drugs; they also report few side effects from EA.[110] Zhou and colleagues report success in treating schizophrenia with EA.[111]

Music Listening

Elderly depressed patients who learned music-listening stress-reduction techniques over an eight-week period showed significant improvements on tests of depression and anxiety. They maintained the improvements during nine months of follow-up.[112]

CONCLUDING COMMENTS

The 1983 film *Lorenzo's Oil* tells the true story of a couple whose young son was diagnosed with the rare disease adrenoleukodystrophy. Doctors said he would die within three years. The couple refused to accept this verdict. They spent long hours in medical libraries, reviewed the results of experiments, contacted researchers and top doctors all over the world, and eventually found a solution. Their son lived at least twenty years longer.

Dedicated detective work would also benefit many people with emotional problems. Rather than accepting drugs for life—till death do they part—patients and doctors should first try to track down and eliminate the causes and explore nonbiological treatments. Their task is much simpler than the one confronting Lorenzo's parents, because so many causes and treatments are already known.

NOTES

1. This comment also applies to alternative treatments that do not get at the root of the problem.

2. H. Lehmann, "Therapeutic Results with Chlorpromazine," *Canadian Medical Association Journal* 72 (1955): 91–99.

3. D. Everitt et al., "Clinical Decision-Making in the Evaluation and Treatment of Insomnia," *American Journal of Medicine* 89 (1990): 357–62.

4. R. Nesse and G. Williams, *Why We Get Sick: The New Science of Darwinian Medicine* (New York: Vintage Books, 1994); R. Nesse, "How Is Darwinian Medicine Useful?" *Western Journal of Medicine* 174 (2001): 358–60.

5. L. Dugatkin, "Tendency to Inspect Predators Predicts Mortality Risk in the Guppy (*Poecilia reticulata*)," *Behavioral Ecology* 3 (1992): 124–27.

6. R. Nesse, "Is Depression an Adaptation?" *Archives of General Psychiatry* 57 (2000): 16.

7. E. Yeats, "Pharmacotherapy from the Perspective of Family Ecology," in *The Psychotherapist's Guide to Pharmacotherapy,* ed. J. Ellison (Chicago: Year Book Medical, 1989), 54.

8. R. Kessler et al., "Lifetime and 12-Month Prevalence of *DSM-III-R* Psychiatric Disorders in the United States: Results from the National Comorbidity Survey," *Archives of General Psychiatry* 51 (1994): 8–19.

9. K. Pajer, "New Strategies in the Treatment of Depression in Woman," *Journal of Clinical Psychiatry* 56 (supplement 2) (1995): 30–37.

10. K. Wells et al., "Psychiatric Disorder in a Sample of the General Population with and without Chronic Medical Conditions," *American Journal of Psychiatry* 145 (1988): 976–81.

11. L. Koran et al., "Medical Evaluation of Psychiatric Patients: I. Results in a State Mental Health System," *Archives of General Psychiatry* 45 (1989):733–40; H. Sox et al., "A Medical Algorithm for Detecting Physical Disease in Psychiatric Patients," *Hospital and Community Psychiatry* 40 (1989): 1270–76.

12. D. Koranyi, "Morbidity and Rate of Undiagnosed Physical Illnesses in a Psychiatric Clinic Population," *Archives of General Psychiatry* 36 (1979): 414–19; C. Thomas, "The Use of Screening Investigations in Psychiatry," *British Journal of Psychiatry* 115 (1979): 67–72; B. Ferguson and K. Dudleston, "Detection of Physical Disorder in Newly Admitted Psychiatric Patients," *Acta Psychiatrica Scandinavica* 74 (1986): 485–89; R. Hall et al., "Physical Illness Manifesting as Psychiatric Disease," *Archives of General Psychiatry* 37 (1980): 989–95.

13. S. Bartels, "Organic Mental Disorder: When to Suspect Medical Illness as a Cause of Psychiatric Symptoms," in *The Psychotherapist's Guide to Pharmacotherapy,* ed. J. Ellison (Chicago: Year Book Medical, 1989), 205–39.

14. G. Schneider et al., "The Prevalence and Differential Diagnosis of Subclinical Depressive Syndromes in Inpatients 60 Years and Older," *Psychotherapy and Psychosomatics* 69 (2000): 251–60.

15. P. Breggin, *Talking Back to Ritalin: What Doctors Aren't Telling You about Stimulants for Children* (Monroe, Maine: Common Courage Press, 1998).

16. B. Charlton, "The Malaise Theory of Depression: Major Depressive Disorder Is Sickness Behavior and Antidepressants Are Analgesic," *Medical Hypotheses* 54 (2000): 126–30.

17. R. Dantzer et al., "Mechanisms of the Effects of Cytokines," in *Cytokines, Stress and Depression,* ed. R. Dantzer et al. (New York: Kluwer Academic/Plenum Publishers, 1999), 83–106; R. Yirmiya, "Behavioral and Psychological Effects of Immune Activation: Implications for 'Depression due to a General Medical Condition,'" *Current Opinion in Psychiatry* 10 (1997): 470–76; R. Dantzer et al., "Cytokines and Depression: Fortuitous or Causative Association?" *Molecular Psychiatry* 4 (1999): 328–32.

18. C. Meyers, "Mood and Cognitive Disorders in Cancer Patients Receiving Cytokine Therapy," in *Cytokines, Stress and Depression,* ed. R. Dantzer et al. (New York: Kluwer Academic/Plenum Publishers, 1999), 75–81; O. Gleason and W. Yates, "Five Cases of Interferon-Alpha-Induced Depression Treated with Antidepressant Therapy," *Psychosomatics* 40 (1999): 510–12.

19. P. Neveu and N. Castanon, "Is There Evidence for an Effect of Antidepressant Drugs on Immune Function?" in *Cytokines, Stress and Depression,* ed. R. Dantzer et al. (New York: Kluwer Academic/Plenum

Publishers, 1999), 267–81; M. Maes et al., "Negative Immunoregulatory Effects of Antidepressants: Inhibition of Interferon-Gamma and Stimulation of Interleukin-10 Secretion," *Neuropsychopharmacology* 20 (1999): 370–79.

20. A. Brown et al., "Affective Disorders in Holland after Prenatal Exposure to the 1957 A2 Influenza Epidemic," *Biological Psychiatry* 38 (1995): 270–73; M. Cannon et al., "Prenatal Exposure to the 1957 Influenza Epidemic and Adult Schizophrenia: A Follow-Up Study," *British Journal of Psychiatry* 168 (1996): 368–71; H. Kunugi et al., "Schizophrenia Following in Utero Exposure to the 1957 Influenza Epidemics in Japan," *American Journal of Psychiatry* 152 (1995): 450–52.

21. R. Yolken and E. Torrey, "Viruses, Schizophrenia, and Bipolar Disorder," *Clinical Microbiology Reviews* 8 (1995): 131–45; E. Torrey and R. Yolken, "Could Schizophrenia Be a Viral Zoonosis?" *Schizophrenia Bulletin* 21 (1995): 167–71.

22. S. Hall and A. Smith, "Investigation of the Effects and Aftereffects of Naturally Occurring Upper Respiratory Tract Illnesses on Mood and Performance," *Physiology and Behavior* 59 (1996): 569–77; A. Smith et al., "Effects of the Common Cold on Mood and Performance," *Psychoneuroendocrinology* 23 (1998): 733–39.

23. R. Waltrip et al., "Borna Disease Virus and Schizophrenia," *Psychiatry Research* 56 (1995): 33–44; L. Bode, "Borna Disease Virus Infection and Affective Disorders in Man," *Archives of Virology—Supplementum* 7 (1993): 159–67; L. Bode, "Human Infections with Borna Disease Virus and Potential Pathogenic Implications," *Current Topics in Microbiology and Immunology* 190 (1995): 103–30; M. Solbrig et al., "Behavioral Disturbances and Pharmacology of Borna Disease," *Current Topics in Microbiology and Immunology* 190 (1995): 93–101.

24. R. Ferszt et al., "Amantadine Revisited: An Open Trial of Amantadine Sulfate Treatment in Chronically Depressed Patients with Borna Disease Virus Infection," *Pharmacopsychiatry* 32 (1999): 142–47.

25. H. Battaglia et al., "Psychiatric Symptomatology Associated with Presumptive Lyme Disease: Clinical Evidence," *Journal of Spirochetal and Tick-Borne Diseases* 7 (2000): 22–25.

26. S. Swedo et al., "Pediatric Autoimmune Neuropsychiatric Disorders Associated with Strep Infections: Clinical Description of the First 50 Cases," *American Journal of Psychiatry* 155 (1998): 264–71.

27. M. Morag et al., "Influence of Socioeconomic Status on Behavioral, Emotional and Cognitive Effects of Rubella Vaccination: A Prospective, Double Blind Study," *Psychoneuroendocrinology* 23 (1998): 337–51.

28. J. Amsterdam et al., "Borna Disease Virus: A Possible Etiologic Factor in Human Affective Disorders?" *Archives of General Psychiatry* 42 (1985): 1093–96.

29. S. Buka et al., "Maternal Infections and Subsequent Psychosis among Offspring," *Archives of General Psychiatry* 58 (2001): 1032–37.

30. L. Jones-Brando et al., "Metabolites of the Antipsychotic Agent Clozapine Inhibit the Replication of Human Immunodeficiency Virus Type 1," *Schizophrenia Research* 25 (1997): 63–70.

31. F. Dohan, "More on Celiac Disease as a Model for Schizophrenia," *Biological Psychiatry* 18 (1983): 561–64.

32. C. Zioudrou et al., "Opioid Peptides Derived from Food Proteins. The Exorphins," *Journal of Biological Chemistry* 254 (1979): 2446–49.

33. S. Fukudome et al., "Effect of Gluten Exorphins A5 and B5 on the Postprandial Plasma Insulin Level in Conscious Rats," *Life Sciences* 57 (1995): 729–34; S. Fukudome and M. Yoshikawa, "Opioid Peptides Derived from Wheat Gluten: Their Isolation and Characterization," *FEBS Letters* 296 (1992): 107–11. See also F. Mycroft et al., "MIF-like Sequences in Milk and Wheat Proteins," *New England Journal of Medicine* 307 (1982): 895.

34. Zioudrou et al., "Opioid Peptides Derived from Food Proteins."

35. Zioudrou et al., "Opioid Peptides Derived from Food Proteins."

36. National Institutes of Health, Publication No. 01-4269 (Washington, D.C.: National Institutes of Health, 1998).

37. For depression, see L. Corvaglia et al., "Depression in Adult Untreated Celiac Subjects: Diagnosis by the Pediatrician," *American Journal of Gastroenterology* 94 (1999): 839–43; C. Ciacci et al.,

"Depressive Symptoms in Adult Celiac Disease," *Scandinavian Journal of Gastroenterology* 33 (1998): 247–50; and G. Addolorato et al., "Anxiety and Depression in Adult Untreated Celiac Subjects and in Patients Affected by Inflammatory Bowel Disease: A Personality 'Trait' or a Reactive Illness?" *Hepatogastroenterology* 43 (1996): 1513–17.

For schizophrenia, see F. Dohan, "Cereals and Schizophrenia: Data and Hypothesis," *Acta Psychiatrica Scandinavica* 42 (1966): 125–52; F. Dohan and J. Grasberger, "Relapsed Schizophrenics: Earlier Discharge from the Hospital after Cereal-Free, Milk-Free Diet," *American Journal of Psychiatry* 130 (1973): 685–88; J. Rice et al., "Another Look at Gluten in Schizophrenia," *American Journal of Psychiatry* 135 (1978): 1417–19; K. Reichelt et al., "The Effect of Gluten-Free Diet on Urinary Peptide Excretion and Clinical State in Schizophrenia," *Journal of Orthomolecular Medicine* 5 (1990): 169–81.

For ADHD, see J. Egger et al., "Controlled Trial of Hyopsensitisation in Children with Food-Induced Hyperkinetic Syndrome," *Lancet* 339 (1992): 1150–53; J. Breakey, "The Role of Diet and Behavior in Childhood," *Journal of Paediatrics and Child Health* 33 (1997): 190–94; M. Boris and F. Mandel, "Foods and Additives Are Common Causes of the Attention Deficit Hyperactive Disorder," *Annals of Allergy, Asthma, and Immunology* 72 (1994): 462–68; I. Colquhoun and S. Bunday, "A Lack of Essential Fatty Acids as a Possible Cause of Hyperactivity in Children," *Medical Hypotheses* 7 (1981): 673–79.

38. Z. Sun and J. Cade, "A Peptide Found in Schizophrenia and Autism Causes Behavioral Changes in Rats," *Autism* 3 (1999): 85–95; Z. Sun et al., "Beta-Casomorphin Induces Fos-like Immunoreactivity in Discrete Brain Regions Relevant to Schizophrenia and Autism," *Autism* 3 (1999): 67–83.

39. R. Cade et al., "Autism and Schizophrenia: Intestinal Disorders," *Nutritional Neuroscience* 3 (2000): 57–72.

40. Medical Letter, Inc., "Drugs That Cause Psychiatric Symptoms," *Medical Letter on Drugs and Therapeutics* 35 (1998): 65–70; Medical Letter, Inc., "Some Drugs That Cause Psychiatric Symptoms," *Medical Letter on Drugs and Therapeutics* 40 (1998): 21–24.

41. E. Brown, "The Psychiatric Side Effects of Corticosteroids," *Annals of Allergy, Asthma, and Immunology* 83 (1999): 495–504.

42. D. Katerndahl, "Nonpsychiatric Disorders Associated with Depression," *Journal of Family Practice* 13 (1981): 619–24.

43. L. Christensen and R. Burrows, "Dietary Treatment of Depression," *Behavior Therapy* 21 (1990): 183–93; H. Reimann, "Caffeinism: A Cause of Long Continued Low-Grade Fever," *Journal of the American Medical Association* (*JAMA*) 202 (1967): 1105–06.

44. A. Parrott, "Does Cigarette Smoking Cause Stress," *American Psychologist* 54 (1999): 817–20.

45. D. Hemenway et al., "Smoking and Suicide among Nurses," *American Journal of Public Health* 83 (1993): 249–51.

46. M. Boris and F. Mandel, "Foods and Additives Are Common Causes of the Attention Deficit Hyperactivity Disorder in Children," *Annals of Allergy, Asthma, and Immunology* 72 (1994): 462–68.

47. C. Carter et al., "Effects of a 'Few Food' Diet in Attention Deficit Disorder," *Archives of Disease in Childhood* 69 (1993): 564–68.

48. I. Bell et al., "Depression and Allergies: Survey of a Nonclinical Population," *Psychotherapy and Psychosomatics* 55 (1991): 24–31; A. Sugerman et al., "A Study of Antibody Levels in Alcoholic, Depressive and Schizophrenic Patients," *Annals of Allergy, Asthma, and Immunology* 48 (1982): 166–71.

49. A. Kant, "Consumption of Energy-Dense, Nutrient-Poor Foods by Adult Americans: Nutritional and Health Implications. The Third National Health and Nutrition Examination Survey, 1988–1994," *American Journal of Clinical Nutrition* 72 (2000): 929–36.

50. A. Hoffer, *Orthomolecular Medicine for Physicians* (New Canaan, Conn.: Keats Pub., 1989).

51. J. Alpert and M. Fava, "Nutrition and Depression: The Role of Folate," *Nutrition Review* 55 (1997): 145–49; R. Crellin et al., "Folates and Psychiatric Disorders: Clinical Potential," *Drugs* 45 (1993): 623–36.

52. A. Coppen and J. Bailey, "Enhancement of the Antidepressant Action of Fluoxetine by Folic Acid: A Randomised, Placebo Controlled Trial," *Journal of Affective Disorder* 60 (2000): 121–30.

53. R. Bell, "B Complex Vitamin Patterns in Geriatric and Young Adult Inpatients with Major Depression," *Journal of the American Geriatrics Society* 39 (1991): 252–57.

54. W. Hawkins and J. Barsky, "An Experiment on Human Vitamin B6 Deprivation," *Science* 108 (1948): 284–86.

55. J. Azuma et al., "Apparent Deficiency of Vitamin B6 in Typical Individuals Who Commonly Serve as Normal Controls," *Research Communications in Chemical Pathology and Pharmacology* 14 (1976): 343–48; J. Stewart et al., "Low B6 Levels in Depressed Outpatients," *Biological Psychiatry* 19 (1984): 613–16; C. Russ et al., "Vitamin B6 Status of Depressed and Obsessive-Compulsive Patients," *Nutrition Reports International* 27 (1983): 867–73.

56. M. Hector and J. Burton, "What Are the Psychiatric Manifestations of Vitamin B12 Deficiency?" *Journal of the American Geriatrics Society* 36 (1988): 1105–12; K. Geagea and J. Ananth, "Response of a Psychiatric Patient to Vitamin B12 Therapy," *Diseases of the Nervous System* 35 (1975): 343–44.

57. G. Milner, "Ascorbic Acid in Chronic Psychiatric Patients: A Controlled Trial," *British Journal of Psychiatry* 109 (1963): 294–99.

58. K. Suboticanec et al., "Vitamin C Status in Chronic Schizophrenia," *Biological Psychiatry* 28 (1990): 959–66.

59. D. Benton and R. Cook, "The Impact of Selenium Supplementation on Mood," *Biological Psychiatry* 29 (1991): 1092–98.

60. C. Bowden et al., "Calcium Function in Affective Disorders and Healthy Controls," *Biological Psychiatry* 23 (1988): 367–76.

61. R. Narang et al., "Levels of Copper and Zinc in Depression," *Indian Journal of Physiology and Pharmacology* 35 (1991): 272–74; I. Mcloughlin and J. Hodge, "Zinc in Depressive Disorder," *Acta Psychiatrica Scandinavica* 82 (1990): 451–53.

62. K. Morgan et al., "Magnesium and Calcium Dietary Intakes of the U.S. Population," *Journal of the American College of Nutrition* 4 (1985): 195–206.

63. C. Shealy et al., "Magnesium Deficiency in Depression and Chronic Pain," *Magnesium and Trace Elements* 9 (1990): 333; D. Frizel et al., "Plasma Magnesium and Calcium in Depression," *British Journal of Psychiatry* 115 (1969): 1375–77.

64. T. Kozielec and B. Starobrat-Hermelin, "Assessment of Magnesium Levels in Children with Attention Deficit Hyperactivity Disorder (ADHD)," *Magnesium Research* 10 (1997): 143–48.

65. B. Starobrat-Hermelin and T. Kozielec, "The Effects of Magnesium Physiological Supplementation on Hyperactivity in Children with Attention Deficit Hyperactivity Disorder (ADHD): Positive Response to Magnesium Oral Loading Test," *Magnesium Research* 10 (1997): 149–56.

66. "Our Multibillion-Dollar Bill for Getting the Lead Paint Out," *Washington Post,* 1–7 July 1991: National Weekly Edition, 32.

67. R. Tuthill, "Hair Lead Levels Related to Children's Classroom Attention-Deficit Behavior," *Archives of Environmental Health* 51 (1996): 214–20.

68. Breggin, *Talking Back to Ritalin.*

69. D. Antonuccio et al., "Psychotherapy versus Medication for Depression: Challenging the Conventional Wisdom with Data," *Professional Psychology: Research and Practice* 26 (1995): 574–85.

70. K. Power et al., "A Controlled Comparison of Cognitive-Behaviour Therapy, Diazepam and Placebo in the Management of Generalised Anxiety," *Behavioural Psychotherapy* 17 (1989): 1–14; K. Power et al., "A Controlled Comparison of Cognitive-Behavior Therapy, Diazepam, and Placebo, Alone and in Combination, for the Treatment of Generalized Anxiety Disorder," *Journal of Anxiety Disorders* 4 (1990): 267–92.

71. J. Glenmullen, *Prozac Backlash* (New York: Simon and Schuster, 2000); S. Fisher and R. Greenberg, eds., *The Limits of Biological Treatments for Psychological Distress* (Hillsdale, N.J.: Lawrence Erlbaum, 1989).

72. R. Mojtabai et al., "Role of Psychosocial Treatments in Management of Schizophrenia," *Schizophrenia Bulletin* 24 (1998): 569–87.

73. J. Pennebaker and S. Beall, "Confronting a Traumatic Event: Toward an Understanding of Inhibition and Disease," *Journal of Abnormal Psychology* 95 (1986): 274–81.

74. J. Smyth and J. Pennebaker, "Sharing One's Story: Translating Emotional Experiences into Words as a Coping Tool," in *Coping: The Psychology That Works,* ed. C. Snyder (New York: Oxford University

Press, 1999), 70–89; J. Smyth et al., "Effects of Writing about Stressful Experiences on Symptom Reduction in Patients with Asthma or Rheumatoid Arthritis," *JAMA* 281 (1999): 1304–09.

75. S. Zeisel, "Dietary Influences on Neurotransmission," *Advances in Pediatrics* 33 (1986): 23–47.

76. W. Poldinger et al., "A Functional-Dimensional Approach to Depression: Serotonin Deficiency as a Target Syndrome in a Comparison of 5-Hydroxytryptophan and Fluvoxamine," *Psychopathology* 24 (1991): 53–81.

77. T. Klaassen et al., "Mood Effects of 24-Hour Tryptophan Depletion in Healthy First-Degree Relatives of Patients with Affective Disorders," *Biological Psychiatry* 46 (1999): 489–97.

78. M. Murray, *5-HTP* (New York: Bantam Books, 1998); S. Steinberg et al., "A Placebo-Controlled Clinical Trial of L-Tryptophan in Premenstrual Dysphoria," *Biological Psychiatry* 45 (1999): 313–20; R. Lam et al., "L-Tryptophan Augmentation of Light Therapy in Patients with Seasonal Affective Disorder," *Canadian Journal of Psychiatry* 42 (1997): 303–06; A. Ghadirian et al., "Efficacy of Light versus Tryptophan Therapy in Seasonal Affective Disorder," *Journal of Affective Disorder* 50 (1998): 23–27.

79. S. Meyers, "Use of Neurotransmitter Precursors for Treatment of Depression," *Alternative Medicine Review* 5 (2000): 64–71.

80. H. Sabelli et al., "Clinical Studies on the Phenylethylamine Hypothesis of Affective Disorder: Urine and Blood Phenylacetic Acid and Phenylalanine Dietary Supplements," *Journal of Clinical Psychiatry* 47 (1986): 66–70; H. Sabelli and J. Javaid, "Phenylethylamine Modulation of Affect: Therapeutic and Diagnostic Implications," *Journal of Neuropsychiatry and Clinical Neurosciences* 7 (1995): 6–14.

81. K. Bell et al., "S-Adenosylmethionine Blood Levels in Major Depression: Changes with Drug Treatment," *Acta Neurologie Scandinavica* 154 (supplement) (1994): 15–18; M. De Vanna and R. Rigamonti, "Oral S-Adenosyl-L-Methionine in Depression," *Current Therapeutic Research* 52 (1992): 478–85; B. Kagan et al., "Oral S-Adenosylmethionine in Depression: A Randomized Double Blind Placebo Controlled Trial," *American Journal of Psychiatry* 147 (1990): 591–95.

82. K. Linde et al., "St. John's Wort for Depression—An Overview and Meta-analysis of Randomized Clinical Trials," *British Medical Journal* (*BMJ*) 313 (1996): 253–58; G. Beaubrun and G. Gray, "A Review of Herbal Medicines for Psychiatric Disorders," *Psychiatric Services* 51(9) (2000): 1130–34.

83. M. Philipp, "Hypericum Extract versus Imipramine or Placebo in Patients with Moderate Depression: Randomized Multicentre Study of Treatment for Eight Weeks," *BMJ* 319 (1999): 1534–39.

84. The 1994 Dietary Supplement Health and Education Act classifies herbs as dietary supplements. Thus, manufacturers can market them without proper safety testing and do not have to report adverse effects to the Food and Drug Administration (FDA). They can make health claims without experimental support. If the FDA receives several adverse effect reports, it usually warns consumers rather than bans the herb. Users of supplements can check a special FDA site for warnings: www.cfsan.fda.gov/~dms/supplmnt.html. Quality control of dosage of active ingredients of herbal preparations is strikingly poor. See Lehmann, "Therapeutic Results with Chlorpromazine"; Everitt et al., "Clinical Decision-Making in the Evaluation and Treatment of Insomnia; B. Gurley et al., "Content versus Label Claims in Ephedra-Containing Dietary Supplements," *American Journal of Health-System Pharmacy* 57 (2000): 963–69; and G. Hasegawa, "Uncertain Quality of Dietary Supplements: History Repeated," *American Journal of Health-System Pharmacy* 57 (2000): 951. See also E. Ernst, "Second Thoughts about Safety of St. John's Wort," *The Lancet* 354 (1999): 2014–16.

85. Hypericum Depression Trial Study Group, "Effect of *Hypericum perforatum* (St. John's Wort) in Major Depressive Disorder: A Randomized, Controlled Trial," *JAMA* 287 (2002): 1807–14.

86. H. Volz and M. Kieser, "Kava-Kava Extract WS 1490 versus Placebo in Anxiety Disorders—A Randomized Placebo-Controlled 25-Week Outpatient Trial," *Pharmacopsychiatry* 30 (1997): 1–5; Beaubrun and Gray, "A Review of Herbal Medicines for Psychiatric Disorders"; M. Cupp, "Herbal Remedies: Adverse Effects and Drug Interactions," *American Family Physician* 59 (1999): 1239–45.

87. M. Peet et al., eds., *Phospholipid Spectrum Disorder in Psychiatry* (Carnforth, U.K.: Marius Press, 1999). Several researchers discussed their findings at the National Institutes of Health "Workshop on Omega-3 Essential Fatty Acids and Psychiatric Disorders" in Bethesda, Md., in September 1998. See also T. Cenacchi et al., "Cognitive Decline in the Elderly. A Double-Blind Placebo-Controlled Multicenter

Study on Efficacy of Phosphatidyl Serine Administration," *Aging—Clinical and Experimental Research* 5 (1993): 123–33; and A. Stoll et al., "Omega 3 Fatty Acids in Bipolar Disorder," *Archives of General Psychiatry* 56 (1999): 407–12.

88. J. Hibbeln and N. Salem, "Dietary Polyunsaturated Fatty Acids and Depression: When Cholesterol Does Not Satisfy," *American Journal of Clinical Nutrition* 62 (1995): 1–9; J. Hibbeln, "Long-Chain Polyunsaturated Fatty Acids in Depression and Related Conditions," in *Phospholipid Spectrum Disorder in Psychiatry,* ed. M. Peet et al. (Carnforth, U.K.: Marius Press, 1999), 195–210.

89. M. Peet et al., "Depletion of Omega-3 Fatty Acid Levels in Red Blood Cell Membranes of Depressive Patients," *Biological Psychiatry* 43 (1998): 315–19; L. Stevens et al., "Essential Fatty Acid Metabolism in Boys with Attention-Deficit Hyperactivity Disorder," *American Journal of Clinical Nutrition* 62 (1995): 761–68; L. Stevens et al., "Omega-3 Fatty Acids in Boys with Behavior, Learning, and Health Problems," *Physiology and Behavior* 59 (1996): 915–20.

90. B. Puri et al., "Eicosapentaenoic Acid Treatment in Schizophrenia Associated with Symptom Remission, Normalisation of Blood Fatty Acids, Reduced Neuronal Membrane Phospholipid Turnover and Structural Brain Changes," *International Journal of Clinical Practice* 54 (2000): 57–63.

91. W. Pahnke and W. Richards, "Implications of LSD and Experimental Mysticism," in *Altered States of Consciousness,* ed. C. Tart (New York: John Wiley, 1969), 410–11.

92. G. Johnson, "LSD in the Treatment of Alcoholism," *American Journal of Psychiatry* 126 (1969): 481–87.

93. C. Naranjo, *The Healing Journey* (New York: Pantheon, 1973).

94. L. Grinspoon and J. Bakalar, "Can Drugs Be Used to Enhance the Psychotherapeutic Process?" *American Journal of Psychotherapy* 40 (1986): 398.

95. G. Greer and R. Tolbert, "The Therapeutic Use of MDMA," in *Ecstasy,* ed. S. Peroutka (New York: Kluver, 1990), 21–36.

96. W. Gallagher, "The Looming Menace of Designer Drugs," *Discover,* August 1986: 34.

97. S. Widmer, "Clinical Work Using MDMA in Switzerland since 1985," trans. Clea Kore, *Newsletter of the Multidisciplinary Association for Psychedelic Studies* 3(3) (summer 1992), available at www.maps.org/news-letters/v03n3/03313swi.html (accessed on 20 May 2001).

98. Grinspoon and Bakalar, "Can Drugs Be Used to Enhance the Psychotherapeutic Process?" 403.

99. Max Fink, in D. Smith, "Shock and Disbelief," *Atlantic Monthly,* February 2001: 80. See also H. Sackheim et al., "Electroconvulsive Therapy," in *Psychopharmacology: The Fourth Generation of Progress,* ed. F. Bloom and D. Kupfer (New York: Raven Press, 1995), 1123–41; R. Lam et al., "Clinical Predictors of Short-term Outcome in Electroconvulsive Therapy," *Canadian Journal of Psychiatry* 44 (1999): 158–63.

100. N. Rosenthal et al., "Seasonal Affective Disorder and Phototherapy," *Annals of the New York Academy of Sciences* 53 (1985): 260–69.

101. A. Ferrell-Torry and O. Glick, "The Use of Therapeutic Massage as a Nursing Intervention to Modify Anxiety and the Perception of Cancer Pain," *Cancer Nursing* 16 (1993): 93–101; S. Sims, "Slow Stroke Back Massage for Cancer Patients," *Nursing Times* 82 (1986): 47–50; T. Field et al., "Massage Reduces Anxiety in Child and Adolescent Psychiatric Patients," *Journal of the American Academy of Child and Adolescent Psychiatry* 31 (1992): 125–31; T. Field et al., "Massage and Relaxation Therapies' Effects on Depressed Adolescent Mothers," *Adolescence* 31 (1996): 903–11.

102. T. Komori et al., "Effects of Citrus Fragrance on Immune Function and Depressive States," *Neuroimmunomodulation* 2 (1995): 174–80; T. Neumann, "Design Trends: Creating a Healing Healthcare Environment," *Journal of Healthcare Design* 7 (1995): 2.

103. M. George et al., "Vagus Nerve Stimulation: A New Tool for Brain Research and Therapy," *Biological Psychiatry* 47 (2000): 287–95.

104. F. Chaouloff, "Effects of Acute Physical Exercise on Central Serotonergic Systems," *Medicine and Science in Sports and Exercise* 29 (1997): 5–62; A. Byrne and D. Byrne, "The Effect of Exercise on Depression, Anxiety and Other Mood States: A Review," *Journal of Psychosomatic Research* 37 (1993): 565–74; E. Ernst et al., "Complementary Therapies for Depression: An Overview," *Archives of General*

Psychiatry 55 (1998): 1026–32; T. Dilorenzo et al., "Long-term Effects of Aerobic Exercise on Psychological Outcomes," *Preventive Medicine* 28 (1999): 75–85.

105. R. Paffenarger, "Physical Activity and Personal Characteristics Associated with Depression and Suicide in American College Men," *Acta Psychiatrica Scandinavica* 377 (supplement) (1994): 16–22.

106. J. Blumenthal et al., "Exercise Treatment for Major Depression: Maintenance of Therapeutic Benefit at 10 Months," *Psychosomatic Medicine* 62 (2000): 633–38.

107. D. Lawlor and S. Hopker, "The Effectiveness of Exercise as an Intervention in the Management of Depression: Systematic Review and Meta-regression Analysis of Randomised Controlled Trials," *BMJ* 322 (2001): 763–66.

108. S. Barker, "Therapeutic Aspects of the Human–Companion Animal Interaction," *Psychiatric Times,* 16 February 1999: 43–45.

109. A. Chen, "An Introduction to Sequential Electric Acupuncture (SEA) in the Treatment of Stress Related Physical and Mental Disorders," *Acupuncture and Electrotherapeutics Research* 17 (1992): 273–83.

110. H. Luo et al., "Advances in Clinical Research on Common Mental Disorders with Computer Controlled Electro-acupuncture Treatment," *Advances in Experimental Medicine and Biology* 363 (1995): 109–22; H. Luo et al., "A Comparative Study of the Treatment of Depression by Electroacupuncture and Amitriptyline," *Acupuncture* 1 (1990): 20–26; J. Dong, "Research on the Reduction of Anxiety and Depression with Acupuncture," *American Journal of Acupuncture* 21 (1993): 327–30.

111. G. Zhou et al., "Comparative Clinical Study on the Treatment of Schizophrenia with Electroacupuncture and Reduced Doses of Antipsychotic Drugs," *American Journal of Acupuncture* 25 (1997): 25–31.

112. S. Hanser and L. Thompson, "Effects of a Music Therapy Strategy on Depressed Older Adults," *Journals of Gerontology* 49 (1994): 265–69.

7

Widely Believed Misperceptions about Drug Addiction Do Great Harm

The concept of drug addiction (drug dependence, substance abuse) evokes images of desperate users committing unspeakable acts to get their next fix or writhing in agony during withdrawal. Their intense cravings are believed to be caused by a biological abnormality, though experts disagree on the precise nature of the abnormality and whether it is inborn or the result of drug use. Their disease robs addicts of rationality and control. As depicted in films such as *Man with the Golden Arm* and *The French Connection,* they become qualitatively different from other people. Cohen writes: "Cocaine-dependent humans prefer it to all other activities. They will continue to use it until they are exhausted or the cocaine is depleted. They will exhibit behaviors markedly different from their precocaine lifestyle. Cocaine-driven humans will relegate all other drives and pleasures to a minor role in their lives."[1]

Some people behave just as Cohen describes. The question is, Why? In the United States, two types of explanations dominate the landscape. One group holds that drugs like heroin and crack cocaine are highly addictive, entrapping casual users and dooming them to progress through stages of increasing abuse and mental and physical deterioration. An alternative view is that addiction is a disease that predates use. Most people can safely use their preferred drugs in moderation, but diseased individuals who start out drinking, snorting, or injecting even occasionally inevitably become addicted. Addicts differ genetically from nonaddicts and without help will deteriorate until they end up in prison or die. Even after years of sobriety, they face loss of control if they ever use again. Thus, moderate drug use is impossible, and treatment requires absolute abstinence.

The origin of the term *addiction* is relatively recent and linked to concerns about alcohol.[2] Throughout history, alcohol and various other drugs played important social and religious roles in many cultures. Through the middle of the nineteenth century, working-class Britons used opiates in great quantities, and cocaine and opium were legal and commonplace in America.[3] Many Americans drank alcohol to start the day, and at every meal, and during an 11:00 A.M. break, and as a nightcap. People of all ages drank. In 1830, per-capita consumption for people over the age of fifteen was three times the current rate. Even New England's Puritans embraced alcohol, calling it the "Good Creature of God."[4] Although habitual drunkards were deemed lacking in moral fiber or self-control, alcohol itself provoked little public concern.

But as the Temperance Movement gained force starting around 1800, its leaders began preaching that habitual drunkenness follows inevitably from use of alcohol. That is, a social movement led to the labeling of a behavior pattern. Levine writes, "The invention of the concept of addiction . . . can be best understood not as an independent medical or scientific discovery, but as part of a transformation in social thought grounded in fundamental changes in social life—in the structure of society."[5] Several professional groups, especially psychiatrists seeking to increase their standing within the medical community, embraced the new concept.[6]

Intellectual descendants of the Temperance Movement may disagree about whether addicts are born or made, but they concur that addiction is a disease. Excerpts from an article written by National Institute on Drug Abuse (NIDA) Director Dr. Alan Leshner summarize the position:

> The most beneficent public view of drug addicts is as victims of their societal situation. However, the more common view is that drug addicts are weak or bad people, unwilling to lead moral lives and to control their behavior and gratifications. To the contrary, addiction is actually a chronic, relapsing illness, characterized by compulsive drug seeking and use.
>
> Not only does acute drug use modify brain function in critical ways, but prolonged drug use causes pervasive changes in brain function that persist long after the individual stops taking the drug. Significant effects of chronic use have been identified for many drugs at all levels: molecular, cellular, structural, and functional. The addicted brain is distinctly different from the nonaddicted brain, as manifested by changes in brain metabolic activity, receptor availability, gene expression, and responsiveness to environmental cues.
>
> That addiction is tied to changes in brain structure and function is what makes it, fundamentally, a brain disease. A metaphorical switch in the brain seems to be thrown as a result of prolonged drug use. Initially, drug use is a voluntary behavior, but when that switch is thrown, the individual moves into the state of addiction, characterized by compulsive drug seeking and use.
>
> Viewing addiction as a chronic, relapsing disorder means that a good treatment outcome, and the most reasonable expectation, is a significant decrease in drug use and long periods of abstinence, with only occasional relapses.

> The individual, once addicted, has moved from a state where drug use is voluntary and controlled to one where drug craving, seeking, and use are no longer under the same kind of voluntary control, and these changes reflect changes in brain function.[7]

The disease concept is widely accepted and has been expanded to apply to excessive eating, sex, gambling, and surfing the Internet.[8] But it is neither based on reliable scientific evidence nor correct. Peele and others have pointed out several flaws.[9] Consider alcoholism. There is no single pattern of uncontrolled drinking. Some drinkers deteriorate over time, and others improve over time. Some learn to drink in moderation, and some drink heavily without incurring serious social consequences.[10] Even chronic alcoholics regulate their drinking in response to external rewards.[11] Many young men mature out of drinking problems or quit entirely, whereas some elderly people who find retirement stressful begin drinking heavily. Real diseases such as hepatitis B and malaria progress independently of their victims' education, values, religiosity, and marital and occupational status. The course of alcoholism depends heavily on such features.

Although addiction is not a disease, it is a real and agonizing phenomenon that dominates some people's lives. Heroin addicts, alcoholics, and other abusers risk terrible consequences to get their drugs, and they experience severe symptoms if deprived. But the symptoms depend more on cultural and environmental factors than biological ones. Schmidt and colleagues compared symptoms of alcohol dependence from sites around the world. Both subjective and physical dependence symptoms were similar in cultures that had similar norms of drinking and drunkenness, but symptoms varied considerably among sites with different norms.[12] Withdrawal patterns from heroin varied tremendously among military units in Vietnam.[13] Street heroin in the United States is usually heavily diluted, so many people unwittingly inject weak doses and do not become pharmacologically dependent. Yet they show pronounced withdrawal symptoms.

Deprived groups often have high addiction rates. If addiction were caused by brain defects, members of the deprived groups would have only their poor, undesirable genes to blame. Social factors such as lack of opportunities, acceptance of the belief that certain substances are highly addictive, values toward addictive involvements, and general life attitudes would be unimportant. Peele, however, emphasizes that these social factors are critical for understanding addiction.[14] For example, many women heroin addicts quit while pregnant, and many Orthodox Jews who are heavy cigarette smokers abstain on the Sabbath.

Despite the impression given by authorities such as NIDA Director Leshner, the vast majority of people who experiment with alcohol, heroin, 3,4-methylenedioxymethamphetamine (MDMA), and crack cocaine do not become addicted. Siegel studied social-recreational cocaine users over a nine-year period plus an additional five-year follow-up. Most occasionally binged but generally used in a moderate, stable pattern. Only five of fifty became compulsive users even briefly.[15] The 2000 *National Household Survey on Drug Abuse* reports that 14.8 percent of adults aged nineteen to forty admitted using cocaine at least once, but only 2.3 percent reported using it in the previous thirty days, and only 0.1 percent reported daily use during the previous thirty days. In other words, less than 1 percent of people who tried cocaine became addicted. The figures for lifetime and thirty-day use for other drugs are as follows: crack cocaine, 6.9 percent and 0.8 percent; heroin, 3.0 percent and 0.2 percent; and marijuana, 58.7 percent and 22.7 percent.[16] Additional evidence that the drugs do not invariably addict comes from a 1998 Australian survey. Only 15 percent of respondents aged fourteen years and over who reported using cocaine recently said that they used it at least once every month; 21 percent used once every few months; and 51 percent used, at most, twice a year.[17] To put the issue in further perspective, in a survey of 278 polydrug abusers, nicotine rated above heroin, amphetamine, barbiturates, marijuana, alcohol, and caffeine as the drug they could least do without.[18]

During the past thirty years, several articles have trumpeted identification of an "alcoholism gene."[19] Lewontin, Hubbard, and Wald exposed many flaws in the entire body of research.[20] The articles have typically been followed by much less publicized failures to replicate. There is no good evidence for genetic causes of abuse of cocaine, heroin, MDMA, marijuana, or any other drug. In the 1800s, most U.S. opiate users were middle-aged, white, highly educated women.[21] The demographics have changed. Similar shifts in usage patterns of other drugs should give pause to those who try to link addiction with specific genotypes or personality traits.

The brains of addicts and nonaddicts certainly differ. Heroin, cocaine, alcohol, nicotine, and marijuana all increase dopamine levels in an area of the brain called the nucleus accumbens.[22] Differences between addicts and nonaddicts in diet, frequency of sex, sleep habits, general health care, and exposure to various experiences may leave indelibly different traces on their brains. But the traces may have no important consequences. Doctors can distinguish between women who have and have not had sex or become pregnant. X-rays may reveal if a person has ever broken a bone even though the break has long healed.

If drug-induced changes in dopamine explained addiction, then all users (including hospital patients who receive morphine and often find the experience pleasurable) would become addicted. As indicated above, that is not the case. Furthermore, many drugs that increase dopamine levels are nonaddicting.[23]

Despite the popular conception that addicts are helpless to resist their drugs, they alter intake in response to environmental factors such as the opportunity to gain privileges, earn money, and receive praise. Many users, even of purportedly highly addictive crack cocaine and heroin, voluntarily abstain on weekends, vacations, and lengthier periods. Some switch drugs or go from heavy use to moderation.

According to the dominant view, users and drugs are the central actors in addiction and environments are largely irrelevant. But surveys and laboratory experiments demonstrate that stress is a major precipitator of drug abuse.[24] Events such as the death of a loved one or a chronic occupational stressor often precede drinking problems.[25] Men in jobs with high physical demands are considerably more likely than other men to become problem drinkers.[26] Alexander speculates that most drug abuse begins with a person's failure to achieve sufficient social acceptance, competence, self-confidence, and personal independence.[27] The person tries to adapt, and drugs seem a possible solution. In support of his view, Alexander cites evidence showing that drug abusers are more likely than other people to come from dysfunctional families and show signs of serious personality disorders prior to abuse.

Even in rats, stressful environments elicit a variety of excessive behaviors including drug abuse. Falk induced stress by feeding rats small food pellets at one-minute intervals during daily three-hour sessions and depriving them of food at all other times.[28] Water was always available. Although the rats remained healthy, they drank ten times their normal twenty-four-hour water intake during the three-hour periods. They also drank excessively when deprived of sawdust or running wheels and then given access to either commodity at one-minute intervals. The same pattern occurred with each of several species tested. Then, instead of water, Falk made drugs available to hungry rats fed at one-minute intervals. Alcohol, amphetamine, cocaine, heroin, methadone, marijuana, chlordiazepoxide, and nicotine all were taken in much greater than normal amounts.

Falk and colleagues did other experiments:

- After inducing excessive water drinking, Falk offered water in one bottle and a diluted solution of alcohol in a second. The rats preferred the alcohol. When he shined a light over the alcohol bottle, the rats continued to choose it in preference to water. Then he replaced alcohol with bottles of other drugs that rats self-administer when given the opportunity, as well as with lidocaine, which they do not self-administer. He always shined a light over the drug bottle. The rats preferred each drug, even lidocaine, to water. But when Falk switched the light to the water bottle, they switched to water. Switching the light back restored their original preferences.

  Naive rats given choices between fluids with and without lights showed no preferences, so Falk concluded that the light became a positive stimulus only because it had been previously associated with alcohol—which the rats initially preferred to water. Later, they chose lidocaine because of its prior association with the light, not because of pharmacological effects.

Furthermore, the light eventually controlled the rats' behavior to a greater extent than any of the drugs did. In humans, too, stimuli previously associated with drug taking may play an important role in producing and maintaining drug habits and evoking strong cravings. The stimuli are not limited to those that occur during or immediately before taking a drug.

- For nine days in a row, rats were fed at one-minute intervals over a three-hour period. Every tenth day they were given their entire daily ration at one time. Throughout the 130-day experiment they had access to alcohol. On those one in ten days when they were fed at one-minute intervals, they drank more than twice as much alcohol as when they were given their food all at once. The factor that determined intake was the current feeding schedule—the environment.
- When phenobarbital solution was offered instead of alcohol, rats fed at one-minute intervals for three hours per day drank so much that they became physically dependent. Then the drug was removed during feeding but made available at all other times. Failure to drink led to signs of painful withdrawal—several rats even died—yet they drank very little during those twenty-one hours of nonfeeding time. Their addiction to phenobarbital was restricted to a specific environment.[29]

Falk and Tang write, "Like the food-limitation condition of the animal experiments, the static niche of the economically marginal ghetto is also impoverished of reinforcing opportunities that could serve as alternatives to drugs. This is not to imply that only economic marginality is the relevant condition. . . . There are hosts of ways lives can be marginal and impoverished."[30]

Falk and Tang's speculations that their rat experiments are relevant to understanding human drug abuse are supported by Robins's work.[31] She investigated the fates of returning war veterans who had become addicted to pure heroin and opium in Vietnam. Despite dire predictions from experts of massive addiction problems, 92 percent stopped using regularly within a year. Goldstein commented, "If we could send most of our addicts 'home' to somewhere else, a lot of them would be cured too."[32]

Ian Hacking argues that the ways in which cultures define and treat psychiatric disorders play a major role in how the disorders are manifested.[33] Schizophrenia occurs in every known society, but schizophrenic behaviors in the twenty-first-century United States differ from those in eighteenth-century China. In nineteenth-century France, many young men wandered the countryside for weeks on end and then awoke in foreign lands with amnesia regarding their travels. Nobody back then discussed multiple-personality disorder. Fugue states are rare nowadays, but many Americans in the 1970s and 1980s came to believe that several different personalities shared their bodies. And Carl Elliott wrote about healthy people who plead with their doctors to amputate a limb. He says that the phenomenon is fairly new and becoming commonplace: "On the Internet there are enough people interested in becoming amputees to support a minor industry. One discussion listserv has 1,400 subscribers."[34]

Hacking and Elliott suggest that psychiatrists help create such epidemics. The questions they ask patients, and their diagnoses, treatments, lectures, and professional and popular articles, all affect patients' self-conceptions and behaviors. The self-conceptions of drug abusers are similarly shaped. Drug abusers are encouraged to believe that they are diseased and powerless to control their habit.

Negative evidence notwithstanding, the concept of addiction plays a major role in attitudes toward drugs. Several generations of people have been (mis)informed about the devastating addictive properties of demon rum, opium, heroin, marijuana, crack cocaine, MDMA (Ecstasy), and other scourges. For example, longtime Federal Narcotic Bureau Commissioner Harry Anslinger enlivened an article for *American Magazine* with several accounts of marijuana users, such as the following:

> An entire family was murdered by a youthful (marijuana) addict in Florida. When officers arrived at the home they found the youth staggering about in a human slaughterhouse. With an ax he had killed his father, mother, two brothers, and a sister. He seemed to be in a daze. . . . He had no recollection of having committed the multiple crime. The officers knew him ordinarily as a sane, rather quiet young man; now he was pitifully crazed. They sought the reason. The boy said he had been in the habit of smoking something which youthful friends called "muggles," a childish name for marijuana.[35]

With more than 20 percent of U.S. adults using marijuana within a thirty-day period, it would appear that the chances of any of us lasting out the week are pretty slim.

CONCLUDING COMMENTS

Incorrect assumptions subvert attempts to solve problems. Misapplication of the addiction concept does damage:

- The disease model of addiction dominates approaches to the treatment of drug abuse in the United States. The long-range success rates of most treatment programs are abysmal. See chapter 12. The disease model demands abstention, so programs that encourage alcoholics to use in moderation, despite documented successes, are underfunded and underused. Heroin and cocaine are illegal, so no programs exist to teach moderate use.

- People convinced that they have a genetic disease are likely to give up hope for a cure. Remaining addicted becomes a self-fulfilling prophecy. See pages 254–57 for further discussion.
- Even addicts who learn to abstain may have occasional lapses. Having been taught that their drug controls them, they are unlikely to use it in the safest way possible and can rationalize misbehavior as caused by the drug. In many legal jurisdictions drug intoxication, like mental illness, can be used in a diminished capacity defense to raise doubt about the intent that is a key element of some crimes. A successful defense results in a lighter sentence. News stories about the defense may become a self-fulfilling prophecy for diminished capacity for some addicts.
- Because users are portrayed as qualitatively different from other people, society marginalizes them. Kolb writes that "the climate . . . was such that an individual might work for 10 years beside an industrious law-abiding person and then feel a sense of revulsion toward him upon discovering that he secretly used an opiate."[36]
- Heroin users in European cities including Liverpool, England, and many in the Netherlands can exchange dirty syringes for clean ones. Health clinic workers in those cities distribute condoms to drug users and treat their contagious diseases. One result is that the incidence of HIV is much lower among Netherland addicts than in the United States. Second, the incidence of severe distress among heavy users of opiates and other drugs is also lower. Third, so are activities that addicts engage in to get money, like prostitution, petty theft, and robbery. Many addicts lead normal lives.[37] See page 167 for further discussion of needle-exchange programs.
- Alcohol industry executives can absolve themselves of blame for any problems caused by their drug. They market their products under the pretense that a small segment of the population has the disease of alcoholism and the rest can indulge with no fear.
- The disease model may promote experimentation with drugs. People without a family history of drug abuse might conclude that they have not inherited an addictive makeup.
- For about one hundred years, the drug industry has expended considerable money and effort to discover a nonaddictive substance that relieves pain and anxiety as effectively as morphine. The first was heroin, whose name derives from *hero* because of its alleged heroic powers in curing morphine addiction. Heroin was followed by supposedly nonaddictive barbiturates, synthetic narcotics such as Demerol and methadone, and nonbarbiturate sedatives. None was successful:

> What brought about this substantial miscalculation was the failure to understand that those who become addicted welcome the elimination of troubling

sensation and the dulling of awareness that all of these drugs produce. This means that any drug which is effective for analgesic or related purposes will by definition be addictive, since it is this very experience the person seeks in an addiction.[38]

NOTES

1. S. Cohen, "Reinforcement and Rapid Delivery Systems: Understanding Adverse Consequences of Cocaine," in *Cocaine Use in America: Epidemiological and Clinical Perspectives,* ed. N. Kozel and E. Adams, DHHS Publication No. ADM 85-1414 (Washington, D.C.: Government Printing Office, 1985), 152.

2. See H. Levine, "The Discovery of Addiction: Changing Conceptions of Habitual Drunkenness in America," *Journal of Studies on Alcohol* 15 (1979): 493–506.

3. V. Berridge and G. Edwards, *Opium and the People: Opiate Use in Nineteenth-Century England* (New Haven: Yale University Press, 1987); D. Courtwright, *Dark Paradise: Opiate Addiction in America before 1940* (Cambridge: Harvard University Press, 1982); C. Earle, "The Opium Habit: A Statistical and Clinical Lecture," *Chicago Medical Review* 2 (1880): 442–46.

4. W. Rorabaugh, "Alcohol in America," *OAH Magazine of History,* fall 1991: 17–19.

5. Levine, "The Discovery of Addiction," 504.

6. C. Acker, *Creating the American Junkie: Addiction Research in the Classic Era of Narcotic Control* (Baltimore: Johns Hopkins University Press, 2002).

7. A. Leshner, "Addiction Is a Brain Disease, and It Matters," *Science* 278 (1997): 45–47.

8. Although the term *addict* has been broadened in recent years to include people in these groups, it is usually restricted in the drug field to only certain types of users. A user of any quantity of heroin is a heroin addict, but people who smoke two packs of cigarettes a day are just heavy smokers.

9. S. Peele, "The Cultural Context of Psychological Approaches to Alcoholism," *American Psychologist* 39 (1984): 1337–51; S. Peele, *The Meaning of Addiction: Compulsive Experience and Its Interpretation* (Lexington, Mass.: Lexington Books, 1985); S. Peele and A. Brodsky, *Love and Addiction* (New York: Taplinger, 1975).

10. D. Rudy, *Becoming Alcoholic* (Carbondale: Southern Illinois University Press, 1986).

11. A. Paredes et al., "Loss of Control in Alcoholism," *Quarterly Journal of Studies on Alcohol* 34 (1973): 1141–61.

12. L. Schmidt et al., "Cross-Cultural Applicability in International Classifications and Research in Alcohol Dependence," *Journal of Studies on Alcohol* 60 (1999): 448–62.

13. N. Zinberg, "Heroin Use in Vietnam and the United States," *Archives of General Psychiatry* 26 (1972): 486–88.

14. S. Peele, "What Addiction Is and Is Not: The Impact of Mistaken Notions of Addiction," *Addiction Research* 8 (2000): 599–607.

15. R. Siegel, "Changing Patterns of Cocaine Use," in *Cocaine: Pharmacology, Effects, and Treatment of Abuse,* ed. J. Grabowski, DHHS Publication No. ADM 84-1326 (Rockville, Md.: Government Printing Office, 1984), 92–110.

16. National Institute on Drug Abuse, *National Household Survey on Drug Abuse: 2000* (Washington, D.C.: Department of Health and Human Services, Substance Abuse and Mental Health Services Administration, 2000).

17. Australian Institute of Health and Welfare, *National Drug Strategy Household Survey* (Bruce: Australian Institute of Health and Welfare, 1998).

18. M. Russell, "Cigarette Smoking: Natural History of a Dependence Disorder," *British Journal of Medical Psychology* 44 (1971): 1–16.

19. M. Schuckit, *Drug and Alcohol Abuse* (New York: Plenum Press, 1984).

20. R. Lewontin, *Biology as Ideology: The Doctrine of DNA* (New York: HarperPerennial, 1991); R. Hubbard and E. Wald, *Exploding the Gene Myth* (Boston: Beacon Press, 1993).

21. C. Terry and M. Pellens, *The Opium Problem* (New York: Committee on Drug Addictions, Bureau of Social Hygiene, 1928).

22. A. Roberts and G. Koob, "The Neurobiology of Addiction: An Overview," *Alcohol, Health and Research World* 21 (1997): 101–06.

23. See pharmacologist John Morgan, quoted in "Marijuana Special Report," *New Scientist*, available at www.newscientist.com/hottopics/marijuana/hooked.jsp (accessed on 5 December 2002).

24. See F. Leavitt, *Drugs and Behavior* (Thousand Oaks, Calif.: Sage Publications, 1995); K. Brady and S. Sonne, "The Role of Stress in Alcohol Use, Alcoholism Treatment, and Relapse," *Alcohol Research and Health* 23 (1999): 263–72.

25. M. Seeman and A. Seeman, "Life Strains, Alienation, and Drinking Behavior," *Alcoholism: Clinical and Experimental Research* 16 (1992): 199–205.

26. R. Crum et al., "Occupational Stress and the Risk of Alcohol Abuse and Dependence," *Alcoholism: Clinical and Experimental Research* 19 (1995): 647–55.

27. B. Alexander, "The Empirical and Theoretical Bases for an Adaptive Model of Addiction," *Journal of Drug Issues* 20 (1990): 37–65.

28. J. Falk, "Drug Dependence: Myth or Motive?" *Pharmacology, Biochemistry, and Behavior* 19 (1983): 385–91.

29. J. Falk and C. Lau, "Oral Cocaine as a Reinforcer: Acquisition Conditions and Importance of Stimulus Control," *Behavioral Pharmacology* 4 (1993): 597–609; J. Falk and M. Tang, "What Schedule-Induced Polydipsia Can Tell Us about Alcoholism," *Alcoholism: Clinical and Experimental Research* 12 (1988): 577–84.

30. Falk and Tang, "What Schedule-Induced Polydipsia Can Tell Us about Alcoholism," 584.

31. L. Robins, *The Vietnam Drug User Returns* (Washington, D.C.: Government Printing Office, 1973).

32. Cited in J. Fort and C. Cory, *American Drugstore* (Boston: Little, Brown, 1975).

33. I. Hacking, *Mad Travelers: Reflections on the Reality of Transient Mental Illnesses* (Charlottesville: University Press of Virginia, 1998).

34. C. Elliott, "A New Way to Be Mad," *Atlantic Monthly*, December 2000: 72.

35. Cited in J. Inciardi, *The War on Drugs: Heroin, Cocaine, Crime, and Public Policy* (Palo Alto: Mayfield Publishing Co., 1986), 22.

36. L. Kolb, "Factors That Have Influenced the Management and Treatment of Drug Addicts," in *Narcotic Drug Addiction Problems*, ed. R. Livingston (Bethesda, Md.: Public Health Service, 1958), 25.

37. P. Cohen, "Junky Elend: Some Ways of Explaining It and Dealing with It. From a Pharmacological Explanation of Junky Behaviour to a Social One," *Wiener Zeitschrift für Suchtforschung* 14 (1992): 59–64.

38. S. Peele, "Reductionism in the Psychology of the Eighties: Can Biochemistry Eliminate Addiction, Mental Illness, and Pain?" *American Psychologist* 36 (1981): 816.

8

Most Citizens Are Harmed Rather than Helped by the Drug Wars

Laws should help the residents of a community feel safer and improve their quality of life, but the laws that make possession and sale of certain drugs illegal do just the opposite. They hurt the vast majority of citizens and take away freedoms that were once a source of national pride. Drug abuse is terrible and has destroyed the lives of individuals and entire families. We should try to eliminate it, minimize the harms it causes, and make treatment available for all in need. But legislating against drugs is not the answer. Child abuse is terrible, yet Congress does not legislate against children.

A SHORT HISTORY OF THE DRUG LAWS

The first U.S. drug laws were motivated by prejudice. Psychoactive drugs had been legal and widely used until, toward the end of the nineteenth century, a few western states introduced legislation banning the sale or possession of opium for smoking. Oral consumption remained legal; the laws targeted smoking because opium smoking was regarded as a habit peculiar to the Chinese. Chinese immigrant workers had come to the United States in large numbers after the Civil War and were exploited as a source of cheap labor for railroad construction and to work in mines. Encouraged by the resentments of white workers, the media presented sensationalized stories of white women being lured to their ruin in opium dens.[1]

The cannabis plant was grown in the United States from colonial times until the 1920s both for its fiber (hemp) and to treat various medical conditions. Few concerns were raised about harmful properties until, starting about 1914, Mexican laborers migrated in great numbers into southwestern and Rocky Mountain states. Seeking to better themselves economically, they competed with whites for various burdensome jobs. Because many used marijuana, marijuana laws were soon introduced in those states. A proponent of Texas's first marijuana law said on the floor of the Texas Senate, "All Mexicans are crazy, and this stuff (referring to marijuana) is what makes them crazy"; a proponent of Montana's first marijuana law said, "Give one of these Mexican beet field workers a couple of puffs on a marijuana cigarette and he thinks he is in the bullring at Barcelona."[2]

In 1930, the Federal Bureau of Narcotics was established. The first commissioner, Harry Anslinger, soon began a campaign to make marijuana use a federal crime. He wrote distorted, fabricated, and blatantly racist anti-marijuana articles for newspapers and magazines. Here are two excerpts:

> Two Negroes took a girl fourteen years old and kept her for two days in a hut under the influence of marihuana. Upon recovery she was found to be suffering from syphillis.
>
> Colored students at the Univ. of Minn. partying with female students (white) smoking and getting their sympathy with stories of racial persecution. Result pregnancy.[3]

Cocaine was legal in the United States until 1914. In fact, prominent neurologist William Hammond extolled its virtues and developed a cocaine wine. Until 1900, cocaine was an ingredient in Coca-Cola. But attitudes changed when cocaine became popular with southern blacks. In 1910, a committee of the House of Representatives heard the following testimony:

> The colored people seem to have a weakness for it [cocaine]. It is a very seductive drug, and it produces extreme exhilaration. Persons under the influence believe they are millionaires. They have an exaggerated ego. They imagine they can lift this building, if they want to, or can do anything they want to. They have no regard for right or wrong. It produces a kind of temporary insanity. They would just as soon rape a woman as anything else and a great many of the southern rape cases have been traced to cocaine.[4]

CONSEQUENCES OF THE DRUG LAWS FOR USERS

The drug laws were not crafted to benefit users. Former drug czar William Bennett (who was a heavy smoker) praised vigilante murder of drug dealers. Former Los Angeles police chief Daryl Gates, testifying before the U.S. Senate, expressed the view that casual users should be taken out and shot. Texas state legislator Al Edwards had a more benign solution—he proposed merely cutting off a finger for each drug conviction.

Drugs became such a focus of the criminal justice system that, by 1992, federal prisons held more people on drug charges than they held in 1980 for all other crimes. While the percentage of violent offenders in state prisons steadily declined from 1978 to 1997, the prison and jail population tripled. In 1997, 1,584,000 people were arrested for drug offenses, 44 percent of them for simple possession or sale of marijuana.[5] By the end of 1998, nonviolent jail, state prison, and federal inmates totaled 1,185,458.[6] One result is that the United States, despite having 100 million fewer citizens than the twelve European Union countries, imprisons six times as many as the EU's combined total.[7]

Treatment for drug abuse is far more cost-effective than imprisonment.[8] Yet, in 1997, fewer than 10 percent of drug offenders in either state or federal prisons had received any treatment since their arrest.[9] (In the past few years, some states passed legislation to send nonviolent first- and second-time drug offenders to community treatment programs instead of prison.)

Hepatitis C has become a major public health concern. Because of overcrowded prisons, all prisoners, including nonviolent drug offenders, are exposed to violence and contagious diseases. The mere threat of imprisonment makes users reluctant to see doctors, so minor problems become serious and overdose deaths keep setting new record highs. Oxman and colleagues interviewed heroin users with a history of overdose. Fear of arrest had kept most of them from calling for emergency assistance following a companion's overdose. Many had attempted to revive overdosed companions on their own, and some had left them in public places, hoping they would be discovered and helped by others.[10] In 1986, basketball star Len Bias died of heart failure after using cocaine. His friends waited until his third seizure before calling an ambulance.[11]

Drug users are not protected by truth-in-packaging laws. Harmful adulterants killed many alcohol drinkers during Prohibition, and they kill or permanently disable many users of illegal drugs today. During recent years the purity level for cocaine ranged between 60 and 70 percent and for heroin, between the high 40s and low 50s.[12] In the early 1980s, an outbreak of parkinsonism symptoms and several deaths among young heroin users were traced to a contaminant in a synthetic heroin.

Drug users and dealers are frequent victims of violence. Once involved in the drug trade, they interact with people they barely know while buying, selling, and distributing illegal substances involving large sums of money. Without recourse to nonviolent methods for settling disputes, they fight over territories and commit assaults to collect debts. Dealers sometimes resort to violence preemptively, to maintain their credibility and deter potential competitors. Under the circumstances, even florists might become violent. Because of the easy availability of powerful automatic weaponry, innocent bystanders are victimized about as often as the protagonists.[13]

In some states, convicted drug users lose the rights to vote, keep firearms, and live near school property. Some have their driver's licenses revoked, which makes it hard for them to hold jobs. They can be evicted from public housing. Anyone convicted of a felony drug violation is denied food stamps for life. The Higher Education Act of 1998 delayed or denied federal financial aid to anyone convicted of any drug offense. In 2000, 8,620 students were denied financial assistance because they admitted to a drug conviction on their financial aid applications; but 300,000 students who did not answer the question about drugs were not penalized. The Bush administration is not so lax. Education Secretary Rod Paige announced that, beginning in spring 2001, applicants who failed to answer the drug question would be rejected. By April 2001, 27,000 students had admitted to a drug offense, and almost fifteen thousand had not answered the question. The act has little relevance to wealthy students but penalizes poor people who cannot attend college without financial aid. It has a strong racist component because black users are much more likely than white users to be convicted of drug charges. See pages 157–58.

Users' families suffer. Many prisons are situated far away from the inmates' homes. For example, about 90 percent of inmates of the Bare Hill Correctional Facility, 15 miles south of the Canadian border, come from New York City or one of its suburbs. The drive takes about eight hours. Buses leave the city for the north every Friday night and carry about eight hundred fare payers for Saturday visits. Most are women and children, and almost all are African American or Hispanic.[14]

CONSEQUENCES OF THE DRUG LAWS FOR POTENTIAL USERS

Many caring people are uninterested in abstract philosophical arguments about victimless crimes.[15] They believe that drug laws protect vulnerable people from becoming addicted, and they may be right. The laws certainly deter some potential users and limit the quantities available to addicts. It is possible that the number of abusers would soar if drugs were sold in neighborhood pharmacies. But the issue is complex. Although legalization would encourage many current abstainers to experiment, the number of *abusers* would in all likelihood not dramatically rise. The extent of addiction is probably fairly stable, with the only changes being in the specific drugs used. When a new drug becomes available on the streets or in pharmacies, use of other drugs declines.

Crack cocaine has been portrayed in the media as an inevitably and instantaneously addicting drug. But according to the 1992 household survey, only about one-third of people who had ever tried crack reported using it in the previous year. See pages 137–38 for further discussion. Alcohol is legal and readily available in the United States, and many people drink moderately. Most people who go on to abuse alcohol had serious problems of adjustment prior to their first drink. The same is true of abusers of other drugs. People without serious problems are unlikely to abuse any drug, regardless of its legal status—as they would be unlikely to attempt suicide if laws against that behavior were repealed.

Legalization might even reduce the number of abusers. Drug sellers, like sellers of other products, try to expand their markets. If drugs were dispensed legally in government stores, there would be little incentive to increase sales. People in the Netherlands can buy marijuana from specialized shops, and the Dutch treat other drug use as primarily a health rather than criminal problem. Yet a smaller percentage of Dutch than U.S. citizens uses marijuana, cocaine, heroin, or inhalants.[16]

Opponents argue that legalization would send a message that drugs are safe. That need not happen. Tobacco is legal, but efforts of government agencies to publicize its dangers have worked. The anti-tobacco campaign has been more effective than the drug laws.

CONSEQUENCES OF THE DRUG LAWS FOR THE GENERAL POPULACE

People who cheer when police arrest drug dealers might be less enthusiastic if they understood the consequences. The worldwide supplies of marijuana and the ingredients for manufacturing cocaine, heroin, and other illegal drugs far outstrip the demands for them, so in a free market they would be inexpensive. Drug selling is profitable only because the laws keep supplies low. A habit that might cost \$10.00 per week in a free market costs about one hundred times that much under present conditions, so habitual users must either renounce drugs for less expensive hobbies or commit crimes to get their drug money. Few users find stamp collecting an adequate substitute, so their response to an increase in drug prices is to commit more robberies, burglaries, petty larcenies, and auto thefts.[17] An additional concern is that, because even minor drug offenses are punished severely, the offenders are more ready to resort to extreme violence to avoid arrest and prosecution. When Switzerland adopted a policy of distributing heroin to addicts, the percentage committing crimes dropped from 66 percent to 10 percent.[18]

Police resources diverted to the drug war are unavailable for protecting communities against other crimes. In 1996, a year in which the FBI helped convict 2,919 people on drug charges, it won two convictions for antitrust laws and thirty-five for environmental crimes.[19] Because so many drug offenders serve lengthy prison sentences, U.S. prisons are bulging at the seams. When capacities are exceeded, some prisoners are released early. The lucky ones are more likely to be rapists or murderers than drug offenders.[20] In an interview, Nobel Memorial

Prize–winning economist Milton Friedman (a political conservative) said, "I have estimated statistically that the prohibition of drugs produces, on the average, ten thousand homicides a year."[21]

EROSION OF PROTECTIONS FROM THE BILL OF RIGHTS

The United States could be more effective in discouraging drug buyers and sellers. We could emulate countries such as Malaysia, Singapore, and Saudi Arabia by executing offenders. The first casualty would be our way of life.

Richard Miller has argued that the war on drugs is analogous in many ways to Nazi Germany's war against Jews.[22] People who may in all respects except drug use be law-abiding citizens are subjected to terrible deprivations and punishments—just as Jews, though they may have been law-abiding citizens in all respects except for their Jewishness, were subjected. The Nazis eventually extended their harsh regime to groups other than Jews. Non-drug-using Americans should also worry about their rights being taken away. For example, forfeiture laws (see below) have been expanded to permit authorities to seize cars from people accused of soliciting sex from prostitutes.

One precious right is free speech, guaranteed by the First Amendment. But legislation introduced in Missouri during the 1990s threatened record dealers with life imprisonment for selling records with lyrics describing drug use. The initial draft of the federal Omnibus Crime Bill declared that it was treason to question drug war policies. Stanford University was pressured into firing a lecturer who criticized the drug war. The Drug Enforcement Administration (DEA) has harassed pro-legalization magazines and their advertisers. Federal drug czar Barry McCaffrey threatened to arrest any doctor who mentioned to AIDS or cancer patients that marijuana might reduce their suffering.

The Office of National Drug Control Policy (ONDCP) pays television networks millions of dollars to run anti-drug commercials. In turn, the networks air either an equivalent number of anti-drug public service announcements or programs with anti-drug messages. Drug czar McCaffrey expressed hope that a similar arrangement could be worked out with filmmakers.[23] Rep. Billy Tauzin (R-La.), chairman of the House Telecommunications Subcommittee, said, "If such a deal exists, it was unconstitutional, and it violated Federal Communications Commission policies, as well as the law that created the ONDCP's anti-drug media campaign. I believe that it puts the government on a horrible slippery slope of interference with First Amendment rights, the likes of which I have never witnessed in my tenure in the United States Congress."[24]

In Kansas City and Denver, drug agents ordered search warrants to obtain records of sales from local bookstores. They hoped that the records would help them convict the buyers of operating illegal drug laboratories. The store owners refused to comply with the warrants, arguing that the First Amendment includes the right to receive information.[25]

The Fourth Amendment protects against unreasonable search. Yet the Supreme Court has ruled that evidence obtained through an invalid search warrant can be used in trials and that police can authorize searches without approval from a judge. Even warrants obtained by perjured police testimony were ruled valid. Judges issued search warrants against citizens on the basis of police claims that they had received anonymous tips. Passengers on Greyhound buses and airplanes and in private cars were searched only because they fit a drug offender profile. (One of the key features of the profile was being black or Hispanic.) Yet the vast majority of people subjected to the inconvenient and humiliating body-cavity searches were not carrying drugs.[26]

Police have invaded homes in the middle of the night, made people undress in front of them, detained innocent people for hours, and vandalized their property. The number of wiretaps has been steadily increasing, and 72.4 percent of them in 1999 were authorized in drug investigations.[27]

Some government Internet sites track the on-line activities of people who surf for information on drugs. To many civil libertarians, the practice is tantamount to conducting searches without a warrant.[28]

The Fifth Amendment's guarantee that citizens do not have to incriminate themselves through compelled testimony has been eviscerated by the war on drugs. Coerced urine tests and police access to previously confidential medical records are now allowable forms of self-incrimination. The Fifth Amendment's guarantee of trials is also a victim. Prosecutors charge people with much more serious crimes than the evidence warrants but then allow the accused to plea-bargain to lesser crimes if they waive trial. The Fifth Amendment used to protect against double jeopardy. Generally, even if local, state, and federal laws all prohibit the same offense, a person charged in one jurisdiction will not be charged in another. That safeguard is often waived in drug cases. After serving one year in prison for a 1985 marijuana cultivation offense, a man returned to the community. In 1991, on the basis of the 1985 search warrant, he was charged with violating federal marijuana conspiracy law and received a mandatory life sentence.[29]

The Eighth Amendment's protection against cruel and unusual punishment has been weakened by laws allowing government agencies to confiscate assets of drug traffickers. Miller cites a Justice Department official who said that 80 percent of federal forfeitures are taken from innocent people who are never even indicted. The innocent must demonstrate that they took reasonable steps to ensure that their assets were not used for illegal purposes. The courts ruled that reasonable steps had not been taken by a mother who lost her car because her son used it for drug transactions; or by a laundromat company whose company car was taken because a store manager used it to travel to a drug deal; or by a family that lost its car because one of the family members gave a ride to someone who, unknown to him, had a small amount of marijuana; or by a rental yacht company that lost a yacht because a marijuana cigarette was found on board.

Courts have supported the government's right to seize property merely by establishing probable cause that the property is subject to forfeiture. The government need not prove that the defendant acted criminally. In fact, property may be forfeited even if the owner is charged and acquitted. It may be forfeited solely for its "intended use" to facilitate a drug offense, that is, for thought. The defendant is not entitled to a presumption of innocence or to an attorney (which the Sixth Amendment guarantees).[30]

Forfeiture can be considered either punishment or remedial. Remedial forfeitures are designed to compensate the public for loss caused by the offense, and they are exempt from Eighth Amendment protection. On those grounds, the courts upheld the forfeiture of a record store owner's inventory, because an employee was found with marijuana in his possession, and of a house, after the owners' repeated but unsuccessful attempts to get their children to stop using drugs. The owner of an apartment building learned that some tenants were guilty of drug violations. He filed criminal trespass charges against them even though he feared that they might retaliate violently. The district attorney's office praised his cooperation, but the DEA ran a forfeiture against the building.[31]

Both prosecutors and police are often awarded the forfeited property, which has included cash, cars, computers, giant-screen television sets, and fitness centers. Not only does the policy encourage zealotry in the pursuit of drug crimes, it also skews priorities. Prosecutors charge people who have the most valuable assets. Police undercover agents pose as drug sellers rather than buyers because they cannot legally profit from seized drugs but can confiscate a buyer's cash or other assets. New York City police focused on stopping people coming to the city to buy drugs in preference to stopping the outward flow of drugs. Police in Florida and Louisiana used traffic violations as a pretext to confiscate money from motorists against whom there was no evidence of wrongdoing. Los Angeles police routinely planted drugs and falsified police reports to establish probable cause for cash seizures.[32]

The "relation back" doctrine holds that government title to forfeited property relates back to the time criminal use of the property occurred. Some of the cash deposited by a firm had a drug odor, so the firm's checking account was forfeited; innocent people who held checks from the firm were told that they had no claim on the money. Police dogs indicated that some money in a food market cash register had a cocaine scent, so police confiscated the store's entire receipts.[33] If you buy a house from a person who grew marijuana in the house last year, the government can subsequently seize it on the grounds that the government owned it (although nobody knew at the time) when it was sold.

Private citizens are given finder's fees for providing information leading to forfeitures. Airline and motel employees who notify DEA agents whenever customers match the drug offender profile get as much as 25 percent of the value of the forfeited property. The practice raises at least three serious concerns: (1) the promise of a large bonus may distract low-paid but essential employees such as x-ray guards in airports from performing their normal duties properly, (2) some employees may be willing to plant drugs on the property of innocent victims, and (3) employees may cite security reasons for routinely opening packages, thereby evading the Fourth Amendment's protection against unreasonable search.

In another activity reminiscent of Nazi Germany, anti-drug crusaders have gone into schools and encouraged children to turn family members in to the police for violating the drug laws. Some parents have been arrested and stripped of custody of their children.[34]

FINANCIAL AND SAFETY COSTS

People arrested for drug offenses must go through the criminal justice system. As noted above, the number of imprisoned nonviolent offenders in 1998 totaled 1,185,458. The costs, both direct and indirect, are staggering. An indirect cost is the diversion of resources from the courts and police for dealing with other matters. Direct costs include an annual estimated $24 billion for imprisoning nonviolent offenders. Zeidenberg and colleagues give some perspective to the numbers by comparing them with other government expenditures: The $24 billion is almost 50 percent larger than the amount the government spends on a welfare program that serves 8.5 million people and six times larger than it spends on child care for 1.25 million children. From 1987 to 1995, state expenditures for prisons increased by 30 percent while expenditures for universities decreased by 19 percent.[35]

The $24 billion figure is probably conservative. Various estimates place the cost of keeping a person in prison at more than $25,000 per year. When prison facility construction costs, health care, other contracted services, and debt services on prison bonds are factored in, the actual annual cost is probably closer to $40,000.[36] Either figure is considerably higher than the annual costs of traditional outpatient drug treatment ($1,800), intensive outpatient care ($2,500), methadone treatment for heroin users ($3,900), and residential drug treatment programs ($4,400–$6,800).[37]

The U.S. prison system was designed to rehabilitate criminals, but today the focus is on punishment. Treatment is available to only about 10 percent of inmate drug abusers.[38] Education and vocational training programs have been substantially curtailed. Brutality prevails in places such as a Texas prison with an isolation unit that houses up to 660 men. The men are kept for about twenty-three hours a day in bathroom-sized quarters, fed through hatches in their doors, provided with virtually no sensory stimuli for months or years on end, deprived of full meals as punishment for breaking rules, and made to dress in paper gowns if they rip up their uniforms.[39]

Even those unsympathetic to prisoners should realize that the vast majority of them will eventually be released—probably between 2.5 and 3.5 million during the next ten years. Seething with rage, with minimal job skills but ineligible for much welfare assistance, drug rehabilitation programs, or access to Medicaid, they will be given little chance to integrate themselves into communities and become law-abiding citizens. They may conclude that criminality is their only means of survival. In fact, recidivism rates are higher for convicted felons sent to prison than for similar offenders placed on probation.[40] Schlosser writes,

> Roughly 124,000 inmates are simply released from prison each year in California, given nothing more than $200 and a bus ticket back to the county where they were convicted. At least 1,200 inmates every year go from a secure housing unit at a Level 4 prison—an isolation unit, designed to hold the most violent and dangerous inmates in the system—right onto the street. One day these predatory inmates are locked in their cells for twenty-three hours at a time and fed all their meals through a slot in the door, and the next day they're out of prison, riding a bus home.[41]

They will spread infectious diseases in the neighborhoods to which they return. They will wreak social and economic havoc.

POLICE CORRUPTION

According to a General Accounting Office (GAO) document, drug-related corruption is a problem for police departments throughout the country. FBI-led investigations have resulted in an average of about sixty-five drug-related convictions of police officers per year, but the total number of cases at all levels of government is unknown. The report indicates that an officer "might view stealing money from a drug dealer as acceptable behavior, while the officer would draw the line at stealing and selling drugs. Over time, behavior, such as dealing in illegal drugs, which was previously viewed as unacceptable by even corrupt officers might become acceptable or at least tolerated."[42] Many officers went further. They (1) conducted unconstitutional searches and seizures, (2) stole money and drugs from drug dealers, (3) sold stolen drugs, (4) protected drug operations, (5) provided false testimony, and (6) submitted false crime reports. Former San Jose, California, police chief Joseph McNamara said, "The sheer hopelessness of the task [the war on drugs] has led many officers to rationalize their own corruption. They say: 'Why should the enemy get to keep all the profits?' Guys with modest salaries are suddenly looking at $10,000 or more, and they go for it."[43]

The Commission on Police Integrity for the city of Chicago reported that New York City police officers stole from street dealers and drug couriers during legitimate raids, warrantless searches, and car stops. Police protected and assisted narcotics traffickers and colleagues who dealt and used illicit drugs themselves. Police in drug cases offered perjured testimony and wrote false crime reports. The authors note that New York is not unique: "Corruption has taken many forms and has continued to plague the police departments of nearly every major city."[44]

CORRUPTION WITHIN PRISONS

According to an Associated Press report, marijuana, methamphetamine, cocaine, and heroin flow freely through California prisons. Most drugs that reach inmates are smuggled inside by friends and relatives, but prison employees are almost always involved with quantities smuggled in bulk. The employees usually have inmate contacts who run their own distribution networks inside.[45]

CORRUPTION OF CUSTOMS DEPARTMENT OFFICIALS AND BORDER SECURITY PERSONNEL

Drug cartels with vast amounts of money can offer huge bribes to customs inspectors. The *New York Times* quoted a Customs Department official as saying: "The large amount of illegal drugs that pass through U.S. Customs land, sea and air ports of entry and the enormous amount of money at the disposal of drug traffickers to corrupt law-enforcement personnel place Customs and its employees at great risk to corruption."[46] The *Fort Worth Star-Telegram* quotes one official, "You hear hints like, 'What would you do if somebody gave you $5,000 just so you could look the other way—would it take $5,000 or $1 million?' It's very hard to get away from it. Sooner or later you're going to talk to someone who will offer you a lot of money."[47]

From 1994 to 1997, forty-six U.S. border law-enforcement officials were indicted on drug-related charges. In 1997, six former law-enforcement officers in Donna, Texas, were indicted for helping traffickers smuggle 1,700 pounds of marijuana across the border. In 1999, three Immigration and Naturalization Service (INS) inspectors were indicted for accepting hundreds of thousands of dollars to allow shipments of cocaine to pass through the Nogales, Arizona, port of entry.[48]

The *Star-Telegram* also reports on a GAO analysis of twenty-eight convictions between 1992 and 1997 of INS and customs employees for drug-related crimes along the Southwest border. The GAO report indicates five ways in which the employees collaborated with drug traffickers:

- Waving vehicles through without inspection. An inspector gave smugglers his work schedule and lane assignment so they could drive marijuana-laden vehicles right through without inspection.
- Coordinating movement of drugs between ports of entry. A Border Patrol agent told marijuana smugglers where loads could be brought across, then picked up the loads in his government vehicle and took them elsewhere.
- Transporting drugs past Border Patrol checkpoints. An agent drove marijuana through checkpoints manned by his friends, then deposited it at a safe location before returning to work.
- Selling the drugs themselves. One Border Patrol agent seized drugs, then sold them to dealers.
- Selling drug intelligence information. A customs operational analysis specialist tipped off smugglers if they came under suspicion.

THE DRUG WAR IS DEVASTATING TO MINORITIES

Officials within the Reagan and George H. W. Bush presidential administrations blamed drugs for urban poverty and crime. Bush's drug czar, William Bennett, wrote, "Crack is responsible for the fact that vast patches of the American urban landscape are rapidly deteriorating."[49] Bush said that cocaine was "turning our cities into battle zones and murdering our children."[50] He eagerly prosecuted a "War on Drugs." The appropriate response would have been to develop strategies for improving the education and health care of minorities—conducting a "War on the Conditions that Breed Drug Abuse."

Michael Tonry documented that the officials knew that their war on drugs would harm the very communities it was supposed to save.[51] Although surveys indicate that whites are the biggest users of illicit drugs, most drug dealing takes place in white suburban neighborhoods, and most drug dealers are white students (see figure 8.1), police enforcement efforts have focused on low-income neighborhoods. They could more easily infiltrate drug distribution organizations in those neighborhoods and, because drug transactions are often conducted on the streets, make more arrests. Sociologist Dina Rose theorizes that neighborhoods in which more than 1 percent of residents are imprisoned per year become so disrupted that community ties crumble and crime rates soar.[52]

Most prisons are located in predominantly white areas. When calculating census figures, the prison populations are added. That increases the areas' eligibility

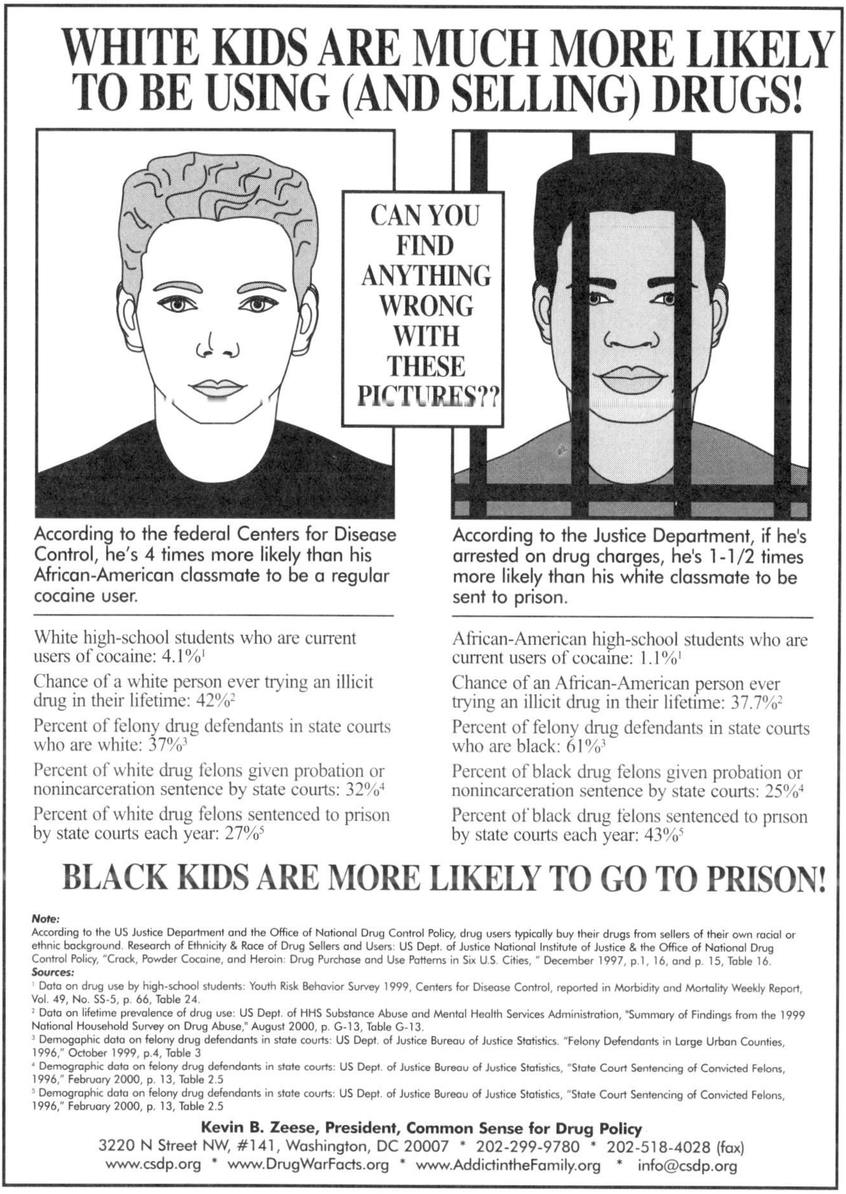

Figure 8.1. A Common Sense for Drug Policy advertisement that appeared in the *National Review, The New Republic,* the *Weekly Standard, The Nation, Reason Magazine,* and *The Progressive* in spring 2001. Reproduced with permission.

for federal funds and political representation while reducing these to an equal extent for the urban communities from which the prisoners come.

Because of the violence associated with illegality and huge monetary transactions, law-abiding residents of low-income neighborhoods live in terror. They find it difficult to get insurance or loans, and local businesspeople cannot attract investors. Their children have few positive role models. The most successful people, if accumulation of material goods is the criterion, are drug kingpins. Selling drugs on a large scale requires creativity and hard work, traits that in most environments help people become respected and influential citizens. Instead, kingpins become criminals. Most eventually end up in prison or die young.

The drug war has encouraged police to harass young black and Hispanic men in airports, buses, and their own cars. For years the New Jersey State Police denied that state troopers discriminated against black motorists by detaining them for drug searches. But in 1999, the state attorney general's department released documents proving otherwise. Evidence from internal audits dating back to 1996 demonstrates widespread illegal racial profiling.[53] New Jersey police were not unique. Tenants in public housing projects in cities across the country were required to submit to repeated inspections of their apartments and all personal belongings.[54]

A March 2002 Supreme Court ruling inflicted further injustice on public housing residents. The Court upheld a government ruling that residents can be evicted if a family member or guest is caught with drugs on or near a housing project. Entire families can be evicted even if only a single offender is caught and nobody else in the household was aware of the offense. Chief Justice William Rehnquist defended the policy on two grounds. He said that it puts all tenants on notice that they can be removed if they do not prevent drug use by their family members; and it protects law-abiding families from crime and violence in the projects.[55]

So young black and Hispanic men were far more likely than white offenders to be arrested. They have been charged with more serious offenses, convicted more frequently, and sentenced to prison more frequently and with longer sentences than whites convicted of the same offenses.[56] By 1997, there were 193 white American prison inmates per 100,000 American whites, 688 Hispanic prison inmates per 100,000 Hispanics, and 1,571 black prison inmates per 100,000 blacks.[57] Imprisonment disrupted their families and reduced their opportunities to attend college or get decent jobs when released. About 13 percent of black men, seven times the national average, have been disallowed from voting because of a felony conviction.[58]

The consequences of racist drug laws are exploited by commentators who blame crime on inferior genetics rather than social, economic, and political factors. See, for example, Rushton, who advances genetic arguments to explain drug addiction and other crime.[59] (Do not see. It is a dishonest and disgraceful book.) He does not explain why most cocaine and opiate users of 100 years ago were middle-aged middle-class white women.

If the genetic view is accepted, it follows that people of color must be biologically predisposed to criminality. After all, they have a higher incarceration rate than whites. But both the genetic view and the inference are without merit. Sociologist Troy Duster writes:

> If we are ignorant of recent history, and do not know that the incarceration rate and the coloring of our prisons is a function of dramatic changes in the last half century, we are far more vulnerable to the seduction of the genetic explanation. Gene pools of humans take centuries to change significantly, but the incarceration rate for blacks in the U.S. in relation to the rate for whites increased dramatically during the past 60 years. Yet in this very period we find a significant increase in scientific journal articles and scholarly books suggesting a greater role for biological explanations of crime.[60]

MINORITY WOMEN

Minority women experience double prejudice. The Partnership for a Drug-Free America (financed heavily by drug companies) creates and displays many clever ads to discourage drug use. Most of the early ads portrayed most drug users as young, foreign, black, and female.[61]

Minority women have been used as unwitting subjects in medical experiments. For example, workers at a family-planning clinic told Hispanic women that they were receiving contraceptives but gave placebos to seventy-six of them. Several became pregnant but were not given abortion services.[62]

A 1989 report that babies born to crack cocaine–addicted women were severely impaired fueled media stories of mothers without parenting instincts. Doomsayers predicted an epidemic of inhuman children who would destroy their schools and then all of society. Although several scientists challenged the initial report, laws were enacted that made pregnant drug users guilty of delivering drugs to a minor. In the decade following, more than thirty states filed charges against women for taking illegal drugs during pregnancy. The range of penalties included imprisonment and loss of custody of the baby. In May 2001, a South Carolina jury found a twenty-four-year-old mother of three guilty of homicide because she used cocaine while pregnant and her unborn child did not survive. Virtually all those prosecuted were poor and nonwhite.

Aware of the severe penalties for testing positive, black female crack users reluctantly stopped going to health clinics and avoided prenatal care. Even delivery became a problem. Hospital staff were often unsupportive and abusive, and when hospitals instituted routine drug testing of newborns, crack users chose to deliver at home. (In March 2001, the Supreme Court ruled that public hospitals cannot test a pregnant woman for drugs and turn the results over to police without the woman's consent. The ruling came after some women who tested positive were arrested from their hospital beds shortly after giving birth.)

Interestingly, the defective cocaine baby scare was unwarranted. Behnke and Eyler studied 300 children from poor families, half born to cocaine-addicted mothers and half to nonaddicts.[63] There were no significant behavioral differences between them. After analyzing thirty-six studies on cocaine babies, Frank and colleagues concluded that a pregnant woman's cocaine use does not cause developmental and behavioral deficiencies in her newborn. Deficiencies previously attributed to cocaine had probably been caused by cigarettes, alcohol, or poverty. Frank and colleagues write,

> When prenatal cocaine and tobacco exposure are compared dispassionately, it becomes clear how sociopolitical forces shape discrepant interpretations of similar scientific data. The mechanisms of nicotine and cocaine effects on the developing brain are similar. . . . Prenatal tobacco exposure has been associated with infant mortality, moderate impairment of cognitive functioning, and a range of behavioral problems (which, unlike those associated with cocaine exposure, are detectable on relatively insensitive epidemiologic measures). . . . Despite increased health care costs imposed by their tobacco use, there are no sterilization campaigns for mothers who use tobacco. No pregnant women have been charged with child abuse for tobacco use in pregnancy.[64]

AIDS

Blacks and Hispanics are far more likely than whites to contract HIV, and AIDS is the number one killer of minority children.[65] Schneider argues persuasively that the reason is the drug war:

> First, intense police surveillance, combined with laws against possession of drug paraphernalia, has made the possession of clean syringes in minority neighborhoods extremely risky. Black users are likely to get rid of their own clean needles to avoid arrest and to rely on syringes borrowed at the moment of injection. They are more likely to shoot up powder cocaine than smoke crack, because powder carries a lower penalty. But it demands frequent injections, so increases the risk of HIV infection. Second, persistent police harassment has promoted the spread of underground shooting galleries. These are the most risky sites of HIV transmission, because of both sharing of infected syringes and sex for drugs exchanges. Third, differential arrest rates have exposed black and Hispanic males to unsafe drugs and sex in prison. Fourth, the frequency of shared syringes, shooting galleries, and unsafe sex and drugs in prison has increased the rate of HIV infection among black and Hispanic males and made it more likely that an adult who borrows a needle from a friend is

much more likely to borrow an infected needle than is the young white adult who borrows a needle from another white.[66]

More than 50 percent of AIDS cases among blacks and Hispanics, and more than 90 percent among black and Hispanic women and children, originate with an infected needle. The risk of needle sharing is greater for women drug users because they are more likely than men to be injected by someone else, thus more likely to be injected with a previously used needle. Unsafe sexual contacts increase women's vulnerability. Many earn drug money through prostitution and live in neighborhoods where a high proportion of potential sexual partners is HIV positive or has AIDS.

Treatment and Imprisonment

Many drug treatment programs either reject pregnant women outright or make no special accommodations for them. Most inpatient programs require lengthy stays but do not have room for children. Women with young children cannot accept spaces in such programs.

During the past two decades, the number of women arrested and imprisoned for drug offenses increased much more rapidly than the rates for men. The greatest increases were for black women. Their young children suffered, being sent to foster homes or shuttled between relatives' homes or institutions. In 2000, 65.3 percent of women in state prisons had children under eighteen.[67]

CLASS BIAS

A *New Republic* article argues that drug laws are class rather than race biased.[68] Most prisoners in the United States held jobs in the year before their arrest, but 90 percent earned less money than the U.S. average, and only 15 percent had attended a year or more of college; the national average is 45 percent. Most are in prison for nonviolent drug offenses. According to a 1994 study, low-level drug offenders constitute 36 percent of federal prison inmates and serve an average of almost six years. Federal judge Stanley Sporkin, after noting that the law gave him no choice but to sentence a working-class first-time drug offender to ten years, said, "If this person were from a different socio-economic background, he would have gone to the Betty Ford Clinic for 60 to 90 days. As I contemplated the sentence I would have to impose, all that came to mind was a modern day version of 'Les Miserables.'"[69]

In the early stages of criminal proceedings, prosecutors and defense attorneys conduct bargaining sessions in private meetings. Wealthy defendants are represented by defense lawyers from top firms who specialize in drug cases. Many are former prosecutors who enjoy negotiating with their ex-colleagues. By contrast, poor defendants have their cases handled by overworked public defenders. Crucial decisions are made at these bargaining sessions, such as the specific charge. Options may include simple possession, sales, sale to a minor, interstate flight, or no prosecution at all. Prosecutors decide whether a mandatory minimum sentence applies and whether to assign the case to a local, state, or federal court. Attorneys in federal courts are generally more skilled and demand longer sentences. Forfeiture laws enable some wealthy defendants to trade property for shorter sentences. A defendant facing a twenty-five-years-to-life indictment had the charge dismissed by agreeing to forfeit over $1 million in assets. In Massachusetts, agreements to forfeit $50,000 bought an average 6.3 year reduction in sentence for dealers, and $10,000 bought elimination or reduction of trafficking charges in almost three-fourths of such cases.[70]

Defendants who supply information that helps the government catch others may have their prison time reduced. With rare exceptions, the only ones with such information are major drug traffickers and dealers. Almost all are men. Women and men with small roles in the drug trade rarely have information to trade. The *New Republic* article notes the case of Anthony Brigham, caught while acting as a lookout at a drug buy in a sting that also caught three major traffickers. The traffickers traded information and received as little as four months of community service. But Brigham knew nothing, had no names to deal, and drew the ten years mandatory minimum. An eighteen-year-old high school student told an undercover agent where to buy lysergic acid diethylamide (LSD). She received a ten-year sentence for conspiracy. The dealer, who had information to give, received five years.[71]

Eric Schlosser has written two chilling articles on the unfairness of the drug war.[72] He cites the case of a young man who lived with his eighty-year-old grandparents and, unbeknownst to them, kept marijuana in the house they had owned for almost forty years. When he was arrested, federal prosecutor Leslie Ohta seized the house on the grounds that people should know what goes on in their own home. Soon afterward, Ohta's eighteen-year-old son was arrested for selling LSD from her car. Her car was not seized. The son of Indiana Congressman Dan Burton, who has argued for life sentences for some marijuana-related crimes, was arrested for transporting nearly 8 pounds of marijuana across state lines in his car. Six months later he was arrested again, in his apartment, where police found thirty marijuana plants and a loaded shotgun. Federal prosecutors did not press charges, Indiana prosecutors dismissed charges, and a Louisiana judge sentenced him to community service, probation, and house arrest. John Baker, the son of future Secretary of State James Baker, sold marijuana to an undercover cop. He faced a felony prison term of between two and twenty years but was charged with only a misdemeanor and fined $2,000. Richard Riley Jr., the son of President

Clinton's secretary of education, was indicted in 1992 on federal charges of conspiring to sell cocaine and marijuana. Facing ten years to life in prison and a fine of $4 million, he received six months of house arrest. Rep. Randy Cunningham of California once said, "We must get tough on drug dealers. Those who peddle destruction on our children must pay dearly." Four months later, his son was arrested for his role in transporting 400 pounds of marijuana across state lines. He confessed to having helped smuggle as much as 10 tons of marijuana throughout the country. He faced a life sentence without parole but instead received a two-and-a-half-year prison sentence. Komp reports that the grandson of former president Ronald Reagan was caught in possession of marijuana, which violated his probation stemming from a conviction for receiving stolen property. He received treatment instead of incarceration. And the nephew of Attorney General John Ashcroft received state probation rather than a federal sentence for marijuana possession.[73]

A Vietnam veteran with an artificial leg owned a business and had a home, wife, and two-year-old son. The man bought a pound of marijuana from an informer who had received the marijuana from the local sheriff's department and was paid $100 for his services. The buyer was arrested, charged as a trafficker, convicted, and sentenced to life in prison without parole. The daughter of the judge who sentenced him was later arrested for selling marijuana. She was granted youthful offender status. Her records have been sealed, but she probably received probation.

BENEFITS DENIED

According to interviews conducted for the National Household Survey,[74] in 1999 an estimated 14.8 million Americans used an illicit drug at least once during the thirty days prior to their interview. The figures for alcohol and tobacco products were 105 million and 66.8 million, respectively. More than seventy-two million Americans (33 percent) twelve years of age and older have tried marijuana at least once in their lifetimes. They are not all crazy. They use drugs because they hope to derive benefits. Some drugs relieve pain, stress, or anger. Psychedelics like LSD and mescaline promote religious feelings and may enhance creativity; LSD and 3,4-methylenedioxymethamphetamine (MDMA/Ecstasy) may facilitate psychotherapeutic healing; and marijuana may be the most effective and least toxic treatment for more than thirty symptoms and syndromes including tetanus, insomnia, labor pain, convulsions, asthma, glaucoma, rheumatism, the intense and prolonged nausea and vomiting induced by cancer chemotherapies, and HIV-associated weight loss.[75] Moreover, marijuana works by different mechanisms than many standard drugs and may thus be especially valuable for people who do not respond to the standards.[76] Each of those claims is disputed, but articles in peer-reviewed journals plus a substantial body of anecdotal evidence make them worth considering. Unfortunately, the illegality of the drugs presents a major hurdle for prospective researchers. The refusal of authorities to acknowledge anticipated benefits sabotages strategies designed to prevent and treat abuse.

Even if drugs brought nothing but brief moments of pleasure, that would be a significant benefit. On medical grounds alone, stress relief is valuable. Psychological stress increases the risk of a variety of illnesses, and drugs like marijuana and heroin relieve stress temporarily in at least some people.[77]

MISINFORMATION AND DISINFORMATION

The drug laws encourage suppression of information and spread of misinformation. Former American Medical Association president Wesley Hall drew national newspaper headlines when he announced that marijuana promotes birth defects and "makes a man of 35 sexually like a man of 70." He later retracted, admitting that his statement was issued to reduce marijuana use and not based on evidence.[78] Arnold Trebach reported that a book he wrote was not included in a government archive because it criticized government policy.[79] After a World Health Organization (WHO) panel of experts concluded that marijuana is more benign than alcohol, the WHO panel was pressured not to publish its findings.[80] William Pollin, administrator of the National Institute on Drug Abuse (NIDA), sent a letter to librarians all over the country listing sixty-two NIDA titles published during the previous twelve years. Calling them outdated or scientifically inaccurate, he wrote, "I strongly suggest that you purge your collection of these old materials." Several of the titles describe the effects of various hallucinogenic drugs and the medical consequences of their misuse. At the time of the letter research on those drugs had been banned for many years, so the information was not outdated and its accuracy had not been challenged. An editorial in *High Times Magazine* accuses Pollin of trying to suppress scientific information about illegal drugs and replace it with anti-drug ideology.[81]

The National Institutes of Health sponsored research on heart disease. Carl Selzer and his colleagues on the project found that men who consumed moderate amounts of alcohol had a lower risk of heart disease than nondrinkers. The information might have encouraged some people to increase their alcohol consumption, a result that institute officials deemed unacceptable. Selzer was denied permission to submit the findings for publication.[82]

The unofficial policy of disinformation sabotages the effectiveness of reports of real dangers. When stories about anabolic steroids first reached the sports pages, most authorities claimed that steroids do not improve athletic performance. The authorities were either misinformed or lying. As a result, subsequent reports documenting real and very serious dangers of steroids were not readily accepted, and steroid use escalated.

Disinformation is the standard for school drug education classes. In the words of Thomas Szasz, drug education is "the name we give to the state-sponsored effort to inflame people's hatred and intolerance of other people's drug habits, which is as indecent as it would be to inflame people's hatred and intolerance of other people's religious habits and call it 'religion education.'"[83]

In a 1989 televised speech, President George H. W. Bush dramatized the scope of the drug problem by holding up a bag of cocaine bought in Lafayette Park. "This is crack cocaine," he announced. "It was seized a few days ago in a park across the street from the White House." Bush claimed that even the White House lawn was not safe from drug dealers. But reporters soon discovered that DEA agents had lured a suspected drug dealer to the area four days before the speech. When first contacted by an undercover DEA agent posing as a drug buyer, the teenaged suspect seemed baffled. "Where the [expletive] is the White House?" he replied.[84]

Figure 8.2 is a reproduction of an advertisement printed in *New Republic* magazine on 5 October 1998. The layout has been altered slightly, but the text is unchanged. See also figure 8.3.

A NATION OF CRIMINALS

If murderers who escape apprehension are still murderers, then people who escape apprehension after committing other felonies are felons nonetheless. The drug laws have made almost half the adult population of the U.S. felons at large, and that includes such prominent citizens as ex-President Bill Clinton, ex–Vice President Al Gore, President George W. Bush, presidential candidate Bill Bradley, Representative Newt Gingrich, New York City Mayor Michael Bloomberg, and Supreme Court Justice Clarence Thomas. All have admitted to youthful experimentation with illegal drugs. That raises several issues:

- Ex-President George H. W. Bush and ex–drug czar William Bennett both said that past marijuana smoking should not disqualify someone from future high office.[85] Then it is hard to understand the rationale for giving convicted nonviolent drug offenders long prison sentences. Bush nominated admitted one-time user Clarence Thomas to the Supreme Court within weeks of a Supreme Court decision upholding a sentence of life imprisonment without parole for mere drug possession.

"There is not a shred of scientific evidence that shows that smoked marijuana is useful or needed. This is not science. This is not medical. This is a cruel hoax."

Gen. Barry McCaffrey, Director of the Office of National Drug Control Policy (Drug Czar), Aug. 16, 1996.

"Smoked marijuana has been shown to lower intraocular eye pressure (IOP) in subjects with normal IOP and patients with glaucoma. . . . Clinical studies and survey data in healthy populations have shown a strong relationship between marijuana use and increased eating. . . . Inhaled marijuana has the potential to improve chemotherapy-related nausea and vomiting."

National Institutes of Health, Department of Health and Human Services (HHS), Workshop on the Medical Utility of Marijuana, 1997.

"In the view of the nation's scientific and medical community, marijuana has a high potential for abuse and no generally accepted therapeutic value."

Gen. Barry McCaffrey, July 22, 1997.

"Federal authorities should rescind their prohibition of the medicinal use of marijuana for seriously ill patients and allow physicians to decide which patients to treat."

Editorial, *New England Journal of Medicine*, January 30, 1997.

"Marijuana is also a gateway drug."

Gen. Barry McCaffrey, July 22, 1997.

"For every 104 people who have used marijuana, there is only one regular user of cocaine and less than one heroin addict."

Department of HHS, *National Household Survey on Drug Abuse*, 1997.

"The murder rate in Holland is double that in the United States. . . . That's drugs."

Gen. Barry McCaffrey, July 23, 1998.

"The Dutch homicide rate in 1995 was one-fourth that of the United States (1.8 vs. 8.0)."

FBI, Uniform Crime Reports/Dutch Bureau of Statistics.

"[Needle exchange] programs are magnets for all social ills—pulling in crime, violence, addicts, prostitution, dealers, and gangs and driving out hope and opportunity."

Gen. Barry McCaffrey, April 24, 1998.[1]

Figure 8.2. ***New Republic*** **Advertisement**

"A meticulous scientific review has now proven that needle exchange programs can reduce the transmission of HIV and save lives without losing ground in the battle against illegal drugs."

Donna Shalala, Secretary of HHS, April 20, 1998.

1. The authors of the studies that McCaffrey cited to show the failure of needle-exchange programs wrote the following letter to the *New York Times*:

Debate has started up again in Washington about whether the Government should renew its ban on subsidies for needle-exchange programs, which advocates say can help stop the spread of AIDS.

In a letter to Congress, Barry McCaffrey, who is in charge of national drug policy, cited two Canadian studies to show that needle-exchange plans have failed to reduce the spread of H.I.V., the virus that causes AIDS, and may even have worsened the problem. Congressional leaders have cited these studies to make the same argument.

As the authors of the Canadian studies, we must point out that these officials have misinterpreted our research. True, we found that addicts who took part in needle exchange programs in Vancouver and Montreal had higher H.I.V. infection rates than addicts who did not. That's not surprising. Because these programs are in inner-city neighborhoods, they serve users who are at greatest risk of infection. Those who didn't accept free needles often didn't need them since they could afford to buy syringes in drug stores. They also were less likely to engage in the riskiest activities.

Also, needle-exchange programs must be tailored to local conditions. For example, in Montreal and Vancouver, cocaine injection is a major source of H.I.V. transmission. Some users inject the drug up to 40 times a day. At that rate, we have calculated that the two cities we studied would each need 10 million clean needles a year to prevent the re-use of syringes. Currently, the Vancouver program exchanges two million syringes annually, and Montreal, half a million.

A study conducted last year and published in *The Lancet*, the British medical journal, found that in 29 cities worldwide where programs are in place, H.I.V. infection dropped by an average of 5.8 percent a year among drug users. In 51 cities that had no needle-exchange plans, drug-related infection rose by 5.9 percent a year. Clearly these efforts can work.

But clean needles are only part of the solution. A comprehensive approach that includes needle exchange, health care, treatment for drug addiction, social support and counseling is also needed. In Canada, local governments acted on our research by expanding needle exchanges and adding related services. We hope the Clinton Administration and Congress will provide the same kind of leadership in the United States. (Julie Bruneau and Martin T. Schechter, "[Letter]," The New York Times, 9 April 1998: 27)

Source: New Republic, 5 October 1998: 13 (paid for by the Common Sense for Drug Policy Foundation, Kevin Zeese, President).

Figure 8.2. ***(continued)***

Recent accounts in the U.S. press about the Netherlands drug policy have included incorrect and misleading statistics about drug use and drug-related crimes in the Netherlands. What follows is a short list of facts and comparisons to refute those accounts. Sources are given to permit and encourage third party verification of facts.

Last month use of cannabis (marijuana) by high school seniors:
18.1% in the Netherlands (1996);
23.7% in the U.S. (1997).
(Sources: The Trimbos Institute, Amsterdam, the Netherlands; Monitoring the Future Survey, University of Michigan and White House Office of National Drug Control Policy)

Any lifetime use (prevalence) of cannabis by older teens (1994):
30% in the Netherlands;
38% in the U.S.
(Sources: Center for Drug Research, University of Amsterdam; Monitoring the Future Survey, University of Michigan and White House Office of National Drug Control Policy)

Recent (last month) use of cannabis by 15 year olds (in 1995):
15% in the Netherlands;
16% in the U.S.;
24% in the U.K.
(Sources: Trimbos Institute, Amsterdam, the Netherlands; Monitoring the Future Survey, University of Michigan and White House Office of National Drug Control Policy; Council of Europe, ESPAD Report)

Any lifetime use of cannabis by 15 year olds (in 1995):
29% in the Netherlands;
34% in the U.S.;
41% in the U.K.
(Sources: Netherlands Institute of Health and Addiction; U.S. National Institute for Drug Abuse; Council of Europe, ESPAD Report)

Heroin addicts as a percentage of population (in 1995):
160 per 100,000 in the Netherlands;
430 per 100,000 in the U.S.
(Sources: Netherlands Ministry of Health, Welfare and Sport; White House Office of National Drug Control Policy)

Murder rate as a percentage of population (in 1996):
1.8 per 100,000 in the Netherlands;

Figure 8.3. Drug Use Statistics: A Comparison

8.22 in the U.S.
(Sources: Netherlands Bureau of Statistics; White House Office of National Drug Control Policy)

Incarceration rate as a percentage of population (1997):
73 per 100,000 in the Netherlands;
645 per 100,000 in the U.S.
(Sources: Netherlands Ministry of Justice; White House Office of National Drug Control Strategy)

Crime-related deaths as a percentage of population:
1.2 per 100,000 in the Netherlands (1994);
8.2 per 100,000 in the U.S. (1995)
(Sources: World Health Organization; Uniform Crime Reports, U.S. Federal Bureau of Investigation)

Per capita spending on drug-related law enforcement:
$27 per capita in the Netherlands;
$81 per capita in the U.S.
(Sources: Netherlands Ministry of Justice; White House Office of National Drug Control Strategy)

Source: "Drug Use Statistics: A Comparison," available at www.netherlands-embassy.org/c_drugstat.html (accessed on 10 May 2001).

Figure 8.3. ***(continued)***

- Bad laws breed hypocrisy. As part of their punishment, many celebrities convicted of drug law violations have been required to publicly condemn use. The rationale is that celebrities are role models, thus highly persuasive. But many become repeat offenders. Their audiences may surmise not that drug use is evil but, rather, that simulated remorse reduces penalties.
- Unfairly administered laws breed resentment. The unfortunate few people arrested for drug crimes (in percentage of user terms, not absolute numbers) must feel unfairly treated.
- Bad laws breed disrespect for law. Law-abiding citizens, by definition, do not break laws. An otherwise law-abiding citizen who breaks a law probably feels less concern about breaking other laws.

CONCLUDING COMMENTS: MISCELLANEOUS CONSIDERATIONS

Here are some interesting statistics: The average number of pupils per public school teacher, nationwide, is thirty; the average number of prisoners per prison guard, nationwide, is three. Two percent of American children have at least one parent in prison.[86]

More than one-third of AIDS cases occur among injection drug users (IDUs), their heterosexual sex partners, and children whose mothers were IDUs or sex partners of IDUs.[87] The rate of IDU-associated AIDS is especially high for minorities: per 100,000 members of the population, the rate is 3.5 for whites, 21.9 for Hispanics, and 50.9 for African Americans.[88]

The enormous profits from the drug trade have enticed the participation of people in several Latin American countries. Exportation of illegal drugs contributes mightily to the economies of Bolivia and Peru and accounts for between one-quarter and one-third of Colombia's exports.[89] It has also led to the killing of thousands of people in those countries.[90]

The United States financed a campaign to spray at least one hundred twenty-five thousand acres of southern Colombia's opium, poppy, and coca fields with the herbicide glyphosate. Many villagers within proximity to the spraying became ill, complaining of nausea, dizziness, vomiting, rashes, blurred vision, and ear and stomach aches. Rohter and Williams cite evidence that glyphosate and related substances impair immune systems, thus increasing the risk of contracting various cancers.[91] Spraying also killed more than twenty-five thousand rainbow trout in fish farms and small animals such as chickens and guinea pigs. Larger farm animals such as cows and horses fell sick. Fields of beans, onions, garlic, potatoes, and corn were inadvertently sprayed, killing the plants. Farmers who had acceded to government pleas to abandon poppy growing were left with nothing.

The wars on drugs have not been total failures. For some they have provided glorious adventure, and for others, have been a financial boon. See chapter 11 for details. Surveys reveal that most Americans want the wars prosecuted even more vigorously, with stiffer penalties for possession and sale of illicit drugs.[92]

NOTES

1. See Charles Whitebread, "The History of the Non-medical Use of Drugs in the United States," available at www.hempfarm.org/Papers/History_of_Drugs_in_the_US.html (accessed on 1 December 2002).

2. Whitebread, "The History of the Non-medical Use of Drugs in the United States."

3. J. Inciardi, *The War on Drugs: Heroin, Cocaine, Crime, and Public Policy* (Palo Alto: Mayfield Publishing Co., 1986), 22.

4. Inciardi, *The War on Drugs,* 72.

5. E. Schlosser, "The Politics of Pot: A Government in Denial," *Rolling Stone Magazine,* 4 March 1999: 47–52; FBI, *Crime in the United States* (Washington, D.C.: FBI, 1997), 221.

6. J. Zeidenberg et al., *America's One Million Nonviolent Offenders* (Washington, D.C.: Justice Policy Institute, 1999).

7. "Prohibition: The So-Called War on Drugs," available at www.cia.com.au/serendipity/wod.html (accessed on 2 January 2001).

8. C. Rydell and S. Everingham, *Controlling Cocaine,* prepared for the Office of National Drug Control Policy and the United States Army (Santa Monica: Drug Policy Research Center, RAND, 1994).

9. U.S. Department of Justice, Office of Justice Programs, Bureau of Justice Statistics, *Substance Abuse and Treatment, State and Federal Prisoners, 1997, 1999,* Correctional Populations in the United States, 1995: Executive Summary, NCJ-163917 (Washington, D.C.: U.S. Department of Justice, Office of Justice Programs, Bureau of Justice Statistics, July 1997), 10.

10. G. Oxman et al., "Heroin Overdose Deaths—Multnomah County, Oregon, 1993–1999," *Morbidity and Mortality Weekly Report* 49 (2000): 633–36.

11. J. Ostrowski, "The Moral and Practical Case for Drug Legalization," *Hofstra Law Review* 18 (1990): 607, 685.

12. White House Office of National Drug Control Policy, "Fact Sheet: Drug Data Summary," available at www.whitehousedrugpolicy.gov (accessed on 2 January 2001).

13. S. Duke and A. Gross, *America's Longest War: Re-thinking Our Tragic Crusade against Drugs* (New York: G. P. Putnam, 1994)

14. E. Schlosser, "The Prison-Industrial Complex," *Atlantic Monthly,* December 1998: 51–77.

15. The only two drugs that routinely victimize nonusers are legal. The health consequences of secondhand smoke are substantial. See page 190. Alcohol increases aggressive tendencies and has been implicated in murders and domestic violence. See National Commission on the Causes and Prevention of Violence, *Crimes of Violence* (Washington, D.C.: Government Printing Office, 1970); and B. Miller, "The Interrelationships between Alcohol and Drugs and Family Violence," in *Drugs and Violence: Causes, Correlates, and Consequences,* ed. M. De la Rosa et al., NIDA Research Monograph 103 (Bethesda, Md.: National Institute on Drug Abuse, 1990). Fell estimates that the risk of a fatal automobile crash, per mile driven, is about eight times higher for legally drunk drivers than sober ones; and many of the victims have not been drinking. See J. Fell, "Alcohol Involvement Rates in Fatal Crashes: A Focus on Young Drivers and Female Drivers," presented at the 31st Annual Conference of the American Association for Automotive Medicine, New Orleans, 1987.

16. Substance Abuse and Mental Health Services Administration, *National Household Survey on Drug Abuse* (Washington, D.C.: Office of Applied Studies, 1997); M. Abraham et al., *Licit and Illicit Drug Use in the Netherlands* (Leiden: Center for Drug Research, University of Amsterdam, 1997).

17. G. Brown and L. Silverman, "The Retail Price of Heroin: Estimation and Application," *Journal of the American Statistical Association* 69 (1974): 595–606.

18. Associated Press, "Swiss Heroin Program Has Good Results," 11 July 1997.

19. D. Burnham, "The FBI," *The Nation,* 11 August 1997: 15–16.

20. B. Benson and D. Rasmussen, *Independent Policy Report: Illicit Drugs and Crime* (Oakland: Independent Institute, 1996).

21. "Friedman and Szasz on Liberty and Drugs" (interview), *America's Drug Forum,* 1991.

22. R. Miller, *Drug Warriors and Their Prey: From Police Power to Police State* (Westport, Conn.: Praeger, 1996).

23. T. Hearn, "ESPN, VH1 Drug Tales Earned $1.7M in Ads," *Multichannel News,* 14 February 2000; P. Albiniak, "McCaffrey Turns to the Movies," *Broadcasting and Cable,* 17 July 2000.

24. Available at http://com-notes.house.gov/cchear/hearings106.nsf/a317d879d32c08c2852567d300539946/58e114bc0e99843185256965007030 6b?OpenDocument (accessed on 1 December 2002).

25. "Bookstore Battles Narcs' Request for Sales Records," *San Francisco Chronicle,* 26 November 2000: A9.

26. Duke and Gross, *America's Longest War*; A. Trebach, *The Great Drug War, and Radical Proposals That Could Make America Safe Again* (New York: Macmillan, 1987).

27. Administrative Office of the U.S. Courts, "1999 Wiretap Report" (Washington, D.C.: Government Printing Office, 2000), 17.

28. L. Gay, "White House Drug Office Tracks Computer Visitors," *Scripps Howard News Service,* 20 June 2000.

29. Miller, *Drug Warriors and Their Prey.*

30. E. Blumenson and E. Nilsen, "Policing for Profit: The Drug War's Hidden Economic Agenda," *University of Chicago Law Review* 65 (14 January 1997): 35–114.

31. Miller, *Drug Warriors and Their Prey.*

32. See Blumenson and Nilsen, "Policing for Profit."

33. Miller, *Drug Warriors and Their Prey.*

34. M. Healy, "Parents Reach Out to Informant Daughter," *Los Angeles Times,* 9 September 1999: A3.

35. Zeidenberg et al., *America's One Million Nonviolent Offenders.*

36. Zeidenberg et al., *America's One Million Nonviolent Offenders.*

37. Associated Press, "Health Experts: Treat, Don't Jail, Drug Abusers," *Dallas Morning News,* 18 March 1998.

38. Schlosser, "The Prison-Industrial Complex."

39. S. Abramsky, "When They Get Out," *Atlantic Monthly,* June 1999: 30–36.

40. J. Petersilia et al., *Prisons vs. Probation in California* (Santa Monica: Rand Corporation, 1981).

41. Schlosser, "The Prison-Industrial Complex," 76.

42. General Accounting Office, *Law Enforcement: Information on Drug-Related Police Corruption,* No. GGD-98-111 (Washington, D.C.: General Accounting Office, 1998), letter 3.1.

43. Page: 18 Available at www.ndsn.org/JULAUG/LAWENF1.html (accessed on 1 December 2002).

44. Commission on Police Integrity, *History of Police Corruption in the United States* (Chicago: Commission on Police Integrity, November 1997), 1.

45. Associated Press, "Drug Inquiry Leads to Prison System's Officers," 10 January 1999.

46. "Customs Admits Its Own Drug Corruption," *New York Times,* 17 February 1999: A13.

47. *Fort Worth Star-Telegram,* 1999 March 8.

48. *Fort Worth Star-Telegram,* 1999 March 8; Pauline Arrillaga, "Six Law Officers Indicted on Drug Charges," Associated Press, available at http://users.tpg.com.au/sparks07/vicstor8.html.

49. The White House, *National Drug Control Strategy* (Washington, D.C.: Government Printing Office, 1989).

50. C. Reinarman and H. Levine, "The Crack Attack: Politics and Media in the Crack Scare," in *Crack in America, Demon Drugs and Social Justice,* ed. C. Reinarman and H. Levine (Berkeley: University of California Press, 1997), 22–23.

51. M. Tonry, *Malign Neglect—Race, Crime, and Punishment* (New York: Oxford University Press, 1995).

52. "The Prison Paradox." Newsweek, 13 November 2000: 40–49.

53. American Civil Liberties Union, press release, 12 October 2000.

54. K. Zeese, "Housing: The New Battleground in the War on Drugs," *Drug Policy Letter,* July–August 1989.

55. Noelle Bush, daughter of Florida Governor Jeb Bush, was arrested in January 2002 and charged with trying to buy a controlled substance (Xanax) with a fraudulent prescription. She called it in while posing as a doctor. Drug prescription fraud is a felony that carries a maximum penalty of five years in prison and a $5,000 fine. She was admitted to a drug treatment program. The governor was not evicted from his government-owned housing.

56. C. Lusane, "In Perpetual Motion: The Continuing Significance of Race and America's Drug Crisis," *University of Chicago Law Review,* January 1994: 96; P. Thomas and P. Davis, "Young Dealers Slip through the Loopholes: Drug Laws, Parental Denial Leave Teens Few Deterrents," *Washington Post,* 15 December 1997: A1; Department of Justice, Office of Justice Programs, Bureau of Justice Statistics, *Sourcebook of Criminal Justice Statistics 1997* (Washington, D.C.: Department of Justice, Office of Justice Programs, Bureau of Justice Statistics, 1998).

57. Zeidenberg et al., *America's One Million Nonviolent Offenders.*

58. M. Mauer and J. Fellner, *Losing the Vote: The Impact of Felony Disenfranchisement Laws in the United States* (New York: Human Rights Watch and the Sentencing Project, October 1998).

59. J. Rushton, *Race, Evolution, and Behavior* (Port Huron, Mich.: Charles Darwin Research Institute, 2000).

60. T. Duster, "Genetics, Race, and Crime: Recurring Seduction to a False Precision," in *DNA on Trial: Genetic Information and Criminal Justice,* ed. P. Billings (Plainview, N.Y.: Cold Spring Harbor Press, 1992), 133.

61. W. Elwood, *The Rhetoric of the War on Drugs: The Triumphs and Tragedies of Public Relations* (Westport, Conn.: Praeger Publishers, 1994).

62. A. Adams and G. Cown, "The Human Guinea Pig: How We Test New Drugs," *World,* 5 December 1972: 21.

63. M. Behnke and F. Eyler, "Rural Pregnant Cocaine Users: An In-Depth Sociodemographic Comparison," *Journal of Drug Issues* 27 (1997): 501.

64. D. Frank et al., "Growth, Development, and Behavior in Early Childhood Following Prenatal Cocaine Exposure: A Systematic Review," *Journal of the American Medical Association* (*JAMA*) 285 (2001): 1620–21.

65. A. Kral et al., "HIV Seroprevalence among Street-Recruited Injection Drug and Crack Cocaine Users in 16 U.S. Municipalities," *American Journal of Public Health* (1998): 108–13; Centers for Disease Control and Prevention, *HIV/AIDS Surveillance Report: U.S. HIV and AIDS Cases through December 1997* (Atlanta: Department of Health and Human Services, Public Health Service, 1998).

66. C. Schneider, "Racism, Drug Policy, and AIDS," *Political Science Quarterly* 113 (1998): 431–32.

67. Schneider, "Racism, Drug Policy, and AIDS."

68. "Run-on Sentencing," *The New Republic,* 26 April 1999: 57–65.

69. S. Sporkin, "Impact of Sentencing Guidelines on Federal Courts," presented at Symposium on 10th Anniversary of Sentencing Guidelines, Judiciary Committee, Washington, D.C., 9 September 1997.

70. Blumenson and Nilsen, "Policing for Profit."

71. Miller, *Drug Warriors and Their Prey.*

72. E. Schlosser, "More Reefer Madness," *Atlantic Monthly* 279 (April 1997): 90–102; Schlosser, "The Politics of Pot."

73. E. Komp, "Downey Case Illuminates Drug War Injustice, Hypocrisy," The Lindesmith Center, 23 January 2001, available at www.drugpolicy.org/news/01_23_01downey2.cfm (accessed on 15 December 2002).

74. We should not place too much faith in survey data, especially surveys concerning illegal, stigmatized activities. For the past thirty years, the *National Household Survey* (*NHS*) has been the primary source of information concerning drug use in the U.S. adult civilian population. But the NHS excludes prisoners, people living in residential drug treatment centers, and the homeless, all of whom have higher than average rates of illicit drug use. So its figures probably consistently underestimate. Contrast the 1990 *NHS* estimates of heavy cocaine and heroin use (662,000 and 200,000 users, respectively) with estimates from a Senate Judiciary Committee study (2.4 million and 1 million). See J. Kelly, "Senator: Survey 'Wildly off the Mark,'" *USA Today,* 20 December 1990: A6.

75. For LSD and mescaline, see F. Leavitt, *Drugs and Behavior,* 3d edition (Thousand Oaks, Calif.: Sage Publications, 1995). For LSD and MDMA, see L. Grinspoon and J. Bakalar, "Can Drugs Be Used to Enhance the Psychotherapeutic Process?" *American Journal of Psychotherapy* 40 (1986): 393–404. For marijuana, see L. Grinspoon, "Whither Medical Marijuana?" *Contemporary Drug Problems* 27 (spring 2000): 3–15 (ADAI jl); and L. Grinspoon and J. Bakalar, *Marihuana, the Forbidden Medicine* (New Haven: Yale University Press, 1997).

76. R. Mechoulam, ed., *Cannabinoids as Therapeutic Agents* (Boca Raton, Fla.: CRC Press, 1986).

77. S. Cohen et al., "Psychological Stress and Susceptibility to the Common Cold," *New England Journal of Medicine* 325 (1991): 606–12; L. Young et al., "Disorders of the Upper Gastrointestinal System: An Overview," *Annals of Behavioral Medicine* 9 (1987): 7–12; S. Maier and L. Watkins, "Cytokines for Psychologists—Implications of Bidirectional Immune-to-Brain Communication for Understanding Behavior, Mood, and Cognition," *Psychological Review* 105 (1998): 83–107; S. Patterson et al., "Stress-Induced Hemoconcentration of Blood Cells and Lipids in Healthy Women during Acute Psychological Stress," *Health Psychology* 14 (1995): 319–24.

78. *San Francisco Chronicle,* 3 April 1971.

79. A. Trebach, "'Socialist Realism' in the Service of the Drug War," *Drug Policy Letter,* May–June 1991.

80. "What the WHO Doesn't Want You to Know about Marijuana," *New Scientist,* 21 February 1998: 4.

81. "Highwitness News," *High Times,* April 1984: 19, 27.

82. C. Selzer, "Second Thoughts: 'Conflicts of Interest' and 'Political Science,'" *Journal of Clinical Epidemiology* 50 (1997): 627–29.

83. Thomas Szasz, *Our Right to Drugs: The Case for a Free Market* (Westport, Conn.: Praeger, 1992), 90.

84. M. Ieikoff, "DEA Set Up Cocaine Purchase for Bush's War-on-Drugs Speech: DEA Lured Seller to Lafayette Park," *Washington Post,* 23 September 1989: A2.

85. M. Kinsley, "TRB: Regrets Only," *New Republic,* 4 April 1990: 49.

86. D. Baum, *Smoke and Mirrors: The War on Drugs and the Politics of Failure* (Boston: Little, Brown and Co., 1996).

87. Centers for Disease Control and Prevention, *HIV/AIDS Surveillance Report, 1995* (Atlanta: Department of Health and Human Services, Public Health Service, 1996).

88. Centers for Disease Control and Prevention, "AIDS Associated with Injecting-Drug Use—United States, 1995," *MMWR: Morbidity and Mortality Weekly Report* 45 (1996): 392–98.

89. L. Rohter, "Colombia Adjusts Economic Figures to Include Its Drug Crops," *New York Times,* 27 June 1999: A3.

90. "Friedman and Szasz on Liberty and Drugs."

91. L. Rohter, "To Colombians, Drug War Is a Toxic Foe," *New York Times,* 1 May 2000: A1, A10; W. Williams, "Killing More Than Coca: Opposition Mounts to Spraying in Colombia," *The American Prospect Online,* 6 August 2001, available at www.prospect.org/webfeatures/2001/08/williams-we-08-06.html.

92. R. Blendon and J. Young, "The Public and the War on Illicit Drugs," *JAMA* 279 (1998): 827–32.

9

Many Drugs Are Dangerous

Virtually any discovery with the power to change people's perspectives about the world has the capacity to do harm. But so many lives have been shattered by improper drug use that the topic of dangers should not be ignored. To do otherwise would be irresponsible. On the other hand, the harms done by various illegal drugs are magnified by their illegality. Therefore, in my view, criminalization is itself criminal (*criminal,* adj. shameful; disgraceful—*American College Dictionary,* 2d edition).

DANGERS BECAUSE OF THE LAW

Users of illegal drugs risk huge financial losses and imprisonment. They buy from sellers unconcerned with truth-in-packaging laws who frequently adulterate their products with dangerous substances. The adulterant problem is magnified when people inject drugs, because injections bypass stomach enzymes and other mechanisms for detoxifying impurities. The illegality of drug paraphernalia makes needles a precious commodity and encourages sharing of unsterile needles. This increases vulnerability to hepatitis, endocarditis, pneumonia, septicemia, and AIDS. Other dangers of illegality are indicated on pages 147–48.

DANGERS BECAUSE OF SMOKING

Smoked substances enter the bloodstream and brain rapidly to produce intense effects, so inhalation is a preferred route of administration for many psychoactive drugs. But drugs undergo chemical reactions when heated to high temperatures in the presence of air, and the resulting compounds often have different toxicities than the parents.[1] Smoking anything exposes the throat and lungs to abnormal heat, and habitual smoking leads to pulmonary problems.

DANGERS BECAUSE OF DRIVING

Drugs that affect psychomotor skills or judgment are likely to affect driving. Fell estimates that the risk of a fatal crash, per mile driven, is about eight times higher for legally drunk drivers (blood alcohol concentration of 0.10 or greater in most jurisdictions) than sober ones.[2] Yet 6.1 percent of U.S. adults have admitted to driving at least once a month when they have had too much to drink.[3]

In blood samples taken from 2,500 injured drivers, alcohol was the drug detected most frequently. Metabolites of marijuana were detected in many drivers; benzodiazepines and stimulants were detected infrequently. Drivers testing positive for alcohol or benzodiazepines were more likely than drug-free drivers to be culpable for the crash. Drivers testing positive for marijuana alone or stimulants alone did not show increased culpability.[4]

DANGERS BECAUSE OF DEPENDENCE

Physical dependence and withdrawal as isolated phenomena are trivial. The narcotic antagonists produce physical dependence but are not abused, whereas many abused drugs—cocaine, lysergic acid diethylamide (LSD), amphetamine, and marijuana among them—produce no or mild physical dependence. Hospital patients made dependent on morphine are not threats to society; but detoxified and hence no longer dependent addicts are still regarded as addicts. Diabetics are physically dependent on insulin. Everybody is physically dependent on food and air. Problems arise only if a drug produces adverse effects or is illegal or expensive, thus requiring users to undertake risky behaviors to obtain it.

Psychological dependence occurs for the simple reason that living organisms try to repeat pleasurable experiences. Dependence also occurs with TV watching, parties, concerts, and sports events. The common thread is that the particular activities bring pleasure. Psychologists accept as a fundamental principle that living organisms try to repeat their pleasurable experiences. Many drugs taken improperly are harmful, but not because of their capacity for giving pleasure. Dependence on anything is of concern if it interferes with normal functioning, but people who impair themselves by voluntarily self-administering massive quantities of drugs must have had problems that preceded drug use. Dependence with impairment is a symptom rather than a cause.

Suppose that scientists develop a drug that increases intelligence, health, creativity, and mood and has no negative side effects. Suppose that the materials for producing the drug are inexpensive and plentiful. Suppose that the drug produces physical and psychological dependence. If such a drug is ever developed, some people will undoubtedly demand that it be made illegal. I see no moral or other reason to justify that position. Dependence by itself is not a problem.

DANGERS TO THE EMBRYO, FETUS, AND DEVELOPING YOUNG

Developing organisms are sensitive to unusual stimuli, including drugs. Some drugs are directly toxic to the fetus, some interfere with fetal metabolism, and some exert effects on the fetus similar to those on the mother. Most substances in the maternal blood cross the placenta, and many reach higher concentrations in fetal than maternal circulation. Low birth weight is the most frequent and clearly documented adverse outcome associated with fetal exposure to a variety of licit and illicit drugs.[5]

Women do not bear the sole burden for the health of their babies. Drugs taken by men prior to mating may damage sperm, change the volume or composition of seminal fluid, remain within the seminal fluid, bind to spermatozoa and be transported into an ovum, or reduce the man's body weight or testosterone level. All of these factors can affect fetal development.[6]

EVALUATING EVIDENCE OF DANGERS

Determining the dangers of drugs is problematic. Estimates of frequency and patterns of use are probably not very accurate, especially for illicit drugs; and many users do not report adverse effects. The media, however, publicize even low-quality studies that report harms. When adverse effects do occur, the reason is often difficult to determine. Effects may be caused by the drug, the wrong dose of the drug, an impurity, or some other drug taken concurrently by a polydrug user. There are further complications:

- Beneficial and side effects may occur at similar doses. Amphetamine taken to control appetite causes insomnia as a side effect. Amphetamine taken to help a person stay awake causes the side effect of appetite suppression.
- All drugs have a therapeutic window—a range between the therapeutic and toxic doses. Because people vary, doses within one person's therapeutic window may be toxic to another.
- Some drugs are effective in extremely small doses. For example, the recreational dose of LSD is about 100 micrograms. One-ounce (about 28 million

micrograms) spice tins hold enough LSD for 280,000 trips. Even with sensitive equipment, it is easy to make a dosage error. Errors are also common when illegal drugs are bought on the street.

- Many drugs that are safe when taken alone interact adversely with other drugs.
- Many drugs are safe for most people but provoke severe hypersensitivity reactions in some.
- Some drugs, such as tobacco, produce few acute effects in experienced users but great harm when taken chronically.

EXPERIMENTAL VERSUS CORRELATIONAL STUDIES

Consider a hypothetical research project in which 100 volunteers are randomly assigned to receive either a caffeine pill or an identical-looking placebo. That is, each volunteer has an equal chance of getting caffeine or placebo, to be determined by a random process such as flipping a coin. While waiting for the caffeine to take effect, the researcher asks the volunteers whether they smoke. Half of the people in each group are nonsmokers, and half smoke exactly one pack per day. (Hypothetical data are great to work with.) The four groups of twenty-five are asked to lift weights, with the following results:

1. caffeine/smoker	100 pounds lifted
2. caffeine/nonsmoker	80 pounds lifted
3. placebo/smoker	60 pounds lifted
4. placebo/nonsmoker	40 pounds lifted

Comparing groups 1 and 2 with 3 and 4 gives the difference between caffeine and placebo, independent of smoking habits. Comparing 1 and 3 with 2 and 4 gives the difference between smokers and nonsmokers, independent of caffeine.

Assuming that the study was well done (another virtue of hypothetical research) and the data are statistically significant, what conclusions can be drawn about the effects of caffeine and smoking on weight-lifting ability?

It is possible that all the heavy lifters received caffeine, and the weaklings, placebo, but random assignment makes such an outcome very unlikely. The researcher could safely assume that the subjects were approximately equal in weight-lifting ability prior to swallowing their pills. So subsequent differences between them would be best explained as a caffeine effect. If a study had actually been done with the results indicated, the researcher could be confident that caffeine increases weight-lifting ability.

But subjects were not randomly assigned to the smoking/nonsmoking groups. They had selected themselves prior to participating in the study because of factors such as gender, genetics, stress, exposure to cigarette advertising, and desire to project a certain image. Those same or other unknown factors may have made them unequal in weight-lifting ability at the outset. If a study had been done with the results indicated, the researcher could safely conclude that smokers can outlift nonsmokers but not that smoking is the reason.

Consider the results of a real study. Puccio and colleagues asked people about their caffeine consumption.[7] Drinkers of caffeinated coffee were less healthy than others, which suggests that coffee drinking impairs health. But drinkers of caffeinated coffee were more likely than nondrinkers to smoke tobacco. They also drank more alcohol, had more saturated fats and cholesterol in their diets, and exercised less. Even if coffee were a health drink, coffee drinkers might be less healthy.

The example illustrates a major difficulty in assessing dangers of drugs. Only results from carefully controlled experiments justify statements such as "Drug X causes symptom Y." Experiments require that subjects be randomly assigned to groups. Random assignment is not a feature of correlational studies. Users and nonusers always differ, and they differed before anyone became a user. It is a logical necessity. Otherwise, either everybody or nobody would use. The initial differences, rather than the drug, might account for other differences between users and nonusers. The limitations of correlational studies should be kept in mind when reading the sections below on coffee drinking, smoking, and suicide.

CASE STUDIES

Consider another hypothetical situation. A psychiatrist reports that over the course of a year she treated ten patients whose lives were disrupted by cocaine. Each had been living a normal existence until a friend offered cocaine. Each then rapidly deteriorated. The psychiatrist concludes that cocaine causes rapid deterioration. Assuming that all the patients are telling the truth, is cocaine dangerous?

Case studies have a long tradition in clinical medicine and psychology. When an individual with unusual symptoms presents him- or herself to a clinical investigator, the investigator typically hypothesizes about possible causes. The first evidence of a smoking/cancer link might have been a 1761 report by Dr. John Hill that two snuff users had swellings of the nose that he believed cancerous.

But although they stimulate ideas, case studies do not establish causes. Knowing that patients with a particular set of symptoms have been exposed to certain stimuli does not justify the conclusion that the stimuli caused the symptoms. If 999 of 1,000 people were to die within a week of receiving a procedure called LR, that would not prove that LR is deadly. LR is my abbreviation for last rites.

Except under rare circumstances, case studies are incapable of showing causal relationships; in fact, they cannot even establish correlations. They do not provide enough information. In the hypothetical example, ten patients used cocaine and had their lives deteriorate. But lots of people use cocaine without developing problems, and lots of nonusers have their lives deteriorate. In order to make any association between cocaine use and subsequent problems, we would have to know the number of cocaine users who do not develop problems and the number of nonusers who do.

DANGERS OF SPECIFIC DRUGS

Much of the information that follows has been taken from the National Institute of Drug Abuse website at www.nida.nih.gov/ResearchReports. For alcohol, caffeine, and nicotine, see pages 185–90.

Amphetamine

Most stimulants do not produce tolerance, but amphetamine and structurally similar drugs such as methamphetamine are exceptions. The usual therapeutic dose is about 10 milligrams, but addicts have taken as much as 1,700 milligrams without ill effect.[8] Withdrawal after high-dose bingeing is marked by depression, anxiety, agitation, and a period of reduced energy that sometimes lasts for weeks. The main problems following moderate use are insomnia and irritability, but high doses damage nerve terminals in the dopamine- and serotonin-containing regions of the brain.[9] They can cause convulsions and dangerously elevated body temperature. Sustained high-dose intravenous use leads to a psychotic state almost indistinguishable from paranoid schizophrenia. The paranoia can result in homicidal and suicidal thoughts.

Cocaine

Even low doses of cocaine constrict blood vessels and increase blood pressure and heart rate. The changes can set off cardiac arrest or seizures followed by respiratory arrest and death, especially in people with hypertension or cardiac problems. But most cocaine-induced heart attack victims have no known history of heart disease.[10] Frequent snorting inflames the mucous membranes of the nose. Other medical complications include chest pain, strokes, seizure, headaches, abdominal pain, and nausea.

High doses of cocaine cause tremors, vertigo, and muscle twitches. Many cocaine users go on binges, taking it repeatedly and in increasingly high doses over a period of several hours or days; paranoid psychosis, in which the user experiences auditory hallucinations, is a common outcome. The paranoia in combination with a temporary increase in energy often leads to violence.

Heroin and Other Opioids

Heroin is less harmful than generally believed. Brecher reported that officials of the U.N. Commission on Narcotic Drugs were unable to cite a single study or offer any data on harmful effects.[11] He devotes a chapter to highly successful people with long-standing addictions.

But heroin is not harmless. Since the publication of Brecher's 1972 book, researchers have identified several medical consequences of chronic heroin abuse. These include depressed immune systems, which probably increase susceptibility to many types of infections; scarred and collapsed veins; and liver and kidney disease.[12] Opioids reduce sensitivity to pain, so users may remain unaware of a disease until it has progressed to a dangerous stage.

Rapid tolerance develops to all opioids except opium, and withdrawal is painful and prolonged. Symptoms include restlessness, muscle and bone pain, insomnia, diarrhea, vomiting, cold flashes with goose bumps, and involuntary leg movements.

Heroin addicts often neglect to take care of themselves, and their poor health makes them vulnerable to lung complications such as pneumonia and tuberculosis. Many additives in street heroin do not readily dissolve; they clog blood vessels, causing infection or even death of cells in vital organs. Immune reactions to additives can cause arthritis or other rheumatologic problems.

Inhalants

Inhalants include antifreeze, cleaning agents, gasoline, kerosene, lighter fluid, spray paints, paint thinner, glues, nail polish remover, deodorant, hair sprays, and industrial solvents such as toluene. Even one session of repeated inhalant abuse can cause death from cardiac arrest or suffocation. Regular abuse can harm vital organs including the brain, heart, kidneys, and liver.

Marijuana

Perhaps in no scientific arena of discussion are biases more clearly displayed than in that on the adverse effects of marijuana. Tennant and Groesbeck characterized heavy users as suffering from apathy, dullness, lethargy, and impairment of judgment, with the implication that marijuana was the cause.[13] But heavy use was defined as smoking seventeen to 200 marijuana cigarettes per day (200 per day over sixteen waking hours is about one every five minutes). The amount is so excessive that the pre-marijuana apathy, dullness, and judgment should certainly have been questioned.

Adverse effects do occur. Smoking is the most popular route of administration, and, as indicated above, smoking anything is unhealthy. Frequent marijuana smokers develop chronic cough and wheezing. Changes occur primarily in the lung's large airways, not the small ones, so they are less serious than changes induced by tobacco smoking; inflammation of the small airways is what causes emphysema.[14] Marijuana smokers may, however, have an increased risk of developing lung cancer.[15]

Nahas and others reported that marijuana impairs the immune system and thus increases the risk of contracting various infectious diseases.[16] Other scientists who repeated the study failed to replicate the findings.[17] There is no clinical or epidemiological evidence that users increase their susceptibility to infections, AIDS, or other diseases.[18] Marijuana temporarily impairs memory but probably has no long-term negative effects on cognitive functions.[19]

3,4-Methylenedioxymethamphetamine (MDMA or Ecstasy)

Ecstasy increases body temperature. When people take it at raves and dance for hours at a time in crowded rooms, they may become dehydrated and hyperthermic. A few people have died after ignoring the danger signs and continuing to dance until they collapsed. More common, milder side effects of MDMA include insomnia, nausea, tight jaw muscles, dry mouth, trouble concentrating, and tremor. High doses of MDMA and related drugs deplete brain serotonin, but no functional or behavioral abnormalities have been reported.[20]

As with many drugs purchased illegally, street MDMA is often impure. Thus, dosage calculations may be incorrect, and some contaminants are dangerous.[21]

Psychedelics

Not all drug experiences turn out as anticipated. Unpleasant outcomes occur often enough to make the term *bad trip* part of the drug culture lexicon. Any potentially enjoyable event may disappoint, as when rainy weather spoils a picnic, but drug users cannot simply run for cover. Bad trips are not easily terminated. The effects of LSD and related drugs last for several hours, and experiences that start out enjoyably sometimes become terrifying.

Concerns have been raised that LSD damages chromosomes, causes brain damage, and leads to prolonged psychosis. The weight of the evidence indicates that the concerns are unfounded.[22]

Steroids

Anabolic steroids—synthetic derivatives of male hormones—enhance athletic performance and muscular appearance. But they increase the risk of heart attack, stroke, liver problems, and sterility and cause breast development and testicular atrophy in men and masculinization of the body in women and hair loss in both sexes. Behavioral effects include depression, irritability, and unpredictable, uncontrollable rage.

CONCLUDING COMMENTS

The wars on drugs pit government agencies against users of illicit drugs. Combatants in war do not typically give good advice to their adversaries, so government warnings about the dangers of various drugs are viewed with suspicion and often go unheeded. That is unfortunate because all psychoactive drugs (all drugs) can cause harm if used improperly. Official reports may exaggerate or mislead—but not always. Compounding the problem, some proponents of legalization have discounted real dangers.

NOTES

1. C. Chiang and R. Hawks, *Research Findings on Smoking of Abused Substances,* NIDA Research Monograph 99 (Bethesda, Md.: National Institute on Drug Abuse, 1990).
2. J. Fell, "Alcohol Involvement Rates in Fatal Crashes: A Focus on Young Drivers and Female Drivers," presented at the 31st Annual Conference of the American Association for Automotive Medicine, New Orleans, 1987.
3. M. Bradstock et al., "Drinking-Driving and Health Lifestyle in the United States: Behavioral Risk Factor Surveys," *Journal of Studies on Alcohol* 48 (1987): 147–52.
4. M. Longo et al., "The Prevalence of Alcohol, Cannabinoids, Benzodiazepines and Stimulants amongst Injured Drivers and Their Role in Driver Culpability. Part I: The Prevalence of Drug Use in Drivers, and Characteristics of the Drug-Positive Group," *Accident Analysis and Prevention* 32 (2000): 613–22; M. Longo et al., "The Prevalence of Alcohol, Cannabinoids, Benzodiazepines and Stimulants amongst Injured Drivers and Their Role in Driver Culpability. Part II: The Relationship between Drug Prevalence and Drug Concentration, and Driver Culpability," *Accident Analysis and Prevention* 32 (2000): 623–32.
5. M. Lifschitz and G. Wilson, "Patterns of Growth and Development in Narcotic-Exposed Children," in *Methodological Issues in Controlled Studies on Effects of Prenatal Exposure to Drug Abuse,* ed. M. Kilbey and K. Asghar, NIDA Research Monograph 114 (Bethesda, Md.: National Institute on Drug Abuse, 1991), 323–39.
6. J. Joffe, "Influence of Drug Exposure of the Father on Perinatal Outcome," *Clinics in Perinatology* 6 (1979): 21–36.
7. E. Puccio et al., "Clustering of Atherogenic Behaviors in Coffee Drinkers," *American Journal of Public Health* 80 (1990): 1310–13.
8. I. Innes and M. Nickerson, "Drugs Acting on Postganglionic Adrenergic Nerve Endings and Structures Innervated by Them (Sympathomimetic Drugs)," in *The Pharmacological Basis of Therapeutics,* ed. L. Goodman and A. Gilman (New York: Macmillan, 1965), 477–520.

9. G. Ricaurte and U. McCann, "Neurotoxic Amphetamine Analogues: Effects in Monkeys and Implications for Humans," *Annals of the New York Academy of Sciences* 648 (1992): 371–82; L. Seiden and G. Ricaurte, "Neurotoxicity of Methamphetamine and Related Drugs," in *Psychopharmacology: The Third Generation of Progress,* ed. H. Meltzer (New York: Raven Press, 1987), 359–66.

10. W. Bunn and A. Giannini, "Cardiovascular Complications of Cocaine Abuse," *American Family Physician* 46 (1992): 769–73.

11. E. Brecher, *Licit and Illicit Drugs* (Boston: Little, Brown, 1972).

12. M. Kreek, "Immune Function in Heroin Addicts and Former Heroin Addicts in Treatment: Pre- and Post-AIDS Epidemic," in *Drugs of Abuse: Chemistry, Pharmacology, Immunology, and Aids,* NIDA Research Monograph 96 (Bethesda, Md.: National Institute on Drug Abuse, 1990), 192–219.

13. F. Tennant and C. Groesbeck, "Psychiatric Effects of Hashish," *Archives of General Psychiatry* 27 (1972): 133–36.

14. D. P. Tashkin et al., "Longitudinal Changes in Respiratory Symptoms and Lung Function in Nonsmokers, Tobacco Smokers, and Heavy, Habitual Smokers of Marijuana with or without Tobacco," in *Marijuana: An International Research Report,* ed. G. Chesher et al. (Canberra: Australian Government Publishing Service, 1988), 25–36.

15. S. Fligiel et al., "Bronchial Pathology in Chronic Marijuana Smokers: A Light Electron Microscope Study," *Journal of Psychoactive Drugs* 20 (1988): 33–42.

16. G. Nahas et al., "Inhibition of Cellular Mediated Immunity in Marijuana Smokers," *Science* 183 (1974): 419–20.

17. R. Lau et al., "Phytohemagglutinin-Induced Lymphocyte Transformation in Humans Receiving Delta-9-Tetrahydrocannabinol," *Science* 192 (1976): 805–7; S. White et al., "Mitogen-Induced Blastogenetic Responses to Lymphocytes from Marijuana Smokers," *Science* 188 (1975): 71–72.

18. L. Hollister, "Health Aspects of Cannabis," *Pharmacological Reviews* 38 (1986): 1–20.

19. J. Page, "Psychosociocultural Perspectives on Chronic Cannabis Use: The Costa Rican Follow-Up," *Journal of Psychoactive Drugs* 20 (1988): 57–65; A. Carlin and E. Trupin, "The Effect of Long-term Chronic Marijuana Use on Neuropsychological Functioning," *International Journal of the Addictions* 12 (1977): 617–24; J. Schaeffer et al., "Cognition and Long-term Use of Ganja (Cannabis)," *Science* 213 (1981): 465–66.

20. G. Ricaurte et al., "Hallucinogenic Amphetamine Selectively Destroys Brain Serotonin Nerve Terminals," *Science* 229 (1985): 986–88; G. Ricaurte et al., "MDMA Selectively Damages Central Serotonergic Neurons in the Primate," *Journal of the American Medical Association* 260 (1988): 51–55.

21. J. Buchanan and C. Brown, "Designer Drugs: A Problem in Clinical Toxicology," *Medical Toxicology* 3 (1988): 1–17; K. Wolff et al., "Contents of 'Ecstasy,'" *Lancet* 346 (1996): 1100–01.

22. R. Strassman, "Adverse Reactions to Psychedelic Drugs: A Review of the Literature," *Journal of Nervous and Mental Disease* 172 (1984): 577–95.

10

Extensive Marketing of Alcohol, Tobacco, and Caffeine Causes Great Harm

Several psychoactive substances are legal and easily obtained in nurseries, supermarkets, and hardware stores. These include various cacti, nutmeg, and inhalants such as antifreeze and paint thinner. Most have a small margin of safety between intoxicating and toxic doses and are used only because they are more accessible than other drugs. On the other hand, three legal psychoactives rank at the top in worldwide popularity. Per-capita consumption of alcohol for adults aged fifteen and over is about 5 liters per year. Per-capita caffeine consumption is about 70 milligrams per day. About 1.2 to 1.5 billion people worldwide use tobacco.[1] Although the first two drugs are safe in moderation, excessive use of any of them can cause serious health problems. The marketing strategies of distributors of all three promote excessive use. Table 10.1 gives estimates of the number of deaths caused each year by tobacco, alcohol, and a few other substances.[2]

ALCOHOL

Excessive drinking is associated with increased risk of hypertension, memory problems, deterioration of cognitive skills, accidents such as burns and falls, and several forms of cancer. It contributes to fatty liver, alcoholic hepatitis, and cirrhosis. After chronic use of alcohol, tolerance and withdrawal symptoms invariably occur. The well-known hangover is a withdrawal symptom. Severe cases are marked by trembling, seizures, hallucinations, delirium, and death.[3] Maternal drinking during pregnancy causes incurable birth defects in approximately sixty thousand babies annually. The child may develop facial deformities and learning disabilities or, in more severe cases, Fetal Alcohol Syndrome, the leading known cause of infant mental retardation.

Table 10.1 Annual Causes of Death in the United States

Cause	Deaths
TOBACCO *Source:* 1996: "Smoking-Attributable Mortality and Years of Potential Life Lost," *Morbidity and Mortality Weekly Report* 46 (20) (23 May 1997): 449.	**430,700**
ALCOHOL *Source:* "Number of Deaths and Age-Adjusted Death Rates per 100,000 Population for Categories of Alcohol-Related (A-R) Mortality, United States and States, 1979–96," National Institute on Alcohol Abuse and Alcoholism, available at www.niaaa.nih.gov/databases/armort01.txt (accessed on 12 February 2001), citing Alcohol Epidemiologic Data System, F. Daadatmand, F. S. Stinson, B. F. Grant, and M. C. Dufour, "Surveillance Report #52: Liver Mortality in the United States, 1970–96" (Rockville, Md.: National Institute on Alcohol Abuse and Alcoholism, Division of Biometry and Epidemiology, December 1999).	**110,640**
ADVERSE REACTIONS TO PRESCRIPTION DRUGS *Source:* J. Lazarou, B. H. Pomeranz, and P. N. Corey, "Incidence of Adverse Drug Reactions in Hospitalized Patients: A Meta-analysis of Prospective Studies," *Journal of the American Medical Association* 279 (1998): 1200–1205; also letters column, "Adverse Drug Reactions in Hospitalized Patients," *Journal of the American Medical Association* 280(20) (25 November 1998), available at http://jama.ama-assn.org/issues/v280n20/ffull/jlt1125-1.html (accessed on 12 February 2001).	**32,000**
ALL LICIT AND ILLICIT DRUG-INDUCED DEATHS *Source:* Sheila L. Murphy, Centers for Disease Control, "Deaths: Final Data for 1998," *National Vital Statistics Reports* 48(11) (24 July 2000): 1, 10, available at www.cdc.gov/nchs/data/nvs48_11.pdf.	**16,926**
NONSTEROIDAL ANTI-INFLAMMATORY DRUGS SUCH AS ASPIRIN *Source:* Robyn Tamblyn, Laeora Berkson, W. Dale Jauphinee, David Gayton, Roland Grad, Allen Huang, Lisa Isaac, Peter McLeod, and Linda Snell, "Unnecessary Prescribing of NSAIDs and the Management of NSAID-Related Gastropathy in Medical Practice," *Annals of Internal Medicine* 127 (15 September 1997): 429–38, available at www.acponline.org/journals/annals/15sep97/nsaid.htm (accessed on 14 February 2001), citing J. F. Fries, "Assessing and Understanding Patient Risk," *Scandinavian Journal of Rheumatology* 92(supplement) (1992): 21–24.	**7,600**
MARIJUANA *Source:* Drug Abuse Warning Network, available at www.samhsa.gov; also see Janet E. Joy, Stanley J. Watson Jr., and John A. Benson Jr., "Marijuana and Medicine: Assessing the Science Base," Division of Neuroscience and Behavioral Research, Institute of Medicine (Washington, D.C.: National Academies Press, 1999), available at www.nap.edu/html/marimed; and U.S. Department of Justice, Drug Enforcement Administration, "In the Matter of Marijuana Rescheduling Petition" (Docket #86-22), 6 September 1988: 57.	**0**

Source: Adapted from a Common Sense for Drug Policy advertisement placed in several magazines.

On the other hand, moderate drinking protects the heart and may improve the health of middle-aged and elderly people;[4] there is no evidence that it does so in men under forty or premenopausal women. The definition of *moderate* varies somewhat but is approximately two drinks per day for men aged sixty-five or under and one drink per day for men over age sixty-five and women. One drink is equivalent to 12 ounces of beer, 5 ounces of wine, or 1.5 ounces of 80-proof liquor. Although drinking small amounts on a regular basis is beneficial, drinking large amounts sporadically is not. Unfortunately, relatively few people drink in moderation.

In the United States, 5 percent of drinkers consume 42 percent of the alcohol sold, while 70 percent of adults average less than one drink per week.[5] Hazardous drinking (defined as five or more drinks in one session) accounts for much of the alcohol industry's market and is practiced primarily by college-aged and underage youth. An American Medical Association policy paper concludes that, despite the alcohol industry's sponsorship of programs to prevent alcohol problems on college campuses and commercials to promote responsible drinking, the industry's aggressive marketing strategies counteract the educational messages and target young people.[6] The industry promotes alcohol's glamour on college campuses and makes it available at low prices. Both factors contribute to hazardous drinking.[7]

Alcohol producers expend huge amounts of money to persuade young people to drink. The nonprofit Center for Media Education has conducted research on alcohol Internet sites.[8] Many present market surveys in the guise of interactive games, chat rooms filled with promotional messages, contests, giveaways such as screensavers featuring product icons, sweepstakes, recipes for sweet drinks that appeal to novices, drinking stories, and merchandise designed to attract high school students and younger children. They use music, personalities, language, and graphic techniques attractive to young viewers. They sell alcohol products over the Web.

Alcohol producers also target minorities. A promotional campaign for "high-octane" malt liquor in African American and Latino neighborhoods prompted the San Francisco city health commissioner to comment: "It is the height of irresponsibility for the beer industry to target poor ethnic communities with these genocidal beer promotions."[9] Community leaders charged that the promotions caused social problems similar to those created by crack cocaine.

CAFFEINE

Although caffeine improves ability to perform certain manual tasks, it slows reaction time and impairs fine muscular coordination. Following ingestion of 750 or more milligrams of caffeine (about seven cups of regular coffee), users may experience restlessness, nausea, headaches, tense muscles, sleep disturbances, irregular heartbeats, ringing ears, and gastrointestinal upsets such as diarrhea. In adults, 1 gram of caffeine taken in the course of a day is likely to produce several unpleasant side effects including insomnia, restlessness, ringing in the ears, muscle tenseness, cardiac irregularities, and diarrhea.[10] Caffeine increases anxiety in anxious, depressed, and normal people.[11] Many people who complain of anxiety plus a variety of unpleasant physical symptoms but have no diagnosable disease probably ingest too much caffeine. Long-range effects on children are uncertain, but Cordes quotes many authorities who have expressed concerns about effects on bones, teeth, and overall mood.[12]

Regular coffee drinking may improve mood and prevent depression. In 1980, Kawachi and colleagues administered questionnaires about coffee and caffeine intake to 86,626 female registered nurses aged thirty-four to fifty-nine years.[13] During the next ten years, fifty-six nurses committed suicide. Women who drank at least two cups of coffee per day were significantly less likely to be victims than nondrinkers of coffee.

Most of the best-selling brands of sodas are laced with caffeine. See table 10.2. When body weight is taken into account, a six-year-old who drinks 12 ounces of soda (many vending machines dispense only the 20-ounce size) receives a caffeine dose roughly equivalent to that received by an adult who drinks 8 ounces of brewed coffee.

Soft drink manufacturers target children and adolescents. Coke and Pepsi paid school districts to sell their products exclusively on school grounds. Mountain Dew distributed free pagers. Other manufacturers gave away textbook covers, computer screensavers, and mouse pads that featured their ads and logos. Not surprisingly, per-capita consumption has increased dramatically in recent years. Children and teens drink on average more than 64 gallons of soda a year, triple the amount of twenty-five years ago.[14]

Table 10.2. Caffeine Content of Carbonated Soft Drinks (Milligrams per 12 Fluid Ounces)

Coca-Cola Classic	34
Diet Coke	42
Dr Pepper	40
Jolt	72
Josta	58
Mountain Dew	55
Pepsi	37
Pepsi One	55
Surge	51
XTC	70

The soft drink manufacturers claim that caffeine is added to sodas to improve taste, but a recent study suggests a different motive. Of twenty-five regular drinkers of cola soft drinks who passed a screening session showing that they could distinguish between Diet Coke and Coke, only two could distinguish between caffeine-free colas and identical beverages with added caffeine (to a concentration of .1 milligram per milliliter, the same as that in most cola soft drinks). The authors write, "It is valuable for the general public, the medical community, and regulatory agencies to recognize that the high rates of consumption of caffeinated soft drinks more likely reflect the mood-altering and physical dependence–producing effects of caffeine as a central nervous system–active drug than its subtle effects as a flavoring agent."[15]

Elementary school children kept a log from which they calculated their daily caffeine intake. Then they abstained from caffeine for a day. The heavy consumers (50 milligrams or more daily, most from soft drinks) reported more symptoms, such as trouble thinking clearly and lack of energy, than the light consumers (10 milligrams or less daily).[16]

Teenagers too young to go to bars hang out at coffee shops. At Starbucks, they drink coffee (about 190 milligrams of caffeine per 12-ounce cup), tea (about 75 milligrams per 12-ounce cup), or sweet coffee drinks such as Frappuccino (93 milligrams per 9.5 ounces).

TOBACCO

Nicotine has many positive effects. It reduces appetite while increasing metabolic activity, thus promoting weight loss. It facilitates certain kinds of learning and memory tasks and benefits victims of Parkinson's disease, ulcerative colitis, Alzheimer's disease, and obstructive sleep apnea. Jarvik writes that nicotine makes people feel good and would be an ideal drug if not for the harmful effects.[17] But tobacco is a major cause of cancer, heart disease, and chronic obstructive lung disease. Cigarette smoking contributes to about 90 percent of cases of lung cancer, the major cancer killer of both men and women. It also contributes to cancers of the mouth, pharynx, larynx, esophagus, stomach, pancreas, cervix, kidney, ureter, and bladder. Smoking causes lung diseases such as chronic bronchitis and emphysema and exacerbates asthma symptoms. Smoking increases the risk of heart disease, including stroke, heart attack, vascular disease, and aneurysm. Tobacco is responsible for more deaths in the United States than the combined total from AIDS, cocaine, heroin, alcohol, fire, automobile accidents, homicide, and suicide.[18] Dropped cigarettes are the leading cause of residential fire fatalities, leading to more than one thousand such deaths each year. The American College of

Chest Physicians called tobacco use the single most important preventable risk to human health in developed countries.[19]

Women who smoke during pregnancy increase their risk for premature delivery and babies of low birth weight. Smoking affects sex ratios. Fukuda and colleagues questioned parents of more than eleven thousand eight hundred babies.[20] Among nonsmoking parents, 1.2 boys were born for every girl. When either parent smoked twenty or more cigarettes per day, the ratio of boys to girls was lowered. And when both parents smoked twenty or more per day, about 0.8 boys were born for every girl. The researchers speculated that Y chromosome–bearing sperm cells are more vulnerable than X chromosome–bearing sperm to the effects of smoking.

Cigarette smokers report more problems than nonsmokers in going to sleep, staying asleep, daytime sleepiness, minor accidents, and depression.[21] Miller and colleagues kept track of 300,000 men in the U.S. Army from January 1987 through December 1996. The risk of suicide increased significantly with the number of cigarettes smoked daily.[22]

The health consequences of passive (secondary) smoking are also substantial.[23] Secondhand smoke is estimated to annually cause approximately three thousand lung cancer deaths and forty thousand deaths related to cardiovascular disease among nonsmokers. Exposure to tobacco smoke in the home is a risk factor for new cases of childhood asthma and sudden infant death syndrome.

The U.S. government, which so assiduously pursues a war on drugs, supports the tobacco industry. In 1999, as part of a broad agriculture bill, the government compensated tobacco growers $328 million for declining cigarette sales. The government sponsors a crop-insurance program to protect growers from risks and allows tobacco companies to take tax deductions for advertising costs.

Tobacco companies, like their counterparts in the alcohol and caffeine businesses, try to entice high school students and younger children to use their products. Marketing is crucial to their success, as so many of their best customers die each year and have to be replaced. So they sponsor rock concerts and sports events. They open Internet sites such as www.smokers.com and offer chat rooms, on-line smoke shops, smoking lifestyle pages, and other amenities.

Congressman Henry Waxman sent a letter to his colleagues and posted it on the Internet (www.house.gov/waxman/L_I/TOB/072998_TOB/072998_tob.html, as of 8 June 2002). He quotes from previously secret tobacco industry documents to emphasize their attempts to market cigarettes to children. Below are some excerpts:

> 1973: "Realistically, if our Company is to survive and prosper, over the long term we must get our share of the youth market. . . .Thus we need new brands designed to be particularly attractive to the young smoker." (RJR Research Planning Memorandum)

1974: "Our strategy becomes clear for our established brands: 1. Direct advertising appeal to the younger smokers." (Presentation by C. A. Tucker, RJR Vice President of Marketing, to the RJR Board of Directors)

1975: "To ensure increased and longer-term growth for CAMEL FILTER, the brand must increase its share among the 14–24 age group which have a new set of more liberal values and which represent tomorrow's cigarette business." (Memorandum to C. A. Tucker, RJR Vice President for Marketing)

1975: "The teenage years are . . . important because those are the years during which most smokers begin to smoke, the years in which initial brand selections are made, and the period in the life-cycle in which conformity to peer-group norms is greatest." (Memorandum to R. B. Seligman, Philip Morris Vice President for Research and Development)

1977: "Kool is heavily oriented toward the young. . . . [I]t will benefit us long-term to develop promotion events that involve the young and especially, to convince the starter group to smoke Kool." (Kool Brand Promotion Plan of Brown & Williamson Tobacco Corp.)

1978: "The base of our business is the high school student. . . . It is the 'In' brand to smoke if you want to be one of the group." (Memorandum to Curtis Judge, President to Lorillard Tobacco Co.)

1981: "Today's teenager is tomorrow's potential regular customer. . . . [T]he overwhelming majority of smokers first begin to smoke while still in their teens. . . . [I]t is during the teenage years that the initial brand choice is made. . . . The smoking patterns of teenagers are particularly important to Philip Morris: . . . Because of our high share of the market among the youngest smokers, Philip Morris will suffer more than the other companies from the decline in the number of teenage smokers." (Memorandum to R. B. Seligman, Philip Morris Vice President for Research and Development)

1987: "Project LF is a wider circumference non-menthol cigarette targeted at younger adult male smoker (primarily 13–24 year old male Marlboro smokers)." (RJR Marketing Memorandum)

1990: "Target smokers are approaching adulthood. . . . Their key interests include girls, cars, music, sports and dancing." (Report by Total Marketing to RJR on Camel Brand Promotion Opportunities)

The marketing works. A substantial proportion of three-year-olds linked cute cartoon character Joe Camel with cigarettes, and Camels garnered a one-third share of the youth market within three years of Joe Camel's introduction.[24] For all brands combined, about three thousand U.S. children per day become regular daily smokers.[25] Many, specifically targeted by brands like Virginia Slims, are adolescent girls. As a result lung cancer became the leading cause of cancer death among women. Rates increased by nearly 400 percent in the past twenty years.[26]

Both the tobacco and the alcohol industries seemed to bow to public pressure by launching campaigns that overtly discourage children from using their products. But the ads, which minimize or ignore health dangers while presenting smoking and drinking as sophisticated, adult activities, actually promote use.[27]

The tobacco industry also targets African Americans, Hispanics, and Asians. Black-owned and black-oriented magazines receive proportionately more revenues from cigarette advertising than other consumer magazines do. In addition, stronger, mentholated brands are more commonly advertised in black- than white-oriented magazines.[28]

Billboards advertising tobacco products are placed in African American communities four to five times more often than in white communities. Hispanics, especially in low-income communities, are targeted.[29] Tobacco companies sponsor community festivals and fairs. An analysis of four New Jersey cities has found that most billboards in racial/ethnic communities promoted alcoholic beverages and tobacco products.[30]

In 1998, a lawsuit against the tobacco industry was filed on behalf of African American smokers. The suit accuses the industry of targeting blacks for sales of menthol cigarettes. The lawsuit claims that menthol compounds, when burned, create additional toxic substances that make such cigarettes more dangerous. Blacks account for about 10 percent of all U.S. cigarette smokers but 60 to 70 percent of the menthol smokers. Black men are at higher risk than white men for heart disease, liver disease, and esophageal cancer, all of which are tied to cigarettes and alcohol.

The *Oakland Tribune* reported that tobacco ads are now commonplace on awnings over storefronts in Vietnamese and Chinese neighborhoods and as glossy full-page spreads in U.S.-based foreign-language magazines. The alluring parts of the ads are in the appropriate foreign languages and aimed at immigrants with little or no English fluency. The surgeon general's health warning is printed in English.[31]

CONCLUDING SPECULATION

If all drugs were legalized and freely available, and people could be persuaded to stop smoking cigarettes and start drinking alcohol and caffeine only in moderation, the country's health would improve dramatically.

NOTES

1. These figures were kindly provided to me by Nina Rehn, a technical officer of Management of Substance Dependence, World Health Organization (WHO), Geneva; Helen Green, of the Tobacco Free Initiative, WHO, Geneva; and Laura Barrett and Donna Hodge, of ask-us@umich.edu.

2. Estimates of numbers of drug users and deaths caused by use may be way off the mark. The most frequently cited research on numbers of users is the National Household Survey on Drug Abuse. Surveyors contact a random sample of people and ask them about their drug use. Although the surveyors promise anonymity, many respondents must be distrustful and give dishonest answers. The small proportion of people who admit to using illegal drugs, that is, committing felonies, becomes the basis for extrapolating to the entire population. Some segments of society with high rates of drug abuse are rarely reached by surveyors: the homeless, school absentees, prisoners, and inmates of psychiatric hospitals.

Small differences in the wording of questions and in statistical analyses can have large effects on estimates of drug use. See R. Room, "Measuring Alcohol Consumption in the United States: Methods and Rationales," in *Alcohol and Drug Problems*, vol. 10, ed. L. Kozlowski et al. (New York: Plenum, 1990), 39–80. In 1990, the National Household Survey estimated 662,000 habitual cocaine users and 200,000 heroin users in the United States. Estimates from a study commissioned by the Senate Judiciary Committee were 2.4 million and 1 million, respectively. See J. Kelly, "Senator: Survey 'Wildly off the Mark,'" *USA Today*, 20 December 1990: A6.

It is often difficult to establish the specific cause of death, especially in multidrug users. Furthermore, even nonsmokers die of lung cancer, but lung cancer victims who smoked will surely have smoking listed as a cause. Another problem is that far more people use alcohol and tobacco than illegal drugs, and on average they are older. The death rates per comparably aged users may not be too different.

3. F. Leavitt, *Drugs and Behavior*, 3d edition (Thousand Oaks, Calif.: Sage, 1995).

4. A. Klatsky, "Alcohol and Cardiovascular Diseases: A Historical Overview," *Annals of the New York Academy of Sciences* 957 (2002): 7–15; M. Thun et al., "Alcohol Consumption and Mortality among Middle-Aged and Elderly U.S. Adults," *New England Journal of Medicine* 337 (1997): 1705–14.

5. T. Greenfield and J. Rogers, "Who Drinks Most of the Alcohol in the U.S.? The Policy Implications," *Journal of Studies on Alcohol* 60 (1999): 78–89.

6. American Medical Association, *Partner or Foe? The Alcohol Industry, Youth Alcohol Problems, and Alcohol Policy Strategies* (Chicago: American Medical Association, 2001).

7. H. Wechsler et al., "Environmental Correlates of Underage Alcohol Use and Related Problems of College Students," *American Journal of Preventive Medicine* 19 (2000): 24–29.

8. Center for Media Education, "Alcohol and Tobacco on the Web: Sites Are Still Hazardous to Your Children's Health," *InfoActive Health* (spring 1998), available at www.cme.org/publications/infoactive_files/iahsp98.html (accessed on 1 June 2002).

9. P. Lang, "Hard Sell to Blacks of Potent Malt Brew Called 'Irresponsible,'" *San Francisco Chronicle*, 3 November 1990: A2.

10. Leavitt, *Drugs and Behavior*.

11. M. Lee et al., "Anxiogenic Effects of Caffeine on Panic and Depressed Patients," *American Journal of Psychiatry* 145 (1988): 632–35; P. Nickell and T. Uhde, "Dose-Response Effects of Intravenous Caffeine in Normal Volunteers," *Anxiety* 1 (1994–95): 161–68.

12. H. Cordes, "Generation Wired: Caffeine Is the New Drug of Choice for Kids," *The Nation*, 27 April 1998: 11–16.

13. I. Kawachi et al., "A Prospective Study of Coffee Drinking and Suicide in Women," *Archives of Internal Medicine* 156 (1996): 521–25.

14. Cordes, "Generation Wired," 11–16.

15. R. Griffiths and E. Vernotica, "Is Caffeine a Flavoring Agent in Cola Soft Drinks?" *Archives of Family Medicine* 9 (2000): 727.

16. A. Goldstein and M. Wallace, "Caffeine Dependence in Schoolchildren," *Experimental and Clinical Psychopharmacology* 5 (1997): 388–92.

17. M. Jarvik, "Beneficial Effects of Nicotine," *British Journal of Addiction* 86 (1991): 571–75.

18. Leavitt, *Drugs and Behavior*.

19. Joint Committee on Smoking and Health, "Smoking and Health: Physician Responsibility; a Statement of the Joint Committee on Smoking and Health," *Chest* 198 (1995): 201–08.

20. M. Fukuda et al., "Parental Periconceptional Smoking and Male:Female Ratio of Newborn Infants," *The Lancet* 359 (2002): 1407–08.

21. B. Phillips and F. Danner, "Cigarette Smoking and Sleep Disturbance," *Archives of Internal Medicine* 155 (1995): 734–37.

22. M. Miller et al., "Cigarette Smoking and Suicide: A Prospective Study of 300,000 Male Active-Duty Army Soldiers," *American Journal of Epidemiology* 151 (2000): 1060–63.

23. S. Glantz and W. Parmley, "Passive Smoking and Heart Disease: Epidemiology, Physiology, and Biochemistry," *Circulation* 83 (1991): 1–12.

24. P. Fischer et al., "Brand Logo Recognition by Children Aged 3 to 6 Years. Mickey Mouse and Old Joe the Camel," *Journal of the American Medical Association* (*JAMA*) 266 (1991): 3145–48; J. Difranza et al., "RJR Nabisco's Cartoon Camel Promotes Camel Cigarettes to Children," *JAMA* 266 (1991): 3149–53.

25. J. Pierce et al., "Trends in Cigarette Smoking in the United States: Projections to the Year 2000," *JAMA* 261 (1989): 61–65.

26. J. Pierce et al., "Smoking Initiation by Adolescent Girls, 1944 through 1988," *JAMA* 271 (1994): 608–11; "Print Ads Push Eve Cigaret[te]s to Black Women," *Advertising Age* 42 (1971): 24; K. Murray et al., "Report of the Tobacco Policy Research Group on Marketing and Promotions Targeted at African Americans, Latinos, and Women," *Tobacco Control* 1(supplement) (1992): S24–S30.

27. J. Difranza and T. McAfee, "The Tobacco Institute: Helping Youth Say 'Yes' to Tobacco," *Journal of Family Practice* 34 (1992): 694–46.

28. K. Cummings et al., "Cigarette Advertising and Black–White Differences in Brand Preference," *Public Health Reports* 102 (1987): 698–701.

29. J. Stoddard et al., "Targeted Tobacco Markets: Outdoor Advertising in Los Angeles Minority Neighborhoods [letter]," *American Journal of Public Health* 87 (1997): 1232–33.

30. O. Mitchell and M. Greenberg, "Outdoor Advertising of Addictive Products," *New Jersey Medicine* 88 (1991): 331–33.

31. A. Le, "Tobacco Merchants of Death Target Asian Communities," *Oakland Tribune*, 9 September 1996: A17.

11

Many Individuals and Organizations Benefit from the Drug Wars

Some laws may strike people as silly. It is illegal in Peru for males to copulate with a female alpaca and for people in Middle Eastern Islamic countries to eat a lamb they have had sex with. In Cicero, Illinois, humming on public streets is prohibited on Sundays.[1] Although laws that make drug use illegal do not accomplish their alleged goals, they are not silly. They benefit many individuals and organizations. A recent estimate puts the global illegal drug industry at $400 billion, about 8 percent of all international trade.[2] Some sponsors of drug laws undoubtedly acted in good although misguided faith, but others cynically pushed legislation to enhance their political standing, increase their personal fortunes, promote racist agendas, and punish dissidents.

TO ENHANCE POWER

Richard Miller argues that Nazi leaders agitated the German public about the Jewish problem to justify a more powerful role for the SS; and U.S. leaders present anti-drug messages to justify more powerful roles for the Drug Enforcement Administration (DEA), the attorney general's office, the prison-industrial complex, and the CIA.[3] They spread disinformation, which includes inflating the size of the problem. Whereas most law-enforcement agencies must wait for crimes to occur before they can respond, drug agents have used informants to entice people who trust them to commit crimes. Because arrest is ensured, police seem more efficient in solving crimes than they otherwise would. Because felony convictions are regarded as more important than misdemeanor convictions, the police have generally favored changing misdemeanor drug offenses to felonies.

TO FINANCE FOREIGN WARS

Starting in the 1950s and continuing to the present, U.S. secret service agencies helped native warlords in several parts of the world mobilize armies to fight the Soviet Union and Communist China. The warlords used profits from illegal drugs to increase their power, and the U.S. agencies conspired with them.[4] An article in the *Montreal Gazette* quotes an anonymous U.S. defense department official: "Name a place where there's conflict and you'll see a linkage between drugs and guns." The official added that drugs have joined guns as an indispensable ingredient of post–Cold War warfare: "When people need money, they tend to market things that pay off big. There's one market that pays off big more than any other, and that's drugs."[5]

When conflicts end, the drug trade usually expands: "War zones have to be rebuilt, usually at enormous expense. Returning refugees have to be reintegrated, despite an often-comatose economy. Drugs, as one of the world's most lucrative commodities, are often one of the only sources of financing available to help war-torn societies get back on their feet." The *Gazette* article quotes Observatoire Geopolitique des Drogues, a Paris-based institute that advises European police forces: "When the objective is peace, drugs are used to finance peace. When the objective is war, they finance war."[6]

Vietnam and Laos

During and after the Vietnam War, the CIA recruited Laotian Hmong hill tribe guerrillas to fight communists. The CIA encouraged the Hmong to grow opium as a cash crop for export instead of rice to feed themselves. The CIA allowed the Laotian Army to open a heroin laboratory and to use a CIA airplane for loading heroin.[7] The CIA air-dropped food but only so long as the Hmong continued supplying recruits to join the fighting. When the CIA eventually pulled out, many Hmong starved.

Afghanistan and Pakistan

In 1979, the Soviets invaded Afghanistan. Soon afterward, the CIA began working with the Afghan resistance in neighboring Pakistan. Before that, opium had been grown on Pakistan–Afghanistan borderlands and sold only in local markets. With CIA help, guerrillas seized territory and demanded that the peasants increase their production of opium poppies. The opium was brought across the Pakistan border and converted to heroin in laboratories protected by Pakistan intelligence. Within two years, the area became the world's top heroin producer, supplying 50 percent of the world's market.[8]

Nicaragua

Journalist Gary Webb has documented the role of the CIA in the spread of crack cocaine.[9] The U.S. supported the dictatorial anti-communist regime of Anastasio Somoza in Nicaragua, but in 1979 Nicaraguan Sandanistas overthrew Somoza. Many leaders of the deposed regime fled to the United States and formed organizations that sought to destabilize the new government and return the old one to power. The CIA, under President Ronald Reagan, authorized $19 million to help them. The CIA picked Agent Enrique Bermúdez to head a new resistance organization, the Contras. Bermúdez met in Honduras with Danilo Blandón and Norwin Meneses. All three men had been powerful figures in the prior regime. A CIA document identified Meneses as kingpin of narcotics trafficking in Central America. Bermúdez told the other two that the operation would require money. He told them to go to California to raise money and not to worry about their methods. They chose cocaine trafficking and began selling in the primarily black neighborhood of South Central Los Angeles. In 1982, Blandón began selling to small-time Los Angeles dealer Ricky Ross.

Although Ross initially sold expensive powdered cocaine, he learned how to cook it into a much cheaper, smokable form—crack cocaine—which was more accessible to poor people. He used small neighborhood gangs, the Crips and the Bloods, to distribute the crack. Business boomed, the gangs grew and set up franchises, and they bought weapons to guard money and supplies. With CIA assistance, the Contras smuggled powerful and sophisticated weapons out of the country to Nicaragua and inside the country to the gangs. Fierce competition erupted between gangs and made drive-by shootings a common Los Angeles occurrence. Then some Crips and Bloods started selling in other cities. They went to black neighborhoods because they were black and knew people in those neighborhoods. In Webb's words, "The fact that a government-connected drug ring was dumping tons of cocaine into the black neighborhoods in L.A.—and to a lesser extent in San Jose, Oakland, San Francisco, Portland, Houston, Oklahoma City, Alabama and New Orleans—goes a long way toward explaining why crack developed such deep roots in the black community."[10] By 1989, crack cocaine was available nationwide. After a lengthy investigation, the Senate Subcommittee on Terrorism, Narcotics, and International Operations wrote:

> There was substantial evidence of drug smuggling through the war zones on the part of individual Contras, Contra suppliers, and Contra supporters throughout the region. . . . In each case, one or another agency of the U.S. government had information regarding the involvement either while it was occurring, or immediately thereafter. . . . Senior U.S. policy makers were not immune to the idea that drug money was a perfect solution to the Contras' funding problems.[11]

President George H. W. Bush's drug czar, William Bennett, frequently lectured on the need to escalate the war on drugs. But during his tenure, U.S. companies exported to Latin American countries an enormous volume of chemicals used for converting coca leaves to cocaine. Federal judicial and legal loopholes permitted such exports. Bennett could have worked to close the loopholes but chose not to.[12]

While poverty-stricken black neighborhoods were being ravaged, CIA agents who supported the Contra activities were protected from prosecution by a secret agreement between the Department of Justice and the CIA. Afterward, George H. W. Bush, while publicly bemoaning the spread of illegal drugs and intensifying the war on drugs, pardoned all the CIA officials responsible for the Contra war.

The Balkans

In Yugoslavia during the mid- and late 1990s, Serbian forces killed as many as one hundred thousand Albanians. The United States and its NATO allies, nervous about Serbian expansion, entered the conflict by launching the heaviest bombing campaign since World War II. Afterward, Western governments backed a band of ethnic Albanians calling themselves the Kosovo Liberation Army (KLA). The KLA proclaimed itself the provisional government of Kosovo. The KLA needed money for arms and ammunition. Alex Roslin in the *Montreal Gazette* summarized evidence indicating that the KLA, with CIA complicity, got much of its funding from sales of heroin.[13]

The Golden Crescent area (Afghanistan and Pakistan's North West Frontier Province) produces more than half of the world's opium. The opium is smuggled into Turkey and refined into heroin. Most of it is then moved through the Balkans (especially Albania and Kosovar) for eventual sale in Europe, the United States, and Canada.

Roslin quotes former DEA agent Michael Levine: "They (the CIA) protected them (the KLA) in every way they could. As long as the CIA is protecting the KLA, you've got major drug pipelines protected from any police investigation." The Observatoire Geopolitique des Drogues said that U.S. priorities in the Balkans "dictate turning a blind eye to a drug trade that finances the arming of Kosovo Albanians."[14]

Colombia, Bolivia, Honduras, Mexico, Panama, Guatemala, the Middle East, Peru . . .

According to a U.N. report, drug money has been exchanged for weapons in Afghanistan and Colombia. A DEA report claims that the CIA blocked it from indicting many members of the ruling government of Bolivia from 1980 to

1983—during a time period that these same people were responsible for producing more than 90 percent of the cocaine consumed in the United States.[15] Cocaine also flowed in from Honduras, where the CIA helped drug traffickers raise money to support Contra forces.[16] Scott and Marshall document similar situations in Mexico, Panama, and Guatemala. They quote Dennis Dayle, the former chief of an elite DEA enforcement unit in the Middle East: "In my 30-year history in the Drug Enforcement Administration and related agencies, the major targets of my investigations almost invariably turned out to be working for the CIA."[17] An op-ed piece in the *New York Times* refers to Peruvian President Alberto Fujimori's chief adviser Vladimiro Montesinos: "Mr. Montesinos built a power base and fortune mainly as a legal strategist for drug traffickers. He has had a close relationship with the CIA and controls the intelligence services and, through them, the military."[18] And former DEA agent Michael Levine is quoted.

> God knows how many secret elements are out there working under the guise of the drug war. Oliver North was the latest example. His operation was hip-deep in Contra drug smuggling. He was banned from Costa Rica for his involvement with drug runners. The DEA documented fifty tons of Contra coke that was being routed into the U.S. by a Honduran connection. An agent bought two kilos in Lubbock, Texas, and made the arrest. The CIA comes quickly to the rescue. A closed hearing is held. Case dismissed.[19]

TO ENHANCE POLITICAL STANDING

Lewis Lapham writes: "The war against drugs provides [politicians] with something to say that offends nobody, requires them to do nothing difficult, and allows them to postpone, perhaps indefinitely, the more urgent questions about the state of the nation's schools, housing, employment opportunities for young black men—i.e. the condition to which drug addiction speaks as a tragic symptom, not a cause."[20] During the past twenty years, people on the political Right became a force in the United States. Right-wing politicians have often attributed homelessness, crime, the spread of AIDS, and other social problems of racial minorities to immorality, weakness, and genetic inferiority. They claim that drug abuse is just another symptom of deviance and a major cause of the problems. They resist calls to develop government programs for solving the problems, preferring instead to expand police powers and impose longer prison terms on drug users. They have succeeded at the polls, which has persuaded Left-leaning politicians that they also have to be tough on drugs or face ouster from office. Thus, the drug war has become self-perpetuating. The right-wing has benefited in two ways: First, it shifted political discourse rightward. Second, the strategy of sending even nonviolent drug abusers to prison resulted in the disenfranchisement of about 13 percent of black men.[21] Those men do not generally subscribe to right-wing ideology.

A subtle benefit to some politicians is that drug laws help make unemployment statistics look good. A considerable percentage of imprisoned, nonviolent drug offenders have limited job skills. They would have trouble finding work but are not counted as part of the labor force.

TO PAY OFF THE LAW-ENFORCEMENT INDUSTRY

The law-enforcement industry benefits from the illegality of drugs in at least four ways. First, the drug war is a good public relations tool. High-profile seizures and arrests convince the public that police are doing their jobs well. Second, the magnitude of the war, as evidenced by the number of arrests and imprisonments, improves job security. Third, the nature of drug work (undercover, reliance on informants) allows police great latitude in exercising power while limiting their need to be accountable. Fourth, the police take advantage of forfeiture laws to enrich themselves. Former California deputy attorney general Gary Schons said, "Much like a drug addict becomes addicted to drugs, law enforcement agencies have become dependent on asset forfeitures. They have to have it."[22] The world press has noticed, as evidenced from the following condensed version of an article in New Zealand's *Dominion Sunday Times*:

> The 1985 drug forfeiture laws allow government agencies to confiscate assets of convicted traffickers. After a police officer in Little Compton, Rhode Island helped capture a major drug baron, the 7-person Little Compton force received a 3 million dollar bonus. The police chief bought the heroic officer a Formula Firebird Pontiac, then added to the police fleet two new cruisers with video cameras on the dashboard. Soon, cars outnumbered officers. The chief—in a town of 3,400 where there has been no murder for 27 years—bought a computer system that gave immediate access to every crime record since 1960. He bought bulletproof vests, guns with laser sights, and a new tower to boost his radio system. After renovating his offices and commissioning architects to design a rifle range, he proposed building a $750,000 police and fire station complex. The town barber filed a lawsuit, however, and a judge froze the remaining money until the next year's town meeting.
>
> Other government agencies have also spent freely, purchasing items such as giant-screen television sets, fitness centers, Christmas parties, amusement park tickets, and Las Vegas junkets. Opponents of the law are concerned that police confiscate assets from people who have committed minor offenses or are merely under suspicion.[23]

In Albuquerque, New Mexico, the Amtrak office provides federal drug agents with details about suspicious passengers. Amtrak police receive 10 percent of any cash that agents seize from arrested drug couriers.[24]

TO CREATE AND SUPPORT BUSINESSES

Prisons

The upward spiraling budget for corrections has spawned a multibillion-dollar industry with its own trade shows, conventions, websites, mail-order catalogs, and direct-marketing campaigns.[25] Competing for business are architecture and construction firms, investment banks that handle prison bond issues and invest in private prisons, and plumbing-supply, health care, and food service companies. A *Corrections Yellow Pages* directory lists more than one thousand vendors. A trade newspaper, *Correctional Building News,* features articles on trends in the prison and jail marketplace and runs ads by companies that build prisons. Correctional officials move on to jobs with firms that supply prisons.

Eric Schlosser describes changes in the North Country in Upstate New York to show how prisons can improve a district's economy. For many years, the North Country's per-capita income was about 40 percent lower than the state's average. The traditional jobs there, such as mining, dairy farming, and logging, were in steady decline. Then came the prison boom—sixteen constructed in the past twenty-five years. Prisons offer year-round employment and are recession-proof. Correctional officers earn about 50 percent more than the typical North Country worker. Today, about 5 percent of the North Country's population are prisoners.

Telephone providers profit from the prison boom. Prison pay phones generate an estimated $1 billion in annual revenues. Profits are so great that MCI installed its phone service throughout the California prison system at no charge and offered the California Department of Corrections a 32 percent share of revenues from inmates' phone calls. MCI adds a $3.00 surcharge to every inmate call.

The surplus of inmates gave rise in the mid-1980s to private, for-profit companies. Companies contracted with government agencies to either operate existing facilities or build and operate their own. Private prisons now house approximately ninety thousand inmates. The governments save money because the for-profit companies have little bureaucratic waste. But the companies' biggest economy is their use of nonunion labor. They usually pay staff less than state government employees doing comparable jobs, and they give fewer benefits and no pensions.

The profits accruing to private prison companies are tied to occupancy rates. This gives them a strong incentive to fill each cell and keep inmates as long as possible, and it has spawned a variety of new industries and occupations. Bed brokers act as middlemen between states with a surplus of inmates and out-of-state facilities with empty beds. In 1996, a private prison in Texas became the State of Hawaii's third largest prison. Delivery services, with nonunion guards making multiple pickups and deliveries on each trip, pick up inmates in one state and deliver them to another. At least one private company, U.S. Corrections Corporation, used another strategy to increase profits. It forced inmates to do unpaid work including painting and maintenance at a country club and painting at a private school attended by a prison warden's daughter.

Commercialized prison labor is a big business. Prisoners throughout the country work for as little as 20 cents an hour and no benefits to produce products for JC Penny, Eddie Bauer, Honda, and McDonalds. Wisconsin Governor Tommy Thompson mailed an information packet to corporate executives telling them that a willing workforce awaits them in Wisconsin prisons. Not only are the prisoners exploited, but their work undermines the wages of free labor.[26]

Drug Testing

Testing for illegal drugs is a billion-dollar growth industry. Large companies that depend for much of their business on federal contracts are viewed unfavorably unless they stay up to the minute on their employees' urine status. Several states offer economic incentives to employers that test. The employers have been told (by the testers) that drug use makes workers less reliable and increases their absenteeism and accident rates.

Many schools test, and advertisements encourage parents to test their children. Home testing kits are available.[27] The prevalence of drug testing has spawned collateral businesses. Newspapers carry advertisements such as "Pamphlet: 'Conquering the Urine Tests,' $5. Our famous Drug Free Powdered Urine, $19.95. Guaranteed."

Workplace testing got an impetus from an assertion by President George H. W. Bush that "drug abuse among American workers costs businesses anywhere from $60 billion to $100 billion a year in lost productivity, absenteeism, drug-related accidents, medical claims and theft."[28] Several authors have since shown that the claim was based on misinterpretation of a single flawed study conducted by the Research Triangle Institute (RTI).[29] In 1982, RTI surveyed 3,700 households. The average income of households with at least one person who admitted to having ever used marijuana daily was 28 percent lower than that of otherwise similar households. The difference was considered to exist because of marijuana use and, when extrapolated to the general population, came to $26 billion. After adding estimated costs of drug-related crime, health problems, and accidents, the RTI researchers concluded that the annual cost to society of drug abuse is $47 billion. Bush used their figure and adjusted it to account for inflation and population increase.

But the RTI study was correlational. Introductory psychology students learn that a correlation between two variables does not prove that one variable affects the other. The RTI researchers did not compare people in similar jobs. Any difference in income between marijuana users and nonusers was attributed to use, even if one person worked as an order taker in a fast food restaurant and the other was the CEO of a major corporation. Users tend to be younger than nonusers, another reason they are likely to have lower-paying jobs. Most of their drug use occurs away from work and does not affect job performance. An unpublicized finding from the RTI study shows no income differential between households without current users of illicit drugs and similar households with current or former users of any illegal drug.

Government officials testified before Congress and at national conferences that employees who use illegal drugs are more likely to injure themselves or others in workplace accidents and to file workers' compensation claims. But their assertions were based on studies that (a) had not been published in peer-reviewed journals and (b) did not support the conclusions. One study involved employees undergoing treatment for alcoholism, not illegal drugs. Another found that employees who tested positive for marijuana had a higher promotion rate and lower absenteeism rate than the company average. In another, 180 hospital employees were hired, tested, and rated one year later. There were no differences in ratings between the twenty-two drug positives and the 158 negatives. But eleven of the negatives had been fired during the year and none of the positives.

Although we want brain surgeons and airline pilots to work at peak efficiency, other employees need not be held to such high standards. Barbara Ehrenreich has written, "In my town, Winn-Dixie tests applicants for a $6-an-hour job stacking Cheerio boxes; Howard Johnson tests applicants for bed-making jobs. *Hudson News*, which can be found in New York area airports, greets customers with a sign boasting that it's a 'drug-free workplace,' but is the newspaper you buy there any more interesting if the cashier is an abstainer rather than a stoner?"[30] Furthermore, drug testing does not achieve its presumed goal of identifying impaired workers. Unlike tests that measure blood alcohol level, urinalyses measure drug metabolites that take several hours to appear in urine. So people under the influence may be missed while those who used several days earlier and are currently drug-free test positive.

Drug testing is expensive. In 1990, the federal government spent $11.7 million to administer nearly twenty-nine thousand tests to workers in federal agencies. One hundred fifty-three were positive, most only for marijuana. That works out to a cost per identified drug user (not necessarily abuser) of approximately $77,000. Employees must temporarily leave their jobs to be tested, which is one of several indirect costs. If use impairs performance, then at least some of the 153 would probably have been detected even without testing.[31] The poor cost-effectiveness has persuaded many companies to stop testing.[32]

Although testing fails to lower absenteeism or improve safety, it does reduce morale and productivity. Shepard and Clifton found that high-tech industries with either pre-employment or random testing of workers are less productive than their counterparts that do not test.[33] An additional concern is that marijuana is easier to detect than amphetamine or cocaine, which may encourage some marijuana users to switch to more powerful drugs.

Some schools require that students who wish to participate in extracurricular activities submit to tests. Although the practice deters some students from further drug use, others are deterred from activities that might ultimately dissuade them from continued use. Thus, if the goal is to reduce long-term drug use, testing may be counterproductive. In June 2002, the Supreme Court overturned a Federal Appeals Court ruling that random drug testing violates students' constitutional privacy protections against unreasonable searches.

Security Firms

Parents who suspect their children of using drugs have an additional resource besides home testing kits. They can arrange for secret surveillance by investigators. Private companies also pay for surveillance services.[34]

Informants

As indicated in chapter 8, people accused or convicted of drug crimes are encouraged to inform on others to get their sentences reduced. Defendants without useful information can secretly buy some from professional informers for fees of up to $250,000. Another moneymaker for informants is the asset-forfeiture program. They receive up to 25 percent of the assets seized from tips that lead to forfeitures. In 1996, the federal government spent more than $100 million on informers.[35]

Primetime Live described the case of a man who was paid as an informant even while he managed a large-scale cocaine-smuggling operation. He was arrested and convicted but served only six weeks in prison and was allowed to keep his illegally gained profits.[36]

Money Laundering

Criminals who accumulate large sums of money have to hide the source. Instead of putting their profits directly into circulation, they turn to money launderers. Launderers collaborate with drug traffickers to put illegally obtained assets beyond the reach of law enforcement and into apparently legal businesses. Cash businesses like restaurants, food delivery establishments, and casinos are excellent fronts for laundering. So are card rooms where the house exchanges chips for cash without keeping records. So are banks that keep transactions secret, as some do in the Cayman Islands, the Netherlands Antilles, Aruba, and Cyprus. According to Treasury Department officials, money laundering plays a role in much of the seemingly legitimate trade between Colombia and the United States.[37] A 1989 *Frontline* television show cited criminal cases of drug money laundering extending from north to south and coast to coast including members of Congress, lobbyists, bankers, lawyers, accountants, college professors, and trade unionists.[38] A Senate subcommittee report concluded that U.S. banks, including some of the largest in the country, are careless about screening the foreign banks they take in as clients; so criminals route billions of dollars of illegal money through them each year.[39] DEA officials suspect that only a small fraction of the participants is caught while the rest reap huge financial rewards.

A laundering ring that was broken in 1994 involved twenty-four people including the honorary consul-general for Bulgaria, a New York City police officer, two lawyers, a stockbroker, an assistant bank manager at Citibank, two rabbis, a firefighter, and two bankers in Zurich:

> A law firm provided the overall guidance for the laundering effort while both a trucking business and a beer distributorship were used as cover. The Bulgarian diplomat, the firefighter and the rabbi acted as couriers picking up drug trafficking proceeds in hotel rooms and parking lots, while money was also transported by Federal Express to a New York trucking business. The two lawyers subsequently placed the money into bank accounts with the assistance of a Citibank assistant manager. The money was then wired to banks in Europe including a private bank in Switzerland, at which two bankers ensured that it was remitted to accounts designated by drug traffickers. During 1993 and 1994 a sum of between \$70M and \$100M was laundered by the group.[40]

Legal Drug Companies

Cocaine, heroin, and marijuana cannot be patented (they have been around too long), and marijuana is easily grown at home. So drug industry profits would suffer if those drugs were legalized. The nonprofit organization Partnership for a Drug-Free America creates and pays for anti-drug messages. Between 1987 and 1997, the partnership spent approximately \$3.3 billion on ads.[41] Two points should be noted. First, the ads frequently distort, exaggerate, and rely on scare tactics rather than reliable evidence. Second, more than 50 percent of partnership financial support has come from manufacturers of legal drugs. Thus, the ads ignore the dangers of tobacco, alcohol, and prescription and over-the-counter drugs. Cotts concludes that "the war on drugs is a war on illegal drugs, and the Partnership's benefactors have a huge stake in keeping it that way. They know that when schoolchildren learn that marijuana and crack are evil, they're also learning that alcohol, tobacco, and pills are as American as apple pie."[42]

Demoss writes, "Ironically, the U.S. government spends billions of dollars on antidrug campaigns . . . while at the same time, it provides tobacco growers with $3 billion per year in subsidies and tax exemptions for cigarette advertising."[43] The United States is the major world supplier of tobacco.

Prevention and Treatment Centers

Many people who might benefit do not receive treatment for their drug abuse. On the other hand, many casual users who are not being harmed by drugs but who fail drug tests or run afoul of the law are ordered to enroll in treatment programs. Although some programs work, many are ineffective and even counterproductive. Yet, as discussed in the next chapter, prevention and treatment programs have become big businesses.

Major Drug Traffickers

Prohibition is what makes the illegal drug industry so profitable. Within the industry, the major beneficiaries are the biggest dealers. In the words of conservative economist Milton Friedman:

> If you look at the drug war from a purely economic point of view, the role of the government is to protect the drug cartel. That's literally true.
>
> What do I mean by that? In an ordinary free market—let's take potatoes, beef, anything you want—there are thousands of importers and exporters. Anybody can go into the business. But it's very hard for a small person to go into the drug importing business because our interdiction efforts essentially make it enormously costly. So, the only people who can survive in that business are these large Medellin cartel kind of people who have enough money so they can have fleets of airplanes, so they can have sophisticated methods, and so on.
>
> In addition to which, by keeping goods out and by arresting, let's say, local marijuana growers, the government keeps the price of these products high. What more could a monopolist want? He's got a government who makes it very hard for all his competitors and who keeps the price of his products high. It's absolutely heaven.[44]

Terrorist Organizations

Shortly after the September 2001 terrorist attacks in New York City and Washington, D.C., House Speaker Dennis Hastert (R-Ill.) said, "The illegal drug trade is the financial engine that fuels many terrorist organizations around the world, including Osama bin Laden. By going after the illegal drug trade, we reduce the ability of these terrorists to launch attacks against the United States."[45]

Television commercials aired during the January 2002 Super Bowl launched a campaign to blame drug users for terrorist acts.

In fact, prohibition benefits terrorists for the same reason it benefits drug dealers. Banning a product in high demand creates a highly profitable commodity. Cocaine, heroin, and other illegal drugs would be inexpensive in a free market, but their illegality ensures enormous profits for successful manufacturers, transporters, and dealers. It gives terrorists the financial wherewithal to carry out their objectives. Terrorists willing to be suicide bombers are unlikely to be deterred from such activities by the threat of prison.

The drug wars provide an additional benefit to terrorists. They strain the resources of the FBI and other agencies that should be trying to infiltrate terrorist organizations and secure our borders.

CONCLUDING COMMENTS

Even readers appalled by the premises of this book should appreciate that the drug wars have enriched and empowered many people. Many of those beneficiaries do their best to ensure that most citizens remain misinformed about drug issues.

NOTES

1. S. Spignesi, *The Odd Index* (New York: Penguin Books, 1994); Dick Hyman, *More Crazy Laws* (New York: Scholastic Inc., 1992).
2. M. Porubcansky, "Drug Trafficking Equals 8 Percent of All World Trade, the U.N. Reports," *Philadelphia Inquirer*, 27 June 1997: 29.
3. R. Miller, *Drug Warriors and Their Prey: From Police Power to Police State* (Westport, Conn.: Praeger, 1996).
4. R. Kelly, ed., *Organized Crime: A Global Perspective* (Totowa, N.J.: Rowman and Littlefield, 1986); P. Scott and J. Marshall, *Cocaine Politics: Drugs, Armies and the CIA in Central America* (Berkeley: University of California Press, 1998).
5. A. Roslin, "Kosovo: KLA, CIA, and Drug Trade," *Montreal Gazette*, 27 November 1999: B1.
6. Roslin, "Kosovo," B1.
7. A. McCoy, *The Politics of Heroin: CIA Complicity in the Global Drug Trade* (New York: Lawrence Hill Books, 1991); A. McCoy, "Casualties of the CIA's War against Communism," op-ed, *Boston Globe*, 14 November 1996.
8. P. Scott, "Cocaine, the Contras, and the United States: How the U.S. Government Has Augmented America's Drug Crisis," *Crime, Law and Social Change* 16 (1991): 97–131.
9. G. Webb, *Dark Alliance: The CIA, the Contras, and the Crack Cocaine Explosion* (New York: Seven Stories Press, 1998). Webb's allegations were originally denied and denounced by CIA officials. The *Washington Post, Los Angeles Times,* and *New York Times* all ran stories attacking his reporting and the series. He lost his job at the *San Jose Mercury News*. But subsequent investigations showed that his charges are correct in all essential details and vindicated him.

10. Webb, *Dark Alliance.*

11. Senate Committee on Foreign Relations, Subcommittee on Terrorism, Narcotics and International Operations, *Drugs, Law Enforcement and Foreign Policy* (Washington, D.C.: Senate Committee on Foreign Relations, 1989), 2.

12. "Between the Lines," *Rolling Stone,* 1 November 1990: 44.

13. Roslin, "Kosovo," B1.

14. Roslin, "Kosovo," B1.

15. M. Levine, *The Big White Lie: The CIA and the Cocaine/Crack Epidemic: An Undercover Odyssey* (New York: Thunder's Mouth Press, 1993).

16. Scott, "Cocaine, the Contras, and the United States."

17. Scott and Marshall, *Cocaine Politics,* xviii–xix.

18. G. Gorriti, "America's Dance with a Dictator," op-ed, *New York Times,* 27 December 1992: E11.

19. M. Kram, "The Betrayal of Michael Levine," *Esquire Magazine,* March 1991: 34–37, 136–39.

20. L. Lapham, "A Political Opiate—The War on Drugs Is a Folly and a Menace," *Harper's Magazine,* December 1989: 45.

21. M. Mauer and J. Fellner, "Losing the Vote: The Impact of Felony Disenfranchisement Laws in the United States," *Human Rights Watch and the Sentencing Project,* October 1998.

22. Quoted in the Drug Policy Foundation, *Policy Briefing: Asset Forfeiture* (Washington, D.C.: Drug Policy Foundation, 1999), 3.

23. *Dominion Sunday Times* (Wellington, New Zealand), 27 September 1992.

24. Associated Press, "N.M. Amtrak Office Is Paid for Tips on Drug Suspects," 12 April 2001.

25. E. Schlosser, "The Prison-Industrial Complex," *Atlantic Monthly,* December 1998: 51–77.

26. "Prison Industrial Complex," *Prevailing Winds Magazine* 5 (1997): 38–39.

27. P. Marks, "New Option for Worried Parents: Drug Testing at Home," *New York Times,* 13 July 1995: B1.

28. J. Horgan, "Science and the Citizen," *Scientific American,* March 1990: 18, 22.

29. Horgan, "Science and the Citizen," 18, 22; J. Normand, *Under the Influence? Drugs and the American Workforce* (Washington, D.C.: National Academy Press, 1994); L. Maltby, *Drug Testing: A Bad Investment* (Washington, D.C.: American Civil Liberties Union, 1999).

30. B. Ehrenreich, "Your Urine, Please," *The Progressive,* March 2000: 15–16.

31. Horgan, "Science and the Citizen"; Normand, *Under the Influence?*; Maltby, *Drug Testing.*

32. American Management Association, *A 2000 AMA Survey: Workplace Testing: Medical Testing: Summary of Key Findings* (New York: American Management Association, 2000).

33. E. Shepard and T. Clifton, "Drug Testing and Labor Productivity: Estimates Applying a Production Function Model," Institute of Industrial Relations, Research Paper No. 18 (Syracuse, N.Y.: Le Moyne University, 1998).

34. M. Davis, "Your Coworker May Be an Undercover Narc," *The Tennessean,* 12 October 1997: 1.

35. E. Schlosser, "More Reefer Madness," *Atlantic Monthly,* April 1997: 96.

36. *Primetime Live,* ABC News, 8 July 1998.

37. A. Marks, "US Firms Unwittingly Aid Drug Lords," *Christian Science Monitor,* 22 October 1997.

38. "Who Profits from Drugs?" *Frontline,* PBS, 12 February 1989.

39. "Report Says Banks Fail to Control Money Laundering," *Oakland Tribune,* 5 February 2001: NEWS 5.

40. P. Williams, "Money Laundering, *The IASOC Magazine,* summer 1997.

41. "The Politics of Denial," *Drug Policy Letter* (Washington, D.C.: Drug Policy Foundation, 1998).

42. C. Cotts, "Hard Sell in the Drug War," *The Nation,* 9 March 1992: 302.

43. B. Demoss, "[Letter to the editor]," *American Family Physician* 46 (1992): 668.

44. "Friedman and Szasz on Liberty and Drugs" (interview), *America's Drug Forum,* 1991.

45. Associated Press, "Hastert Forms Task Force on Drugs," 21 September 2001.

12

Popular Programs for Combating Drug Abuse Are Unsuccessful, While Effective Programs Are Underused

In the year 2000, the federal government allocated $18.4 billion for drug control problems. The biggest chunk ($9 billion) went to law enforcement, but $2.4 billion was allocated toward prevention efforts and $3.6 billion toward treatment. (Three federal agencies overstated their spending on drug abuse treatment by $1 billion.)[1] States spent an additional $3 billion on prevention and treatment.[2] The programs for prevention and treatment of drug abuse provide jobs for substance abuse counselors, employee assistance counselors, residential counselors, social workers, and parole officers. They have made some people wealthy. One of the first therapeutic communities, Synanon, gained as much as $50 million in assets from the late 1950s to 1980. Proponents claim that the programs are highly effective, but national surveys show that more people than ever are using legal and illegal drugs. And the prison population keeps growing.

PREVENTION

Goals

Despite the very real horrors of drug abuse, the goal of reducing use to zero in the adult population may be neither attainable nor desirable. Proponents of legalization claim that various drugs confer benefits such as mood enhancement, relief from stress and depression, facilitated psychotherapeutic healing, and religious and mystical insights. There is considerable, although strongly disputed, evidence to support each claim. Furthermore, among adolescents, moderate users tend to be psychologically healthier than abstainers.[3] Therefore, enlightened democratic societies might serve their citizens best by providing honest information about drugs while striving to reduce the harms from abuse. A zero-tolerance, just-say-no approach that lumps all drugs in the same category is both irresponsible and ineffective.

Causes of Drug Abuse

Whereas treatments for certain conditions are effective even when the cause is unknown, prevention programs are unlikely to succeed without attacking causes. In fact, they take resources away from efforts to end societal causes such as poverty, racism, and lack of opportunity. (Most Americans do not believe that difficult social conditions are a major cause of drug use.)[4] Spokespersons for Alcoholics Anonymous (AA) claim that alcoholism is a disease caused by inborn, predisposing characteristics. As discussed in chapter 7, the disease concept is incorrect.

Evaluation of Prevention Programs

General Issues

The rationales for most prevention programs seem plausible, and participants and administrators generally express satisfaction with outcomes. As a result, public support for anti-drug education programs has grown in recent years.[5] But evaluations of effectiveness have uncovered serious methodological deficiencies:

- Only rarely have people been randomly assigned to participate or not participate, and nonrandom assignment makes unambiguous interpretation impossible. For example, volunteers for a program may be more motivated than people who decline to participate. The differential motivation rather than the program itself may account for subsequent differences in drug-seeking behavior.
- Most programs that measure drug abuse rely on subjects' self-reports rather than urine tests. Many do not do even that—they measure behaviors possibly related to drug abuse but not drug use itself. But socially sensitive behaviors such as drug use are often underreported. When the dangers of cigarette smoking became widely publicized, self-reports of smoking declined substantially; but sales records showed that smoking behaviors had not changed much.[6] Harrell interviewed former drug treatment clients in their own homes and promised that no one would ever know how they responded. Although all of them had been through treatment, fewer than 40 percent reported that fact.[7]
- Program participants may feel more pressure than nonparticipants to underreport their drug use.

Literature Reviews

Few school-based drug prevention programs reduce future drug use. Most have been poorly designed for proper evaluation, and the more methodologically sound among them show the weakest results.[8] There have been successes. Characteristics of effective programs include interactive delivery, a focus on improving social and general life skills rather than teaching about drugs, and periodic booster sessions.[9] These will not be discussed further, because this book is about exposing abuses so they can be corrected.

The Drug Abuse Resistance Education (DARE) program has been the leading drug prevention program in the United States. In 1997, total funding exceeded $750 million annually. The seventeen-week course taught by uniformed police uses lectures, role-playing, and other techniques to teach children to avoid drugs. The focus is on fifth graders, with seventh and tenth grade boosters. But DARE graduates do not differ from students in control groups in the percentage of new users of cigarettes, smokeless tobacco, alcohol, cocaine, glue, phencyclidine (a.k.a. PCP), or marijuana.[10] DARE graduates were *more* likely to use hallucinogens, which led Wysong and colleagues to consider the possibility that drug education programs increase student curiosity about drugs and lead to earlier and greater drug experimentation.[11]

The failure of drug education programs should not be too surprising. Being well informed has not persuaded doctors to renounce illicit drugs; to the contrary, they use at a high rate.[12] In one survey, more than 11 percent said they used benzodiazepines or other sleeping pills, more than 17 percent said they used opiates, and more than 90 percent self-prescribed the drugs.[13] The knowledge and expertise of some pharmacists may contribute to rather than prevent their abuse of prescription drugs.[14] Cincinnati carefully tracks prescription drug abuse, and 30 percent of arrests have involved medical employees.[15]

The dangers of cigarette smoking have been known for decades, but sixty million Americans still smoke. Some people share the sentiment expressed by a quote attributed to Henny Youngman: "When I read about the evils of drinking, I gave up reading."

Programs rarely provide objective, fully accurate information. According to a National Institute of Drug Abuse publication, the purpose of information programs is to specify "the harmful physical and psychological consequences of drug consumption."[16] This fundamentally dishonest approach results in young adults who learn to distrust the warnings of parents, school personnel, police officers, and clergy. So information programs have been resounding failures.[17] So too have programs based on values clarification, attitude change, and decision making.[18] Programs that teach cognitive and behavioral skills training produced some positive but usually short-lived effects.[19]

Some studies showed positive effects of DARE on students' social skills, self-esteem, and knowledge and attitudes about drugs. But the effects were small and dissipated over time. Rosenbaum concludes his extensive review by noting an inverse relationship between strength of research design and reported impact on drug use measures.[20]

Then why is DARE so popular? The answer, as is so often the case when current approaches to drugs seem irrational, is money. Schools' choices of programs have been influenced more by commercial marketing than by demonstrated effectiveness. University researchers generally conduct effectiveness studies, and those who develop successful programs have neither the time nor the knowledge to market the programs commercially.

The Drug Reform Coordination Network listed the names of several people affiliated with DARE who earn substantial amounts of money. DRCN explains how DARE personnel profit:

> DARE America is the California nonprofit corporation which develops and licenses the Drug Abuse Resistance Education curricula. When local police departments and school districts decide to implement the DARE program, they must get the curriculum and workbooks from DARE America. But the tee-shirts, pens, lapel pins, gym bags, and other nonacademic DARE materials are not purchased from the nonprofit organization. They are sold instead by four licensed distributors nationwide. Each distributor pays royalties to DARE America, ranging from 5 percent on some items to 10 percent on others. Unlike DARE America, these licensed distributors are for-profit businesses.
>
> Royalties were 71 percent of DARE America's income in 1992, or $1,020,995. Royalties for 1993 rose to $1,280,162, yet this was only 45 percent of DARE America income in that year. Royalties in 1994 were $1,802,516, or 42 percent of its income. These figures indicate that nonacademic DARE materials are at least a $10–20 million per year business in the United States (IRS 990 tax returns 1992–1994).[21]

DARE officials have responded to the criticisms by planning modifications. A new DARE program that will target seventh and ninth graders is being created at the University of Akron with a $13.7 million grant from the Robert Wood Johnson foundation.

A Radical Rethinking of Prevention

As noted in chapter 7, Peele contrasted southern European countries such as Italy, Portugal, and Spain with Scandinavian and English-speaking countries.[22] In southern Europe, alcohol drinking is commonplace and pleasurable. Drinking is integrated into social activities, and teenagers drink freely in public establishments. In the northern countries, the age at which people can drink and the times and places of consumption are strictly regulated. But drinking in southern Europe, though much greater per capita, leads to far fewer alcohol-related problems. In 1990, Iceland had the lowest per-capita alcohol consumption in Europe and almost eight hundred Alcoholics Anonymous groups per million population; Portugal had the highest per-capita consumption and 0.6 AA groups per million. Similarly in the United States, religious groups that encourage abstinence and, thus, have very low per-capita drinking rates, have above-average problem drinking rates among those who ever touch alcohol. Peele's explanation is that such groups have no norms for moderate consumption.

In light of the foregoing, Peele and his colleagues recommend that the following information be disseminated in campaigns to prevent problem drinking; of course, similar recommendations will not work for illegal drugs:

1. Alcohol is a legal beverage widely available in most societies throughout the world.
2. Alcohol may be misused with serious negative consequences.
3. Alcohol is more often used in a mild and socially positive fashion.
4. Alcohol used in this fashion conveys significant benefits, including health, quality of life, and psychological and social benefits.
5. It is critical for the individual to develop skills to manage alcohol consumption.
6. Some groups use alcohol almost exclusively in a positive fashion, and this style of drinking should be valued and emulated.
7. Positive drinking involves regular moderate consumption, often including other people of both genders and all ages and usually entailing activities in addition to alcohol consumption, where the overall environment is pleasant—either relaxing or socially stimulating.
8. Alcohol, like other healthful activities, both takes its form and produces the most benefit within an overall positive life structure and social environment, including group supports, other healthful habits, and a purposeful and engaged lifestyle.[23]

PROBLEMS WITH TREATMENT PROGRAMS

Too Few Needy People Have Access

Only about 15 percent of people who need treatment for drug abuse receive it. Many pregnant abusers cannot afford the fees or are unable to find an inpatient program that will accept their children. As a result, only 5 to 20 percent of them get treatment.[24] Methadone clinics for heroin addicts are unavailable in some U.S. states, and most have waiting lists. About 85 percent of California prison parolees are drug abusers who must pass periodic drug tests or risk being remanded to custody. In 1997, about 65 percent of people sent to prison were parole violators, and about 70 percent of them had failed a drug test.[25] Yet fewer than 10 percent of state and federal prison inmates with histories of drug abuse receive treatment.[26] (Conversely, many people are forced into treatment. The treatment is not always confidential and often stigmatizes. Being labeled and stigmatized may produce a self-fulfilling prophecy of addictive behavior.)

The Effectiveness of Treatment Programs Is Questionable

Goals Vary

More than 93 percent of alcoholism treatment centers in the United States involve some form of twelve-step program, as do most programs for treating abusers of illicit drugs. Twelve-step programs require participants to admit that they are powerless over their addiction and can never use the addictive substance in moderation. They must strive for total abstinence. At least 99 percent of treatment programs in the United States have total abstinence as the goal.[27]

But drug use dominates addicts' lives, and being weaned from the drugs leaves a void. If they are not taught skills for coping with the problems that caused the abuse, their lives may deteriorate even further. They may become irritable, begin abusing other drugs, or develop marriage, work, or health problems. In one recent study, patients in methadone maintenance treatment were tracked over a six-month period; their use of crack cocaine, marijuana, and nonprescribed methadone had increased considerably.[28] People in a smoking cessation program, especially those with a history of depression, were at serious risk of experiencing depressive episodes after treatment.[29] More than 50 percent of addicts who stopped using illegal drugs developed drinking problems.[30]

So some programs de-emphasize reductions in drug use in favor of promoting their clients' overall ability to function in society. Comparisons of program effectiveness are difficult when one measures success by global lifestyle changes and another by cleanliness of urine.

Virtually All People Involved with Programs Are Biased

Granting agencies, therapists, clients, and program administrators all prefer positive treatment outcomes. Unfavorable results can cost therapists and administrators their jobs. (Treatment of alcohol problems alone is a $10 billion a year industry.)[31] Clients who revert to drugs risk losing jobs, spouses, and freedoms. Workers at granting agencies want to show that they made wise decisions about where to stake their monies. So each interested party may regard precautions for catching relapsers as counterproductive. Failed drug tests are potential catastrophes for all.

Evaluations Are Difficult

Proper experiments require at least two groups, experimental and control, that are similar at the outset and then handled identically except for the treatment. Recall from chapter 1 that bias is likely in non-double-blind experiments and even more likely in studies without control groups. Most existing programs for treating drug abuse have not been evaluated with double-blind experiments or even with nonblinded studies with a control group.

Evaluations are further complicated by several features of treatment programs:

- Success is often measured by comparing pre-treatment with post-treatment use. If pre-treatment use is exaggerated for the purpose of gaining sympathy or qualifying for a program, outcomes will appear better than they really are. (I once watched a man dig a ballpoint pen into his arm over a period of several hours. He was scheduled to appear in court the next day on a burglary charge and wanted to show "track marks" to persuade the judge that he was a heroin addict. His ploy worked, and he received a relatively lenient sentence.)
- Participants lie about post-treatment use (which is typically measured by self-reports, on which lying is easy, or urine tests, which can be fooled) so they can claim to be satisfying the terms of their parole.
- Many go at a low point in their lives—they have been arrested, been sentenced, lost a job, lost a spouse, and so on. They may improve because the only way is up.
- The type of program may not matter as much as the amount of treatment provided. In one study, crack cocaine smokers were randomly assigned to six different treatments. The best predictors of success were days in treatment and number of treatment sessions.[32] But users who bounce from program to program before finally quitting drugs for good might give credit only to the last one.
- Many comply as long as failure to comply would be detected; they are prone to relapse as soon as participation in the program ends.
- All programs require a high level of commitment. In one large-scale study, potential clients were so carefully screened that only 24 percent met the criteria for inclusion, yet 62 percent of them refused to participate.[33] Only about 5 percent of eligible heroin users accepted treatment with a narcotics antagonist.[34] And millions of U.S. smokers are insufficiently motivated to take advantage of an abundance of inexpensive cessation programs. So (a) successes may be due primarily or solely to clients' strong motivations rather than specific program elements, and (b) generalizations from successful results are problematic.
- Dropout rates are high and often caused by drug use.[35] The dropouts, that is, the failures, typically form the group with which those who stay are compared.

For example, Kleinman and colleagues evaluated a large-scale methadone program.[36] The estimated heroin use by people who remained in the program declined from a high of 38 percent toward the end of the first year to 21 percent at the end of the fourth. It might appear that the treatment worked. But, as the authors emphasize, 1,042 of the original 1,774 enrollees dropped out during the first two years, and each year's dropouts were among the worst offenders the previous year. Imagine a program for increasing people's height, in which the shortest 25 percent are dismissed each year. The remaining participants would on average be taller, but that would not prove the program a success. In the program, estimated heroin use by specific individuals *increased* with each year in attendance.

- Treating addicts and then returning them to their previous environments may do more harm than good. Many heroin abusers who complete methadone programs or undergo enforced abstinence while incarcerated start injecting again upon release. Their tolerance is lower than previously, and they often use drugs such as sedatives and alcohol that contribute to central nervous system depression. So they have a high risk of overdose.[37]

Treatment versus No Treatment

Research does not support the conclusion that the popular treatments for drug abuse are effective, but the multibillion-dollar U.S. treatment industry constantly spins data to persuade the public otherwise.[38] Miller and his colleagues reviewed the scientific literature and concluded that "the negative correlation between scientific evidence and application in standard practice remains striking, and could hardly be larger if one intentionally constructed treatment programs from those approaches with the least evidence of efficacy."[39]

Consider a program for treating fictitious disease X. Several sufferers are identified, and their symptoms are measured. They are treated over the course of a month and then measured again. If 99 percent of them have fewer symptoms, can we conclude that the treatment works?

The answer is no. The results prove little, as can be appreciated by imagining that disease X is the common cold. The study lacks a standard of comparison for success—a control group. In drug abuse evaluations, the key question is whether people undergoing treatment are more likely to stop abusing than equally motivated people left on their own. Keep in mind that approximately three million Americans stop smoking each year, the vast majority without formal treatment.[40] Smokers who wanted to quit did equally well whether or not they attended a treatment program, and more than 90 percent of the approximately forty million ex-smokers in the United States quit without treatment.[41]

Although cocaine, heroin, amphetamine, and alcohol abusers have been portrayed as out-of-control people in thrall to their urges, they often quit or cut down if problems arise; most do so without seeking formal treatment.[42] Dawson interviewed 4,585 adults who had once been diagnosed as alcohol dependent.[43] Approximately one-quarter had received alcoholism treatment. Although their problems on average had probably been more severe than those of the untreated, it is still worth noting that the treated were slightly *more* likely than the untreated to have had a recent drinking problem. Walters reviewed the literature on recovery from addictions without treatment and reported an incidence ranging between 4 and 56 percent.[44] (The variability was partly caused by differences between studies in definition of spontaneous remission and length of follow-up.)

Controlled Drug Use versus Abstinence

The harms caused by tobacco increase with dose, so all use is abuse and total abstinence should be the goal. Abstinence is also the safest course for illicit drugs, because users risk arrest and imprisonment unless the laws are changed. But moderate use of alcohol confers several health benefits,[45] so problem drinkers and their therapists have reason to consider the options of abstinence and controlled drinking as goals. For almost three decades a virulent debate has raged between advocates and opponents of the idea that many problem drinkers can be taught to drink responsibly. Stanton Peele, a strong advocate of controlled drinking, shows that financial and power considerations outweigh scientific findings in the controversy.[46] See Nathan and McCrady for the (in my view unconvincing) opposition point of view.[47]

Alcoholics Anonymous

Just as DARE dominates the prevention field, twelve-step programs dominate approaches to treatment. More than 93 percent of alcoholism treatment centers in the United States involve some form of twelve-step program, with Alcoholics Anonymous as the prototype.[48] Twelve-step programs are free and available worldwide for life, which must be reassuring to participants. But evaluation is difficult, because the tradition of anonymity precludes accurate counts of current members, curiosity seekers, dropouts, and former problem drinkers who attend meetings for fellowship or to sustain their recoveries.

People who voluntarily attend a twelve-step program have recognized that they have a problem and are attempting to solve it. If such people stay sober, the credit may be due less to AA than to their initial awareness and motivation. AA does not help those forced to attend meetings after being convicted of offenses such as drunk driving.[49] Yet most Americans enter the programs involuntarily,[50] including defendants in drug-related crimes given the choice between a twelve-step program and jail. Some states have passed laws requiring nonviolent individuals guilty of drug crimes to receive treatment for addiction instead of jail time. (In 1996, the New York Court of Appeals ruled that a prison inmate may not be deprived of expanded family visitation privileges for refusing to participate in a drug addiction program. The program entailed mandatory attendance at and participation in a curriculum based on the religious-oriented practices and precepts of Alcoholics Anonymous.)[51]

AA supporters claim that alcoholism is a disease and that treatment requires total abstinence. They argue that people must hit bottom before they can accept treatment. Research findings are at variance with these tenets. Among recovering alcoholics, one of the strongest predictors of relapse is belief in the disease concept.[52] And over a ten-year period, problem drinkers who entered treatment earliest had the best outcomes.[53]

After analyzing various data sources, Bufe concluded that between 50 and 90 percent of U.S. alcoholics have attended at least one AA meeting, but only 5 to 8 percent return often enough to be counted as members.[54] Only about 5 percent of people who begin AA in any given year are still in AA and sober a year later. Bufe cites studies that compared outcomes for people who participated in AA or received no treatment; the untreated groups did better.

Money is a key factor in the promotion of AA. Jack Trimpey writes:

> While AA appears to the casual observer as a nonprofit corporation that sponsors autonomous, community-level cell groups, it has evolved far beyond that level of organization. Its members, shielded by anonymity and presenting themselves as concerned addictions experts, have infiltrated federal and state bureaucracies, where they manipulate social policies and funding patterns affecting America's social service system. Hundreds of nonprofit organizations exist purely for the purpose of disseminating disease/treatment propaganda and networking within communities to create political support for the 12-step agendas described in AA doctrinal literature. Now in possession of the American social service system, including the prisons and courts, the professional disciplinary and licensing boards, the Medicaid and social welfare programs, and the military health care system, AA can be seen as a powerful hierarchy of professional AAers employed in positions of social responsibility. AA is a cult which has spread into a bureaucracy, which I call a "cultocracy," for the lack of a standard word to describe this anomaly. The funding for the AA cultocracy is not only from the free-will donations of grateful alcoholics, but taken from each taxpayer by the force of national tax laws. The AA cultocracy enlarges AA's membership by using the authority of social institutions to force vulnerable people into their recovery groups, where they are indoctrinated under conditions that should interest Amnesty International. The penalty for resisting AA participation may be imprisonment, death by the lack of organ transplant, imprisonment as in parole and early-release policies, alternative to substance abuse diversion programs, loss of child custody as in domestic court cases, loss of livelihood as in impaired professional programs, and loss of employment as in employment assistance programs.

The incestuous relationship of the recovery groups and the treatment centers, where the referral traffic sustains the interests of each, has run up bills that no person or family can pay. Treatment centers have materials for credit applications and mortgage arrangements to pay for readmissions of chronic relapsers. If the services were in any way effective, the cost would not be exploitive, but treatment centers are acutely aware that only about 5 percent of those who come through the turnstiles will remain abstinent for long. Repeat business is the best business in the addiction treatment industry, but claims of "success rates" of 60 percent to 70 percent are common by the treatment centers.

AA itself has set a suggested limit on how much members can give at meetings (in 1990 it was $500 per year), but in the atmosphere of meetings this is akin to a pledge goal. In just one of AA's many districts, the amount actually sent to AA, not just dropped in the basket, in 1989 was $11 million.[55]

SUCCESSES

Psychologists at the University of Washington developed an inexpensive program aimed specifically at those who need it most. The program offers nonthreatening services, requires little commitment, and is therefore usually accepted. Freshmen at the university who report having ever engaged in risky drinking or alcohol-related problems are asked to meet for one hour with a staff member. They receive feedback concerning their drinking risks, review practices for reducing harm, and are told that additional help is available if needed. But often the single session is enough. Among the more than four hundred students in the initial group, program participants drank less and had fewer alcohol-related problems than a randomly assigned control group over a two-year follow-up period.[56]

Several similar programs show that at-risk or nondependent problem drinkers respond well to even briefer sessions (five–twenty minutes) of outpatient counseling with regular follow-ups.[57] Follow-ups are important; Wutzke and colleagues report short-term benefits of brief interventions but no significant reductions in drinking behavior or mortality at ten-year follow-up.[58] Kristenson and colleagues gave brief interventions with regular follow-ups and reinforcing advice and reported positive effects lasting at least five years.[59] Sending occasional letters explaining how users can monitor themselves, set goals, and protect against relapse reduced alcohol consumption substantially.[60] The successes target people most in need with brief, inexpensive treatments. A meta-analysis confirms that brief interventions are as effective as lengthier treatments for alcohol problems,[61] and they also work with cigarette smokers. Guidelines for doctors state that the first step in eliminating tobacco use is to routinely question patients about their smoking habits.[62] Questioning also helps identify alcohol users but will not work well for users of illegal drugs.

The Community Reinforcement Approach (CRA) emphasizes stress management, family counseling, job preparation, social skills training, and recreational planning. Clients are trained to recognize antecedents and consequences of drug use. They are reinforced for drug-free urine tests with approval from spouses and friends and vouchers redeemable for recreational and consumer items. Peele and DeGrandpre cite many references showing that CRA is both effective and cost-effective in treating drug abusers.[63]

But this book is about abuses. One abuse is that no type of brief, inexpensive treatment or CRA is used in standard treatments.[64] Of 887 psychiatrists surveyed by Montoya and colleagues, 756 had drug-abusing patients in their caseloads. Fewer than 50 percent of them used any of the CRA strategies or cognitive behavioral therapy, which also has demonstrated effectiveness.[65]

Transtheoretical Model

Velicer and colleagues argue that quitting a drug habit (and other types of behavior change) is not a one-time event.[66] They construe change as a process involving progress through a series of five stages. People in stage 1 may not acknowledge that they have a problem and do not intend to take action in the foreseeable future. Stage 2 people hope to change within the next six months but are often ambivalent. They recognize the benefits of changing but also the difficulties. People in stage 3 intend to take action within the next month and typically have a plan, such as consulting a counselor or doctor or reading self-help materials. Stage 4 people make specific lifestyle changes according to criteria established by professionals. In maintenance stage 5, people work to prevent relapse.

Regression occurs when individuals revert to an earlier stage. Relapse involves regression from stage 4 or 5 to an earlier stage, but regression can occur from any stage to any earlier stage.

Assessments on three large samples showed that about 40 percent of smokers were in stage 1; 40 percent, in stage 2; and 20 percent, in stage 3. The stage distributions for other problem behaviors are not known. People in either of the first two stages do not respond well to programs demanding immediate behavior change, that is, traditional treatment programs. Only stage 3 people are appropriate candidates. By tailoring their recruitment strategies to the needs of individuals, Velicer and colleagues achieved high participation rates. By individualizing their interventions, they were able to keep the dropout rates low.[67]

CONCLUDING COMMENTS

All vertebrate species can be conditioned. Rats, pigeons, and monkeys respond to rewards and punishments, and we should expect no less of drug abusers. They can learn to stop abusing. But not only do the most popular treatment programs start with incorrect assumptions about addiction, they fail to use well-established principles of learning. Not surprisingly, their success rates are low. We must start supporting programs that work.

NOTES

1. J. Donnelly, "US Is Said to Overstate Spending on Drug Care. Report Cites $1b in Discrepancies," *Boston Globe,* 24 January 2001: A01.

2. "Mapping Addiction," *Newsweek Magazine,* 12 February 2001: 43.

3. J. Shedler and J. Block, "Adolescent Drug Use and Psychological Health: A Longitudinal Inquiry," *American Psychologist* 45 (1990): 612–30.

4. R. Blendon and J. Young, "The Public and the War on Illicit Drugs," *Journal of the American Medical Association* (*JAMA*) 279 (1998): 827–32.

5. Blendon and Young, "The Public and the War on Illicit Drugs."

6. K. Warner, "Possible Increases in the Understanding of Cigarette Consumption," paper presented at the 105th Annual Meeting of the American Public Health Association, Washington, D.C., 1977.

7. A. Harrell, "The Validity of Self-Reported Drug Use Data: The Accuracy of Responses on Confidential Self-Administered Answer Sheets," in *The Validity of Self-Reported Drug Use: Improving the Accuracy of Survey Estimates,* NIDA Research Monograph 167, ed. L. Harrison and A. Hughes (Rockville, Md.: Department of Health and Human Services, 1997), 37–58.

8. R. Bangert-Drowns, "The Effects of School-Based Substance Abuse Education: A Meta-analysis," *Journal of Drug Education* 18 (1988): 243–65; R. Battjes, "Prevention of Adolescent Drug Abuse," *International Journal of the Addictions* 20 (1985): 1113–24; G. Botvin, "Substance Abuse Prevention: Theory, Practice, and Effectiveness," in *Drugs and Crime,* ed. M. Tonry and J. Wilson (Chicago: University of Chicago Press, 1990), 461–519; N. Tobler, "Meta-analysis of 143 Adolescent Drug Prevention Programs: Quantitative Outcome Results of Program Participants Compared to a Control or Comparison Group," *Journal of Drug Issues* 16 (1986): 537–67.

9. M. Falco, *Making of a Drug-Free America* (New York: Times Books, 1993); N. Tobler and H. Stratton, "Effectiveness of School-Based Prevention Programs: A Meta-analysis of the Research," *Journal of Primary Prevention* 18 (1997): 71–128; National Institute on Drug Abuse, *Preventing Drug Use among Children and Adolescents: A Research-Based Guide,* NIH Publication No. 97-4212 (Rockville, Md.: Department of Health and Human Services, March 1997); G. Botvin et al., "Long-term Follow-up Results of a Randomized Drug Abuse Prevention Trial in a White Middle-Class Population," *JAMA* 273 (1995): 1106–12; P. Ellickson et al., "Preventing Adolescent Drug Use: Long-term Results of a Junior High Program," *American Journal of Public Health* 83 (1993): 856–61.

10. D. Lynam et al., "Project Dare: No Effects at 10-Year Follow-Up," *Journal of Consulting and Clinical Psychology* 67 (1999): 590–93; R. Clayton et al., "The Effectiveness of Drug Abuse Resistance Education (Project Dare): 5-Year Follow-up Results," *Preventive Medicine* 25 (1996): 307–18; S. Ennett et al., "Long-term Evaluation of Drug Abuse Resistance Education," *Addictive Behaviors* 19 (1994): 113–25.

11. E. Wysong et al., "Truth and DARE: Tracking Drug Education to Graduation and as Symbolic Politics," *Social Problems* 41 (1994): 448–72.

12. G. Domenighetti et al., "Psychoactive Drug Use among Medical Doctors Is Higher than in the General Population," *Social Science and Medicine* 33 (1991): 269–74.

13. P. Hughes et al., "Prevalence of Substance Use among US Physicians," *JAMA* 267 (1992): 2333.

14. D. Dabney and R. Hollinger, "Illicit Prescription Drug Use among Pharmacists: Evidence of a Paradox of Familiarity," *Work and Occupations* 26 (1999): 77–106.

15. C. Kalb, "Playing with Pain," *Newsweek,* 9 April 2001: 44–48.

16. W. Bukoski, *A Framework for Drug Abuse Prevention Research,* NIDA Research Monograph 107 (Washington, D.C.: Department of Health and Human Services, 1991), 14.

17. D. Fejer et al., "Sources of Information about Drugs among High School Students," *Public Opinion Quarterly* 35 (1971): 235–41; Tobler, "Meta-analysis of 143 Adolescent Drug Prevention Programs."

18. A. Mauss et al., "The Problematic Prospects for Prevention in the Classroom: Should Alcohol Education Programs Be Expected to Reduce Drinking by Youth?" *Journal of Studies on Alcohol* 49 (1988): 51–61.

19. B. Flay, "Psychosocial Approaches to Smoking Prevention: A Review of Findings," *Health Psychology* 4 (1985): 449–88.

20. D. Rosenbaum, "Assessing the Effects of School-Based Drug Education: A Six-Year Multilevel Analysis of Project Dare," *Journal of Research in Crime and Delinquency* 35 (1998): 381–412.

21. Drug Reform Coordination Network, "How Much Money Is Spent on D.A.R.E.," available at www.drcnet.org/DARE/daremoney.html (accessed on 12 December 2002).

22. S. Peele, "Utilizing Culture and Behavior in Epidemiological Models of Alcohol Consumption and Consequences for Western Nations," *Alcohol and Alcoholism* 32 (1997): 51–64; S. Peele, "Promoting Positive Drinking: Alcohol, Necessary Evil or Positive Good?" in *Alcohol and Pleasure: A Health Perspective,* ed. S. Peele and M. Grant (Philadelphia: Brunner/Mazel, 1999), 1–7.

23. E. Harburg et al., "Towards a Concept of Sensible Drinking and an Illustration of Measure," *Alcohol and Alcoholism* 29 (1994): 439–50.

24. Associated Press, "Health Experts: Treat, Don't Jail, Drug Abusers," *Dallas Morning News,* 18 March 1998.

25. E. Schlosser, "The Prison-Industrial Complex," *Atlantic Monthly,* December 1998: 51–77.

26. C. Mumola, *Substance Abuse and Treatment, State and Federal Prisoners, 1997,* Bureau of Justice Statistics Special Report (Washington, D.C.: Department of Justice, January 1999).

27. P. Roman and T. Blum, *National Treatment Center Study* (Athens: Institute of Behavioral Research, University of Georgia, 1997); Substance Abuse and Mental Health Services Administration, *National Admissions to Substance Abuse Treatment Services: The Treatment Episode Data Set (TEDS) 1992–1995,* Advance Report No. 12 (Rockville, Md.: Substance Abuse and Mental Health Services Administration, Office of Applied Studies, February 1997).

28. D. Best et al., "Use of Non-prescribed Methadone and Other Illicit Drugs during Methadone Maintenance Treatment," *Drug and Alcohol Review* 19 (2000): 9–16.

29. J. Tsoh et al., "Development of Major Depression after Treatment for Smoking Cessation," *American Journal of Psychiatry* 157 (2000): 368–74.

30. Elliott Currie, *Reckoning: Drugs, the Cities, and the American Future* (New York: Hill and Wang, 1993).

31. S. Peele, "Recovering from an All-or-Nothing Approach to Alcohol," *Psychology Today,* September–October 1996: 35–43, 68–70.

32. J. Hoffman et al., "Psychosocial Treatments for Cocaine Abuse: Treatment Intensity as a Predictor of Long-term Clinical Outcomes," in *Problems of Drug Dependence 1994: Proceedings of the 56th Annual Scientific Meeting,* ed. L. Harris (Rockville, Md.: National Institute on Drug Abuse, 1995).

33. R. Fuller et al., "Disulfiram Treatment of Alcoholism: A Veterans Administration Cooperative Study," *JAMA* 256 (1986): 1449–55.

34. R. Greenstein et al., "Predictors of Favorable Outcome Following Naltrexone Treatment," *Drug and Alcohol Dependence* 12 (1983): 173–80.

35. G. Leon, "Retention in Drug-Free Therapeutic Communities," in *Improving Drug Abuse Treatment,* ed. R. Pickens et al., NIDA Research Monograph 106 (Rockville, Md.: National Institute on Drug Abuse, 1991); R. Hubbard et al., *Drug Abuse Treatment: A National Study of Effectiveness* (Chapel Hill: University of North Carolina Press, 1989); J. Zweben and J. Payte, "Methadone Maintenance in the Treatment of Opioid Dependence—A Current Perspective," *Western Journal of Medicine* 152 (1990): 588–99.

36. P. Kleinman et al., "The Magic Fix: A Critical Analysis of Methadone Maintenance Treatment," *Social Problems* 25 (1977): 208–14.

37. K. Seal et al., "Predictors and Prevention of Nonfatal Overdose among Street-Recruited Injection Heroin Users in the San Francisco Bay Area, 1998–1999," *American Journal of Public Health* 91 (2001): 1842–46.

38. See S. Peele, "Bait and Switch in Project Match: What NIAAA Research Actually Shows about Alcohol Treatment," *PsychNews International* 2 (May–June 1997).

39. W. Miller et al., "What Works? A Methodological Analysis of the Alcohol Treatment Outcome Literature," in *Handbook of Alcoholism Treatment Approaches*, 2d edition, ed. R. Hester and W. Miller (Boston: Allyn and Bacon, 1995), 33.

40. National Cancer Institute, *Clearing the Air*, NIH Publication No. 91-1647 (Washington, D.C.: National Cancer Institute, 1991); M. Fiore et al., "Methods Used to Quit Smoking in the United States," *JAMA* 263 (1990): 2760–65.

41. S. Cohen et al., "Debunking Myths about Self-Quitting: Evidence from 10 Prospective Studies of Persons Who Attempt to Quit Smoking by Themselves," *American Psychologist* 44 (1989): 1355–65; Fiore et al., "Methods Used to Quit Smoking in the United States."

42. P. Erickson et al., *The Steel Drug: Cocaine in Perspective* (Lexington, Mass.: Lexington Books, 1987); D. Waldorf et al., *Cocaine Changes: The Experience of Using and Quitting* (Philadelphia: Temple University Press, 1991); P. Biernacki, *Pathways from Heroin Addiction: Recovery without Treatment* (Philadelphia: Temple University Press, 1986); C. Winick, "Maturing Out of Narcotic Addiction," *Bulletin on Narcotics* 14 (1962): 1–7; G. Woody et al., "Clinical-Behavioral Observations of the Long-term Effects of Drug Abuse," in *Residual Effects of Abused Drugs on Behavior*, ed. J. Spencer and J. Boren, NIDA Research Monograph 101 (Rockville, Md.: National Institute on Drug Abuse, 1990); R. Smart, "Spontaneous Recovery in Alcoholics: A Review and Analysis of the Available Research," *Drug and Alcohol Dependence* 1 (1975–76): 277; W. Saunders and P. Kershaw, "Spontaneous Remission from Alcoholism: A Community Study," *British Journal of Addiction* 74 (1979): 251–65.

43. D. Dawson, "Correlates of Past-Year Status among Treated and Untreated Persons with Former Alcohol Dependence: United States, 1992," *Alcoholism: Clinical and Experimental Research* 20 (1996): 771–79.

44. G. Walters, "Spontaneous Remission from Alcohol, Tobacco, and Other Drug Abuse: Seeking Quantitative Answers to Qualitative Answers to Qualitative Questions," *American Journal of Drug and Alcohol Abuse* 26 (2000): 443–60.

45. See F. Leavitt, *Drugs and Behavior* (Thousand Oaks, Calif.: Sage Publications, 1995).

46. S. Peele, "Alcoholism, Politics, and Bureaucracy: The Consensus against Controlled-Drinking Therapy in America," *Addictive Behaviors* 17 (1992): 49–62; S. Peele, "Why and by Whom the American Alcoholism Treatment Industry Is under Siege," *Journal of Psychoactive Drugs* 22 (1990): 1–13.

47. P. Nathan and B. McCrady, "Bases for Use of Abstinence as a Goal in the Behavioral Treatment of Alcohol Abusers," *Drugs and Society* 1 (1987): 109–31.

48. Roman and Blum, *National Treatment Center Study.*

49. J. Morgenstern et al., "Affiliation with A.A. after Treatment: A Study of Therapeutic Effects and Mechanisms of Action," *Journal of Consulting and Clinical Psychology* 65 (1997): 768–77.

50. C. Weisner, "Coercion in Alcohol Treatment," in *Broadening the Base of Treatment for Alcohol Problems*, ed. Institute of Medicine (Washington, D.C.: National Academy Press, 1990), 579–610; C. Weisner and R. Room, "Financing and Ideology in Alcohol Treatment," *Social Problems* 32 (1984): 167–84.

51. *Griffin v. Coughlin*, 88 N.Y. 2d 674 (11 June 1996).

52. W. Miller, "Is a Belief to Blame?" *Psychology Today*, January–February 1998: 10.

53. C. Timko et al., "Long-term Treatment Careers and Outcomes of Previously Untreated Alcoholics," *Journal of Studies on Alcohol* 60 (1999): 437–47.

54. C. Bufe, *Alcoholics Anonymous: Cult or Cure*, 2d edition (Tucson: See Sharp Press, 1997).

55. Jack Trimpey, "Alcoholics Anonymous: Of Course It's a Cult!" available at www.positiveatheism.org/rw/ofcourse.htm (accessed on 12 December 2002).

56. G. Marlatt et al., "Preventing Alcohol Abuse in College Students: A Harm-Reduction Approach," in *Alcohol Problems among Adolescents: Current Directions in Prevention Research*, ed. G. Boyd et al. (Hillsdale, N.J.: Lawrence Erlbaum Associates, 1995), 147–72.

57. H. Kristenson et al., "Serum Glutamyl-Transferase in Screening and Continuous Control of Heavy Drinking in Middle-Aged Men," *American Journal of Epidemiology* 114 (1981): 862–72; J. Persson and

P. Magnusson, "Early Intervention in Patients with Excessive Consumption of Alcohol: A Controlled Study," *Alcohol* 6 (1989): 403–08; O. Nilssen, "The Tromso Study: Identification of and a Controlled Intervention on a Population of Early-Stage Risk Drinkers," *Preventive Medicine* 20 (1991): 518–28; R. Maheswaran et al., "Effectiveness of Advice to Reduce Alcohol Consumption in Hypertensive Patients," *Hypertension* 19 (1992): 79–84; M. Fleming et al., "Brief Physician Advice for Problem Drinkers: Long-term Efficacy and Benefit-Cost Analysis," *Alcoholism: Clinical and Experimental Research* 26 (2002): 36–43.

58. S. Wutzke et al., "The Long-term Effectiveness of Brief Interventions for Unsafe Alcohol Consumption: A 10-Year Follow-Up," *Addiction* 97 (2002): 665–75.

59. H. Kristenson et al., "Identification and Intervention of Heavy Drinking in Middle-Aged Men: Results and Follow-up of 24–60 Months of Long-term Study with Randomized Controls," *Alcoholism: Clinical and Experimental Research* 7 (1983): 203–9.

60. D. Kavanagh, "An Evaluation of Brief Correspondence Programs for Problem Drinkers," *Behavior Therapy* 30 (1999): 641–56.

61. A. Moyer et al., "Brief Interventions for Alcohol Problems: A Meta-analytic Review of Controlled Investigations in Treatment-Seeking and Non-Treatment-Seeking Populations," *Addiction* 97 (2002): 279–92.

62. M. Fiore et al., *Treating Tobacco Use and Dependence: Clinical Practice Guideline* (Rockville, Md.: Department of Health and Human Services, Public Health Service, 2000). One tip for women: Quit smoking during the follicular phase (days one–fourteen after menstrual onset) of the menstrual cycle. Women who tried to quit smoking during the luteal phase (day fifteen or longer after menstrual onset) reported stronger tobacco withdrawal symptoms and depressive symptoms than women quitting during the follicular phase. Although the study concerned smoking, changes during the menstrual cycle probably affect attempts to control any addictive behavior. K. Perkins et al., "Tobacco Withdrawal in Women and Menstrual Cycle Phase," *Journal of Consulting and Clinical Psychology* 68 (2000): 176–80.

63. S. Peele and R. DeGrandpre, "Cocaine and the Concept of Addiction: Environmental Factors in Drug Compulsions," *Addiction Research* 6 (1998): 235–63.

64. Peele and Degrandpre, "Cocaine and the Concept of Addiction."

65. I. Montoya et al., "Substance Use Disorders in Routine Psychiatric Practice," presented at the 153rd Annual American Psychiatric Association Meeting, Chicago, 13–18 May 2000; H. Pincus et al., "Psychiatric Patients and Treatments in 1997: Findings from the American Psychiatric Practice Research Network," *Archives of General Psychiatry* 56 (1999): 441–49.

66. W. Velicer et al., "Smoking Cessation and Stress Management: Applications of the Transtheoretical Model of Behavior Change," *Homeostasis* 38 (1998): 216–33.

67. W. Velicer et al., "Distribution of Smokers by Stage in Three Representative Samples," *Preventive Medicine* 24 (1995): 401–11.

13

How Drugs Work

WHAT IS A DRUG?

There is no universally accepted definition for *drug.* An adequate one for most purposes defines drugs as chemicals that affect body functions or organs. Psychoactive drugs affect thinking, perceiving, memory, mood, and overt behavior. All illegal drugs and drugs prescribed by psychiatrists are psychoactive. Doctors and unsavory characters on dimly lit street corners are not the only purveyors of psychoactive drugs. Any supermarket will do. A sixteenth-century representative to the Egyptian sultan called coffee an exhilarating drink that inspired men and women to break Islamic laws.[1] Nicotine and alcohol have powerful effects on the brain, as do many vitamins, herbs, and spices. Yet many books and articles, even those published by government agencies, include the phrase "drugs and alcohol." The false implication is that alcohol is something other than a drug. Perhaps that is why fewer than 40 percent of adults surveyed considered either alcohol or tobacco a drug.[2]

PHARMACOKINETICS

Pharmacokinetics is the branch of pharmacology that describes how drugs move around the body. It comprises the processes of absorption, distribution, metabolism, and excretion. These affect how quickly a drug acts and its intensity and duration of action.

Absorption

Unless a drug is placed directly onto its site of action, it must first be absorbed into the bloodstream. Drugs administered as capsules or other solid forms must dissolve before being absorbed, so solubility is important. Almost all solid dosage forms of drugs contain ingredients besides the active agent that increase chemical stability, mask unpleasant tastes, or add bulk to agents active in minute quantities. These fillers may affect solubility and absorption rate. Generic preparations of brand-name products contain identical amounts of active drug and often cost considerably less, but they may have different fillers and thus, occasionally, differ in effectiveness.

In many cases only a small proportion of administered drug is absorbed. Absorption rate increases when a drug is administered in high concentration and blood flow is rapid. The rate of blood flow can be increased by massage, heat, or vasodilation. Rate of absorption is speeded up by drugs that dilate blood vessels and slowed by vasoconstrictors like cocaine. The rate is also affected—in different ways for different drugs—by quantity of food in the stomach and contents of the intestines.

The route by which a drug is administered influences both rate and extent of absorption. Swallowing a pill is convenient and pain free, but many drugs taken orally are destroyed by stomach enzymes or inactivated by the liver before reaching the bloodstream. Drugs administered sublingually (under the tongue) do not go to the liver first, which is why sublingual nitroglycerin relieves angina pain whereas the same dose, if swallowed, is ineffective. For the same reason, cocaine acts rapidly when snorted into the nostrils. The large surface area of the lungs promotes rapid absorption of inhaled drugs, but smoking may modify the drug's composition; in addition, some drug is invariably lost in sidestream smoke. Intravenously injected drugs act rapidly because they go directly into the bloodstream. If they have been adulterated, as is the case with many illegal drugs, they may carry potentially dangerous germs and additives along with them. Exotic new routes of administration are being developed to speed up or slow down absorption rate or release the drug at precise times of day.

Distribution

Most behaviorally active drugs act on the brain. Drugs that reach the bloodstream are distributed throughout the body in about one minute, but two barriers retard entry into the brain. First, many drugs combine with proteins while in the bloodstream, and while bound they cannot diffuse out. The unbound drug and the protein-drug complex eventually reach an equilibrium. Then, as the unbound drug is metabolized and excreted, the equilibrium changes and the bound drug is released to reestablish it. People with impaired kidneys or liver often have fewer than normal numbers of plasma proteins, so drugs leave the bloodstream and reach the target organs rapidly. Such people may experience abnormally intense drug effects.

The second barrier, the blood–brain barrier, is composed of a capillary wall that prevents most substances from entering the brain. A dye injected into a laboratory animal will color the animal's internal organs but leave its brain pristine. Substances that dissolve readily in fats get through the blood–brain barrier relatively easily, whereas water-soluble substances do not, which explains why the common drugs of abuse are fat soluble. Altering a drug's molecular structure may change its solubility and, thus, its effectiveness. Certain drugs increase the permeability of the blood–brain barrier to other drugs.

Lorenzo and colleagues injected a drug into cats and then exposed the animals to either rapid flashes of light or various tones.[3] The drug concentrated in the brain's visual system in those cats that had received visual stimulation and in the auditory system in the cats exposed to tones. Interestingly, music festivals with light shows as accompaniment are common settings for drug users. The study suggests intriguing possibilities for getting legal drugs efficiently to their sites of action.

Metabolism

The primary mechanisms for terminating drug effects are metabolism and excretion. Metabolism, which occurs primarily in the liver, converts fat-soluble into water-soluble substances because the kidneys process water-soluble substances more readily. Rapidly metabolized drugs generally have smaller effects than those metabolized more slowly. Many drugs have many metabolites (marijuana has about eighty), some of which may be more active than the parent compound. Differences in metabolic rates and pathways account for much individual variation in response to drugs. Some people metabolize certain drugs so rapidly that their blood and tissue concentrations do not reach therapeutically effective levels; others metabolize the same drugs so slowly that usual doses are toxic.

Excretion

Although the primary excretory pathway is via the kidneys, drugs can be excreted in feces, expired air, sweat, and mothers' milk. Nitrous oxide (laughing gas) and the hallucinogenic mushroom *Amanita muscaria* are excreted unchanged. In societies where *Amanita* is prized, the urine of a recent user may become a valuable commodity. Because reindeer also like the mushroom and have a keen sense of smell, Wasson writes that it is dangerous to relieve oneself in the open when reindeer are around.[4] (This book is full of practical information.)

The rate of excretion is pH dependent. Basic drugs are excreted most rapidly when the urine is acidic; and acidic drugs, when the urine is alkaline. Thus, a weak base such as sodium bicarbonate can be lifesaving to an overdose victim of an acidic drug such as pentobarbital; and ascorbic acid can treat overdoses of the weakly basic amphetamine. (Sophisticated amphetamine users prolong the effects by first ingesting sodium bicarbonate.)

Rebound and Residual Effects

Using a drug has something in common with pulling a rubber band. Just as a rubber band shoots off in the opposite direction when let go, discontinuation of a drug may cause bodily functions to rebound in the opposite direction from the original drug effect. Withdrawal from a central nervous system depressant may precipitate seizures. Cocaine-induced euphoria is often a prelude to depression. Withdrawal from a drug that suppresses the frequency and vividness of dreams may cause rebound nightmares and then addiction—because the easiest way to reduce the discomfort of the nightmares is to take more drug.

Drugs can have other types of residual effects. Reserpine was once used to both lower high blood pressure and treat schizophrenia. But a significant proportion of reserpine-treated people became depressed, so doctors stopped prescribing it. Unfortunately, the depression often persisted so long after drug discontinuation that some people committed suicide.

Hospitalized drug abusers were grouped into three categories according to their primary drugs: stimulants, depressants, or opioids. Some patients became frequent repeat offenders over the next six years and were given repeated psychiatric evaluations while drug free. Over time, the stimulant abusers increased in schizophrenia-like symptoms, especially paranoia. The depressant group increased in depressive symptoms, cognitive impairment, and anxiety. The opioid abusers did not increase in psychiatric symptoms.[5]

Drugs may have residual effects on behavior even into the next generation. Five-day-old female rats were injected daily for fifty days with either saline or one of three antipsychotic drugs. Then they were put aside. At 120 days they were bred with males that had never received drugs. Their offspring were never exposed to drugs. But when tested in a conditioning apparatus at seventy-five days, the offspring did not learn as well as offspring of control mothers.[6]

NEUROTRANSMITTERS

Pharmacologists must learn where a drug acts to understand how it works. Identifying sites of action helped neuroscientists understand the origins of hallucinations and enabled clinical pharmacologists to develop new psychiatric drugs. Scientists seeking to unravel the mechanisms of reward and pleasure located the brain sites activated by cocaine and other drugs of abuse. Others followed a similar strategy to deepen their understanding of sleep, dreams, learning, and memory.

The brain, being the site of action for most psychoactive drugs, is the primary object of study for psychopharmacologists. The functional unit of the brain and the rest of the central nervous system is the nerve cell (neuron). Neurons vary considerably in size and shape, but all have three principal parts: a cell body, many slender dendrites that carry nerve impulses into the cell body, and one relatively thick axon that carries impulses from the cell body. The number of neurons within the human brain has been estimated at one hundred billion, and each neuron may connect with several thousand others.

Impulses that travel along neurons from dendrites to axon are propagated by tiny electric currents. However, transmission between neurons is primarily chemical. Small sacs (synaptic vesicles) at the end of each axon hold chemicals called neurotransmitters (NTs). There are probably at least one hundred different NTs. When a neuron is stimulated sufficiently, its synaptic vesicles release one or as many as six different NTs. These diffuse across a tiny gap (the synaptic cleft) to receptor molecules on nearby neurons. The first neuron is called presynaptic, and the others, postsynaptic. Excitatory NTs make postsynaptic neurons more likely to discharge their own NTs, and inhibitory NTs have the opposite effect.

After an NT acts on a postsynaptic neuron it must be inactivated. One process is metabolism, but the primary means of inactivation involves moving the NT away from the receptors and back into the presynaptic neuron's synaptic vesicle. The process, called reuptake, conserves NTs for subsequent reuse. Many psychoactive drugs affect reuptake. Cocaine, for example, blocks the reuptake of the NTs norepinephrine, dopamine, and serotonin. Thus, the NTs continue to stimulate postsynaptic neurons and augment their normal effects. The immediate effect is mood elevation, but the NTs are eventually metabolized and depleted, so depression follows. Reserpine causes a slow depletion of the same NTs, which is why it depresses.

Disruption of the reuptake mechanism is one way that psychoactive drugs affect NTs. There are at least nineteen others. Here are some examples:

- L-tyrosine is needed for producing norepinephrine, that is, L-tyrosine is a norepinephrine precursor. Norepinephrine elevates mood and is deficient in some depressed people. They often benefit from L-tyrosine supplements.[7]
- Amphetamine promotes the release of several NTs, which accounts for its stimulating effects.
- Norepinephrine increases blood pressure. Some drugs that have weaker effects on blood pressure can displace norepinephrine from synaptic vesicles, so they are used to lower blood pressure.
- Many scientists believe that schizophrenia is caused by excessive dopamine activity. Most drugs used to treat schizophrenia inhibit the activity of dopamine receptors.

- The enzyme monoamine oxidase (MAO) is crucial for metabolizing serotonin, norepinephrine, and dopamine. All three NTs affect mood. Drugs called monoamine oxidase inhibitors block the actions of MAO and so increase NT levels. They are used as antidepressants.

Several features of synaptic transmission allow for an almost infinite complexity and gradation of response. NTs act on specific receptors, but most receptors occur in several subtypes that produce different effects. Because of receptor diversity, an NT that stimulates one neuron may inhibit another. Because receptor subtypes differ in their sensitivity to NTs, some NT effects are reversed as dosage is increased. For example, acetylcholine (ACh) stimulates two receptor subtypes, called muscarinic and nicotinic. Muscarinic receptors are highly sensitive and have a small blood pressure–lowering effect. Nicotinic receptors are less sensitive but more powerful, and they raise blood pressure. So low doses of ACh lower blood pressure by acting only on muscarinic receptors, whereas high doses stimulate both types of receptors and raise blood pressure. Drugs that interact with more than one receptor subtype or receptors for more than one NT are likely to produce unwanted side effects. Drugs of the future will be designed to act on single receptors only.

Receptors on presynaptic neurons, some of which come from other neurons, respond to released NTs and influence further NT release. Some NTs release substances called second messengers that change the activity of postsynaptic neurons. Neurosteroids are substances synthesized within the brain that interact with receptors to alter synaptic transmission extremely rapidly. Various cell membrane proteins called G proteins convert incoming chemical messages to different kinds of messages. If a postsynaptic neuron is stimulated excessively, its receptors decrease in number (called down-regulation); conversely, the number of receptors increases when level of stimulation is low.

There is still another level of complexity. Although neurons make up only 10 percent of the brain's cells, neuroscientists until recently believed that they were the only cells that transmit chemical signals. The more numerous brain glial cells were thought to serve only supporting and clean-up functions. But Parpura and Haydon discovered that a type of glial cell—the astrocyte—is also important to the brain's communication network.[8] Astrocytes release the NT glutamate under normal conditions.

Specific Neurotransmitters and Their Probable Physiological and Psychological Functions

In light of the preceding paragraphs on the complex workings of the human brain, it should be obvious that there are few one-to-one relationships between NTs and behaviors. Memory, for example, is a product of the simultaneous functioning of many neurotransmitters; altering any one will alter learning and memory.[9]

Psychoactive drugs act initially on the synthesis, release, metabolism, and receptor sites of NT systems. Unfortunately, notes Khan, most explanations of how drugs work limit themselves to the initial actions and ignore secondary effects that result from interactions among NTs, neuropeptides, and hormones.[10] For example, because dopamine normally inhibits the release of ACh, drugs that interfere with the dopamine system produce, as a secondary effect, an increased release of ACh. Drugs also have tertiary effects—the final changes in behavior, emotions, and cognition. Khan writes that it is impossible to predict a drug's tertiary or therapeutic effects from its primary pharmacological actions: "The pharmaceutical industry evaluates hundreds of compounds with similar chemical structures and primary actions, but only a few of these prove to be clinically effective. For example, not all chemicals that inhibit reuptake of serotonin are effective antidepressants."[11] Please keep these comments in mind as you read about a few NTs and their probable functions. (There is a deeper limitation. We shall probably never know how the brain transforms tiny packets of chemicals into the entire panoply of human emotions and experience.)

Some NTs produce effects similar to those of psychoactive drugs. The best known belong to a group of substances collectively called endorphins, a contraction of "endogenous (produced within the body) morphines." Endorphins have morphine-like effects: They block emotional responses to pain while creating a sense of well-being. Another endogenous substance, anandamide, acts much like marijuana. Another is called CART (cocaine- and amphetamine-regulated transcript) peptide. In rats, CART injections produced effects similar to those observed with cocaine; and CART levels increased following cocaine administration. Kuhar suggests that CART gives a potential therapeutic target for drugs designed to treat addiction.[12]

Acetylcholine

ACh acts within the parasympathetic division of the autonomic nervous system to promote relaxation (reduced heart rate, lowered blood pressure, constricted pupils of the eyes, etc.). Substances that interfere with the actions of ACh are called anticholinergic. These include several antipsychotic, antianxiety, and antidepressant drugs and over-the-counter drugs containing an antihistamine. Side effects from these drugs include rapid pulse, agitation, and sensitivity to light (because of dilated pupils).

ACh also acts on the skeletal system to promote muscle contraction. The drug curare prevents ACh receptors at neuromuscular junctions from delivering their messages, so curare causes paralysis. Many insecticides and nerve gases stimulate excessive skeletal system ACh activity and thus lead to convulsions and death.

ACh is distributed throughout the brain and plays a key role in memory. Drugs that interfere with brain ACh, such as plants of the genus *Datura* and the *Amanita muscaria* mushroom, cause memory loss and hallucinations. Alzheimer's disease is associated with ACh dysfunction.[13]

Norepinephrine

Norepinephrine (NE) acts on the sympathetic division of the autonomic nervous system to promote arousal. The effects are essentially opposite to those of ACh and similar to those of anticholinergics (increased heart rate, elevated blood pressure, dilated pupils, etc.). Most stimulant drugs cause sympathetic side effects such as sensitivity to light, headache, and sweating. NE within the brain affects several behaviors, including mood.

NE is one of several compounds with a common molecular structure that are collectively called catecholamines. Dopamine and epinephrine are two other catecholamine NTs. All are excitatory and linked to the basic reward system in the brain. However, overactivity of any of these NTs may cause agitation and paranoid delusions.

Dopamine

Volkow and colleagues found a strong correlation in healthy volunteers between dopamine-receptor density and performance on an array of mental and motor tests.[14] All known addictive drugs cause dopamine release in a key structure in the brain's reward system, the nucleus accumbens. That observation led to the hypothesis that dopamine release mediates pleasurable experiences. A study by Garris and colleagues, with rats as subjects, upset this long-held view.[15] The researchers administered a pleasurable stimulus to the rats and observed significant dopamine release; but when the rats administered the stimulus to themselves, they released little dopamine. Garris and colleagues concluded that dopamine is involved in learning or anticipation of reward rather than reward itself.

A separate circuit of dopamine neurons in the midbrain is crucial for normal motor functioning. The neurons gradually die off as people age, and if dopamine levels fall below about 20 percent of normal, then symptoms of Parkinson's disease appear. Although Parkinson's disease occurs primarily in elderly people, several young heroin users in California, Maryland, and Vancouver, British Columbia, developed severe and usually irreversible parkinsonism symptoms in the early 1980s. The outbreaks were eventually traced to a contaminant in a synthetic heroin that was being sold on the streets and injected intravenously. The contaminant, N-methyl-4-phenyl-1, 2, 3, 6-tetrahydropyridine (MPTP), kills dopamine neurons. A frightening aspect for the general population is that

MPTP is structurally similar to some herbicides and pesticides. Subsequent studies showed an increased incidence of Parkinson's disease in areas with exposure to pesticides and herbicides.

Serotonin

Serotonin, also called 5-hydroxytryptamine or 5-HT, is widely distributed in the brain and regulates mood, appetite, sleep, and the perception of pain. Many hallucinogenic drugs act on a subtype of serotonin receptor. Serotonin dysfunction is implicated in several psychiatric disorders, and serious suicide attempters typically have impaired serotonin systems. Many psychiatric drugs affect the availability of serotonin at synapses. About 95 percent of the body's serotonin is outside the brain, so most serotonergic psychiatric drugs used to treat psychiatric conditions produce a variety of side effects.

Peptides

Peptides are chains of amino acids. Chains of at least one hundred amino acids are called proteins; smaller chains are called polypeptides. The endorphins are peptides. Others include substance P, which influences the experience of pain, and vassopressin, which is involved in memory formation.

Gamma-aminobutyric Acid

The amino acid gamma-aminobutyric acid (GABA) is probably the major inhibitory NT of the cerebral cortex, limbic system, and midbrain. That is, GABA release reduces the likelihood that a postsynaptic neuron will fire. A GABA receptor subtype links with receptors for the most popular antianxiety drugs. People with anxiety disorders have a diminished number of GABA receptors in brain areas associated with fear responses. When a gene that leads to the production of GABA receptors in mice was inactivated, the mutant mice showed a variety of symptoms of severe anxiety.[16]

Glutamate

Glutamate is an excitatory amino acid transmitter involved in many processes, including memory formation. Recent research suggests that glutamate plays a critical role in drug addiction. Rats repeatedly injected with amphetamine or cocaine run rapidly around their cages, make exaggerated movements, and show other signs of extreme excitation. The behaviors do not appear in rats pretreated with drugs that interfere with glutamate.[17] Grant and colleagues asked cocaine addicts to watch films of people using drug-related objects such as glass pipes and razor blades. During the procedure, the addicts' brains were scanned with positron-emission tomography. The degree of craving they reported paralleled the activity in brain regions that release glutamate in the nucleus accumbens.[18]

Others

Adenosine sedates by inhibiting the release of several excitatory NTs. Caffeine blocks adenosine receptors. And glycine is an inhibitory NT important for muscle relaxation.

NOTES

1. P. Quimme, *The Signet Book of Coffee and Tea* (New York: Signet, 1976).
2. G. Uelmen and V. Haddox, eds., *Drug Abuse and the Law Sourcebook* (New York: Clark Boardman Co., 1988).
3. A. Lorenzo et al., "Physiologically Induced Alteration of Sulfate Penetration into Brain," *Archives of Neurology* 12 (1965): 128–32.
4. G. Wasson, *Soma, Divine Mushroom of Immortality* (New York: Harcourt, 1968).
5. A. McLellan et al., "Development of Psychiatric Disorders in Drug Abusers," *New England Journal of Medicine* 301 (1979): 1310–14.
6. E. Gauron and V. Rowley, "Effects on Offspring Behavior of Mothers' Early Chronic Drug Experience," *Psychopharmacology* 16 (1969): 5–15.
7. I. Goldberg, "L-tyrosine in Depression," *Lancet* 2 (1980): 364.
8. V. Parpura and P. Haydon, "Physiological Astrocytic Calcium Levels Stimulate Glutamate Release to Modulate Adjacent Neurons," *Proceedings of the National Academy of Sciences* 97 (2000): 8629–34.
9. J. Martinez, "Memory: Drugs and Hormones," in *Learning and Memory,* ed. J. Martinez and R. Kesner (New York: Academic Press, 1986).
10. A. Khan, "How Do Psychotropic Medications Really Work?" *Psychiatric Times* 16 (12–20 October 1999): 16–20.
11. Khan, "How Do Psychotropic Medications Really Work?" 13.
12. M. Kuhar et al., "CART Peptides: Novel Addiction- and Feeding-Related Neuropeptides," *Trends in Neurosciences* 22 (1999): 316–20.
13. N. Woolf and L. Butcher, "Cholinergic Synapses: Synopsis of Anatomy and Overview of Physiology and Pathology," in *The Biological Substrates of Alzheimer's Disease,* ed. A. Scheibel and A. Wechsler (New York: Academic Press, 1989), 73–86.
14. N. Volkow et al., "Evaluation of the Human Brain Dopamine System with PET," *Journal of Nuclear Medicine* 37 (1996): 1242–56.
15. P. Garris et al., "Dissociation of Dopamine Release in the Nucleus Accumbens from Intracranial Self-Stimulation," *Nature* 398 (1999): 67–69.
16. F. Crestani et al., "Decreased $GABA_A$-Receptor Clustering Results in Enhanced Anxiety and Bias for Threat Cues," *Nature Neuroscience* 2 (1999): 833–39.
17. M. Wolf, "The Role of Excitatory Amino Acids in Behavioral Sensitization to Psychomotor Stimulants," *Progress in Neurobiology* 54 (1998): 679–720.
18. S. Grant et al., "Activation of Memory Circuits during Cue-Elicited Cocaine Craving," *Proceedings of the National Academy of Sciences* 93 (1996): 12040.

14

Classification of Psychoactive Drugs

Classification systems provide frameworks around which to organize facts and thinking, so the system chosen should reflect the classifier's interests. None is best under all circumstances. In the drug field, the federal government, law-enforcement agencies, judges, and lawyers classify by legal status, whereas some users classify all drugs as uppers or downers. Classification according to molecular structure helps chemists plan syntheses of new compounds and pharmacologists uncover relationships between structure and effects. But structural similarity does not guarantee pharmacological similarity—the powerful hallucinogen lysergic acid diethylamide (LSD) has a close relative, 2-bromo-LSD, which is only weakly active. The reason is that 2-bromo-LSD does not reach the brain after being taken orally.

Box 14.1 gives the government schedules of controlled substances. Then follows a classification of drugs used clinically to treat psychiatric disorders and a classification of drugs used recreationally. Note three points. First, all drugs have many actions. Although chlorpromazine is classified as an antipsychotic drug, it also affects the heart, kidneys, eyes, endocrine system, autonomic nervous system, sleep and dream patterns, learning, motor activity, proneness to seizures, and many other physiological and psychological functions. Second, many factors including cultural ones influence drug actions. For example, although 75 percent of U.S. respondents reported that marijuana increases their appetite and enjoyment of food, 60 percent of Jamaican users reported that marijuana reduces hunger.[1] Jamaican fieldworkers and fishermen often go many hours without food and use marijuana in part to suppress their appetites. Third, classification systems are rapidly dated. My book *Drugs and Behavior* has gone through three editions, and the classification chapter of each edition lists an almost entirely new group of drugs. As patent protections expire and generics enter the market, companies develop new drugs so they can once again have exclusive rights. The only drugs used in the United States by a substantial number of people over a period of more than thirty years are caffeine, nicotine, alcohol, and several illegal substances such as marijuana, cocaine, heroin, and LSD.

DRUGS USED CLINICALLY

The Diagnostic and Statistical Manual of Mental Disorders is published by the American Psychiatric Association and periodically revised. The 1994 revision, *DSM-IV,* lists more than four hundred disorders. Conditions listed in the *DSM-IV* that afflict large numbers of people and are frequently treated with drugs form the basis of the drug classification system below.

Anxiety Disorders

Sufferers from generalized anxiety disorder experience excessive anxiety and tension. Although they do not dwell on any one specific worry, they spend much of their lives worrying. Panic disorder is characterized by recurrent sudden attacks of overwhelming anxiety. Victims of obsessive-compulsive disorder experience persistent, uncontrollable, unwanted thoughts and urges to perform senseless rituals.

The most widely used drugs to treat anxiety disorder are derived from the compound benzodiazepine. In the 1970s, benzodiazepines (BZs) became the most frequently prescribed psychiatric drugs in the United States. In addition to treating anxiety, short-acting BZs are prescribed for people who have trouble falling asleep. Intermediate-acting BZs are used for people who awaken early in the morning, and long-acting ones are prescribed when severe anxiety accompanies insomnia. When used for sleep problems, the drugs are called hypnotics. BZs are also used to treat muscle strains and seizures. Their effects include lowered pulse, temperature, and respiration; lack of coordination; lethargy; and drunken behavior (very much like alcohol). At low doses they often stimulate. Commonly used benzodiazepines for treating anxiety disorders (brand names in parentheses) include the following:

Short acting: midazolam (Dormicum, Versed) and triazolam (Halcion)
Intermediate acting: alprazolam (Xanax), bromazepam (Lectopam), estazolam (ProSom), halazepam (Paxipam), lorazepam (Ativan), oxazepam (Serax, Seresta), and temazepam (Restoril)

Box 14.1. Government Schedules of Controlled Substances

The Federal Controlled Substances Act of 1972 divided drugs into five schedules based on their potential for abuse and physiological or psychological dependence.

- Schedule I: No accepted medical use and high abuse potential. Not obtainable by prescription. Examples—heroin, LSD, psilocybin, peyote, marijuana,[1] methaqualone
- Schedule II: Some currently accepted medical use and high abuse potential. Prescription required. Examples—cocaine, amphetamines, opium, morphine, and methadone
- Schedule III: Some currently accepted medical use and moderate abuse potential. Prescription required. Examples—glutethimide, nalorphine, some anabolic steroids, certain stimulants, and depressants not listed in Schedules I or II
- Schedule IV: Some currently accepted medical use and lower abuse potential than Schedule III drugs. Prescription required. Examples—benzodiazephines, fenfluramine
- Schedule V: Some currently accepted medical use and low abuse potential. No prescription required, but certain conditions must be met, for example, the drug must be sold by a pharmacist, who must keep an official record of the sale, and the purchaser must be at least eighteen. Examples—buprenorphine, propylhexedrine, and preparations containing limited amounts of certain opioids

NOTE

1. In May 2001, the U.S. Supreme Court ruled that a federal law classifying marijuana as illegal has no exception for ill patients. Justice Clarence Thomas wrote for the unanimous court: "In the case of the Controlled Substances Act, the statute reflects a determination that marijuana has no medical benefits worthy of an exception (outside the confines of a government-approved research project)."

Long acting: chlordiazepoxide (Librium), clonazepam (Klonopin, Leponex), clorazepate (Tranxene, Tranxilene), diazepam (Valium, Stesolid), flurazepam (Dalmane), nitrazepam (Mogadon), prazepam (Centrax, Reapam), and quazepam (Doral)

Nonbenzodiazepine antianxiety drugs include buspirone (Buspar), clonidine (Catapres), and meprobamate (Miltown). Unlike the benzodiazepines, buspirone has no anticonvulsant or muscle-relaxant properties.

Depression

Clinically depressed people are extremely sad, demoralized, and often suicidal. Drugs used to treat depression are of three main types, though several atypical antidepressants (ADs) have been developed in recent years. Tricyclics (TCAs) increase brain activity of norepinephrine and serotonin. Monoamine oxidase inhibitors (MAOIs) block the enzyme that metabolizes norepinephrine, dopamine, and serotonin, and so MAOIs enhance the activity of those neurotransmitters. There are two similar enzymes, monoamine oxidase A and B. The first generation of MAOIs blocked both enzymes. The more recently developed selective MAOIs block only one or the other. In addition, selective MAOIs are reversible. These two properties make them much safer. The third and most recently developed large class of ADs is the serotonin selective reuptake inhibitors (SSRIs), which increase serotonin activity. Following are the names of commonly used drugs to treat depression (brand names in parentheses):

TCAs: amitriptyline (Elavil, Typtanol), amoxapine (Asendin), ciralopram (Seropram), clomipramine (Anafranil), desipramine (Norpramin, Pertofrane), doxepin (Adapin, Sinequan), imipramine (Tofranil), isocarboxazid (Marplan), maprotoline (Ludiomil), mirtazepine (Remeron), nortriptyline (Aventyl, Pamelor), parosetine (Aroxat), pramipexole (Mirapex), prazepam (Centrax, Reapam), protriptyline (Vivactil), reboxetine (Edronax, Vestral), and trimipramine (Surmontil)

MAOIs: brofaromine, moclobemide (Manerix, Aurorix), pargyline, phenelzine (Nardil), selegiline (also called deprenyl; Eldepryl), and tranylcypromine (Parnate) (the three italicized are selective inhibitors)

SSRIs: citalopram (Celexa, Prisdal), fluoxetine (Deprax, Prozac, Veritina), fluvoxamine (Luvox, Faverin), sertraline (Altruline, Lustral, Zoloft, Sercerin), paroxetine (Aropax, Paxil, Seroxat)

Miscellaneous ADs: bupropion (Wellbutrin), lithium (Eskalith), nefazodone (Serzone, Dutonin), reboxetine (Edronax), trazodone (Desyrel), venlafaxine (Dobupal, Effexor)

Bipolar Disorder

Manic people are full of energy and enthusiasm, although they frequently fail to finish what they start. They typically alternate between periods of mania and depression, so the condition was once called manic depression. The current term is *bipolar disorder.* Following are the names of commonly used drugs to treat bipolar disorder and stabilize mood (brand names in parentheses): carbamazepine (Tegretol), lithium (Cibalith-S, Eskalith), felbamate (Felbatol), gabapentin (Neurontin), lamotrigine (Lamictal), topiramate (Topamax), and valproic acid (Depakene).

Schizophrenia

The most widely used drugs for treating schizophrenia are called antipsychotics. Older antipsychotics block a subset of dopamine receptors, the D2 receptors. Newer ones are called atypical because they have relatively weak actions on D2 receptors and greater serotonin blockade. Some older antipsychotics (brand names in parentheses) include chlorpromazine (Thorazine), fluphenazine (Prolixin, Anatensol), haloperidol (Haldol), loxapine (Loxitane), mesoridazine (Serentil), molindone (Moban), perphenazine (Trilafon), pimozide (Orap), sertindole (Serlect), thioridazine (Mellaril), and trifluoperazine (Stelazine). Atypical ones include clozapine (Clozaril), olanzapine (Zypreza), quetiapine (Seroquel), and risperidone (Risperdal).

Other Disorders

Attention deficit/hyperactivity disorder (ADHD) is marked by a group of symptoms that usually includes hyperactivity and difficulty in concentrating. Drugs used to treat ADHD include the stimulants methylphenidate (Ritalin), dextroamphetamine (Dexedrine), methamphetamine (Desoxyn), and an amphetamine-dextroamphetamine combination (Adderall). Clonidine, a drug normally used to treat hypertension, is another popular choice, and caffeine has also been used.

Various drugs are used to treat drug abuse. Antidepressant and antianxiety drugs help abusers endure withdrawal and may reduce coexisting psychiatric pathology. Some drugs substitute for the abused drug but with more favorable properties. Methadone, for example, prevents withdrawal symptoms from heroin and other opiates. Whereas heroin must be injected, often several times a day, methadone can be taken orally, and a single dose lasts about twenty-four hours. Antagonists block the pharmacological effects of the abused drug. Unlike substitutes, antagonists have no abuse potential themselves. Naloxone and naltrexone are heroin antagonists; they reverse its effects and prevent users from experiencing pleasure from heroin. Mecamylamine reduces craving for tobacco. Deterrents cause unpleasantness when combined with the abused drug. People experience several unpleasant effects if they drink alcohol within several days of having taken disulfiram (Antabuse).

Sales of prescription painkillers (analgesics) have tripled since 1996 and reached $1.8 billion in 2000. In 1999, an estimated four million Americans used analgesics, not only for pain relief but also because analgesics induce a worry-free euphoric state.[2] Abuse of analgesics containing opioids is a rapidly growing problem. OxyContin alone is believed responsible for more than one hundred twenty fatal overdoses among drug misusers in recent years in the United States.[3] Drugs in this category include hydrocodone (Vicodin), hydromorphone (Dilaudid), meperidine (Demerol), oxycodone (Percodan), propoxyphene (Darvon), and oxycodone controlled release (OxyContin).

DRUGS USED RECREATIONALLY

Stimulants

Stimulants such as amphetamine, methamphetamine, methylphenidate (Ritalin), cocaine, and caffeine increase alertness, tension, and activity of the sympathetic division of the autonomic nervous system. They impair sleep and suppress appetite (which accounts for their popularity among dieters). The most prominent psychic changes include euphoria, increased self-confidence, and feelings of great muscular strength. Wadler suggests that Roman gladiators in 600 B.C.E. used stimulants in the famed Circus Maximus to stave off fatigue.[4] Nicotine has much in common with drugs in this category.

Powdered cocaine hydrochloride can be treated with ammonia or sodium bicarbonate (baking soda) and water and heated. The process transforms it into a substance that produces a crackling sound when smoked and is called crack cocaine. Crack users experience a high within ten seconds.

Central Nervous System Depressants

Alcohol, barbiturates, benzodiazepines, and related drugs are used extensively outside of medical practice. On the street they are called downers. Users enjoy their disinhibiting, antianxiety, and sleep-promoting effects. Although small doses produce a sense of well-being, larger doses cause slurred speech, motor incoordination, mood swings, reduced attention span, and impaired memory.

Psychedelics

These drugs, also called hallucinogenic and psychotomimetic, change mood and thinking at doses that produce just minor physiological effects. They heighten awareness of sensory stimuli so that perceptions become brilliant and intense, but they reduce the ability to control what is experienced. Users often experience intense emotions and increased suggestibility. The psychedelics promote introspection and feelings of profound religious and philosophical insight.

Drugs in this category include LSD, peyote, mescaline, and psilocybin. Many species of plants and mushrooms are hallucinogenic. LSD's effects include mood changes, intensification of colors and other sensory intake, merging of senses (synesthesia) so that sounds may be seen as color patterns, distortions in the perception of space and time, and release from the subconscious of repressed material.

Mescaline, the chief psychoactive ingredient of the peyote cactus, is related chemically to norepinephrine and amphetamine. Peyote contains about sixty alkaloids besides mescaline that contribute to its effects. Many other cacti contain hallucinogenic alkaloids. The initial phase after ingestion of peyote or mescaline lasts one to two hours and is unpleasant, characterized by nausea, tremor, perspiration, and elevated pulse rate and blood pressure. Shulgin describes it as an experience in which the hangover precedes the drunk.[5] The primary psychic effects are visual. Both substances induce vivid hallucinations consisting of brightly colored lights, geometric designs, and brilliantly colored objects that are treated as sources of wonder. Mitchell writes that "these shows are expensive. . . . The experience, however, was worth one such headache and indigestion, but was not worth a second."[6]

3,4-Methylenedioxymethamphetamine (MDMA or Ecstasy) has been classified as a psychedelic, but it does not produce cognitive or perceptual distortion. It intensifies mood, accentuating both anxiety and feelings of euphoria. Imagery becomes dreamlike and can be dispelled by opening the eyes. Most people become aware of a sense of physical and mental well-being.

Psychedelic Anesthetics

Phencyclidine (PCP, angel dust) is a once-popular veterinary anesthetic, and ketamine has been used in surgery on both human and nonhuman animals. Both drugs are hallucinogenic and cause users to feel dissociated from themselves and their environments. Acute effects include elevated pulse, temperature, and respiration; muscle rigidity; and reduced sensitivity to pain. Some people enjoy the experience.

Inhalants

The intoxicating effects of nitrous oxide (laughing gas) and ethyl ether have attracted users for more than a century. Nitrous oxide is still used by doctors and dentists to relax patients. Other often-abused inhalants include antifreeze, cleaning agents, gasoline, kerosene, paint thinner, various forms of glue, and industrial solvents such as toluene. All the inhalants are generalized central nervous system depressants. They induce giddiness, euphoria, a feeling of floating, slurred speech, and visual and auditory hallucinations.

Narcotic Analgesics (Opioids, Opiates)

Narcotic analgesics relieve pain. They lower pulse, temperature, and respiration; constrict pupils; and cause drooping of the upper eyelids, low raspy speech, and itchy skin because of a histamine reaction. They generally induce a feeling of euphoria. The narcotic analgesics include opium, heroin, morphine, methadone, and codeine. Note, cocaine and marijuana do not belong in this category.

Marijuana

The hemp plant synthesizes at least four hundred chemicals, including more than sixty cannabinoids. One, delta-9-tetrahydrocannabinol, is responsible for most of the psychological effects of marijuana (pot, weed, Mary Jane). During the past twenty-five years, growers developed sophisticated cultivation methods for increasing levels of delta-9-tetrahydrocannabinol and, thus, the potency of marijuana. Marijuana induces a relaxed pleasant state that facilitates social interactions. It produces a host of other effects including hilarity, occasional anxiety, confusion, difficulty in concentration, flights of ideas, and distortions of space and time. Appreciation of music and colors is enhanced. There is often (an illusion of?) profound insight. Physical effects include increased pulse and heart rate, reddening of the conjunctiva of the eye, dry mouth, drooping eye, muscular weakness, and sleepiness. At high doses, users may experience hallucinations. The effects often appear within seconds of smoking marijuana but considerably more slowly when it is eaten.

Miscellaneous Drugs

Kava, which initially stimulates and then induces a pleasant sleeplike state, and the powerful psychedelic *Amanita muscaria* are used in many parts of the world. Indians of Northern Canada ingest asarone, the active principle of the plant *Acorus calamus,* to stave off fatigue. Ethiopians and Yemenites chew on the amphetamine-like drug khat. The related household spices nutmeg and mace produce marijuana-like and even LSD-like effects but only at doses dangerously close to those that can cause severe toxicity and death. Jimson weed and other members of the plant genus *Datura* are anticholinergic. Their effects include impaired memory and motor ability, slurred speech, and confusion. They are popular among various Native American tribes of the American Southwest.

NOTES

1. C. Tart, *On Being Stoned* (Palo Alto: Science and Behavior, 1971); V. Rubin and L. Comitas, *Ganja in Jamaica* (Garden City, N.Y.: Anchor, 1976).
2. C. Kalb, "Playing with Pain," *Newsweek,* 9 April 2001: 44–48.
3. F. Charatan, "News Roundup," *British Medical Journal* 322 (2001): 1143.
4. G. Wadler, *Doping in Sport: From Strychnine to Genetic Enhancement, It's a Moving Target,* available at www.law.duke.edu/sportscenter/wadler.pdf (accessed on 15 March 2001).
5. A. Shulgin, lecture, California State University, Hayward, January 1980.
6. Mitchell in A. Hoffer and H. Osmond, *The Hallucinogens* (New York: Academic, 1967), 4.

15

Variability

The *Physicians' Desk Reference* (*PDR*) is a yearly publication, updated with periodic supplements, whose contents are written by each drug's manufacturer after negotiated discussions with representatives of the Food and Drug Administration. The *PDR* lists drugs by class and includes information on dosages and contraindications. Approximately five hundred thousand copies are delivered free to doctors, and five hundred thousand more are sold to the general public. According to the publisher, 90 percent of doctors consider the *PDR* their most used reference book, and 97 percent consult it when prescribing a drug about which they have limited information. But information in the *PDR* is not entirely trustworthy:[1]

- Drug companies sell more of their products if doctors prescribe high doses, so they often omit studies showing that lower-than-recommended dosages are equally or more effective. In some cases the *PDR* reports the effectiveness of a low-dose preparation, but the manufacturer markets only higher doses.
- Doctors can prescribe approved drugs for any conditions they choose. But for each condition listed in the *PDR* as treatable by a drug, manufacturers must go through a lengthy and costly application procedure. So although their sales representatives and advertisements encourage doctors to use the drug in multiple ways, the *PDR* may list it as treating only one condition. That creates a problem because even if the drug is effective for two separate conditions, the appropriate dosages may differ, and doctors may prescribe the inappropriate dose.
- Many drugs are recommended in the one or two dosages that worked best for most subjects in a research study or are effective in typical middle-aged

adults with only the condition being treated. But if special characteristics or circumstances of individual patients are ignored, a standard dose can be ineffective or harmful.

- The *PDR* may cite a study showing that patients with a particular condition, treated with the drug, improved on average 50 percent more than patients treated with placebo. Such information is ambiguous and easily misinterpreted. The drug might improve all patients about 50 percent, or might improve every patient with a specific form of the condition and nobody else, or might improve 100 percent of patients with a certain genotype and nobody else.
- Reactions to drugs are influenced by many factors, and people respond variably. Stimulants sometimes sedate, depressants stimulate, euphoriants cause anguish, and placebos duplicate virtually any action of any drug. When volunteers were injected with precise amounts of cocaine, or smoked cocaine base or marijuana under controlled conditions, their peak plasma levels varied about fivefold.[2] Greenblatt and colleagues write, "Even within a diagnostically and demographically homogeneous group of patients receiving the same daily dose of the same drug for the same length of time, therapeutic and/or toxic response may vary greatly. Explanation of these differences is beyond the scope of controlled clinical trials as customarily designed."[3]

I occasionally give my psychopharmacology class a multiple choice question. No matter what I put for A, B, and C, the correct answer is always D:

Which of the following affects response to drugs?
A. __________
B. __________
C. __________
D. All of above

The influences on drug response can be grouped under five somewhat arbitrary and overlapping sets of variables: organismic, drug, environmental, task, and expectational.

ORGANISMIC VARIABLES

Age

Several bodily functions change with age, such as the efficiency of the liver and kidneys; pH of gastric acids; percentage of lean muscle mass, water, and fat; level of plasma proteins; and permeability of the blood–brain barrier. Each factor can affect pharmacokinetics (see pages 225–28) and, thus, the intensity and duration of action of many drugs. Pediatric and geriatric pharmacology are important medical specialties.

Weight

Other things being equal, heavier people need more drug than lighter people. Clinical researchers typically express dosages in milligrams of drug per kilogram of body weight. People who administer drugs should calculate dosages according to body weight. Clinical practitioners often require greater precision, so they consider proportion of body fat to muscle. (Many drugs are stored in fat and remain active longer in overweight people than in more muscular people of the same weight.)

Gender

Women produce less alcohol dehydrogenase, the enzyme that breaks down alcohol before it enters the bloodstream, so they absorb about 30 percent more alcohol than men of equal weight who drink the same amount. Women require smaller doses per body weight of antipsychotics, and they eliminate certain antianxiety and hypnotic drugs more slowly than men do. Women on average have slower metabolic rates. Pentazocine and related opioids produce greater pain relief in women than in men.[4] Drug effects change throughout the menstrual cycle and during pregnancy.[5]

For a given dosage, adjusted for body weight, plasma levels of the antidepressants fluvoxamine, sertraline, and amitriptyline are lower in men than in women.[6] Schizophrenic women have higher plasma levels of clozapine per unit of dose than schizophrenic men.[7]

The sexes may react differently even at the neurotransmitter level. Male mice that lack the gene that produces the neurotransmitter nitric oxide become hyperaggressive. Females without the gene are less aggressive than normal females.[8]

Doctors should be sensitive to the widespread gender differences, but most drugs for adults come in only a few dosages based on a standard male weight. That may at least partially explain why more women than men suffer adverse drug reactions.[9]

Biological Rhythms

Every physiological process of every living organism that has been tested shows rhythmic cycles of activity. Some cycles repeat each second (heartbeat), every ninety minutes (the nighttime sleep cycle), each day (thousands of circadian rhythms have been documented), every month (the menstrual cycle), annually (reproductive behavior and hibernation in various animals), and over many intermediate time periods. The rhythms affect many body processes, including responsiveness to drugs. Time of administration influences the effectiveness of over-the-counter analgesics, anticancer and antibacterial drugs, and drugs used in cardiology, neurology, and psychiatry. In fact, more than one hundred drugs vary significantly in concentrations or effects depending on when they are taken during the day.[10]

Chronopharmacologists study the effectiveness of drugs as a function of time of administration and believe that prescriptions should routinely indicate when to take the drug. Certain processes crucial to cell division either speed up or slow down at different times of the day or night. For example, the activity of an enzyme that breaks down the anticancer drug fluorouracil, and thus improves its tolerability, increases by 40 percent around midnight. In a study of women with advanced ovarian cancer, one group received doxorubicin at 6 a.m. and cisplatin at 6 p.m. A second group received the same drugs at the same times but in reverse order. Four times as many women in the first group as in the second survived for at least five years.[11] Patients with colorectal cancer were given either regular chemotherapy or the same drugs administered with a programmable pump that provided the drugs at optimal times. Chronotherapy reduced the rate of severe adverse effects on the lining of the gastrointestinal tract fivefold and halved the rate of functional nerve damage, such as loss of sensitivity in fingertips or feet.[12]

Theophylline, used to treat asthmatics, is usually given in a divided dose that produces a steady blood concentration throughout the day. But most asthmatics experience their worst attacks between 3 a.m. and 5 a.m. A sustained-release preparation of theophylline, given in a single dose between 5 p.m. and 8 p.m., reaches peak blood concentration in the early morning and produces better results than the traditional method.[13]

Blood pressure is higher during waking hours and lower during sleeping hours. Upon awakening, blood pressure increases rapidly, which may account for the increased incidence of stroke, heart attack, and sudden death between the hours of 6 a.m. and 9 a.m. Patients at risk have been encouraged to take blood pressure–lowering drugs before breakfast, but the drugs would be more effective if taken immediately upon awakening.[14]

Personality

Personality variables affect both proneness to drug use and responsiveness. Amphetamine and related drugs amplify existing mood, so that anxious people become more anxious, mild depression becomes pronounced, and cheerful people reach great heights of euphoria. There is an axiom among users of psychedelic drugs: "If you have a garden in your mind (before you take the drug), you will find yourself in a garden. If you have a garbage pail, you will find yourself in the garbage." On the other hand, drugs that raise the level of a physiological or psychological function usually produce smaller effects if the initial level is high rather than low. Most drugs that depress the function produce greater effects if the initial level is high. For example, antihypertensive drugs reduce blood pressure most in people with high blood pressure, and blood pressure–raising drugs have strongest effects on people with low blood pressure.

Physiological State

People with impaired kidney or liver function have altered pharmacokinetics, so they are likely to have prolonged or intense reactions to a variety of drugs. Pharmacokinetics is also affected by body build, ratio of muscle to fat, gastric pH, and many other factors. Chronic drinkers become tolerant to alcohol's effects because the enzymes that metabolize alcohol become more numerous. The drinkers then become tolerant to other drugs metabolized by the same enzymes. Cigarette smokers metabolize many drugs more rapidly than nonsmokers do. Pregnancy reduces activity of the enzyme CYP1A2, which metabolizes caffeine. Thus, pregnant women show increased sensitivity to caffeine.

Handedness

The literature is sparse on drug effects as a function of handedness. In several studies, left-handers showed a greater drug-related change in their electroencephalograms than right-handers did. The magnitude of the changes correlated with handedness scores.[15]

Genetics

Certain drugs are active in rats but not humans, in women but not men, and in people of some races but not others. Genetic variations play a huge role. Pharmacogeneticists try to identify specific genes and gene products associated with diseases that might act as targets for new drugs, as well as genetic variations that affect all phases of drug activity. Metabolic differences are the most important. Individuals differ much more in drug metabolizing enzymes than in excretory rates or pathways, so drug effects are most variable for drugs whose primary means of elimination is metabolism rather than excretion. Drugs are ineffective if metabolized too quickly and potentially toxic if metabolized too slowly. Pharmacogenetic DNA testing may someday help doctors choose the right dose of the right drug for each patient.

A family of roughly thirty enzymes found mostly in the liver, the cytochrome P450s, plays an important role in the metabolism of most drugs listed in the *PDR.*[16] One member of the family, P450 CYP2D6 (debrisoquine hydroxylase), metabolizes about 25 percent of all drugs, including many prescribed by psychiatrists. The antidepressant nortriptyline, given to people with an inactive form of the gene (slow metabolizers), is effective at one-twenty-fifth to one-fiftieth the dose of nortriptyline given to people with multiple copies of the CYP2D6 gene (rapid metabolizers).[17] Slow metabolizers do not convert the mild painkiller codeine into the much more powerful morphine. Identifying slow metabolizers in advance would make their dental visits less unpleasant, as they do respond to other analgesics. Compared with non-redheaded women, redheads required more of a commonly used anesthetic, desflurane, to suppress movement in response to small electric shocks.[18]

Many adverse drug reactions have a genetic basis. Kalow describes a particularly tragic case in which a young boy died following general anesthesia. Some time later his sister required an operation, and the anesthesiologist assured the parents that the boy's death had been an extremely rare occurrence. He said that no special precautions were needed. He was mistaken, and she died under the same circumstances.[19]

Ethnicity

Racial and ethnic groups vary in their proportion of slow and rapid CYP2D6 metabolizers, but genetic explanations sometimes obscure other factors such as cultural practices that affect drug experiences. Some drugs are metabolized differently by Indians living in India compared with both British whites and Indian emigrants to Great Britain. But the emigrants who follow their traditional vegetarian diet respond like Indians in India. For those drugs, diet, not genetics, is the key.[20]

DRUG VARIABLES

Dose–Response Relations

Strychnine in minute doses improves memory, but higher doses kill. A can of beer may enhance the pleasure of watching football, but the person who guzzles two six-packs may confuse the football game with lawn bowling. More generally, the response to a drug depends on how much is taken. Because people vary, no single dose fits all. The potency of a drug is often defined as the minimum dose needed to produce positive effects in 50 percent of subjects. Maximum efficacy refers to the strongest positive effect not accompanied by adverse side effects in

50 percent of subjects. Maximum efficacy is the more important characteristic. Consider the following: Drugs X and Y both relieve headaches but cause nausea as a side effect. The nausea occurs in 50 percent of users who take a 1milligram dose of X or 100 milligram dose of Y. Which drug is better?

The question cannot be answered with the information given. Suppose that 0.001 milligrams of X and 100 milligrams of Y relieve pain in 50 percent of users. Drug X would be preferred. The therapeutic index is the ratio of the dose that causes side effects in 50 percent of users to the dose that is effective with 50 percent. The higher the therapeutic index, the better, although there are no hard-and-fast rules—it depends to a great extent on the condition being treated. For X, the therapeutic index would be 1/.001 = 1,000; and for Y, an unacceptable 100/100 = 1. Lithium and old tricyclic antidepressants have therapeutic indexes of 5 or less. The therapeutic index of many of the newer antidepressants is much higher.

Now suppose that 0.1 milligrams of X and 10 milligrams of Y relieve pain in 50 percent of users. The therapeutic index would be the same for X and Y (for X, 1/.1 = 10; for Y, 100/10 = 10). Yet advertisers might try to persuade unwary consumers to buy X on the grounds that it is more powerful or Y because each pill contains more active ingredient.

Repeated Administrations of the Same Drug

Tolerance occurs when a given dose of drug produces smaller effects than it did initially. *Pharmacokinetic (dispositional) tolerance* refers to changes in processes such as absorption, binding with plasma proteins, and metabolism that reduce a drug's concentration at its site of action. *Pharmacodynamic tolerance* refers to changes within systems affected by the drug, such as the number of receptors or their sensitivity, that reduce responsiveness to the drug. Behavioral tolerance occurs through learning, as demonstrated by Chen. He injected alcohol into rats either before training them in a maze or afterward. He trained the rats for six days. The impairing effects of alcohol diminished each day as the rats became tolerant—but only in animals that received the alcohol prior to training. Unless they ran in the maze while in the alcohol state, they did not become tolerant to it.[21]

A different type of behavioral tolerance occurs when certain stimuli reliably precede administration of a drug. The stimuli, such as drug paraphernalia, the presence of certain people, being in a particular room, and so forth, may come to elicit anticipatory responses that partially cancel the drug effect. For example, alcohol lowers body temperature. Rats given alcohol repeatedly and then a placebo under identical conditions typically respond to the placebo with a brief rise in temperature.

Tolerance does not develop equally to all aspects of drug action, so effectiveness can change over time. Alcoholics become resistant to alcohol's sedating and intoxicating effects but not to the lethal dose. The constipating effects of heroin persist long after the same dose no longer produces euphoria.

Heroin users become tolerant to morphine, and morphine users to heroin, a phenomenon called cross-tolerance. Other related drugs, such as mescaline and lysergic acid diethylamide (a.k.a. LSD), and alcohol and many central nervous system depressants, also produce cross-tolerance. Reverse tolerance (sensitization) occurs to some drugs, especially stimulants; with repeated exposure, responsiveness to the drug increases. Drugs given repeatedly over a short period of time may promote very rapid tolerance, called tachyphylaxis.

Dosage Regimen

If a drug's concentration at its site of action is too low, the drug will be ineffective. Too high a concentration may cause adverse effects. Sadly, the standard intervals prescribed for many drugs, such as three times per day with meals, result in plasma levels outside the therapeutic range for much of the day. If the drug is taken three times during the roughly twelve hours between breakfast and dinner, plasma levels during that time period are likely to be too high; during the other twelve hours they will be too low.[22] On the other hand, schedules that require multiple daily doses may inconvenience or confuse patients and reduce their compliance. For many psychiatric drugs, proper compliance is more important than a steady state of plasma concentration.

Drug Interactions

Drug company research almost always involves comparing the company drug with a placebo or a competitor's product. Rarely are drug combinations studied, and if so, then almost exclusively on healthy young volunteers. Despite lack of information about drug cocktails, and even though the presence of one drug may affect the actions of a second in unknown ways, combinations are frequently prescribed by doctors (polypharmacy) and mixed by street users (polydrug abuse). Survey data indicate that about 25 percent of psychiatric patients (diagnosis not specified) in outpatient settings receive two antipsychotic drugs.[23] The actual frequency is probably substantially higher. Yet there are few controlled studies supporting antipsychotic drug polypharmacy. Stahl calls it a "dirty little secret."[24]

To ease the agitation produced by cocaine, users often snort heroin. Benzodiazepines are used to heighten the euphoriant effects of opioids, to relieve withdrawal symptoms between heroin doses, to temper cocaine highs, and to enhance alcohol highs. About 80 percent of alcoholics under the age of thirty regularly use at least one other drug.[25]

Some drug combinations are desirable. For example, naloxone reverses the effects of opiates and is used to treat overdose. Pindolol may improve the response to selective serotonin reuptake inhibitors. Disulfiram interferes with the metabolism of alcohol, so a person who takes disulfiram and then alcohol within five days will have a violently unpleasant reaction. The interaction has been used to help motivated alcoholics quit.

But interactions can occur in unpredictable ways and cause adverse reactions. For example, various drugs taken with the analgesic phenacetin block phenacetin's major metabolic pathway. The secondary pathway produces a toxic product, so the combination of phenacetin with another drug had serious consequences for many people.[26] Many antidepressant and antianxiety drugs bind tightly to plasma proteins. A normally safe dose, if administered after the anticoagulant (blood-thinning drug) warfarin, may displace warfarin into the bloodstream and cause toxicity.

Taking two drugs simultaneously increases the risk of an adverse effect, taking another drug increases the risk more, and taking eight drugs doubles it.[27] The more sites of action affected by a drug, the greater is the potential for interactions. Polypharmacy has been predicted to soon become the principle safety issue for elderly people with chronic health problems.[28] Hospital patients typically get ten to fifteen drugs during their stay.[29]

Serotonin syndrome, a potentially fatal disorder, can result from combining highly serotonergic drugs such as the newer antidepressants with each other or with other strongly serotonergic drugs. About 90 percent of heroin-related deaths in 1995 involved heroin in combination with other drugs, most often cocaine.[30] A substantial proportion of people admitted to emergency departments for heroin abuse and to publicly funded treatment programs for heroin also used cocaine and alcohol.[31] Alcohol interacts with anesthetics, antianxiety drugs, antibiotics, antidepressants, antihistamines, antiseizure drugs, and cardiovascular drugs. Alcohol-related interactions are by far the leading cause of emergency room drug episodes.[32] Many nonprescription drugs, especially antacids, antihistamines, and decongestants, interact with other drugs. Aspirin enhances the effect of anticoagulants and can promote excessive bleeding. Cigarette smoking, by increasing the production of liver enzymes that metabolize caffeine and many other drugs, weakens their effects. Plasma levels of caffeine may rise considerably and cause severe anxiety in coffee drinkers who stop smoking; this may sabotage their attempt to quit.

Several popular herbs interact with standard drugs. Ginkgo, ginseng, feverfew, garlic, and ginger may cause spontaneous and excessive bleeding in patients taking the anticoagulant warfarin (Coumadin). Ephedra may cause sedation, heart attack, seizure, or death when used with various decongestants or stimulants, including caffeine. Kava can produce deep sedation and coma when combined with alcohol, sleeping pills, or antianxiety drugs. St. John's wort taken with tetracyclines increases sensitivity to the burning effects of the sun. Taken with some antidepressants, St. John's wort may produce serotonin syndrome. It intensifies or prolongs the effects of some anesthetic and narcotic drugs.

Drugs are absorbed into the bloodstream primarily from the intestines. If the stomach is too acidic, some drugs dissolve there before reaching the intestine. Therefore, drugs should not be taken with substances such as soda pop and high-acid fruit and vegetable juices that increase stomach acidity. On the other hand, many drugs are metabolized in the intestines before being absorbed, so they never get into the bloodstream. Grapefruit juice inhibits the intestinal enzyme cytochrome P450 3A4, thus increasing absorption and raising peak levels of benzodiazepines, triazolam, and other drugs by up to 900 percent.[33]

Calcium-containing foods such as milk interfere with the absorption of tetracycline and other antibiotics. Milk reduces the absorption of some drugs but enhances absorption of water-insoluble ones. The interaction can be beneficial or harmful. A person who takes a drug occasionally with water and occasionally with milk may experience highly variable reactions. Cruciferous vegetables such as cabbage, cauliflower, and Brussels sprouts affect the metabolism of many drugs. So does vitamin deficiency or excess. Vitamin K helps promote blood clotting; green leafy vegetables contain the vitamin and, thus, decrease the effect of anticoagulants.

Lithium is used to treat bipolar disorder. Because it is similar chemically to sodium, the level of sodium in the body affects the level of lithium. Eating salty foods may cause lithium levels to fall. Conversely, sweating, vomiting, and diarrhea reduce sodium levels and cause a corresponding rise in lithium levels. Lithium has a narrow therapeutic index, so even small changes may induce toxicity.

ENVIRONMENTAL VARIABLES

The temperature of the room in which a drug is administered, the temperature of the drug, levels of noise and illumination, and the size of the group being studied all affect responsiveness under some circumstances. Vesell and colleagues let urine and feces accumulate under the cages of one group of rats and cleaned a second group's cages daily. The rats in the dirty cages showed less liver enzyme activity, which may explain some discrepancies among laboratories studying drug metabolism.[34] Another implication is that people who want to maximize drug effects might consider moving to New York or Los Angeles.

TASK VARIABLES

Drug actions are influenced by what the recipient is doing. Several animal experiments have demonstrated that a drug might increase activity under some circumstances and decrease it under others.[35] Steele and Josephs gave one group of volunteers enough alcohol to intoxicate them and kept another group sober. Then the volunteers were given the anxiety-provoking news that they would have to give a speech on "what I dislike most about my body and physical appearance." Some had to sit quietly while waiting to speak, and others were given a distracting task. Intoxicated subjects who were distracted showed reduced anxiety, whereas those who waited quietly had their anxiety increase. The interim activities did not affect sober subjects.[36]

VARIABLES THAT INFLUENCE THE MEANING OF THE DRUG

Some psychoactive drugs facilitate the production of neurotransmitters (NTs), but the vast majority act on already available NTs and receptors. Although drug company literature routinely implies that the molecular structures of the drugs determine the entire effects, psychological factors modify the same systems and can play a huge role. Expectations account for much of the placebo effect. Placebos—substances without specific activity for the condition being tested—influence both subjective measures like mood and objective measures like reaction time and composition of the blood. Typically in drug studies, between 35 and 75 percent of patients in the placebo control group benefit. Benson and McCallie contend that many new medical treatments are effective because they generate enthusiasm, but their initial 70 to 90 percent effectiveness declines to 30 to 40 percent as skeptical investigators test them under circumstances that minimize the placebo effect. Treatments that had been helping 70 to 90 percent are then abandoned. Benson and McCallie quote nineteenth-century physician Trousseau: "Treat as many patients as possible with the new drugs while they still have the power to heal."[37]

When people become sick because of their expectations, the phenomenon is called the "nocebo" effect. Voodoo death is the most dramatic example. Vomiting is a common side effect of women given placebo estrogen but is rare with other placebos. Luparello and colleagues sprayed asthma patients with a harmless saline solution and told them they were inhaling an allergen.[38] Several immediately developed breathing difficulties. Some had full-blown attacks that disappeared when they were sprayed with the same substance and told it was therapeutic. In a chemotherapy study, 30 percent of the placebo control group members lost their hair, and 56 percent had "drug-related" nausea or vomiting.[39] Box 15.1 tells about one of the most famous placebo effects in medical history.

Moerman reconceptualizes the placebo effect as a response to the meaning of the situation. The worldviews of patients affect their responses to treatments, which is why treatment effectiveness varies between individuals and especially between different cultures and time periods. Moerman tells of a man who murdered several people. His trial defense, widely described in the media, attributed his behavior to Prozac. As a result, both ordinary citizens and doctors came to think of Prozac as an enormously powerful drug. Moerman argues that such cultural factors influence the effects of both active drugs and placebos: "If physicians prescribed placebos alone, their effect would be significantly reduced because doctors would have little confidence in them."[40] Moerman's view rests on two propositions for which he provides ample evidence.

Meanings Vary

A Harvard diploma in a doctor's office might imply his competence to most American patients but not to people from traditional Asian and African cultures.

Box 15.1. One of the most famous placebo effects in medical history

In 1957, shortly after being diagnosed with orange-sized cancer tumors and given only days to live, a man heard that scientists had discovered a miracle substance for treating cancer. He begged for the substance, Krebiozen, and on a Friday afternoon received an injection. By Monday, he was out of bed joking with the nurses. His doctor wrote that the tumors "had melted like snowballs on a hot stove." But two months into his remarkable recovery, upon reading medical reports that Krebiozen was a quack remedy, he suffered an immediate relapse. The doctor told him not to believe what he read in the papers and then injected him with what he said was "a new superrefined double-strength" version of the drug. Actually, it was water. But the tumor masses once again melted. The man stayed healthy for two more months. Then he read a definitive report stating that Krebiozen was worthless. He died two days later.

Source: S. Blakeslee, "Placebos Prove So Powerful Even Experts Are Surprised," *New York Times*, 13 October 1998: F1.

A healer's credentials and costume—headdress or white coat with stethoscope hanging out of her pocket—affects meanings. So too does her manner (enthusiastic or not); her language; whether the treatment is administered in an office, clinic, hospital, or elsewhere; and her final diagnosis and prognosis. If she prescribes a drug, the extent to which it has been advertised and written about will affect meanings.

Meanings Have Biological Consequences

Factors that affect meanings affect physiological systems as well as subjective responses. Little and colleagues analyzed outcomes for 579 patients who presented with sore throats and were randomly assigned to receive antibiotics or no antibiotics.[41] About two-thirds in each group got better within five days. The factor most closely associated with rapid improvement was satisfaction with the visit with the doctor. Attitudes about illness and treatment vary from country to country, and so do placebo effects. In one study, only 7 percent of Brazilian ulcer patients but 59 percent of German patients healed on placebo. But Germans experienced less improvement than people in other countries from placebos for treating high blood pressure. People in different countries also varied widely in placebo response to generalized anxiety disorder.[42]

Responses to both active drugs and placebos are influenced by biological rhythms, color of pills, routes of administration (injection or pill), association with a well-known brand, and dosage.[43] Patients with ulcers, generalized anxiety disorder, and depression who respond well to drugs generally also respond well to placebos.[44]

Moerman cites a study by Blackwell in which subjects given packets containing either one or two blue or red placebo pills were told that they were receiving either a tranquilizer or a stimulant.[45] The red tablets induced reports of stimulation, and the blue, of sedation. For both groups, two pills had more effect than one. Moerman's explanation is that red in our culture is associated with excitement and blue, with coolness and quiet. Two pills imply a higher dosage than one.

Moerman cites a study by Branthwaite and Cooper in which women who suffered frequent headaches were randomly assigned to one of four groups.[46] Group 1 received aspirin labeled with a widely advertised brand name; group 2, the same aspirin in a plain package; group 3, a placebo marked with the widely advertised brand name; and group 4, a placebo in a plain package. Group 1 experienced more headache relief than group 2, and group 3 experienced more relief than group 4. Aspirin helps, but so does a popular brand name.

Moerman also cites the authors of two meta-analyses who conclude that chiropractic therapy for lower back pain is no better than placebo. However, according to several other studies, chiropractic patients express more satisfaction than patients of family doctors with treatment receive for lower back pain. Yet the analgesics and muscle relaxants prescribed by family doctors are more effective than placebo for pain and muscle stiffness. The apparent paradox can be resolved by considering meaningfulness. Physicians typically advise patients with lower back pain to "'take aspirin, rest in bed, take it easy.' Of course, the patient has been doing that for ten days before the appointment, and is there because those things have made no difference." By contrast,

> the chiropractor immediately carries out a focused, pointed, attentive examination asking pertinent questions about history, injury, mobility and so on, asking you to bend this way and that, usually taking *x* ray films and showing them to you, pointing out misaligned vertebrae, explaining the course of treatment, its goals and likelihood of success. The walls in a chiropractor's office are frequently hung with large posters displaying the spine, explaining its function and workings; there are colorful brochures explaining the history and value of chiropractic treatment. Occasionally one finds articles, popular or scholarly, photocopied perhaps, showing the results of studies on the effectiveness of chiropractic. One may even see a model of an actual spine with simulated spinal nerves arrayed along it, hanging from a doorknob. The entire experience is validating, encouraging, supportive and positive. We have not yet had an adjustment and we feel better already. The adjustment, on an elaborate adjustable table, is itself replete with satisfying pops and snaps, rolling over, and just enough pain to suggest that something good may come from it.[47]

The evidence that meanings have biological consequences should persuade doctors to polish their bedside manners. Patients treated with warmth and enthusiasm are most likely to heal rapidly. The evidence bolsters the position taken in earlier chapters that certain common practices are abuses:

- Children diagnosed with Attention Deficit/Hyperactivity Disorder and prescribed Ritalin learn that (a) they have a psychiatric disorder and (b) drugs solve behavioral problems.
- People shorter, or taller, or shyer than most of their contemporaries but still within the normal range are persuaded by aggressive marketing campaigns that they have a serious problem that can be cured by drugs.
- Drug abusers are taught that they have an incurable disease and can never use in moderation. One-time problem drinkers who have not touched liquor in a decade are still considered alcoholics. They become poor candidates for cure.

NOTES

1. J. Cohen and P. Insel, "*The Physicians' Desk Reference.* Problems and Possible Improvements," *Archives of Internal Medicine* 156 (1996): 1375–80.

2. R. Jones, "The Pharmacology of Cocaine Smoking in Humans," *NIDA Research Monograph* 99 (1990): 30–41; M. Perez-Reyes, "Marijuana Smoking: Factors That Influence the Bioavailability of Tetrahydrocannabinol," *NIDA Research Monograph* 99 (1990): 42–62.

3. D. Greenblatt et al., "Pharmacological Considerations," in *Clinical Evaluation of Psychotropic Drugs: Principles and Guidelines/in Association with the NIMH and the ACNP,* ed. R. Prien and S. Robinson (New York: Raven Press, 1994), 123–38

4. N. Gordon et al., "Enhancement of Morphine Analgesia by the GABA Agonist Baclofen," *Neuroscience* 69 (1995): 345–49; R. Gear et al., "Kappa-Opioids Produce Significantly Greater Analgesia in Women than in Men," *Nature Medicine* 2 (1996): 1248–50; R. Gear et al., "Gender Difference in Analgesic Response to the Kappa-Opioid Pentazocine," *Neuroscience Letters* 205 (1996): 207–09.

5. A. Kimberly et al., "Gender Differences in Pharmacokinetics and Pharmacodynamics of Psychotropic Medication," *American Journal of Psychiatry* 149 (1992): 587–95.

6. I. Godfroid, "Des variations intersexuelles relative aux traitements en psychiatrie," *Revue Canadienne de Psychiatrie* 44 (1999): 362–67.

7. H. Lane et al., "Effects of Gender and Age on Plasma Levels of Clozapine and Its Metabolites: Analyzed by Critical Statistics," *Journal of Clinical Psychiatry* 60 (1999): 36–40.

8. S. Gammie and R. Nelson, "Maternal Aggression Is Reduced in Neuronal Nitric Oxide Synthase Deficient Mice," *Journal of Neuroscience* 19 (1999): 8027–35.

9. J. Hamilton and B. Parry, "Sex-Related Differences in Clinical Drug Response: Implications for Women's Health," *Journal of the American Medical Association (JAMA)* 38 (1983): 126–32.

10. A. Reinberg and M. Smolensky, *Biological Rhythms and Medicine* (New York: Springer, 1983); B. Lemmer, "Chronopharmacology: Time, a Key in Drug Treatment," *Annales de Biologie Clinique* 52 (1994): 1–7.

11. W. Hrushesky et al., "Circadian Chronotherapy: From Animal Experiments to Human Cancer Chemotherapy," in *Chronopharmacology: Cellular and Biochemical Interactions,* ed. B. Lemmer (New York: Markel Dekker, 1989), 439–73.

12. F. Levi et al., "Randomized Multicentre Trial of Chronotherapy with Oxaliplatin, Fluorouracil, and Folinic Acid in Metastatic Colorectal Cancer," *Lancet* 350 (1997): 681–86.

13. R. Bogin and R. Ballard, "Treatment of Nocturnal Asthma with Pulse-Release Albuterol," *Chest* 102 (1992): 362–66.

14. T. Umeda et al., "Timing for Administration of an Antihypertensive Drug in the Treatment of Essential Hypertension," *Hypertension* 23 (1994): 1212–14.

15. P. Irwin, "Greater Brain Response of Left-handers to Drugs," *Neuropsychopharmacology* 23 (1985): 61–67.

16. C. Wolf and G. Smith, "Pharmacogenetics," *British Medical Bulletin* 55 (1999): 366–86.

17. L. Bertilsson et al., "Molecular Basis for Rational Mega-prescribing in Ultrarapid Hydroxylators of Debrisoquin," *Lancet* 341 (1993): 63.

18. E. Liem et al., "Increased Anesthetic Requirement in Subjects with Naturally Red Hair," *American Society of Anesthesiologists Meeting Abstracts,* 15 October 2002.

19. W. Kalow, "Pharmacogenetics and the Predictability of Drug Responses," in *Drug Response in Man,* ed. G. Wolstenholme and R. Porter (Boston: Little, Brown, 1967), 220–46.

20. K. Lin and R. Poland, "Ethnicity, Culture, and Psychopharmacology," in *Psychopharmacology: The Fourth Generation of Progress,* ed. F. Bloom and D. Kupfer (New York: Raven Press, 1995), 1907–17.

21. C. Chen, "A Further Note on Studies of Acquired Behavioral Tolerance to Alcohol," *Psychopharmacologia* 27 (1972): 265–74.

22. P. Niebergall et al., "Potential Dangers of Common Drug Dosing Regimens," *American Journal of Hospital Pharmacy* 31 (1974): 53–58.

23. S. Stahl, "Selecting an Atypical Antipsychotic by Combining Clinical Experience with Guidelines from Clinical Trials," *Journal of Clinical Psychiatry* 60(S10) (1999): 31–41.

24. S. Stahl, "Antipsychotic Polypharmacy, Part 1: Therapeutic Option or Dirty Little Secret?" *Journal of Clinical Psychiatry* 60 (1999): 425–26.

25. M. Gold et al., "Epidemiology of Benzodiazepine Use and Dependence," *Psychiatric Annals* 25 (1995): 146–48.

26. T. Fischbach and W. Lenk, "Additional Routes in the Metabolism of Phenacetin," *Xenobiotica* 15 (1985): 149–64.

27. A. Shaughnessay, "Common Drug Reactions in the Elderly," *Emergency Medicine* 24 (1992): 21–32; G. McInnes and M. Brodie, "Drug Interactions That Matter: A Critical Reappraisal," *Drugs* 36 (1988): 83–110.

28. Healthy People 2000, "Food and Drug Safety," available at www.odphp.osophs.dhhs.gov/pubs/hp2000/12food2.htm (accessed on 12 December 2000).

29. D. Bates, "Incidence of Adverse Drug Events and Potential Adverse Drug Events: Implications for Prevention," *JAMA* 274 (1995): 29–34.

30. Drug Abuse Warning Network Series: D-2, "Mid-Year Preliminary Estimates from the 1996 Drug Abuse Warning Network, Public Health Service" (Rockville, Md.: Department of Health and Human Services, 1996).

31. Data from the 1994 Treatment Episode Data Set, Office of Applied Studies, Substance Abuse and Mental Health Services Administration, Washington, D.C.

32. Alcohol Alert, No. 27, Ph-355 (Washington, D.C.: National Institute on Alcohol Abuse and Alcoholism, January 1995).

33. S. Hukkinen et al., "Plasma Concentrations of Triazolam Are Increased by Concomitant Ingestion of Grapefruit Juice," *Clinical Pharmacology and Therapeutics* 58 (1995): 127.

34. E. Vesell et al., "Hepatic Drug Metabolism in Rats: Impairment in a Dirty Environment," *Science* 179 (1973): 896–97.

35. P. Dews, "Studies on Behavior. I. Differential Sensitivity to Pentobarbital of Pecking Performance in Pigeons Depending on the Schedule of Reward," *Journal of Pharmacology and Experimental Therapeutics* 113 (1955): 393–401; J. Barrett, "Differential Drug Effects as a Function of the Controlling Consequences," *NIDA Research Monograph* 37 (1981): 159–81.

36. C. Steele and R. Josephs, "Alcohol Myopia: Its Prized and Dangerous Effects," *American Psychologist* 45 (1990): 921–33.

37. H. Benson and D. McCallie, "Angina Pectoris and the Placebo Effect," *New England Journal of Medicine* 300 (1979): 1424.

38. T. Luparello et al., "Influences of Suggestion on Airway Reactivity in Asthmatic Subjects," *Psychosomatic Medicine* 30 (1968): 819–25.

39. J. Fielding et al., "An Interim Report of a Prospective, Randomized, Controlled Study of Adjuvant Chemotherapy in Operable Gastric Cancer: British Stomach Cancer Group," *World Journal of Surgery* 7 (1983): 390–99.

40. D. Moerman, "Explanatory Mechanisms for Placebo Effects: Cultural Influences and the Meaning Response," in *The Science of the Placebo,* ed. H. Guess et al. (London: BMJ Books, 2002), 80–107; D. Moerman, *Meaning, Medicine, and the "Placebo Effect"* (London: Cambridge University Press, 2002); D. Moerman and W. Jonas, "Deconstructing the Placebo Effect and Finding the Meaning Response," *Annals of Internal Medicine* 136 (2002): 471–76.

41. P. Little et al., "Clinical and Psychosocial Predictors of Illness Duration from Randomized Controlled Trial of Prescribing Strategies for Sore Throat," *British Medical Journal* (*BMJ*) 319 (1999): 736–37.

42. D. Moerman, "Cultural Variations in the Placebo Effect: Ulcers, Anxiety, and Blood Pressure," *Medical Anthropology Quarterly* 14 (2000): 51–72.

43. For biorhythms, see Pollman, reported in A. Reinberg and M. Smolensky, *Biological Rhythms and Medicine* (New York: Springer, 1983). For pill color, see A. de Craen et al., "Effect of Color of Drugs: Systematic Review of Perceived Effect of Drugs and of Their Effectiveness," *BMJ* 313 (1996): 1624–26. For administration route, see A. de Craen et al., "Placebo Effect in the Acute Treatment of Migraine: Subcutaneous

Placebos Are Better Than Oral Placebos," *Journal of Neurology* 247 (2000): 183–88. For brand association, see A. Branthwaite and P. Cooper, "Analgesic Effects of Branding in Treatment of Headaches," *BMJ* 282 (1981): 1576–78. For dosage, see A. de Craen et al., "Placebo Effect in the Treatment of Duodenal Ulcer," *British Journal of Clinical Pharmacology* 48 (1999): 853–60.

44. Moerman, "Cultural Variations in the Placebo Effect."

45. See B. Blackwell et al., "Demonstration to Medical Students of Placebo Responses and Non-drug Factors," *The Lancet* 1 (1972): 1279–82.

46. See Branthwaite and Cooper, "Analgesic Effects of Branding in Treatment of Headaches."

47. Moerman, "Explanatory Mechanisms for Placebo Effects," 97.

Epilogue

There is hope. Courageous men and women, many whose names appear throughout the book, have called attention to and tried to correct the various abuses described. They have had several minor and a few major successes. Below I give examples of progress and then suggestions for further improvement.

EXAMPLES OF PROGRESS

There has been some progress:

- Academic institutions and drug companies appoint review boards to determine if proposed research provides adequate safeguards for subjects. There is much room for improvement, but their existence is a sign of progress, and dedicated people both within and outside the scientific community are working to make needed changes.
- In 1991, the United Nations published a statement of rights for the protection of persons with mental illness. Principle 10 specifies that psychiatric drugs shall never be administered as a "punishment or for the convenience of others."
- Tests on the effectiveness of new drugs increasingly include women and people of different ethnic and racial groups among their subjects.
- Hospitals, pharmacies, and individual medical personnel have been sensitized to the problem of medical errors. Systems have been overhauled to reduce their incidence. Several books and articles with tips on minimizing errors can be accessed on the Internet. See, for example, www.medicalerrors.ca/links.html, which lists many sources.

- Doctors are now required to offer their patients adequate medication for relieving pain.
- Doctors are becoming increasingly familiar with alternatives to psychiatric drugs.
- Several drug companies have pledged to discount prices of expensive products to needy developing countries.
- In 1997, South Africa enacted legislation aimed at lowering the cost of drugs to its citizens. The focus was on drugs for treating HIV and AIDS, and included other provisions such as facilitating generic substitution on prescriptions. Shortly afterward, thirty-nine large international drug companies filed a lawsuit against the South African government to stop it from implementing the law. But the suit proved to be a public relations disaster and was withdrawn in April 2001.
- Reimportation of drugs is now allowed, which means that Americans can buy them more cheaply.
- Asset-forfeiture laws have come under scrutiny and in some states have been changed.
- Many politicians, judges, and community leaders have questioned the effectiveness of the wars on drugs. They are grappling with alternatives.
- Medical marijuana is legal in some places.
- Pregnant women are no longer routinely tested for illegal drugs.

Many fine organizations have emerged with the goal of correcting abuses. Listing them all would take too much space, but three exemplary ones will be mentioned. Drug Policy Alliance (www.drugpolicy.org) works to broaden the public debate on drug policy and promote realistic alternatives to the war on drugs. The alliance was formerly known as the Lindesmith Center–Drug Policy Foundation. The Lindesmith Center and the Drug Policy Foundation merged in 2000 with the objective of building a national drug policy reform movement. The Drug Reform Coordination Network (www.drcnet.org) is a national network of concerned citizens working for drug policy reform from a variety of perspectives, including harm reduction, reform of sentencing and forfeiture laws, medicalization of currently Schedule I drugs, and promotion of an open debate on drug prohibition. Its Internet site has an excellent library. And Public Citizen (www.citizen.org) is a consumer advocacy organization that fights for safe, effective, and affordable prescription drugs and health care.

SUGGESTIONS

Much more must be done. The introductory chapter lists three major causes of abuse. Each cause should be minimized. One general strategy is to be an active citizen. Identify abuses and write your congressional representatives to legislate against them. One person cannot do much, but there may be a critical mass. Implementation of some of the suggestions below would require granting bigger budgets to various government agencies. The monies would have to come from taxes. But the gains would easily offset the relatively miniscule tax increases.

Human Error

Patients can do little to prevent certain types of errors, such as botched surgeries, but they are not entirely helpless. In addition to following the suggestions given on pages 66–67, patients should check out the credentials of their doctors, pharmacists, and hospitals. They should appreciate that many adverse drug effects are not recognized until after the drug has received Food and Drug Administration (FDA) approval and has been administered to a large number of patients. So they should not rush to try new drugs.

Encourage legislation to identify and suspend medical personnel who commit frequent or severe errors. Although many errors could be eliminated inexpensively, for example, by requiring doctors to print rather than write out prescriptions, reducing the frequency of others would necessitate expenditures of time, personnel, and equipment. Several states have legislated ceilings on the monetary amounts that victims of medical error can recover in lawsuits. This reduces the motivation of doctors and hospital administrators to correct errors, because they can maximize profits by accepting higher insurance premiums rather than implementing costly safeguards. In addition, defendants in medical malpractice cases typically insist that out-of-court settlements be confidential, with no information divulged about either the amounts paid out or the facts of the case. This practice also reduces incentive to change. Legislation should be enacted to outlaw confidential settlements, and legislation imposing ceilings should be repealed.

Lack of Information, Misinformation, and Disinformation

Several remediable practices result in the spread of faulty information to doctors and the general populace.

Shoddy Research

Students in science Ph.D. programs attend graduate school for several years and are trained extensively in research methodology. Then they do an original dissertation project under the tutelage of experienced mentors. Yet many graduate without grasping important methodological concepts. Their subsequent projects are poorly conceived and designed, with inaccurate measurements, improper statistical analyses, and unjustified interpretations.[1]

Medical school curricula have few courses in research methodology, so newly graduated physicians are not nearly as well prepared as new science Ph.D.s to do independent research. Yet they are legally entitled to do research on humans, and many do so.

Government funding agencies carefully evaluate the competency of applicants and the feasibility of their projects, but monetary awards from drug companies are often based on less-stringent criteria. Giving the government agencies bigger budgets to evaluate and fund projects would lessen the influence of drug companies and improve research quality.

Dishonest Research

It is debatable whether incompetence or dishonesty poses a bigger threat to the integrity of the medical literature. The system offers strong incentives to cheat, and not only financial ones. Bruno Bettelheim built an international reputation from his work on childhood autism, and Cyril Burt—Sir Cyril—was knighted for his contributions to the field of intelligence testing. Both men fabricated data.[2]

Fraudulent studies impede progress and lead to ineffective and harmful medical procedures. Yet, while thousands of young men and women convicted of cultivating marijuana plants for personal use languish in prisons, the punishment for fraudulent research is rarely more severe than being made ineligible to receive additional funding for a few years. We should criminalize fraudulent medical research. Researchers should be considered fraudulent if they fail to disclose financial ties with companies whose products they are testing.

Censorship

The work of Carl Selzer, described on page 164, was censored because it did not fit the objectives of the National Institutes of Health. Arnold Trebach's work was censored for a similar reason, as were the findings of a World Health Organization panel of experts (see page 164). The public has a right to know. We should demand an end to censorship. We should also demand that drug companies be forbidden to censor publication of work they have sponsored that shows their products unfavorably.

The Influence of Money

The best way to understand drug policies is to ignore rhetoric from all sides and focus on the flow of money. Ask, for example, Who profits from advertisements and commercials condemning marijuana and other illegal drugs, from the promotion of psychiatric drugs by "grassroots organizations" such as the National Alliance for the Mentally Ill, and from relegating the most effective treatments for drug abuse to minor status in the United States? Once citizens recognize how money has corrupted the drug field, they can urge their elected representatives to pass legislation to

- require that drug ads directed at both doctors and consumers be truthful,
- enforce restrictions on drug company gifts to doctors,
- expand the powers of the FDA and ensure that it is independent of drug company influence,
- use Institutional Review Boards more effectively,
- criminalize improper experimentation on human subjects,
- eliminate continuing medical education courses or, if the American Medical Association deems them necessary, make them independent of drug company influence, and
- use tax dollars to support public interest organizations such as the ones mentioned above.

Despite these suggestions, and the many positive changes in recent years, I am pessimistic on two fronts. The variety of drug abusers is considerable. Many are rich, powerful, deceitful, and corrupt. They commit crimes daily, and, in contrast to those who use illegal drugs, their crimes are not victimless. Yet our society will probably continue to displace blame onto poor young African American and Hispanic men and women who seek solace in cocaine, heroin, or marijuana.

As long as drug companies are allowed to operate like other businesses, with profit as the bottom line, they will conduct dishonest research, distort results, market their products aggressively, and price their drugs out of the range of many who desperately need them. The solution can be given in five words, but they are an obscenity to many Americans. Women and children, close your eyes: Free health care for all.

NOTES

1. For examples, see F. Leavitt, *Evaluating Scientific Research: Separating Fact from Fiction* (Upper Saddle River, N.J.: Prentice-Hall, 2001).

2. R. Pollak, *The Creation of Dr. B: A Biography of Bruno Bettelheim* (New York: Simon and Schuster, 1997); Leavitt, *Evaluating Scientific Research.*

Index

About the Author

Fred Leavitt received his Ph.D. in psychopharmacology from the University of Michigan and had a postdoctoral fellowship at the University of California in Berkeley. Since 1970 he has taught at Cal State University in Hayward. He has been a visiting professor at universities in Nairobi, Kenya; Vancouver, Canada; Palmerston North, New Zealand; Bushey, England; Utrecht, the Netherlands; and Istanbul, Turkey.

Leavitt has written journal articles and five textbooks. He has appeared on radio and television and testified before the California State Senate Committee on Drugs and Licensed Sports concerning the consequences of drug abuse for professional athletes. Leavitt is married and has two daughters. His daughter Melanie created the index for this book. Leavitt encourages his readers to e-mail him at fleavitt@csuhayward.edu.